Handbook of the Psychology of Interviewing

Handbook of the Psychology of Interviewing

Edited by
Amina Memon
University of Aberdeen, UK
and
Ray Bull
University of Portsmouth, UK

JOHN WILEY & SONS

Chichester · New York · Weinheim · Brisbane · Singapore · Toronto

Paperback edition 2000
Copyright © 1999 by John Wiley & Sons Ltd,
                  Baffins Lane, Chichester,
                  West Sussex PO19 1UD, England

          National   01243 779777
          International (+44) 1243 779777
          e-mail (for orders and customer service enquiries):
          cs-books@wiley.co.uk
          Visit our Home Page on http://www.wiley.co.uk
                       or http://www.wiley.com

Other Wiley Editorial Offices

John Wiley & Sons, Inc., 605 Third Avenue,
New York, NY 10158-0012, USA

WILEY-VCH Verlag GmbH, Pappelallee 3,
D-69469 Weinheim, Germany

Jacaranda Wiley Ltd, 33 Park Road, Milton,
Queensland 4064, Australia

John Wiley & Sons (Asia) Pte Ltd, 2 Clementi Loop #02-01,
Jin Xing Distripark, Singapore 129809

John Wiley & Sons (Canada) Ltd, 22 Worcester Road,
Rexdale, Ontario M9W 1L1, Canada

Library of Congress Cataloging-in-Publication Data

A catalogue record for this book is available from the Library of Congress

British Library Cataloguing in Publication Data

A catalogue record for this book is available from the British Library

ISBN 0-471-49888-2

Typeset in 10/12pt Times by Dorwyn Ltd, Rowlands Castle, Hants.
Printed and bound by Antony Rowe Ltd, Eastbourne
This book is printed on acid-free paper responsibly manufactured from sustainable forestation, in
which at least two trees are planted for each one used for paper production.

Contents

About the Editors

Amina Memon is a senior lecturer in Social Psychology at the University of Aberdeen. She has published widely on topics such as police interviewing, face recognition, eyewitness identification, child witness memory and jury decision-making. Amina recently completed her first book: *Psychology and Law: Truthfulness, Accuracy and Credibility* (with Ray Bull & Aldert Vrij). Amina has held several research grants and her current project funded by the National Science Foundation is an investigation of eyewitness testimony in older adults. This text was completed while she was a visiting research scientist in the School of Human Development at the University of Texas at Dallas.

Ray Bull is Professor of Criminological and Legal Psychology in the Department of Psychology at the University of Portsmouth. He has published extensively on investigative interviewing, particularly of children. He has advised a large number of organisations in various countries, especially police forces, on how best to conduct interviews both with ordinary people and those with special needs. He, with collaborators, has received funding for research on interviewing from the Home Office and the Economic and Social Research Council, with the latter supporting doctoral students to be supervised by Ray and colleagues. Together with the lawyer David Carson he is co-editor of Wiley's *Handbook of Psychology in Legal Contexts* and of the Kluwer journal *Expert Evidence*. Ray has been recognised by various courts as an Expert Witness.

Contributors

Andrew R. Block, The Well Being Group, Texas Back Institute, 6300 W. Parker Road, Plano, Texas 75093, USA

Susan M. Bögels, Department of Experimental Abnormal Psychology, University of Maastricht, PO Box 616, 6200 MD, Maastricht, the Netherlands

Ray Bull, Department of Psychology, King Henry Building, University of Portsmouth, PO1 2DY, UK

Constance J. Dalenberg, Trauma Research Institute, California School of Professional Psychology, 6160 Cornerstone Court East, San Diego, California 92121, USA

Ian Diamond, Department of Social Statistics, University of Southampton, Southampton SO17 1BJ, UK

Judy J. Epstein, Trauma Research Institute, California School of Professional Psychology, 6160 Cornerstone Court East, San Diego, CA 92121, USA

Phillip W. Esplin, Private Practice, 7220 North 16th Street, Building K, Phoenix, AZ 85020, USA

Hubert S. Feild, Auburn University, Department of Management, 415 W. Magnolia, Suite 401, Lauder Building, Auburn, AL 36849-5241, USA

Gisli Gudjonsson, Department of Psychology, Institute of Psychiatry, De Crespigny Park, Denmark Hill, London, SE5 8AF, UK

Owen Hargie, University of Ulster, Newton Abbey, County Antrim, BT37 0QB, Northern Ireland

Monique Hennink, Department of Social Statistics, University of Southampton, Southampton SO17 1BJ, UK

Irit Hershkowitz, School of Social Work, University of Haifa, Mount Carmel, Haifa, Israel

Roger Ingham, Centre for Sexual Health Research, University of Southampton, Southampton SO17 1BJ, UK

Denise Kirkland, Centre for Sexual Health Research, University of Southampton, Southampton SO17 1BJ, UK

Irving Kirsch, Psychology Department, University of Connecticut, Storrs, CT 06269–1020, USA

Michael E. Lamb, National Institute of Child Health and Development, 9190 Rockville Pike, Bethesda, MD 20814, USA

Steven Jay Lynn, Department of Psychology, University of Binghamton, Binghamton, NY 13902, USA

Lisa Marmelstein, Department of Psychology, University of Binghamton, Binghamton, NY 13902, USA

Michael A. McDaniel, Department of Psychology, University of Akron, Akron, Ohio 44325-4301, USA

Amina Memon, Department of Psychology, University of Aberdeen, Kings College, Old Aberdeen, Scotland, AB24 2UB, UK

Rebecca Milne, Institute of Police and Criminological Studies, University of Portsmouth, Ravelin House, Ravelin Park, Portsmouth PO1 2QQ, UK

Anna Mortimer, Investigative Science, Wych End, The Spinney, Ford Lane, East Hendred, Oxfordshire, OX12 8LS, UK

Yael Orbach, National Institute of Child Health and Development, 9190 Rockville Pike, Bethesda, MD 20814, USA

Sheila Payne, Health Research Unit, School of Occupational Therapy and Physiotherapy, University of Southampton, Southampton, SO17 IBJ, UK

Cynthia Pladziewicz, The Well Being Group, Texas Back Institute, 6300 W. Parker Road, Plano, Texas 75093, USA

Amelia J. Prewett-Livingston, PRIDE Learning and Development Center, Southern Natural Gas, 1501 Meadowcraft Road, Birmingham, Alabama 35215, USA

Judith Rhue, Department of Family Medicine, College of Osteopathic Medicine, Ohio University, Athens, Ohio 45701, USA

Paul C. Rosenblatt, Department of Family Social Science, University of Minnesota, St Paul, Minnesota MN 55108, USA

Eric Shepherd, Investigative Science, Wych End, The Spinney, Ford Lane, East Hendred, Oxfordshire OX12 8LS, UK

Neville A. Stanton, Department of Design, Brunel University, Egham, Surrey, TW20 0JZ, UK

Kathleen J. Sternberg, National Institute of Child Health and Development, 9190 Rockville Pike, Bethesda, MD 20814, USA

Ann Terry, 16 Fourth Avenue, Selly Park, Birmingham B29 7EU, UK

Dennis Tourish, University of Ulster, Newton Abbey, County Antrim, BT37 0QB, Northern Ireland

Ine Vanwesenbeeck, Department of Women's Studies, Tilbury University, PO Box 90153, 5000 LE Tilburg, The Netherlands

Aldert Vrij, Dept Psychology, King Henry Building, University of Portsmouth, Portsmouth PO1 2DY, UK

Deborah L. Whetzel, US Postal Service, 475 L'Enfant Plaza SW, Room IP650, Washington, DC 20260–4215, USA

Daniel B. Wright, School of Computing & Cognitive Sciences, University of Sussex, Falmer, Brighton, BN1 9QH, UK

Mark S. Young, Department of Design, Brunel University, Egham, Surrey, TW20 0JZ, UK

Preface

The interview is one of the most used methods within psychology, and one of the psychological methods least analysed within the theory of science (Kvale, 1983, p.171).

Effective interviewing skills can be described as one of the most useful qualities a professional can possess. Although our aims may be diverse there are few of us who do not require to collect information of one sort or another using interviews. Those who work in the field of medicine rely on accurate case histories from patients, social workers rely on detailed case notes including family histories, market researchers rely on accurate information obtained from public surveys and therapists rely on eliciting accurate personal histories from their clients. For instance, we may use the interview as a therapeutic technique (exploring an individual's current attitudes and emotions) or as an investigative technique (attempting to retrieve information from an individual's memory). The interview is a valuable tool in data collection whether it is used on its own or in combination with other techniques. The interview is indispensable when relevant information cannot be observed directly or be obtained by means of psychometric tests or questionnaires (Koehnken, 1995). The interview is also very important in testing theories. The interview provides the researchers with an in-depth and quality analysis of the subject matter that is of interest to them and allows them to build new theories and ideas.

This handbook examines the psychology of interviewing from varying perspectives and for different purposes: clinical, forensic, organisational and social. Contributors provide detail on interview methodology, how their procedure relates to theory and the practical uses to which their special techniques can be put.

In the first section of the book, experts in the field of interviewing in mental health discuss the role of diagnostic and assessment interviews in the clinical context. Susan Bögels reviews methods of diagnostic interviewing in mental health care as well as the teaching and assessment of the diagnostic interviewing skill in the mental health professions. Steven Lynn and colleagues look specifically at the use of clinical hypnosis in psychotherapeutic contexts and note important caveats in terms of suggestibility and leading procedures. Constance

Dalenberg and Judy Epstein examine the therapeutic potential of the interview in talking to Holocaust survivors.

Part Two explores how different types of interviews can be used to address specific theoretical questions and to gather in-depth information about a particular topic in the health and social sciences field. Ann Terry examines the potential of motivational interviewing, which she describes as "a specific interpersonal style involving the application of appropriate counselling skills to initiate the process of behavioural change". Owen Hargie and Dennis Tourish examine the interview as a form of skilled behaviour. They present a transactional model of interviewing based upon a skills paradigm. This model highlights the importance of the goals of the participants, their strategies and plans for achieving these goals, related behavioural routines and associated perceptual concerns. It takes cognisance of personal factors relating to interviewer(s) and interviewee(s) as well as the situated features of the actual interviewing encounter. Sheila Payne provides an overview of the process of interviewing for qualitative research analysis. Daniel Wright reviews the survey interview, focusing in particular on cognitive aspects of survey methodology. Monique Hennink and Ian Diamond detail a procedure for conducting focus groups in social research.

Part Three examines the role of interview methodology, whether gathering information on sensitive issues where sensitivity could be due to the nature of the topic, the vulnerability of the population being studied, or both. Roger Ingham and colleagues describe how the interview method has been used to obtain information about the sexual conduct of young people in the UK and the Netherlands. Rebecca Milne explores the various techniques that can be used to gather information from children with learning disabilities. Cynthia Pladziewicz and Andrew Block describe the procedure they use in screening candidates for spine surgery. Their research-based approach, termed "presurgical psychological screening", uses a prepared, specialised clinical interview format and psychological testing to identify emotional, behavioural and psychosocial difficulties that negatively impact surgical outcomes. Paul Rosenblatt examines the ethical dilemmas researchers may face in interviews with grieving families including the ethics of recruiting people, the ethics of causing pain, informed consent, the ethical boundary between research and therapy and confidentiality issues.

Part Four comprises three chapters which examine the role of interviewing in organisational contexts. Deborah Whetzel and Michael McDaniel describe the psychometric characteristics of the employment interview which includes threats to the reliability and validity of the interview. Variables that can impact on decisions made by employers such as impression management are also discussed. Mark Young and Neville Stanton discuss how the interview may be used to improve usability in the design of consumer products. Amelia Prewett-Livingston and Hubert Feild examine the effects of interviewer race, candidate race and racial composition of interview panels on interview ratings.

The final section of the book looks at the role of the interview in forensic contexts. Michael Lamb and colleagues evaluate various types of investigative interview procedures used by researchers and clinicians in obtaining evidence

from young children. Ray Bull describes how the incorporation into police interviewing of psychological principles has resulted in a major change in the way that
such interviews can be conducted. Anna Mortimer and Eric Shepherd evaluate
the schemata that guide cognition and conduct in the investigative interview of
suspected offenders. Aldert Vrij examines the potential of the interview in catching a liar. Gisli Gudjonnson provides a framework for the psychological evaluation of the defendant who confesses to a crime in the police interview. Finally,
Amina Memon provides a review of research on cognitive interviewing techniques and their potential in increasing the amount of information that can be
obtained from child and adult witnesses.

Amina Memon
Ray Bull

References

Koehnken, G. (1995). Interviewing adults. In R. Bull and D. Carson (Eds.), *Handbook of
Psychology in Legal Contexts*, Chichester, Wiley.
Kvale, S. (1983). The qualitative research interview: a phenomenological and a hermeneuti-
cal mode of understanding. *Journal of Phenomenological Psychology*, 14, 171–196.

Part 1

Interviews in Mental Health

Diagnostic Interviewing in Mental Health Care: Methods, Training and Assessment

Susan M. Bögels
University of Maastricht, the Netherlands

Abstract

This chapter describes the method of diagnostic interviewing in mental health care. First, the tasks and skills of the diagnostic interviewer are described. Secondly, empirical evidence on effective diagnostic interviewing styles is reviewed. Thirdly, a model for conducting the diagnostic interview in mental health care is presented. Fourthly, training methods related to the teaching of diagnostic interviewing are outlined, and a training programme, developed to teach diagnostic interviewing to undergraduates, is described. Fifthly, research on effects of training programmes to teach diagnostic interview skills to novices is reviewed. Finally, the assessment of diagnostic interview performance of mental health professionals is discussed.

INTRODUCTION

The diagnostic interview is the main assessment tool in mental health care. The goals of the diagnostic interview are to arrive at a diagnosis and a rational treatment plan. The diagnostic interview traditionally has been a task of the psychiatrist. However, because of the increasing involvement of professionals from other disciplines (psychologists, social workers, doctors and psychiatric

Handbook of the Psychology of Interviewing. Edited by A. Memon and R. Bull.
© 1999 John Wiley & Sons Ltd.

nurses) in the provision of mental health care, diagnostic interviewing has become an important skill for all mental health professionals.

Most educators agree that diagnostic interviewing is an important skill that mental health professionals should master during their formative years. Although basic interviewing and counselling skills tend to be included in training (Baker & Daniels, 1989), the teaching of *diagnostic* interviewing is often ignored, in clinical psychology education, counsellor training, and psychiatric residency training (McCready & Waring, 1986; McGuire, 1982). Little is known about how to teach these skills effectively to novices in this field.

The purpose of this chapter is to review recent developments in diagnostic interviewing for the mental health professions. A model for conducting, teaching and assessing diagnostic interviewing will be described.

TASKS AND SKILLS OF THE DIAGNOSTIC INTERVIEWER

The major goals of the diagnostic interview are to arrive at a diagnosis and treatment plan. Usually, a diagnosis is formulated in terms of psychopathology (the *descriptive* diagnosis), generally by means of the *Diagnostic and Statistical Manual of Mental Disorders* (DSM-IV, American Psychiatric Association, 1994). In addition, the interviewer seeks to reformulate patients' problems by reconstructing patients' life histories and analysing their present circumstances and the organization of their personalities (Siassi, 1984). For this aetiological formulation, or *explanatory* diagnosis, no universally used language is available. The interviewing task thus consists of gathering relevant information from patients for descriptive and explanatory diagnosis, as well as other information necessary for planning treatment. Establishing a working alliance with the patient is another goal of the diagnostic interview (Reiser, 1984). Whether or not the interviewer becomes engaged in the treatment of the patient following the diagnostic interview, agreement between interviewer and patient, based on mutual rapport and comprehension, is important for compliance.

To teach a complex professional skill such as diagnostic interviewing, it is necessary to divide the skill into behavioural units (Authier & Gustafson, 1982). Mumford et al. (1987) distinguished two types of skills in the overt behaviour of psychiatrists interviewing a patient: skills focusing on the relational and communicative aspects of the encounter (*process* skills) and skills focusing on information gathering (*content* skills).

Process skills reflect the ability of interviewers to show interest in the problems of the patient, to elicit information in an open and natural way, to communicate their understanding of the problem to the patient, and to provide the patient with as much information as possible about the purpose of the interview, the therapy, and so forth. Process skills aim to establish a working relationship with the patient. Process skills can be subdivided into two main categories:

listening skills and regulating skills (Lang & van der Molen, 1990). Listening skills are required to encourage patients to tell their story. We distinguish the following listening skills: attending, asking questions, concreteness, paraphrasing of content, reflection of feelings, summarizing. Regulating (or meta-communicative) skills are necessary to safeguard order and clarity of the interview. The following regulating skills are distinguished: giving information, asking feedback, structuring and thinking aloud.

Content skills reflect the way interviewers handle their agenda (e.g. the topics important to cover during the interview). The literature on psychiatric interviewing suggests that there is consensus on the topics to be covered during the initial diagnostic interview. Interviewers' agenda should contain the following: identification of the patient, clarification of the presenting complaint, history of main problem, personal history, medical history, history of prior treatments, mental status (or psychiatric) examination, assessment of the premorbid personality, present circumstances, and request for help (Gelder, Gath & Mayou, 1989; Ginsberg, 1985; MacKinnon & Michels, 1971; Nicholi, 1978; Nurcombe & Gallagher, 1986; Othmer & Othmer, 1994; Reiser, 1984; Rosenthal & Akiskal, 1985; Shea, 1988; Siassi, 1984; Thompson, 1979).

So far the overt behaviour of interviewers has been described. We now turn to the mental activities during the interview. Interviewers have to process substantial patient information from verbal and non-verbal sources simultaneously, select diagnostic hypotheses based on this information, and develop questions to test and progressively refine their hypotheses (Nurcombe & Gallagher, 1986). To select diagnostic hypotheses, they may compare the case to other cases stored in memory. Furthermore, they may use their knowledge of diagnostic classifications to select and test hypotheses. Finally, they decide which diagnosis is most probable. These activities are referred to as *cognitive* skills or problem-solving skills.

The cognitive process of hypothesis selection and testing in novices has been described by Othmer and Othmer (1994). Starting with the first contact, interviewers assemble a running list of all possible diagnoses, based on observations and symptoms that are compatible with major mental disorders. During the same screening process, interviewers make observations and obtain clues that exclude other mental disorders, to make a list of excluded disorders. The third list concerns the unexplored disorders. The diagnostic process can then be conceptualized as follows: from the long list of unexplored disorders, a list of included and a list of excluded disorders is derived. This process continues until the list of unexplored disorders is empty. During the first step of this process ("diagnostic clues"), interviewers use overinclusive questions, which have high sensitivity but low specificity, to screen the main diagnostic areas of mental disorders: psychotic symptoms, mood disturbances, irrational anxiety, physical complaints and cognitive impairment. They also screen psychosocial and environment problems, and lifelong patterns of maladjustment. During the second step of this process ("diagnostic criteria") interviewers use questions of high diagnostic specificity to identify all essential signs and symptoms of a disorder.

The third step consists of gaining more supportive evidence via information on the course of the disorder, premorbid personality, treatment history, medical, family and personal history. These steps are not necessary consecutive steps. As long as patients' elaborations contribute to any of these steps, interviewers may follow their leads (Othmer & Othmer, 1994).

The result of the diagnostic interview in mental health care is generally a multi-axial evaluation of patients' problems according to DSM-IV. Axis I is reserved for the clinical disorders, and other conditions that may be a focus of clinical attention (so-called V-codes), like a partner relationship problem. Axis II includes personality disorders and mental retardation. On axis III general medical conditions are described that are potentially relevant to the mental disorder (on axis I or II). Axis IV is for reporting psychosocial and environmental problems that may affect the diagnosis, treatment and prognosis of mental disorders (axis I and II) such as a life event or occupational problems. Axis V, finally, considers a global assessment of psychological, social and occupational functioning on a hypothetical continuum of mental health–illness. Interviewers who do not wish to use the multi-axial evaluation may simply list the appropriate diagnoses. The principal diagnosis or reason for visit should be listed first. In addition to the diagnostic formulation in DSM terms, other data that are relevant to understanding the patient's problem and considering the best treatment, such as the patient's request for help, personality traits, relevant findings from the patient's personal, social, intellectual, and treatment history, and ability to self-reflect, should be described on a form. Finally, an argued proposal for treatment (or no treatment) evolves from the diagnostic interview, as well as a prognosis. The results of the diagnostic interview – the diagnostic formulation, treatment plan and prognosis – should be shared with the patient, at some point during the diagnostic interviewing process.

EFFECTIVE DIAGNOSTIC INTERVIEWING STYLES

Research in the medical domain has consistently indicated that interpersonal and communication skills affect the adequacy of the medical interview. These skills have a positive effect on the working relationship (Pendleton et al., 1984), and on patient satisfaction (Kraan & Crijnen, 1987). They also promote compliance with treatment (DiMatteo & DiNicola, 1982), and improve diagnostic accuracy (Evans et al., 1991). Goldberg and Huxley (1980) found that interviewing skills by general practitioners associated with a high detection of mental health problems include (a) good eye contact, (b) clarification of patients' presenting complaints, (c) picking up verbal and non-verbal cues, (d) using open-ended questions, and (e) being able to direct the course of the interview.

Surprisingly little empirical evidence is available on what constitutes effective diagnostic interviewing in mental health care. Cox and his colleagues (Cox, Holbrook & Rutter, 1981a; Cox, Hopkinson & Rutter, 1981b; Cox, Rutter & Holbrook, 1981c) conducted a series of studies to evaluate the efficiency of different diagnostic interviewing styles. Their subjects were psychiatrists interviewing parents of children referred to a clinic. In both a naturalistic study (Cox et al., 1981b) and an experimental study (Cox et al., 1981c), they found that directive and non-directive approaches produced equal numbers of reported problems. However, directive interview styles, consisting of specific probes and inquiry for detailed information, produced fuller and more detailed information on each problem and more information on topics where there was no abnormality. Furthermore, systematic questioning had no negative effects on the expression of emotions by the patient (Cox et al., 1981a).

The two interviewing styles that are generally distinguished, a non-directive, counselling approach and a directive, structured approach, have not been well integrated into training courses (Shea & Mezzich, 1988). McCready and Waring (1986), for example, noticed that, as a result of education that focused only on data collection, diagnostic formulation and management, psychiatric interns appear to be preoccupied with these issues at the expense of empathic listening. Interviewers using a counselling approach, by contrast, may not cover all important issues for accurate diagnostics. Shea and Mezzich (1988) furthermore observed that psychiatric interns tend to err in one of two ways: performing the interview in an overly structured way or allowing the patient to ramble unproductively.

Hak and de Boer (1996) distinguish three interviewing styles: the investigatory, explorative and collaborative type. The psychiatric interview is characterized as an exploratory type of interviewing. In the exploratory interview, the interviewer uses the "formulation–decision pair" for exploring the patient's problems, i.e. formulating the information received according to the interviewer's understanding, and exposing it to the patient's assessment, who decides whether this is the right formulation. The function of the formulation–decision pair is to create a shared understanding of "facts" of the patient's life, an understanding that can be subsequently transformed into a diagnostic formulation. The interest in the patient's talk, however, is restricted merely to the delivery of symptoms. The exploratory type is contrasted to the investigatory type (typically occurring in the medical interview), which is characterized by the absence of formulations, and to the collaborative type of interviewing (typically found in psychotherapy), in which the formulation–decision pair is used for translating the patient's problems into a joint problem definition.

Since the introduction of the DSM, structured and semi-structured interview schedules, based on the DSM classification, have been developed (see Friedman, 1989, for an overview of the frequently used types). Although there is general agreement that structured interviews improve the reliability of psychiatric diagnoses (Siassi, 1984), they have some disadvantages. First, they are time-consuming. Secondly, they do not allow experienced diagnosticians to take shortcuts, whereas experts generally gather far less data than novices to diagnose cases accurately (Schmidt, Norman & Boshuizen, 1990). Thirdly, they do not pay attention to the interpersonal and communication skills of the helper, and, as a result, patients may not feel understood by the interviewer. Furthermore, structured interviews do not cover themes such as request for help, life history and premorbid personality.

To summarize, the few empirical studies directed at effective diagnostic interviewing techniques and styles in mental health care point to the importance of integrating non-directive/counselling and directive/structured techniques. Clinical impressions of educators are that trainees have difficulty integrating these two techniques, suggesting that training should focus explicitly on using non-directive and directive interviewing techniques in conjunction. The exploratory style of interviewing, which characterizes the psychiatric interview, integrates both techniques.

A MODEL OF THE DIAGNOSTIC INTERVIEW IN MENTAL HEALTH CARE

Based on the above analysis of the tasks and skills of the interviewer, as well as the literature on effective interviewing styles, a schematic model of the diagnostic interview in mental health care is proposed, in which content, process and cognitive skills are defined (Table 1).

Content of the Interview

The content of the diagnostic interview (or: the agenda of the interviewer) is divided into four stages: (1) problem clarification and history of the main problem; (2) psychiatric examination; (3) personal history; and (4) present functioning.

Problem Clarification and History of the Main Problem

Problem Clarification

Interviewers start with a short introduction, in which they introduce themselves, mention the purpose of the interview, how much time it will take, summarize what they already know about the patient, etc. Then they invite patients to clarify what brought them here: what is the problem, when, where, and with whom does it occur, and how does the patient experience it? The frame of reference of the patient is central.

Exploration of Other Problems

When the presenting problem is clarified, interviewers ask whether there are other problems, and clarify them in the same way.

Reason for Encounter and Request for Help

Interviewers explore the immediate cause for clients asking for help, which may also shed more light on the present suffering of the patient. Furthermore, they

Table 1 A model of the diagnostic interview in mental health care: content, process and cognitive skills

Content skills	Process skills	Cognitive skills
Introduction	Giving information Asking for feedback	
1. *Problem clarification and history of the main problem*		Formulating hypotheses about axis I and II diagnoses
1a. Problem clarification Clarification of presenting problem Exploration of other problems Reason for encounter and help request	Attending behaviour Open-ended questions Reflections of feelings Paraphrasing of content	List 1: possible diagnoses List 2: excluded diagnoses List 3: unexplored diagnoses
1b. History of present problem(s) Analysing main problem(s) Causal factors Duration and course Consequences for daily life Prior treatments and medical history	Open- and close-ended questions Concreteness Thinking aloud Summarizing Structuring	Selecting questions to test the diagnostic hypotheses
2. *Psychiatric examination* Orientation in time, place, person Concentration and memory Perception Thinking and insight Mood and affect	Giving information (introducing the second stage) Specific open- and close-ended questions Thinking aloud Structuring	Formulating (differential) diagnosis axes I, II and III
3. *Personal history* Childhood Adolescence Adulthood Intrapsychic, social, intellectual and sexual development Premorbid personality	Giving information (introducing the third stage) All listening skills Thinking aloud Structuring	Formulating precipitating, predisposing and maintaining factors (explanatory diagnostics) Testing axis II diagnosis
4. *Present functioning* Quantity and quality of social relations Occupational functioning, work satisfaction, financial situation	Giving information (introducing the fourth stage) All process skills	Diagnosis axes IV and V
Closing the interview	Summarizing Giving information Asking for feedback	Formulating plan for further management

explore patients' requests for help: what kind of help do they want for their problem, what do they hope to achieve, and in case of more than one problem: which problem needs to be treated first?

Analysing Main Problem(s)

Next, the present problem(s) is (are) further explored, now from the frame of reference of the interviewer. Interviewers ask about the nature and intensity of the main problem(s), and ask for symptoms that may accompany them (the diagnostic criteria).

Causal Factors

Interviewers ask for the cause of the problem: which circumstances and events accompanied the onset of the problem, and what ideas the patient has about the causes of the problem?

Course

Interviewers also explore the duration of the problem as well as the development of the problem from onset to present. Did the problem get worse or did it improve during certain periods, and what factors were connected with such fluctuations?

Consequences for Daily Life

The impact of the problem on the daily life of the patient is explored. It concerns the consequences for the patient as well as for his/her environment. Also, it is important to assess the reaction of the environment to the patient's complaint. The possible function of the problem can become clear in this way.

Prior Treatments and Medical History

Finally, interviewers explore prior treatments for the present or other mental problems, including medical, paramedical, psychiatric and psychotherapeutic treatment. Use of medication, alcohol, and drugs is also checked, and the medical history is examined. The effects of all "treatments" on the problem are assessed.

Psychiatric Examination

During the second stage of the interview, interviewers assess the mental status of the patient. Information can be derived in three ways: by observing, testing and exploring.

Appearance and Psychomotor Behaviour

From the first moment of confrontation with the patient, interviewers need to observe the patient's behaviour, appearance and presentation. The way the patient waits in the waiting room (sitting, standing) already gives important information. Interviewers specifically observe appearance, including nutritional status, hygiene and eye contact. They observe patient's psychomotor behaviour, and look for abnormalities like tremors, tics or catatonic stupor.

Orientation

During the psychiatric interview, tests are made to see how well the patient is oriented in time, place and person, that is, whether the patient knows what date it is, when the appointment was made, how long they have been in the hospital, how they found the office, and who the interviewer is.

Attention and Memory

Interviewers also observe and ask for possible problems in concentration and consciousness, like drowsiness or sleepiness. They assess memory, by informal tests such as spelling their name while introducing themselves and observing whether the patient uses the interviewer's name afterwards, and by asking about problems in remembering.

Perception

Interviewers assess disturbances in perception: does the patient see, hear, feel, or smell things that other persons do not perceive?

Speech and Thinking

Speech is encoded thought, and disturbances in speech may indicate disturbances in thinking but not always. Interviewers observe tempo of speech, disturbances in articulation, speed and flow. Disturbances in form of thinking are explored: is the thinking slow, circumstantial, or too fast? Many mental disorders are characterized by a pathological content of thinking. Are there delusions, overvalued ideas, suicidal or extremely guilty thoughts? Does the patient suffer from irrational fear, obsessions or compulsions?

Mood and Affect

Finally, interviewers explore the mood of the patient, that is the emotion experienced by the patient during a longer period. The mood can be depressed, anxious, euphoric or irritated, or there can be a lack of emotion. The affect of the patient, that is the patient's emotional response to external and internal events during the interview, is observed. Indications for (change in) affect are auto-nomic responses like blushing, trembling, sweating, voice tone, posture and movement.

Personal History

Interviewers explore the life history of the patient in different periods; the early childhood (0–4), childhood (4–12), adolescence (12–18) and adulthood. They question the psychological, social, intellectual (i.e. educational and occupational) and sexual development of the patient during the different periods. Life events during different periods, like moving, hospitalization, divorce, are asked for. Lifelong patterns of maladjustment are assessed. The family background and comparable mental disorders in the family are explored.

Present Functioning

The fourth stage of the interview concerns the present functioning of the patient.

Social Situation

Interviewers need to explore the presence and quality of social contacts within the family (the primary group) as well as contacts outside of the family. In this way social functioning and social support is assessed.

Societal Situation and Pursuits

The patient's occupational functioning, financial situation, housing and hobbies are examined, as well as patient's satisfaction with his/her societal situation and pursuits.

At the end of the interview, interviewers share their insights with the patient. They summarize their understanding of the problem of the patient, the diag-nosis, possible causes, and the request for help. Also, they give information about the prognosis and treatment possibilities.

Process Skills

The process skills that are mainly used in different phases of the interview are listed in Table 1. Firstly, it is important that interviewers structure the interview in a way which is clear for the patient. Therefore, they have to introduce the different stages of the interview, give information about the purpose of each stage, and clarify what kind of questions they will ask and what they expect from the patient. Thus, they communicate as much as possible about their way of

working. During the whole interview they use the regulating skills "giving information", "asking for feedback", and "thinking aloud" (that is clarifying considerations and questions from the interviewers' perspective). In the first phase of
the interview, when the reference of the patient is the central focus (problem
clarification), interviewers use the process skills "attending behaviour" (that is:
non-verbal and verbal minimal encouragements to talk), "open-ended questions", "reflection of feelings" and "paraphrasing of content". During the second part of the first phase of the interview (history of present problem) as well as
during the second phase (the psychiatric examination) interviewers use more
specific open- and close-ended questions, and structure the interview more. In
the third and fourth stage of the interview, all process (listening and regulating)
skills are used.

Cognitive Skills

The interviewers' cognitive processes during the different stages of the interview
are listed in the third column of Table 1. During the first stage of the interview,
while clarifying the present problem and exploring other problems (stage 1a),
interviewers formulate hypotheses about axis I and II diagnosis (list 1 of all
possible diagnoses from list 3 of unexplored disorders). However, they do not
test their hypotheses yet, since the frame of reference of the patient is central
during this first stage. When interviewers further analyse the main problem(s)
(stage 1b) they select questions to test their diagnostic hypotheses. As a result,
they refine their list of all possible diagnoses and make a list of excluded disorders (list 2). During the second stage of the interview, the psychiatric examination, they further investigate their list of unexplored disorders (by posing specific
questions about their mental status). At the end of the psychiatric examination,
they generally have enough information to formulate a (differential) diagnosis
on axis I and III. At the end of the third stage of the interview, the personal
history, interviewers are able to formulate precipitating, predisposing and maintaining factors, combining the information from stage 1 of the interview with
personal history information. Also, life-long patterns of maladaptive behaviour
generally become clear after reviewing the patient's personal history, enabling
interviewers to make an axis II diagnosis, if any. After the fourth stage of the
interview, interviewers have gained the information to make a diagnosis on axis
IV (psychosocial and environmental problems) and on axis V (global assessment
of social, occupational and psychological functioning). For an overview of the
content and process skills during the diagnostic interview see also Table 1.

TRAINING METHODS

Research on teaching medical interviewing suggests that highly structured training programmes in which specific skills are identified, demonstrated, practised

and evaluated are more effective than less structured programmes in influencing behaviour and are more positively evaluated by students (Carrol & Monroe, 1979). Ivey's (1971) microcounselling approach is an example of such a highly structured training programme. Microcounselling is a model of instruction that subdivides complex human behaviours into discrete behavioural units and then teaches those units through didactic instruction, behavioural practice, observation and immediate feedback. In microcounselling, skills are practised through role-playing. Patient roles are impersonated by fellow trainees. Although substantial evidence indicates that microcounselling is an effective training approach, the method has also been criticized. Robinson and Halliday (1987), for instance, argued that microcounselling concentrates too much on the overt behaviour of the counsellor and that the complex cognitive skill of reaching a deeper understanding of a client's problem needs to be given far more emphasis in training. Robinson and Halliday (1988) studied the interview behaviour of counsellors interviewing two simulated patients. They found that the frequency of reasoning out loud was highly predictive of problem-analysis quality, suggesting that the skills of on-the-spot information processing need to be emphasized more in counsellor training.

A second training approach, applied in psychiatric education, relies on direct supervision of residents interviewing "real" patients (Salvendy, 1987). In the traditional method of indirect supervision, the interviewer informs the supervisor of the interview process and the patient's problems. The supervisor, therefore, must rely on secondhand information that may be unreliable. In the direct supervisory approach, by contrast, the supervisor observes the initial interview directly (by means of a one-way mirror or by sitting in with the interviewer) and gives feedback at the end of the interview. An alternative direct supervision approach, described by Lovett, Cox and Abou-Saleh (1990), is to interview a patient in front of a small group of peers and a supervisor. Peer feedback is given afterwards, and group discussion is facilitated by the supervisor. Jaynes et al. (1979) found that, compared to patients whose therapists had indirect supervision, more than twice as many patients of therapists with direct supervision remained in active treatment or successfully completed treatment. The effectiveness of indirect supervision may be enhanced when the supervisor gives immediate feedback on audio- or video-recordings of the patient–interviewer sessions. Moreover, roleplaying parts of the (forthcoming or already conducted) interview during supervision may also improve the effectiveness of indirect supervision. A roleplay in which the supervisor is the interviewer and the trainee the patient enables modelling of effective interview behaviour, whereas the supervisor can provide the trainee with immediate feedback during a roleplay in which the supervisor is the patient and the trainee the interviewer.

Shea (1988) developed a method to analyse the flow of the psychiatric interview, the facilics system (*facilis* is Latin for "ease of movement"). Residents learn to recognize the various clinical topics (called regions) explored in interview situations and the various methods of making transitions (called gates) between these regions. Two types of regions – process and content – are distinguished. Process regions focus on such issues as engagement, patient opinion and patient perspective. Content regions refer to areas of conversation in which the focus is on data gathering. Facilics analysis, thus, provides a means for structuring the interview and making it more manageable for trainees.

A third approach, mainly practised in medical education, is to use simulated patients in teaching diagnostic skills. A simulated patient is a person who has been trained to effectively simulate a patient or any aspect of a patient's illness, depending on the educational need (Barrows, 1971). Simulated patients have important advantages over real patients. First, the trainee can practise without the risk of hurting or exhausting the patient. Secondly, a simulation allows for controlled learning. For example, a complex diagnostic problem can be presented to the trainee in more manageable units. Thirdly, simulated patients are in a better position to give objective feedback about the quality of the care they have received, because their perspective on the interviewer is not influenced by real troubles and need for help. Compared to roleplaying in which a fellow trainee simulates a patient, standardization and life-likeness of simulated patients is high (Norman et al., 1985; Rethans & van Boven, 1987; Sanson-Fisher & Poole, 1980). As a result, skills learned during interactions with simulated patients may generalize easily to real practice.

To summarize, the published literature suggests that effective training in diagnostic interviewing should (a) focus on the acquisition and the integrated application of process, content, and cognitive skills, (b) be highly structured, following microteaching principles, and (c) use simulated patients or direct supervision.

A STRUCTURED APPROACH TO TEACHING DIAGNOSTIC INTERVIEWING

A training programme has been developed at Maastricht University in The Netherlands, based on the model presented in Table 1, to teach clinical psychology undergraduates to conduct a diagnostic interview and produce an accurate diagnosis and plan for further management (see also Bögels, 1994a).

First of all, students receive a training course in problem clarification, in which all process skills are practised. In each session, one or two process skills are taught by means of video-modelling, roleplaying and immediate feedback. During this training, no emphasis is put on diagnostic issues; feedback is directed only to the proper and functional use of process skills.

Thereafter, students receive training in diagnostic interviewing, first with regard to neurotic problems, then with regard to psychotic problems. In the first course, the four stages of the diagnostic interview are taught separately by means of video-modelling, roleplaying and feedback. Each session starts with a video-taped demonstration of one of the stages of the diagnostic interview. Role-playing takes place in triads, with one of the students playing a patient, another being the interviewer, and a third being the observer. Trainees impersonating a patient are provided with written scripts. Student-observers and the trainer give feedback with regard to the content skills to be used during this stage of the interview. Also, videotaped feedback is provided. At the end of the training, students are trained to use process and content skills in conjunction.

Diagnostic reasoning (cognitive skill) is taught by showing a large number of short videotaped vignettes of actual and simulated patients with mental disorders. Students formulate hypotheses about the diagnosis in DSM-IV terms. They motivate their (differential) diagnostic hypotheses on the basis of observed signs and symptoms, and formulate questions they would ask in order to test their hypotheses. Diagnostic reasoning is also encouraged during roleplaying. After a "patient" has been interviewed, the trainer (or student-observer) asks the interviewers which diagnostic hypotheses went through their mind during the interview. It is then evaluated whether these diagnostic hypotheses have been tested during the interview. Other interventions are suggested to gather information for further verification of the hypotheses. The roleplaying is then continued to try out the suggestions.

Simulated patient encounters are organized in two ways: during training sessions and at the end of a training course. Psychiatric nurses are used as simulated patients, because their experience in communication with psychiatric patients is helpful in simulating mental disorders. Plenary sessions with a simulated patient in the group allow for discussion before and during the encounter on which interview strategy to follow. These encounters are occasions to confront trainees with new and difficult problems, such as dealing with hostile or paranoid patients, in a supportive learning environment. For each student, an individual encounter with a simulated patient is organized at the end of every training course. The room is equipped with a one-way screen, and the encounter is videotaped. The trainer and a fellow trainee observe the encounter from behind a one-way screen. After the interview, the trainee receives feedback from the patient, fellow-student and trainer. The latter two provide feedback using a structured rating form. These encounters are meant to evaluate the level of skills a student has attained after training.

EFFECTS OF DIAGNOSTIC INTERVIEW TRAINING

In the last decade, training programmes have been developed to teach diagnostic interviewing skills to future mental health professionals (e.g. Bögels, 1994a; Shea & Mezzich, 1988). However, controlled studies on the effects of these training programmes are scarce. Diagnostic interview training has been found to be effective in improving family physicians' recognition of mental disorders (Goldberg et al., 1980) and their interviewing skills (Gask et al., 1987, 1988). Effects of a psychiatric clerkship for medical students were evaluated by Mumford et al. (1987). They found a modest improvement of residents' process skills, with no improvement on their content skills.

The immediate and long-term effects of diagnostic interview training for psychology undergraduates were studied by Bögels (1995). Students were trained first in diagnostic interviewing with regard to mood disorders, and six months later they received training focusing on psychotic disorders. Both training courses consist of six group sessions of three hours. After the first training, students' performance improved significantly with regard to content skills, cognitive skills (diagnostic accuracy) and recall of relevant patient information. No improvement was found on process skills, but this may be caused by students' high level of process skills before training, due to prior training in process skills. However, students' performance deteriorated significantly with regard to content skills and recall of relevant patient information after six months during which they received no training. The second training did not improve performance. The results indicated that diagnostic interviewing can be taught effectively in a short period with regard to (for example) mood disorders, but students may need more practice in conducting a diagnostic interview with psychotic patients. Also, the results show that diagnostic interview training, like other forms of skills training, suffers from the loss of effect over time (Baker & Daniels, 1989; Engler et al., 1981; Graig, 1992).

EVALUATION OF TRAINEES' EMERGING COMPETENCIES

To measure diagnostic interviewing performance, two instruments are presented: the Diagnostic Interviewing Rating Scale in Mental health care (DIRSM) and a questionnaire to assess diagnostic accuracy (Bögels et al., 1995).

The DIRSM measures two dimensions of diagnostic interviewing: process and content skills. Process scores reflect ratings on 10 aspects of interpersonal and communication skills, whereas content scores reflect ratings on 13 aspects of information gathering ability (see Table 1). Aspects are defined in behavioural terms and criteria of inadequate and adequate behaviour are described. Each aspect is scored on a 5-point scale ranging from unacceptable (1) to advanced (5).

Research (Bögels et al., 1995) has indicated that the process and content interviewing skills can be reliably measured, as far as interrater reliability is concerned. The intraclass correlation was 0.79 for process skills, and 0.72 for content skills ($n = 20$). However, interviewer performance on one case proved to be a poor predictor of performance on other cases. Therefore, at least four encounters with simulated patients with different categories of mental disorders are necessary to obtain reliable scores of general diagnostic interviewing ability. Evidence supporting the concurrent validity of the DIRSM was also produced; process skills were strongly related to patient satisfaction ($r = 0.68$), whereas content skills correlated with the amount of relevant information given by the patient ($r = 0.57$) and diagnostic accuracy ($r = 0.45$). By means of the DIRSM experts could be discriminated from novices: experts (12 psychiatrists and clinical psychologists) outperformed novices (15 third-year clinical psychology undergraduates who were trained in diagnostic interviewing) on process skills ($p < 0.01$) as well as content skills ($p < 0.001$) (Bögels, 1994b). These results support the external validity of the DIRSM.

Diagnostic accuracy of the trainees, an indicator of their cognitive skills, is measured by means of a problem-solving questionnaire. Using the information gathered during the simulated patient contact, students write a (differential) diagnosis in DSM-IV terms. They also formulate precipitating, predisposing and maintaining factors that can explain the present problem. Based on the descriptive and explanatory diagnoses, they describe their plan for further management. The interrater reliability for diagnostic accuracy was high (intraclass correlation = 0.84). However, like the process and content skills, at least four cases are necessary to obtain reproducible results (Bögels et al., 1995). Experts outperformed novices on diagnostical accuracy ($p < 0.001$), lending support for the external validity of the questionnaire (Bögels, 1994b).

CONCLUDING COMMENTS

A number of issues with regard to diagnostic interviewing need further clarification. First, more research is required on what constitutes effective diagnostic interviewing in the mental health field. As a result of extensive research on the diagnostic expertise of physicians, utilizing the novice–expert paradigm, a fairly detailed understanding now exists of what goes on during the medical interview and how expertise in this field develops (Schmidt et al., 1990). In the same way, by comparing the performance of mental health workers of different level of expertise, insight can be obtained concerning the nature of diagnostic expertise in the mental health field. Secondly, the development of effective methods to teach complex skills, such as diagnostic interviewing, needs further attention. Cognitive training strategies, in which students are specifically trained to formulate, test and refine their growing comprehension of a case, may be especially important in the acquisition of diagnostic interviewing. Thirdly, there is an urgent need for empirical evaluation of training programmes in higher-order skills such as diagnostic interviewing. Without controlled outcome studies, the value of diagnostic interview training programmes remains questionable. Fourthly, it is important to study how diagnostic interviewing ability develops through training in the context of a curriculum and through clinical clerkships, in order to establish the relative effects of both approaches to skills acquisition. Finally, in order to handle the phenomenon of relapse of skills, strategies need to be developed to efficiently retrieve or reactivate earlier acquired skills.

REFERENCES

American Psychiatric Association (1994). *Diagnostical and Statistical Manual of Mental Disorders* (4th edn). Washington: American Psychiatric Association.

Authier, J. & Gustafson, K. (1982). Microtraining: Focusing on specific skills. In E.K. Marshall & P.D. Kurtz (Eds.), *Interpersonal Helping Skills* (pp. 93–131). San Francisco: Jossey-Bass.

Baker, S.B. & Daniels, T.G. (1989). Integrating research on the microcounselling program: A meta-analysis. *Journal of Counselling Psychology*, **36**, 213–222.

Barrows, H.S. (1971). *Simulated Patients (Programmed Patients): The Development and Use of a New Technique in Medical Education*. Springfield Il.: Thomas.

Bögels, S.M. (1994a). A structured approach to teaching diagnostic interviewing. *Teaching of Psychology*, **21**, 144–150.

Bögels, S.M. (1994b). *Teaching and assessing diagnostic interviewing skills: An application to the mental health field*. Thesis. Maastricht: Datawyse.

Bögels, S.M. (1995). Immediate and long-term effects of psychiatric interview training on students' skills. *Medical Teacher*, **18**, 279–287.

Bögels, S.M., van der Vleuten, C.P.M., Blok, G.A., Kreutzkamp, R., Melles, R. & Schmidt, H.G. (1995). The diagnostic interview in mental health care: Assessment and validation of process and content skills. *Journal of Psychopathology and Behavioral Assessment*, **17**, 217–230.

Carrol, J.G. & Monroe, J. (1979). Teaching medical interviewing: A critique of educational research practice. *Journal of Medical Education*, **54**, 498–500.

Cox, A., Holbrook, D. & Rutter, M. (1981a). Psychiatric interviewing techniques: VI. Experimental study: Eliciting feelings. *British Journal of Psychiatry*, **139**, 144–158.

Cox, A., Hopkinson, K. & Rutter, M. (1981b). Psychiatric interviewing techniques: II. Naturalistic study: Eliciting factual information. *British Journal of Psychiatry*, **138**, 283–291.

Cox, A., Rutter, M. & Holbrook (1981c). Psychiatric interviewing techniques: V. Experimental study: Eliciting factual information. *British Journal of Psychiatry*, **138**, 283–291.

DiMatteo, M.R. & DiNicola, D.D. (1982). *Achieving Patient Compliance*. New York: Pergamon.

Engler, C.W., Saltman, C.A., Walker, M.L. & Wolf, F.M. (1981). Medical skills acquisition and retention of communication and interviewing skills. *Journal of Medical Education*, **56**, 572–579.

Evans, B.J., Stanley, R.O., Mestrovic, R. & Rose, L. (1991). Effects of communication skills training on students' diagnostic efficiency. *Medical Education*, **25**, 517–526.

Friedman, J.M.H. (1989). Structured interviews: The expert's vantage. In S. Wetzler & M.M. Katz (Eds.), *Contemporary Approaches to Psychological Assessment: Vol. 1. Clinical and Experimental Psychiatry* (pp. 83–98). New York: Brunner/Mazel.

Gask, L., McGrath, G., Goldberg, D. & Millar, T. (1987). Improving the psychiatric skills of established general practitioners: evaluation of group teaching. *Medical Education*, **21**, 362–368.

Gask, L., Goldberg, D., Lesser, A.L. & Millar, T. (1988). Improving the psychiatric skills of the general practice trainee: An evaluation of a group training course. *Medical Education*, **22**, 132–138.

Gelder, M., Gath, D. & Mayou, R. (1989). *Oxford Textbook of Psychiatry* (2nd edn). Oxford: Oxford University Press.

Ginsberg, G.L. (1985). Diagnosis and psychiatry: Examination of the psychiatric patient. In H.I. Kaplan & B.J. Sadock (Eds.), *Comprehensive Textbook of Psychiatry/IV* (pp. 482–494). Baltimore: Williams & Wilkins.

Goldberg, D. & Huxley, P. (1980). *Mental Illness in the Community: The Pathway to Psychiatric Care*. London: Tavistock Publications.

Goldberg, D.P., Steele, J.J., Smith, C. & Spivey, L. (1980). Training family doctors to recognise psychiatric illnesses with increased accuracy. *Lancet*, **8193**, 521–523.

Graig, J.L. (1992). Retention of interviewing skills learned by first-year medical students: a longitudinal study. *Medical Education*, **26**, 276–281.

Hak, T. & de Boer, F. (1996). Formulations in first encounters. *Journal of Pragmatics*, **25**, 83–99.

Ivey, A.E. (1971). *Microcounselling: Innovations in Interviewing Training.* Springfield, Il: Thomas.

Jaynes, S., Charles, E., Kass, F. & Holzman, S. (1979). Clinical supervision of the initial interview: Effects on patient care. *American Journal of Psychiatry*, **11**, 1454–1457.

Kraan, H.F. & Crijnen, A.A.M. (1987). *The Maastricht History and Advice Checklist: Studies of instrumental utility.* Thesis, Amsterdam: Velden van den Hazelaar.

Lang, G. & van der Molen, H., with Trower, P. & Look, R. (1990). *Personal Conversations: Roles and Skills for Counsellors.* London: Routledge.

Lovett, L.M., Cox, A. & Abou-Saleh, M. (1990). Teaching psychiatric interview skills to medical students. *Medical Education*, **24**, 243–250.

MacKinnon, R.A. & Michels, R. (1971). *The Psychiatric Interview in Clinical Practice.* Toronto: Saunders.

McCready, J.R. & Waring, E.M. (1986). Interviewing skills in relation to psychiatric residency. *Canadian Journal of Psychiatry*, **31**, 317–322.

McGuire, P. (1982). Psychiatrists also need interview training (Comments). *British Journal of Psychiatry*, **141**, 423–424.

Mumford, E., Schlesinger, H., Cuerdon, T. & Scully, J. (1987). Ratings of videotapes and four other methods of evaluating a psychiatric clerkship. *American Journal of Psychiatry*, **138**, 316–322.

Nicholi, A.M. (1978). History and mental status. In M.A. Nicholi (Ed.), *Harvard Guide to Modern Psychiatry.* Cambridge: Harvard University Press.

Norman, G., Neufeld, V., Walsh, A., Woodward, C. & McConvey, G. (1985). Measuring physicians' performance by using simulated patients. *Journal of Medical Education*, **60**, 925–934.

Nurcombe, B. & Gallagher, R.M. (1986). *The Clinical Process in Psychiatry: Diagnosis and Management Planning.* New York: Cambridge University Press.

Othmer, E. & Othmer, S.C. (1994). *The Clinical Interview Using DSM-IV, Vol. I: Fundamentals.* Washington: American Psychiatric Press.

Pendleton, D., Schofield, T., Tate, P. & Havelock, P. (1984). *The Consultation: An Approach to Learning and Teaching.* Oxford: Oxford University Press.

Reiser, D.E. (1984). The psychiatric interview. In H.H. Goldman (Ed.), *Review of General Psychiatry* (pp. 197–205). Los Altos: Lange.

Rethans, J. & van Boven, C. (1987). Simulated patients in general practice: A different look at the consultation. *British Medical Journal*, **294**, 809–812.

Robinson, V.M.J. & Halliday, J. (1987). A critique of the microcounselling approach to problem understanding. *British Journal of Guidance and Counselling*, **15**, 113–124.

Robinson, V.M.J. & Halliday, J. (1988). Relationship of counsellor reasoning and data collection to problem-analysis quality. *British Journal of Guidance and Counselling*, **16**, 50–62.

Rosenthal, R.H. & Akiskal, H.S. (1985). Mental status examination. In M. Hersen & S.M. Turner (Eds.), *Diagnostic Interviewing* (pp. 25–52). New York: Plenum.

Salvendy, J.T. (1987). Supervision of the initial interview: A choice of methods. *Journal of Psychiatric Education*, **11**, 121–126.

Sanson-Fisher, R.W. & Poole, A.D. (1980). Simulated patients and the assessment of medical students' interpersonal skills. *Medical Education*, **14**, 149–253.

Schmidt, H.G., Norman, G.R. & Boshuizen, H.P.A. (1990). A cognitive perspective on medical expertise: Theory and implications. *Academic Medicine*, **65**, 611–621.

Shea, S.C. (1988). *Psychiatric Interviewing: The Art of Understanding.* Philadelphia: Saunders.

Shea, S.C. & Mezzich, J.E. (1988). Contemporary psychiatric interviewing: New directions for training. *Psychiatry*, **15**, 385–397.

Siassi, I. (1984). Psychiatric Interview and Mental Status Examination. In G. Goldstein & M. Hersen (Eds.), *Handbook of Psychological Assessment* (pp. 259–275). New York: Pergamon.

Tanner, L.A. & Silverman, G. (1981). A teacher's guide to teaching medical interviewing. *Medical Education*, **15**, 100–105.

Thompson, M.G.G. (1979). *A Resident's Guide to Psychiatric Education.* New York: Plenum.

Turner, S.M. & Hersen, M. (1985). The interviewing process. In M. Hersen & S.M. Turner (Eds.), *Diagnostic Interviewing* (pp. 3–23). New York: Plenum.

The Hypnotic Interview: Conceptual and Technical Considerations

Steven Jay Lynn, Lisa Marmelstein
Binghamton University, USA
Irving Kirsch
University of Connecticut, USA
and
Judith Rhue
Ohio University College of Osteopathic Medicine, USA

In much of the public eye, hypnosis is nothing more than a gimmicky and potentially dangerous technique, as much associated with legerdemain and stage tricks as it is with Svengali-like powers, including the ability to rob a person of his or her willpower. These stereotypes and misconceptions are residues of beliefs that can be traced to nineteenth century mesmerism and later investigators who maintained that hypnotized participants could see without the use of their eyes, perform complex actions while asleep, travel mentally to distant planets and report back accurately about the inhabitants, spot disease by seeing through the skin to the internal organs of sick individuals, and communicate with the dead – all special abilities manifested by persons who lose control of their ability to respond independently of the operator during hypnosis (see Lynn, Rhue & Spanos, 1994).

Although most of these outlandish ideas are no longer taken seriously by scientific investigators, unusual claims for hypnosis continue to be made. For example, some investigators argue that the use of hypnotic procedures enables people to recall their earlier abduction by space aliens, other investigators argue that hypnosis has special power to recover forgotten memories of childhood, and

Handbook of the Psychology of Interviewing. Edited by A. Memon and R. Bull.
© 1999 John Wiley & Sons Ltd.

still others argue that hypnotic regression to past lives supports the theory of reincarnation. Whereas there is no scientific evidence to support these notions, they persist and are invigorated by cultural narratives disseminated by the media. Because of such claims and the fact that inaccurate and misleading cultural stereotypes about hypnosis abound, it is no wonder that many professionals are poorly educated about hypnosis and either exclude hypnosis from their armamentarium of therapeutic techniques or minimize the utility of hypnosis.

This state of affairs is unfortunate for at least two reasons. First, contemporary hypnosis researchers have shown that hypnosis is a safe technique (Lynn, Martin & Frauman, 1996b) that cannot create a will-less automaton who experiences a sleep-like state of consciousness where he or she is putty in the hands of an unscrupulous or incompetent operator. To the contrary, hypnotized participants retain the ability to control their behavior. Furthermore, participants are aware of their surroundings and typically remember much or all of what occurred during hypnosis. It is also worth noting that suggestions can be responded to with or without hypnosis, and that the function of an hypnotic induction is merely to increase suggestibility to a minor degree. Contrary to popular opinion, hypnosis does not increase the accuracy of memory and does not foster a literal re-experiencing of childhood events. In fact, hypnotic procedures can increase confidence in memories regardless of whether they are accurate or inaccurate.

Most hypnosis researchers and clinicians agree that the impressive effects of hypnosis stem from social influence and personal abilities. How participants respond to suggestions depends less on the nature and success of a particular induction than on the following variables: (a) participants' prehypnotic attitudes, beliefs, intentions and expectations about hypnosis; (b) their ability to think, fantasize and absorb themselves in suggestions; (c) their ability to form a trusting relationship with the hypnotist; (d) their ability to interpret suggestions appropriately and view their responses as successful; (e) their ability to discern task demands and cues; (f) the hypnotist and participant's ongoing interaction; and (g) the appropriateness of the therapeutic methods and suggestions to treating the presenting problem (see also Barber, 1985).

Second, hypnotic interviewing techniques can provide clinicians with a wide range of creative opportunities for enhancing treatment gains and treating a diversity of conditions ranging from anxiety and personality disorders to schizophrenia (Rhue, Lynn & Kirsch, 1993). With the impetus from managed health care systems for clinicians to use empirically validated treatments, it is appropriate to ask whether there is any reason to believe that hypnosis is an efficacious procedure. The answer to this question is "Yes": meta-analyses (see Kirsch, Montgomery & Sapirstein, 1995; Smith, Glass & Miller, 1980) reveal that the addition of hypnosis to cognitive-behavioral and psychodynamic treatments substantially enhances their efficacy. In this chapter we define clinical hypnosis, argue that hypnosis can play an important, if not pivotal role in many psychotherapeutic ventures, provide a sample hypnotic induction, and proffer guidelines for assessing clients' psychological and hypnotizability status and using hypnotic interviews to maximize treatment outcomes.

WHAT IS CLINICAL HYPNOSIS?

The American Psychological Association Division of Psychological Hypnosis has adopted a definition of hypnosis as a procedure during which changes in sensations, perceptions, thoughts, feelings, and/or behavior are suggested (see Kirsch, 1994). Clinical hypnosis can be defined as the addition of hypnosis to accepted psychological or medical treatment. Thus, hypnosis is not a treatment in itself. Rather, hypnosis is a specialized technique that can be used as an adjunctive intervention integrated into a more encompassing treatment package. Indeed, the term "clinical hypnosis" refers to a wide variety of nonstandardized and changeable methods that can serve as a catalyst to an equally wide variety of psychotherapies (Barber, 1985). Only professionals who have the appropriate training and credentials to provide the treatment that is being augmented by hypnosis should practice it.

WHY USE HYPNOSIS?

Why might therapists incorporate hypnotic interview methods into their treatment of choice? The following reasons are adapted from Lynn, Kirsch and Rhue (1996a):

1. Hypnosis as a Means of Providing Structure and Increasing Salience

Hypnosis provides an excellent context for experiential psychotherapeutic techniques. In this context, clients can detach from the external world and devote their full attention to therapeutic ideas and suggestions (see Barber, 1985). Hypnosis can thus provide a structure for therapeutic suggestions and activities, facilitating a focus on selected thoughts, feelings and images.

2. Disinhibition of the Client and Therapist

Defining interview methods as "hypnotic" affords the therapist and the client with a remarkable degree of flexibility. Clients tend to imbue the hypnotic situation with virtually magical properties that they believe will set in motion important changes in consciousness, feelings and behavior. Therapists, in turn, "have a chance to talk to their patients in a very personal and meaningful way that is difficult to do in a two-way conversation. They can now say virtually anything they believe will be beneficial to the patients" (Barber, 1985, p. 349). During hypnosis, the interviewer can suggest therapeutic images and experiences that could never occur in reality and talk with the client in metaphoric, rather than strictly literal terms.

3. Hypnosis as a Nondeceptive Placebo

For clients who have positive attitudes and wish to experience hypnosis, the hypnotic context may enhance their confidence in the effectiveness of therapy and thereby produce a placebo effect without the deception that is generally associated with placebos (see Kirsch, 1993).

4. Facilitating the Therapeutic Relationship

Hypnosis can foster a positive collaborative working alliance with the client. For instance, during hypnosis with adult survivors of sexual abuse, a positive relationship with the therapist can be rapidly established in which she or he is experienced as attentive, benign and respectful of the client's need for control (Smith, 1996). Murray-Jobsis (1996) maintains that hypnosis is the treatment of choice with persons with borderline personality disorder because hypnotic imagery is an ideal vehicle for presenting and rehearsing a corrective process of separation and individuation against a background of bonding and connectedness with the therapist.

5. Relaxation and "Ego Strengthening"

Specific and individualized suggestions can promote self-soothing, mental and physical relaxation, ego strengthening, creativity, a sense of well-being, and feelings of mastery and self-control (see Kirsch, Lynn & Rhue, 1993; Lynn et al., 1996a). Such suggestions constitute the building blocks upon which interventions for various disorders are based. In working with patients with depression, hypnotic procedures can be used to increase frustration tolerance, help a person to separate past and present events, recognize ongoing experience as changeable and malleable, and shift from a reactive to a proactive position in life (see Yapko, 1996). Hypnosis and relaxation techniques can also be used in cognitive-behavioral treatments to treat somatoform disorder (see Chaves, 1996), public speaking anxiety (see Schoenberger, 1996), and destructive habits such as cigarette smoking (Lynn et al., 1993).

6. Containing Strong Affect

Hypnotic suggestions can be used to contain strong affect. For instance, clients can be asked to hold their hand out, let their negative feelings of discomfort, tension, conflict and strong emotion coalesce on their palm and make a fist around the dysphoric sensations, thereby containing and controlling them. The client can then be asked to squeeze the feelings and compress them until they are insubstantial, and to release whatever remaining tensions exist as the fist is gradually relaxed and the hand returns to an open position. At this point, feelings of lightness in the hand can be suggested, and suggestions for hand levitation can be administered, along with suggestions to achieve a "lightness of being". Suggestions for full body relaxation, well-being, and ego strengthening can also be administered in this context.

Hypnosis can be combined with exposure techniques to titrate the level of affect experienced during or after the procedure and to integrate past traumatic experiences into a more encompassing and positive sense of the self in the present. Hypnotic visualization techniques wherein the client observes traumatic incidents on video or television screens and uses knobs or other dampening devices to regulate dysphoria can assist in controlling affect and regressive experiences during abreactions. However, the focus of the hypnotic interview should be on consciously available memories and never on the recovery of memories with hypnotic procedures.

7. Accessing and Building Resources

Hypnotic interviews often focus on accessing and building personal resources. For instance, persons can be age regressed to times when they felt they were strong, competent, intelligent, or kind or caring, attributes the individual may be unaware of during depressive or anxious episodes or even in the course of daily life. Alternately, clients can simply be asked to get in touch with their feelings of strength, competence, or caring for others.

8. Therapeutic Rehearsal

One way that clients can be encouraged to enact behaviors is by having them mentally rehearse the target action or task while they feel relaxed, confident, and engaged in positive self-talk that enhances performance. During hypnosis, imagined actions can be speeded up, slowed down, or stopped, while affect can be muted or accentuated as clients watch their actions on imagined television screens, computers, or videos, for example.

9. Imagery Techniques

Many imagery techniques are useful and are limited only by the therapist's and the client's imaginations. One widely used imagery technique is to invite clients to have a dream during hypnosis, which resembles a daydream or nightdream. Of course, the dream is designed to serve a therapeutic purpose (e.g. "Have a dream about 'X' in which its meaning to you is revealed in direct or symbolic form."). Such dreams can serve as vehicles to learn about personally meaningful life themes, problems and conflicts (e.g. see Spanos et al., 1980) as well as about the parameters of interpersonal relationships and hypnotic rapport (Frauman et al., 1984).

Age progression techniques, in which clients project themselves into the future (e.g. "after you solve your problem"), can stimulate creative thought and solution-focused attempts to cope in the present (and near future) to achieve a more distal goal. Clients can be asked to reflect on what small, achievable, steps they took on the path to achieving their goals. In one variation of this intervention, clients can be asked to contact an "inner advisor" or "wise part of the self" that can provide commentary or advice on how obstacles can be surmounted and solutions achieved.

10. Hypnotic Desensitization

Hypnotic techniques can desensitize clients to fears and provide an optimum level of exposure to anxiety eliciting stimuli in a gradual, safe, and controlled manner. When graduated tasks are administered and calibrated to the client's readiness to move forward in treatment, a sense of personal efficacy can be cultivated or enhanced. For example, hypnosis can be used to enhance the effectiveness of a standard, empirically validated, cognitive-behavioral treatment for phobias (Schoenberger, 1993).

11. Self-Hypnosis

Often, perhaps in the majority of the cases in which hypnosis is used clinically, hypnotic procedures are framed in terms of self-hypnosis (Orne & McConkey, 1981). In fact, it is not misleading to inform clients that "all hypnosis is self-hypnosis". Ultimately, it is the client's choice to accept or reject a particular suggestion, and it is the client who must create the suggested experience and perform the suggested action. Additionally, there are generally little or no differences in responsiveness to hypnotic suggestions when they are administered by an independent operator or by the participant herself (Orne & McConkey, 1981).

Self-hypnosis is most frequently taught by first introducing the client to hetero-hypnotic techniques and related experiences and then encouraging the client to assume increasingly greater responsibility for devising suggestions appropriate to achieving treatment goals. In self-administering therapeutic suggestions, the client replaces the therapist as the active agent in the therapeutic proceedings. Barber (1985) noted that labeling procedures as self-hypnosis minimizes many fears often encountered when the situation is labeled as hypnosis (e.g. fear of being under the control of another, fear of not coming out of hypnosis, fear of being unaware or unconscious). The therapist can be defined as a coach or as a guide, and the client can be encouraged to devise creative suggestions for self-administration.

Hypnotic procedures can be defined as "self-hypnosis" to enhance perceptions of treatment success and the likelihood that what is learned during the therapy hour will be implemented in everyday life (Barber, 1985).Therapists often make customized tapes for clients to listen to at home or at work that capture the essentials of the hypnotic session and crystallize important learnings. This is done in order to minimize dependency on the therapist, generalize treatment gains, and encourage mastery of self-suggestions. When instructions for self-hypnosis are given, therapists instill the idea that suggested responses will get easier with practice and that additional resources will become available to cope with problems in living.

12. Posthypnotic Suggestions

Posthypnotic suggestions can also be used to generalize treatment gains. It is often helpful to administer posthypnotic suggestions for relaxation, ego enhancement and mastery that are linked with a physical movement or gesture such as touching the thumb and forefinger together. As will be exemplified in the sample induction below, when a particular feeling state or sense of mastery regarding a situation is achieved during hypnosis, clients can be instructed to touch their thumb and forefinger together, for example, and to do so in an actual life situation in which they would like to replicate the feelings or sense of mastery (e.g. later, when you are taking the test, you will feel particularly relaxed yet alert when you touch your thumb and forefinger together).

This technique of cue-controlled relaxation, or "anchoring", as it is sometimes termed, is widely used. Many therapists use cue-control techniques that pair an image or verbal cue with a well practiced or conditioned response to relaxation or other suggested experiences. "Key phrases" (e.g. relax completely, safe, secure) can be used to trigger or elicit specific feelings and cognitions. Typically, key phrases are first suggested by the therapist or developed by the client during hypnosis and then later self-administered in relevant situations.

ASSESSMENT

The decision to incorporate hypnosis into any treatment should not be finalized before a thorough evaluation of the client has been conducted. At a minimum, the assessment should include information pertinent to the client's mental and physical status, life history, resources, motivation for treatment, current psychological problems and dynamics, and beliefs and misconceptions about hypnosis that hamper the client's ability to trust the hypnotist and to participate fully in the hypnotic proceedings.

It is imperative to initiate hypnosis only with the participant's explicit consent, to demystify hypnosis and bolster positive expectancies, and to help the participant feel tangibly in control of the events that unfold. Before hypnosis is undertaken, it is essential that therapists establish a strong therapeutic alliance, know what they wish to accomplish, and have a clear idea about how hypnotic communications can facilitate treatment. Ideally, the therapist and client should have congruent perceptions and mutual goals in this regard.

It is important to know what hypnosis represents to the client and what he or she hopes to accomplish. In addition, the therapist should determine if the client is requesting hypnosis because she is dissatisfied with the therapeutic work that has been done so far or because she is trying to avoid issues that are emerging in therapy. Furthermore, the therapist must make certain that the client maintains realistic expectations and is not viewing hypnosis as the "magic" cure.

Correspondingly, examining the therapist's motive is equally important. For example, hypnosis should not be undertaken solely because the therapist feels guilty that he or she is not doing more for the client or because the therapist is bored or angry with the client and hungering for "fireworks" in therapy that only hypnosis can provide. In short, one or more issues may need to be examined and resolved before hypnotic treatment is initiated.

Assessment of the client is necessary to screen out candidates who are inappropriate or less than ideal for hypnotherapy. Clients who are vulnerable to psychotic decompensation (Meares, 1961), those with a paranoid level of resistance to being influenced or controlled (Orne, 1965), unstabilized dissociative or posttraumatic clients, and those with borderline character structure for whom hypnosis may be experienced as a sudden, intrusive and unwanted intimacy, may all be poor candidates for hypnosis or require special attention or modification of typical hypnotic procedures to emphasize safety, security and connectedness. Ultimately, the pros and cons of hypnosis must be carefully weighed against those of nonhypnotic treatment.

Hypnotizability Assessment

Certain persons are more responsive to hypnotic suggestions than others. Most clients are able to respond to relatively simple nondemanding suggestions. This is important because many therapeutic suggestions can be so described: much good therapeutic work can be done with suggestions for comfort, security, peace of mind and imaginative rehearsal of specific events. However, virtually every experienced therapist has encountered the rare client who can not or will not respond to even simple suggestions. Given this, many therapists conduct a brief informal assessment by observing their clients' responses to simple suggestions such as for eye closure or relaxation. It is impossible to know precisely how a client will respond to a hypnotic intervention prior to inducing hypnosis itself.

It is always advisable to explore carefully the reasons why the client failed to respond to suggestions in keeping with the treatment agenda. Failures to respond may include the failure to establish rapport, misinterpretation of hypnotic communications, unconscious resistance to relinquishing symptoms, and the persistence of popular misconceptions about hypnosis that interfere with responding (e.g. you lose control during hypnosis).

Another reason to assess hypnotic responsiveness is if substantial costs are incurred with failure to hypnotize someone. Consider the case of a request to hypnotize a dental patient who is contemplating undergoing painful dental procedures without analgesia due to an allergic response to analgesics. It would be foolhardy to hypnotize such a patient in a dental situation who failed to demonstrate appreciable hypnotic analgesia, in a relatively less demanding situation, prior to the dental procedure.

If therapists assess hypnotic responsiveness, they must decide whether to use formal, standardized tests of hypnotic responsiveness, or to use nonstandard tests of responsiveness carefully tailored to the treatment at hand. If the clinician decides to use a standardized test, then he or she must further decide about whether to use a relatively long formal test of hypnotizability, such as the Stanford Hypnotic Susceptibility Scale, Form C (SHSS: C; Weitzenhoffer & Hilgard, 1962), or a shorter yet potentially diagnostic assessment of hypnotizability, such as the "induction" (IND) score of the Hypnotic Induction Profile (HIP; Spiegel

& Spiegel, 1978), for which moderate to high correlations with other hypnotizability scales have been shown (Perry, Nadon & Button, 1992).

If treatment is brief and involves only relaxation or generic ego-strengthening suggestions, a thorough assessment of hypnotizability and an examination of responses to a variety of suggestions may not be required. Furthermore, if the therapist knows in advance which suggestions will be relevant to treatment, he or she may decide to limit hypnotizability testing to specific, treatment-relevant target suggestions. It may not be essential to test clients on a complete hypnotizability scale if we are only interested in determining the robustness of hypnotic amnesia, for example, or how a person might respond to an age regression, analgesia or hypnotic dream suggestion. Because there is variability in how even highly hypnotizable individuals experience and respond to suggestions, a high hypnotizability score does not obviate the need to evaluate clients' responses to specific suggestions that are germane to treatment. It is useful to assess not only observable hypnotic responses, but subjective responses as well. Although each therapist must weigh the costs and benefits of any assessment procedure with each client, we would argue that some form of assessment of hypnotizability, whether formal or informal, brief or extensive, can provide the clinician with valuable data.

HYPNOSIS IN PRACTICE: AN ILLUSTRATIVE SELF-HYPNOSIS SCRIPT

It is useful to think of suggstions as being divided into two phases – induction and application – although in practice they may not be entirely distinct. The following induction was created by one of the authors (SJL) and is permissive and nondemanding. It can be used with a wide clientele for purposes of achieving a sense of safety, well-being, security and peace. The induction contains suggestions that are particularly useful in working with chronically anxious persons, in assisting individuals who have experienced recent traumas or have difficulties separating their "presents and pasts", and in working with persons who wish to achieve a sense of well-being in a variety of stressful life situations. The induction that follows, like any other scripted narrative, is really only a scaffolding for a more individually tailored induction that can be adapted to the unique needs of each client and type of psychotherapy.

> Please make yourself comfortable. Let us begin by your simply closing your eyes. Please close your eyes and take a deep breath. And as you breathe out you can begin to feel a sense of calm, feel the calmness spreading. You will not fall asleep, although just how relaxed or awake you are really doesn't matter, because there are always lessons to be learned, and in learning . . . growing, and in evolving as a person, reminding yourself that you are in charge now, you can do or not do, think or not think, as you wish. And whether your mind drifts or wafts or whether thoughts break up in no particular order or flow like a stream, you can always listen to my voice, and talk if you have the desire to do so. I wonder whether you would

like to experience what it might be like to move to an even deeper state of calm, moving and moving and moving, you doing it, you creating it, in your own mind, in your own body, in your own way, peace, easy, comfortable, at ease, as deep as you like into your experience, nothing to disturb, nothing to bother, lots of time, lots and lots of time to experience what you need to, what you want to, with no one to make decisions for you, to tell you just how to be the person you are or can be, or what you need to know to do what needs to be done or exactly when and how you will go even deeper into your experience of who you are and what you can be, with freedom to write the story more and more as you wish, you the author, your hand writing, in your own hand, taking with you, from this experience, what interests and absorbs you, what piques your curiosity, even surprises you, noticing what you need to, discovering what is really important . . . what you want . . . in your own time, in your own way, with you the author, you the creator of it all. Whatever you experience is alright. It is your experience and you own it. Nothing in particular to do unless you want to.

I wonder if you have the experience of time slowing down . . . time slowing down to a most comfortable pace. Are you aware that your breathing has altered, perhaps slowed down, perhaps speeded up slightly; it just doesn't matter at all . . . not for now . . . at any rate . . . at any speed. No matter how you breathe, no matter whether you might wish to move around to adjust your position, what matters is that you are aware of what you can experience. And are you willing to experience a certain level of comfort, a level that is good enough for you? Just enough, if not a little more, to have an experience of safety and security? Wouldn't it be nice to feel at perfect peace? Wouldn't it be nice to be quiet inside? Wouldn't it be wonderful to experience body, mind, at ease . . . safe . . . secure . . . comfort . . . for now . . . As if enveloped by some sort of protective bubble, in charge of what comes in and goes out, able to write the script as you choose? Would you like to modify your experience in some way? Do you give yourself permission to do so? Go ahead, and do so, if you wish, make yourself comfortable.

Perhaps even images and thoughts are slowing down to a trickle . . . or maybe some thoughts are a bit faster than others, yet catching up with the slow ones . . . slowing down . . . I wonder whether you can experience a place where you are complete, whole, where you are aware of your strength, and ability to care and be kind, to support and care for yourself and others. A place of peace and safety . . . safety and peace . . . a place protected from any past tensions or worries or situations you have felt or experienced . . . a place protected from the past and fully in the present . . . any concerns you have that get in the way of this sense of perfect peace and safety are moving farther and farther away, breaking up like clouds in the wind . . . moving and moving and moving . . . as you breathe and feel even more connected . . . resting so comfortably and peacefully . . . bringing your sense of well-being into focus . . . more and more . . . more and more . . .

Imagine yourself moving closer and closer to this perfect place . . . this sense of safety and well-being . . . with each step you take, you become more centered, grounded, focused . . . relaxation flowing . . . flowing relaxation . . . waves of relaxation . . . open and receptive . . . safe and secure. Nothing to bother . . . do you feel more heavy and warm or an easy floating feeling? I don't know, it is your experience.

To help us move toward this goal, I will count from one to five. And with each step, you can remember to take a deep breath and move closer to that sense of perfect peace and safety . . . If you are there already, why then your conscious mind does not even need to listen fully to what I say, as I count from one to five, as you move and flow with this sense of peace and safety.

One. And take your first step. More and more focused on your experience of what you are and can be as you gain a sense of inner peace. And wouldn't it be nice to really let go to the point where you feel this sense of serenity enveloping you? Is this alright?

Two. And with your second step, are you more relaxed than when you are asleep or would you rather not think at all? Are you willing to go deep and deep and deeper into your own experience as you move toward that level of being where you know you can let yourself experience comfort . . . safety . . . security? Your breathing is so relaxed at this point. Would you like to go even deeper? Nothing to bother, nothing to disturb . . .

Three. And with your third step you discover a pull toward this place within yourself . . . gently drawing you toward it . . . moving closer . . . soon you discover even more aspects of peace and serenity . . . as you feel cushioned and protected.

Four. You are almost there. Touching that inner part of yourself, almost one with it, even as you breathe. You don't really have to do anything . . . more and more at peace, serene.

Five. And with that fifth and final step, feel a new sense of wholeness emerging . . . a sense of yourself as good and lovable. And can you feel a sense of strength you can draw on enveloping, comforting and nurturing you? Get in touch with this. Sense the ability to decide what is truly important to you. When you can sense this, nod gently . . . very gently yet visibly. Can you sense your ability to separate the past from the present? The ability to live more and more in the present . . . feeling safe and secure . . . able to make good decisions . . . more and more trusting yourself to take care of yourself? Can you realize deep within your being that you can act in terms of your own best good? I know that you can . . . nod now to let me know that you know this.

Think of a key phrase that captures for you a sense of safety, peace, strength and wisdom. I don't know what your key phrase is . . . but you do . . . look deep inside and you will discover it . . . let it come to you . . . if it is not already there . . . You can access this key phrase in your mind . . . whenever you need to . . . peace of mind and inner strength . . . It is so easy . . . three very simple things . . . three very simple things . . . One, you will take a deep breath. Two, as you breathe in, you will think of your key phrase. And three, you will make a fist, drawing on all your inner strength and will and determination and love and caring for yourself.

When I say the word anchor, you will breathe in, think of your key phrase, and make a fist, all at the same time. Then, you will breathe out, release your fist, and think of your key phrase again. And now, anchor: Breathe, phrase, fist . . . and release, and say your key phrase. Do this again . . . and when you release your fist, you will feel your body and your mind letting go and relaxing even more . . . even more . . . if that is possible.

This is a place to remember when you are stressed or disturbed or simply wish to feel good. And you can use this anchor any time you need it. Once again, anchor and release. Feel the calmness spread as you breathe out. Whatever you experience is alright, it is perfectly fine.

In a minute, I will suggest another anchor you can use. You will bring your thumb and forefinger together, creating a circle or a ring. That circle stands for oneness . . . with all aspects of yourself . . . of a coming together in peace . . . of all your feelings . . . and an acceptance of who you are and all that you can be . . . of serenity that flows from self-acceptance and caring for yourself and for others . . . the circle represents your inner self.

You will anchor in the same way you did when you made a fist. You will do three things at once. You will bring your thumb and forefinger together, breathe in, and think of your key phrase, strength is within. Then breathe out and think of your key phrase again. Strength is within.

Once again, anchor.

You can use this anchor at times when you need to focus on strength, when you want to go deep inside. You can access your inner self this way.

Feel yourself so relaxed, notice how comfortable and peaceful you are now. You have a sense of peace, of being at one with yourself, of being at one with your inner self. You can return to this place anytime you want. You can come back to this state of calm at even the most distressing times. Remember to use your anchors when you are distressed or upset, as well as any other times. And remember that your inner self is more than your experiences, more than your thoughts, more than your feelings, more than your past.

And in a minute, you will begin to leave this special place, but you will bring your inner self with you. And you will come back slowly. You will bring your strength, your renewed sense of self, coming together, more whole and complete, your inner calmness, and you will bring all of your tools, all of your ways of coping with you. I will count back slowly from five to one. You will gradually come back, so that, by the time I say two, you will open your eyes. When I reach the count of one, you will be wide awake, alert, no longer hypnotized.

And now, I am counting back . . . Five . . . You are getting a sense of moving away very, very slowly. You are very calm. Four . . . You're moving a little further away. Your inner self is coming with you, and you feel so safe and secure. Three. You're becoming more aware of your body. You're more aware of your surroundings. Maybe you are aware of light beyond your closed eyelids. You're more aware of sensations in your body that you might not have been aware of before. Two . . . You are slowly opening your eyes. Can you continue to feel very calm and relaxed? Have a sense of wholeness, of completeness? It can feel so good, and it can stay with you. You're becoming reoriented to where you are right now. Your inner self is coming with you. One . . . You are becoming wide awake again. Fully alert. Let yourself move your body . . . begin to move slowly. Stretch and let it come back to a state of wakefulness. Your inner self is with you. You can come back to this hypnosis exercise again and again, when you wish, when you want to. You can develop even more skills and abilities to calm and soothe yourself as you practice using your self-hypnosis. The idea here is that practice makes perfect. Practice at night, the morning, and the afternoon, at least once or twice a day, or more, as you choose, as you wish, at any time you need to, want to. If you wish, you can also keep a record of what works best for you as you learn and grow, learn and grow.

Let's practice using the anchor now.

Let's close our eyes again. Place yourself in self-hypnosis. Use your anchor now, be sure to breathe and say your key phrase. Take a minute or so.

Now bring yourself out. Count to yourself from 5 to 1 and you will gradually become fully alert. Ready? Count to yourself, and at the count of one, wide awake. How do you feel?

TREATMENT ISSUES AND RECOMMENDATIONS FOR MAXIMIZING TREATMENT GAINS

In this section we consider how therapists can maximize treatment gains in hypnotic interviews. The following discussion is adapted from Lynn et al. (1996a).

Bolstering Positive Expectancies

Expectancies are important determinants of what clients experience and how they behave in hypnotic situations (see Kirsch, 1990, 1994). In fact, expectancy is one of the few stable correlates of hypnotizability (Kirsch & Council, 1992). Like placebos, hypnosis produces therapeutic effects by changing the client's expectancies. And as noted earlier, unlike placebos, hypnosis does not require deception in order to be effective. It is important to monitor and influence expectations throughout the course of therapy and to provide clients with feedback indicating that treatment is successfully producing sought-after changes. Expectancies vary along two independent dimensions. One is the degree of certainty that change will occur. The other is the speed and amount of change that is expected. Ensuring that positive feedback will be experienced during treatment is facilitated by certainty that improvement can occur, but also by the expectancy that it will begin with small, gradual changes. This allows small increments, such as those produced by random fluctuations, to be interpreted as signs of therapeutic success, in much the same way as a twitch of a finger is interpreted as the beginning of arm levitation. Similarly, the assignment of easy initial tasks ensures early successes, which bolster the client's confidence in treatment.

Conversely, perceived failure to comply with suggestions may lead to a vicious cycle of negative expectancies and failure to respond to subsequent suggestions (Lynn & Hamel, 1995). Clinicians who imply that a certain depth of hypnosis must be reached in order to experience hypnosis successfully are setting their clients up for failure. Rather, the therapist should be permissive and define tasks so that failure is impossible. Finally, the therapist should prepare clients for setbacks by labeling them in advance as inevitable, temporary and useful learning opportunities (Kirsch, 1994).

Interpersonal Issues

Interpersonal issues and concerns can dampen clients' response expectancies, elicit counterproductive response sets and provoke outright resistance to treatment. Some clients' histories with parents, authority figures or helping professionals predispose them to view the hypnotist with mistrust, anger and fear. Given cultural associations of the hypnotist as having control, power and authority over the client, the hypnotic situation may accentuate clients' negative reaction tendencies (Fromm, 1980). Not only may the client be reluctant to become involved in hypnosis, but hypnosis also may be experienced as an emotionally charged, aversive event. Of course, this is most likely to occur when the hypnotherapy is imbued with connotations of personal dominance and control. Therefore, it is important to carefully assess clients' expectancies, attitudes and beliefs about hypnosis and to demystify hypnosis and portray it as a therapeutic tool that can increase personal control. When concerns about being dominated or out of control during hypnosis are salient, the therapist should consider defining hypnotic procedures as "imagery work", "goal-directed fantasies" or self-hypnosis.

Alternately, clients might develop a highly charged positive, idealized, archaic, or even sexualized transference (Shor, 1979) *vis-à-vis* the therapist, which can be equally counterproductive. The therapist must strive to establish a resilient, working alliance with the client as a deterrent against such negative or idealized transference reactions (Lynn, Martin & Frauman, 1996b).

Orne (1965) has noted that the hypnotist-directive nature of hypnosis might amplify countertransference difficulties. When the therapist is aware of having particularly strong positive, sexualized, or hostile feelings toward the client or feels a need to control the therapeutic encounter with little regard for the client's well-being, it is appropriate for the therapist to seek consultation, supervision, or individual psychotherapy.

Direct Suggestions to Relinquish Symptoms

Symptoms may represent coping or adaptive mechanisms that are associated with potent yet unconscious secondary gains. In order to assess any secondary gains or reinforcement contingencies that maintain or exacerbate current symptoms, the therapist ought to consider the following questions. What, in the past, has increased and decreased the behavior or problem at issue? How ready is the person to try something new or to make requisite life changes? How would the person's life be changed if the symptom were no longer a part of the clinical picture? What would have to change in the person's life in order to relinquish the symptom?

Because forceful directives to abandon symptoms may engender significant conflict and outright rebellion in the client, in general, the therapist should avoid direct suggestions to relinquish symptoms in the absence of a foundation of adequate psychological defenses and coping skills. Suggestions for symptom reduction may be safer and more effective than suggestions for symptom elimination, and permissive wording can forestall a sense of failure and provide respect for the client's intuitive sense of timing.

Suggestions May Instigate or Reveal Unexpected Affect

Like many psychotherapeutic procedures, hypnotic suggestions may impinge on a person's current concerns or conflicts, trigger painful memories, and provide an avenue for the expression of suppressed or possibly repressed affect (Fromm, 1980). Certain suggestions (e.g. age regression, hypnotic dreams) about particular events or issues imply that access to early life events can be achieved, and that insight into important psychological dynamics can be gained. Given this focus and the demands upon the client, it is not surprising that unexpectedly intense abreactions can ensue following such suggestions.

The dictum, "never treat anything with hypnosis that you are not trained or equipped to treat in nonhypnotic therapy", is an indispensable hedge against unmanageable reactions. Of course, abreactions, when managed with skill and sensitivity, can have therapeutic benefit in the context of master-based treat- ments. However, therapists should have specialized and supervised training in using abreactive techniques (with or without hypnosis) before they incorporate such techniques into their clinical practice.

Pseudomemory Risk

Rather than being a playback of a recorded event, remembering has been shown to be a constructive process, in which memories and imaginings can be mixed indistinguishably (Lynn & McConkey, 1998). As a result, suggestive and leading information can create false memories that are mistaken for historical truth. Because hypnosis involves suggestions, some of which may be leading in nature, and because hypnosis can increase confidence of recalled events with little or no change in the level of accuracy (Lynn et al., 1997), therapists employing hypnosis must be vigilant to the problem of false memory creation. Clients' memory reports during age regression, for example, can seem compelling because the reported images and emotions are vivid and intense. However, neither vivid nor emotional narrative content guarantees historical veracity.

The bottom line for us is that hypnosis should not be used to recover historically accurate memories. Whereas hypnosis can increase the number of accurate memories, it comes at the expense of a tradeoff of increased errors. Although we can find no credible justification for using hypnosis to enhance recall, this should not deter therapists from adding hypnosis to the clinical procedures they use. Hypnosis is a valuable adjunctive technique that can be used by skilled and well-trained therapists to ameliorate many problems in living.

REFERENCES

American Psychological Association, Division of Psychological Hypnosis. (1993). Hypnosis. *Psychological Hypnosis*, **2**, 3.

Barber, T.X. (1985). Hypnosuggestive procedures as catalysts for all psychotherapies. In S.J. Lynn & J.P. Garske (Eds.), *Contemporary Psychotherapies: Models and Methods* (pp. 333–376). Columbus: Merrill Press.

Chaves, J.F. (1996). Hypnotic strategies for somatoform disorders. In S.J. Lynn, I. Kirsch & J.W. Rhue (Eds.), *Casebook of Clinical Hypnosis* (pp. 131–152). Washington, DC: American Psychological Association.

Frauman, D.C., Lynn, S.J., Hardaway, R. & Molteni, A. (1984). Effect of subliminal symbiotic activation on hypnotic rapport and susceptibility. *Journal of Abnormal Psychology*, **93**, 481–483.

Fromm, E. (1980). Values in hypnotherapy. *Psychotherapy: Theory, Research and Practice*, **17**, 425–430.

Kirsch, I. (1990). *Changing Expectations: A Key to Effective Psychotherapy*. Pacific Grove, CA: Brooks/Cole.

Kirsch, I. (1993). Cognitive-behavioral hypnotherapy. In J.W. Rhue, S.J. Lynn & I. Kirsch (Eds.), *Handbook of Clinical Hypnosis*. Washington, DC: American Psychological Association.

Kirsch, I. (1994). Clinical hypnosis as a nondeceptive placebo: Empirically derived techniques. *American Journal of Clinical Hypnosis*, **37**, 95–106.

Kirsch, I. & Council, J. (1992). Situational and personality correlates of suggestibility. In E. Fromm & M. Nash (Eds.), *Contemporary Hypnosis Research* (pp. 267–292). New York: Guilford.

Kirsch, I., Lynn, S.J. & Rhue, J.W. (1993). Introduction to clinical hypnosis. In J.W. Rhue, S.J. Lynn & I. Kirsch (Eds.), *Handbook of Clinical Hypnosis* (pp. 3–22). Washington, DC: American Psychological Association.

Kirsch, I., Montgomery, G. & Sapirstein, G. (1995). Hypnosis as an adjunct to cognitive behavioral psychotherapy: A meta-analysis. *Journal of Consulting and Clinical Psychology*, **63**, 214–220.

Lynn, S.J. & Hamel, J. (1995). *Age regression and negative effects*. Unpublished manuscript, Ohio University.

Lynn, S.J. & McConkey, K.M. (1998). *Truth in Memory*. New York: Guilford.

Lynn, S.J., Neufeld, V., Rhue, J.W. & Matorin, A. (1993). Hypnosis and smoking cessation: A cognitive-behavioral treatment. In J.W. Rhue, S.J. Lynn & I. Kirsch (Eds.), *Handbook of Clinical Hypnosis* (pp. 555–586). Washington, DC: American Psychological Association.

Lynn, S.J., Rhue, J.W. & Spanos, N.P. (1994). Hypnosis. In I. Ramachadran (Ed.), *Encyclopedia of Human Behavior*. New York: Academic Press.

Lynn, S.J., Kirsch, I. & Rhue, J.W. (1996a). Maximizing treatment gains: Recommendations for the practice of clinical hypnosis. In S.J. Lynn, I. Kirsch & J.W. Rhue (Eds.), *Casebook of Clinical Hypnosis* (pp. 395–406). Washington, DC: American Psychological Association.

Lynn, S.J., Martin, D. & Frauman, D.C. (1996b). Does hypnosis pose special risks for negative effects? *International Journal of Clinical and Experimental Hypnosis*, **44**, 7–19.

Lynn, S.J., Lock, T., Myers, B. & Payne, D. (1997). Recalling the unrecallable: Should hypnosis be used for memory recovery in psychotherapy? *Current Directions in Psychological Science*, **6**, 79–83.

Meares, A. (1961). An evaluation of the dangers of medical hypnosis. *American Journal of Clinical Hypnosis*, **4**, 90–97.

Murray-Jobsis, J. (1996). Hypnosis with a borderline patient. In S.J. Lynn, I. Kirsch & J.W. Rhue (Eds.), *Casebook of Clinical Hypnosis* (pp. 173–192). Washington, DC: American Psychological Association.

Orne, M.T. (1965). Undesirable effects of hypnosis: The determinants and management. *International Journal of Clinical and Experimental Hypnosis*, **13**, 226–237.

Orne, M.T. & McConkey, K.M. (1981). Toward convergent inquiry into self-hypnosis. *International Journal of Clinical and Experimental Hypnosis*, **29**, 313–323.

Perry, C., Nadon, R. & Button, J. (1992). The measurement of hypnotic ability. In E. Fromm & M.R. Nash (Eds.), *Contemporary Hypnosis Research* (pp. 459–490). New York: Guilford.

Rhue, J.W., Lynn, S.J. & Kirsch, I. (1993). *Handbook of Clinical Hypnosis*. Washington, DC: American Psychological Association.

Schoenberger, N.E. (1996). Cognitive-behavioral hypnotherapy for phobic anxiety. In S.J. Lynn, I. Kirsch & J.W. Rhue (Eds.), *Casebook of Clinical Hypnosis* (pp. 33–50). Washington, DC: American Psychological Association.

Shor, R.E. (1979). A phenomenological method for the measurement of variables important to an understanding of the nature of hypnosis. In E. Fromm & R.E. Shor (Eds.), *Hypnosis: Developments in Research and New Perspectives* (2nd edn, pp. 105–135). New York: Aldine.

Smith, W. H. (1996). When All Else Fails: Hypnotic Exploration of Childhood Trauma. In S.J. Lynn, I. Kirsch & J.W. Rhue (Eds.) *Casebook of Clinical Hypnosis*. Washington, D.C.: American Psychological Association.

Smith, M.L., Glass, G.V. & Miller, T.I. (1980). *The Benefits of Psychotherapy*. Baltimore, MD: Johns Hopkins University Press.

Spanos, N.P., Nightingale, M.E., Radtke, H.L. & Stam, J.J. (1980). The stuff hypnotic "dreams" are made of. *Journal of Mental Imagery*, **4**, 99–110.

Spiegel, H. & Spiegel, D. (1978). *Trance and Treatment: Clinical Uses of Hypnosis*. New York: Basic Books.

Weitzenhoffer, A.M. & Hilgard, E.R. (1962). *Stanford Hypnotic Susceptibility Scale: Form C*. Palo Alto, CA: Consulting Psychologists Press.

Yapko, M.D. (1996). A brief therapy approach to the use of hypnosis in treating depression. In S.J. Lynn, I. Kirsch & J.W. Rhue (Eds.), *Casebook of Clinical Hypnosis* (pp. 75–98). Washington, DC: American Psychological Association.

Interviewing the Survivor of the Holocaust: Lessons for the Advancement of the Understanding of the Effects of Extreme Child Trauma

Constance J. Dalenberg *and* Judy J. Epstein
Trauma Research Institute, California School of Professional Psychology, San Diego, USA

Any attempt to give meaning or purpose to the Holocaust, or to "learn lessons" from its survivors, as we attempt to do here, places the authors at legitimate risk for the receipt of many accusations. The lesson, our critics might point out, was not worth the price. The level of abstraction necessary to accomplish the task of description or ascription of meaning trivializes and distances us from the horror of the event. The monstrous nature of the Holocaust transcends words, and therefore any communication about it is a lie. We agree with Roiphe (1988) that in the best of Holocaust writing, one feels the tension in the author between speaking and not speaking, "the hand held over the mouth" as the words are spoken (p. 40). And yet survivors have spoken, and in the authors' opinion, they have much to say to students of trauma, to clinicians and researchers desperate to find a way to reach the (often inarticulate) victims of extreme events, and to child abuse scholars in particular. It is the purpose of this chapter to draw out some of these connections.

The choice of the Holocaust literature as a source for clinical direction and material to understand child abuse experience is justified for at least two reasons,

Handbook of the Psychology of Interviewing. Edited by A. Memon and R. Bull.
© 1999 John Wiley & Sons Ltd.

aside from the many clinical parallels which the reader will later find apparent. First, the trauma literature has been incomparably enhanced by the magnitude, the sheer number of Holocaust survivor cases that can be studied, often from detailed first person accounts, allowing analysis of the variety of responses to a single horrific experience. Attempts can be and have been made to tie these responses to premorbid personality (Dimsdale, 1980; Niederland, 1968), "severity" of experience (Kuch & Cox, 1992), defensive strategy (Modai, 1994; Salamon, 1994), or availability and use of coping mechanisms (Shanon & Shahar, 1983). While not making the case for the objective equivalence of all Holocaust experiences, the study of the vast array of outcomes to living through "the same hell [with] different horrors" (Rittner & Roth, 1993) is in and of itself invaluable to the traumatologist.

Second, child abuse victims have been seen as a special class of traumatic survivor, not only by virtue of their developmental differences from adults, but also due to their *social* differences. The child, particularly the young child, is virtually wholly dependent on adult society. To be forced to depend for safety and sustenance on the very people who cause the greatest pain is a mind-fragmenting experience (Shengold, 1979) and one relatively unique to the experience of children. But it is not, we are arguing here, wholly unique. The European concentration camps were organized in such a manner that all aspects of the inmates' lives, including when and if prisoners ate and slept, were highly controlled by malignant others (see Kogon, 1980). Bettleheim (1960) presented the survivors as childlike, regressive and primitive in thought and behavior, but this controversial observation is not necessary to the argument here. Rather, we would argue that Holocaust survivors have emerged from a period of enforced removal from adult social, professional and personal obligation. They survived an often extended time in which the major life tasks were to learn the rules, to anticipate the wishes of a hostile environment, and to protect the physical and psychic self through public obedience and private disobedience. Similar tasks face the children of chaotic, mentally ill and abusive parents. However, lacking both (a) the adequate comparison data (a former life as a responsible adult) that would make the deprivations salient and (b) the intellectual capacity to reflect analytically upon this comparison, the child abuse victim is often less articulate in his or her description of the immediate and long-term consequences of violence. From the survivors of the camps, in contrast, have come complex, passionate and vivid portraits of the transformation from competent and productive adult citizen to abused and disenfranchised slave. These treatises may contain therapeutic directions for those clinicians and scholars who can tolerate listening.

This chapter is also built on the personal experiences of the authors in speaking to the Holocaust survivors and their families, from very different perspectives. The first author is a director of the Trauma Research Institute (TRI), and teaches a course on Holocaust scholarship. She has interviewed survivors as research subjects, has investigated the consequences of extreme trauma for 15 years, and has conducted long-term psychotherapy with both Holocaust survivors and victims of abuse. She is a converted Jew and student of philosophical Judaism. The second author is a child of Holocaust survivors, a woman who grew up surrounded by relatives and friends who had emigrated to the United States soon after World War II had ended. She is now an associate researcher at TRI and a doctoral candidate in clinical psychology, participating in our Holocaust research project for her dissertation. We hope that the generalizations below are more reliable given the disparity in our backgrounds and differences in our circle of interview subjects.

In addition to information provided by the testimonial and research literature and by five Holocaust survivor patients who have been treated by the first author, the recommendations and thoughts below are based on three structured interview samples, two Holocaust survivor samples ($n = 27$ thus far) and one group of adults with experience of severe child trauma ($n = 52$ thus far). The Holocaust survivors had been held in the concentration camps of Poland and Germany in the 1940s, and had for the most part come to America shortly after their release. The survivors were 65 to 78 at the time of their interviews, and were adolescents or young adults (in their twenties) at the time of their internment. They were part of two TRI projects, the Holocaust History project (aiding the first author in developing a Holocaust History course for psychologists) and the Holocaust Narration project (a part of which will serve as the second author's dissertation). The child survivors were participants in the Countertransference Project, and were 25 to 58 at the time of their interviews. All scored at least three standard deviations above the mean on the Violence History Questionnaire, a measure of physical violence experience in childhood. The focus of this chapter will be on the Holocaust survivor themes as they might apply to other populations.

FINDING THE WORDS

> here in this carload
> i am eve
> with abel my son
> if you see my other son
> cain son of man
> tell him that i
> > Don Pagis

The response of many readers to Don Pagis' poem, entitled *Written in Pencil in the Sealed Railway Car*, is to visualize interruption of the writer's desperate message. The pencil has been jolted from her hands, and it is lost in the darkness. She has paused, weakened from hunger and thirst, and no longer can stand to finish her work. She has arrived at Auschwitz. Similarly, the literature on trauma tends to focus on the *obstacles* to the survivor's transmission of his or her story to the therapist, evaluator or interviewer. Subtle or obvious messages are sent to the survivor to be silent (see Pearlman & Saakvitne (1995) for a general description of countertransference responses to extreme trauma and Danieli (1984) for a discussion specific to Holocaust victims). Words are unavailable because the full experience is dissociated, repressed or fragmented (Dalenberg, 1996a; van der Kolk et al., 1996). The survivor has a story to tell, many therapists argue, and we must remove the obstacles that prevent the telling.

Certainly, these mechanisms describe real pieces to the problem of communication of trauma. However, it is the Holocaust literature that most clearly raises the alternative explanation that the essence of the difficulty may be not that the survivor cannot share these words, *but that there are no words.* "From the first days on", writes French author and survivor Romaine Anteime, "it seemed impossible for us to bridge the gap that we discovered between the language available to us and this experience which was still continuing in our bodies . . . Hardly did we begin to tell the tale than we choked. What we had to say began to appear unimaginable, even to ourselves" (Fine, 1988, p. 42). Charlotte Delbo (1995), survivor of Auschwitz and Ravensbruck, in some of the most eloquent descriptions of the Holocaust experience we have encountered, similarly vents her frustration at the inadequacy of the words she must use to engage with us. She wonders how the term "thirst" could cover both today's mild wish for a lemonade, and the sensations she felt after three days without water in Auschwitz.

More than one survivor whom we have interviewed, and all of the therapy patients, at times were moved to anger at the imprecision in communication that they often attributed to their own lack of verbal skill. Survivor after survivor cursed their perceived failure to describe fully, "accurately", their life in an unimaginable world. Typically, they finally slip into what Langer (1991) calls "a controlled inaccuracy, not as a calculated breach of truth, but as a concession to what words cannot do, an assent to the partial collapse of verbal power" (p. 105). "It was as if I were dead, a walking dead person", Anna N. told us. "What do you mean?" we asked her. "I don't know what I mean", she answered. "Because it wasn't like that at all. It's just the best I can do."

Holocaust scholars remind us that the silence of the brutalized victim is not always pathology, not always a failure of memory, courage, or capacity for coherence. When this message is communicated to the subjects of our interviews, the tension in the process of sharing is somewhat dissipated, and both interviewer and interviewee can come to acknowledge the tenuous bridge that is built between life-in-extremity and ordinary existence by the giving of some initial set of words to the experiences. Further, it can be acknowledged that the problem of climbing outside of language, "using it to get beyond itself" (Delbanco, 1997, p. 14), is an ancient one, unlikely to be solved to one's complete satisfaction.

Understanding the paucity of our trauma vocabulary can aid the listener in overcoming his or her own discomfort in finding the words to communicate with the survivor. Yael R., one of the survivor patients interviewed, chastised her doctor for not making the analogies her therapist usually offered when other material arose. Like Anna, it is important for us as interviewers to do the best that we can with our deficient language base, trying not to give in to our frustration with the clear insufficiency of available vocabulary. Elie Weisel attributes the high suicide rate among Holocaust writers to this despair. "Where language fails", he asks, "what can be its substitute?" (Weisel, 1993, p. 161).

The eloquent testimony of the Holocaust survivor echoes a theme in the extreme trauma sample, in which survivors spoke positively and negatively about the emotional consequences of their failure to find words and their therapists' inability to recognize this phenomenon. When asked to describe the hardest part of therapy for trauma symptoms, Ellen E. responded:

> The hardest thing? I think the hardest thing was when she'd ask me how something felt and I'd think of like 100 things at once but none were exactly right and it would make me cry.

On the more positive side, underlining the role of the therapist in giving words to amorphous concepts, Joseph F. stated:

> I guess the most helpful thing my doctor did . . . well, this is going to sound strange, but he tried to guess what it must have felt like to me as a kid. And when he was groping around for the words he just hit on a couple that worked. And until that happened, I couldn't grip them in my mind, you know? They kept slipping away. His descriptions weren't exactly right, but they were like sandpaper. My own truth stuck to his words well enough for me to trap it and talk about it.

RESPECTING THE WORDS

It is a seeming contradiction to confront again and again in the vast Holocaust literature a questioning of the survivor's right to describe the Holocaust. Survivor authors repeatedly state not only that they do not understand, but that they refuse to understand their own experience. Elie Weisel (1995), who has done as much to clarify and enhance Holocaust understanding as any modern author, still claims that to understand well enough to describe would be to "blaspheme – the frightened smile of that child torn away from his mother and transformed into a flaming torch. Nor have I been able, nor will I ever be able", he continues, "to grasp the shadow which, at that moment, invaded the mother's eyes" (p. 142). One of our interviewees quoted a Holocaust author as stating that "no words should be spoken about the Holocaust that cannot be uttered in front of burning children". But that, of course, forces all of us into silence, since again there are no words that should be uttered in front of burning children. One turns, and takes the children from the fire, no matter what the cost.

Many of our interviewees, both Holocaust survivors and their children, immediately and chronically disparage their ability to relate their trauma. One is struck by how important it is for the survivor to "tell it right", as if they have a duty to the trauma itself. A Yiddish poet, Aron Tsaytline wrote: "Were Jeremiah to sit by the ashes of Israel today, he would not cry out a lamentation. The almighty Himself would be powerless to open his well of tears. He would maintain a deep silence. For even an outcry is now a lie, even tears are mere literature, even prayers are false" (Howe, 1988, p. 179). In general, survivors not only feel that they lack adequate words, but also that there is something morally questionable about describing their trauma poorly. Interestingly, although this theme rarely emerges verbally in child abuse testimony (in our research), 92% of the extreme child abuse victims answered "true" to the interview question "Do you ever feel as if you have an obligation or duty to accurately describe your traumatic experience to your therapist?"

Silence, then, is not always avoidance, and not always the enemy. At times silence is a gesture of respect of the survivor toward the enormity of the pain and loss involved. The many pauses and gaps in Holocaust testimony are part of the aftermath of trauma, and deserve the understanding of the skilled practitioner. It is the survivor's choice, or it should be, to wait for some degree of self-understanding or faith in the ability to self-contain (Slochower, 1996) before dialogue about the trauma can take place.

Therapists often describe part of their role to be facilitating the ability of the client to face the trauma. But Holocaust survivors as often state that they are protecting their listeners as well as protecting themselves by not speaking. While there is evidence that the pouring out of extreme and painful Holocaust stories is of help to the survivor (Pennebaker, Barger & Teibout, 1989; Traue & Pennebaker, 1993), there is also compelling evidence that listening to such stories is stressful for the listener. In fact, one study showed that while survivors were recounting their most traumatic memories, their skin conductance levels were dropping (Pennebaker et al., 1989). Their listeners, however, were becoming more aroused, and skin conductance levels were increasing (Shortt & Pennebaker, 1992). Those who provide social support to people in distress, although their presence is a positive health predictor for the survivor, also experience negative health and distress outcomes themselves (Coyne et al., 1987; Kessler et al., 1985).

Both authors had profound emotional reactions to listening to the Holocaust stories. This was true for the second author particularly, who grew up seeing the untold story of the Holocaust in the faces of dozens of relatives and friends. She was concerned that her questions would crack the protective walls that the survivors had built, and was extremely attentive in designing each question in the 62-item structured interview in a manner that would not offend or disturb her subjects. As she continued her work, she began to explore the possibility that her fear of the survivor's fragility was based less on the interviewee's lack of capacity and more on her unwillingness to face the depth of their losses, which were inferentially the losses of her own parents.

The skeptical response of the survivor to the therapist's common denials that extreme trauma will be burdensome thus not only is understandable but also is quite valid. Survivors often are well acquainted with the discomfort of those who are asked to listen to trauma, and just as often interpret it as the wish not to hear, rather than the wish not to cause further pain by reacting badly. Listening to Holocaust survivors has helped us learn to disclose that listening is burdensome, is hurtful, and is painful, and that this must be so if a true connection is present. But this is different than stating that the traumatic experience is not worth hearing, or that receiving the disclosure is not an affirmative choice on the part of the helper. In a sense, the helper is hoping for the outcome described in a Midrash story. We are told that when God gave Adam the gift of fire, He directed him to take two stones, called in the legend Darkness and the Shadow of Death, and to rub them together. The meaning of the legend is said to be that with the proper environment, one can take even darkness and death and turn them to light (Wolpe, 1992, p. 120).

Survivors of the Holocaust also speak with articulation about the timing of effective speech (the word "effective" meaning both persuasive to the listener and healing for the victim). Elie Weisel is one of a dozen Holocaust survivors who spoke of the period of silence after release that seemed a necessary part of recovery (Wolpe, 1992). He needed the time, he said, to know that what he said was true (or perhaps to gain the inner strength to defend against an assault on that truth). Similarly, our interviewees spoke of the timing of disclosure and the titration of exposure to Holocaust reminders.

Tanya J., an interviewee who spent her teenage years in the camps, for instance, accompanied her daughters to Yad Vashem, as did Yael R., a therapy patient who was in work camps in her twenties. Tanya was also one of the first visitors to the Holocaust museum in Washington. In Yad Vashem, both women found the experience overwhelming. Visitors can turn a corner after looking at disturbing (but relatively benign) photographs of honoring the resistance only to be confronted with a mountain of human hair. "Pieces of death on the floor", Yael called them. "I thought I was done with that."

The Washington museum was an easier experience for Tanya, who then was in the company of her young grandsons. Here, the visitor is warned of upcoming events, and Tanya chose not to go into the simulated cattle car or to peer into the realistic replicas of the bunks of Auschwitz. Her confrontation was held to a level she could tolerate, and she and her family were very moved by the experience. Such discussions underline for therapists and interviewers (a) the importance of pacing and (b) the importance of client participation in determining this pacing. The first author has used the analogy of running along with the child on his new bicycle, holding onto the handlebars and assuring him that it is safe while speed is increased, and then letting go precipitously as the session ends, leaving the client barreling off toward a cliff. Mastery of an event of extreme traumatic significance is a long-term task, and must be undertaken with attention to strengthening the ego capacity concomitantly as the events are disclosed (such that disclosure may continue safely). Yael disclosed the loss of her son, the loss of her husband, and a brutal attack by a guard on the first session with her first therapist. Living with lethal authorities for years in the camps left her unable, or at least unlikely, to inform this therapist that she could not psychically tolerate the images she was being forced to face (Davies & Frawley, 1994). Instead, she never went back. Her second therapist, the first author, welcomed her into her office 20 years later.

BELIEVING THE WORDS

The experience of the Holocaust victim and the experience of the adult victim of extreme child trauma are remarkably in parallel when we discuss the reactions of the listeners. Despite the rancorous discussions between groups on both Judaism and child abuse, it would be unfair to state that large numbers of Americans doubt either the existence of the Holocaust or the fact that the child abuse is an important and widespread problem. Yet, when individual persons tell individual stories, disbelief is common. The second author recalls when her father disclosed that he had lost 11 siblings to the Holocaust. An adult daughter of two Holocaust survivors, she still could not believe him. It was not that she thought he was lying; it was simply an impossible statement to digest.

Stories about refusal to hear are so common in the Holocaust literature that they must be conceded to be the norm (Danieli, 1984; Hass, 1995). Yet a theme also emerges that it is not the telling of the Holocaust story that is resisted, it is the telling of the survivor's tale. Somehow it seems that the Holocaust story, the general overview of the themes of the camps, can leave us enraged and overwhelmed and yet amazed and vaguely proud of these people we do not know who could demonstrate humankind's capacity for survival. But when the single survivor begins to speak, as Rabkin (1976) states, "his tales of the night side of human experience, of the insidious ripping away of humanity, of the perverse evil man can wreck upon his own kind – all put into question the continuity of existence and evoke our profoundest anxieties. The more the survivor insists on being heard, the more do we feel threatened and indicted" (p. 593).

Interviews with survivors have helped the authors understand how much easier it is to make sweeping statements about child abuse survivors, and to declare our wish to help them, than it is to listen and believe a single survivor standing before us. For a few professional listeners, the result will be disbelief in each specific voice together with declarations of belief in the many. For most interviewers, however, the internal struggle between the tendency to believe and the wish not to believe is quite consciously experienced, *and it is important to understand that it is a wish the interviewer shares with the survivor.* Limited disclosure by the interviewer/clinician of this struggle (see Maroda's (1991) general discussion of countertransference disclosure) potentially blocks the survivor's alternative explanation that the listener's "disbelief" is a disparagement of the survivor's honesty or integrity.

The active wish not to believe has a number of transferential and countertransferential sources for the participants in the extreme trauma survivor interview. A type of shame enters the interaction when the survivor begins to speak, but we think that it is wrong to label it "survivor guilt" (Chodoff, 1997; Garwood, 1996), as much of the literature tends to do. The shame shared by interviewer and survivor can be an indictment of the event, not of the survivor's role in it, the shame "that the just man experiences at another man's crime: the feeling of guilt that such a crime should exist, that it should have been introduced irrevocably into the world of things that exist, and that his will for good should have proved too weak or null, and should not have availed in defense" (Levi, 1976, p. 426). But Levi, in the above quote, still intertwines the two types of shame that must be disentangled in the clinical setting.

The first type of shame at sharing is the legacy of the survivor, and is unlikely to disappear with therapy, time or integration of memory. It is akin to the humiliation that the good person feels when forced to embarrass another publicly – a shared experience that this event damages the worldview of both participants as well as any who must witness it. The survivor does not *wish* to wield the sword that cuts apart the listener's comfortable and rosy view of the possibilities and impossibilities of life. To pepper another individual's life with the horrors of your own feels like an assault to the survivor, and can feel so to the listener, although both would admit that this is in some sense unfair. Both participants reasonably wish to protect cherished beliefs, even beliefs that already have been seriously undermined. One is reminded of the apocryphal story of Thomas Jefferson, who when confronted with evidence from two academic scientists that meteors were actual objects that could be studied, supposedly responded "It is easier to believe that two Yankee professors would lie than that stones fall from heaven" (Bryan, 1995).

The countertransferential danger, however, enters the picture most strongly when the first type of shame is confused and combined with the second. Here, both survivor and listener can feel shame for the survivor's *role* in the story. What kind of man is he, wonders Wilkomirski (1996), when he could step over bodies of dead babies and feel nothing? How could he watch a Kapo beat his father, wonders Amery (1995) and not throw himself into the fight? "I took bread from a dying woman's mouth", Yael admits in tears. "How could I do that?"

Struggling with the shame of sharing a world that contains the Holocaust, the clinician or interviewer who does not understand this dilemma may be ineffective in communicating that the shame of the survivor regarding his or her own acts is *not* shared. The moral reasoning of the nontraumatic world is simply inapplicable to the traumatic world, and it is not worthwhile to attempt to apply the former rules to the latter situation. It is here that the Holocaust writers urge their readers not to try to use their Holocaust decision-making to illustrate their present character.

Interviews with Holocaust survivors render our glib statements about blame quite obviously inadequate. "I don't think I can judge her", Isaac N. tells his therapist, discussing his wife's decision to leave their child in a camp with a friend while she volunteered for a work detail. Both therapist and client become silent for a moment, both silently fighting recognition and the urge to admit that they *do* judge her, as she judges herself. They are each ashamed of their own inability to understand fully the woman's actions, and the cost of this shame can be an increase in dishonesty (by omission of unpleasant thoughts and feelings) in the clinical interview. Professionals can learn from the Holocaust literature to encourage the view that resisting the urge to judge is therapeutic *work*, not a simple decision expected of any good human being listening to another's pain.

On this same point, the interviewer must remember that trauma, by its definition, is not a known part of the world. It is an impossible history, a seeming
falsehood or "displacement of meaning" (Caruth, 1995, p. 5). Repeatedly,
Holocaust victims speak of their self-doubts. "I, being, myself, when I think back
sometimes, doubt that I went through [the Holocaust]. It's not possible", Louis
Weintraub writes (Hass, 1995, p. 86). "Today I am no longer sure that what I
have written is true", notes Charlotte Delbo, commenting in Langer (1988) on
her work, "but I am sure that it happened". It is often the pain of these self-
doubts that drive the survivor to begin again to speak. "It is easy to make a child
mistrust his own reflections", continues Wilkomirski (1996), "to take away his
voice. I wanted my own certainty back, and I wanted my voice back, so I began
to write" (pp. 153–154).

Listeners, whether they are therapists, researchers or clinicians, easily misuse and mistreat the survivors' doubts, which are in fact symptoms of their
impossible history rather than symptoms of the unreliability of their accounts.
"Chronic doubts about what did and did not happen", Davies and Frawley
(1994) write, discussing the parallel process in child abuse victims, "along with
a persistent inability to trust one's perceptions of reality, are perhaps the most
permanent and ultimately damaging long-term effects of childhood sexual
abuse" (p. 109). And certainly we agree. Trauma does relate empirically to
both a sense of unreality (Allen & Coyne, 1995; Santonastaso et al., 1997;
Simeon et al., 1997) and an increased confusion of nightmare and truth (Dalenberg, Hyland & Cuevas, 1997). This is easily seized upon by those less familiar
with trauma as a sign that the individual is exaggerating or confabulating, if the
times are ripe for a distrust of a particular type of disclosure (see Ofshe &
Watters' (1994) discussion of "sexual hysteria" among psychotherapy
patients). By illustrating that uncertainty, doubt and the experience of unreality are normative to the experience of trauma, Holocaust survivors (who are
less often now doubted as to the essence of their accounts), underline for us the
necessity not to treat the extreme trauma survivor's sense of unreality as a sign
of the falsity of the account.

DIFFERENT VOICES

A final point should be raised regarding the variety in methods of coping with
trauma that were championed by survivors in our interviews. First, we wish to
emphasize that 80% of the survivors felt that they were doing very well, and
reported no significant mental health problems. This group answered affir-
matively to our question about whether they felt that the pain and trauma had
strengthened them. Yet, in listening to them speak, and in analyzing results of
questionnaires that they filled out, there appear to be two important caveats to
their statement that are important to interviewers and clinicians.

First, while there was tremendous variety in the way in which the survivors
thought about their history, it appeared that some way of putting together the

fragments into a meaningful account was a prerequisite (or at least a strong correlate) of the subjective feeling of having triumphed over the ordeal. When we asked the survivors which of ten factors were important in their own individual experience of living through the Holocaust, there was almost no agreement on the relative weight of support, will to live, luck or other factors. However, the sum of the weights, which might be seen as the summated degree of explanatory power that the survivor accorded these factors, were highly related ($r = 0.93, p < 0.001$) to the survivors' sense of having "grown" beyond the pain of the past. This phenomenon is well-documented in the child abuse literature (Dalenberg & Jacobs, 1994; Silver, Boon & Stones, 1983), in which success in the search for meaning seems to be adaptive to long-term healthy survival.

Moniak K., one of our interviewees, when asked for a free response to the question of why he survived, said that it was because he had hope. We believe that hope is intimately tied to believing that one can understand and predict one's future. Helping the survivor come to any understanding of the past, rather than ensuring that some favored explanation is accepted, might be the best we have to offer as supporters of the extreme trauma victim. Unfortunately, some of the survivors' beliefs about themselves or other survivors offend or disturb the listener (e.g. that the most righteous among them did not live). Yet these beliefs may be part of a general explanatory framework that is part of the survivor's coping mechanism, one that should be attacked or even challenged by an interviewer with some caution (see Dalenberg & Jacobs (1994) discussion of the functions of self-blame).

Second, although it is too complex a topic to deal with in depth here, survivors almost uniformly reported that they never did fully integrate their trauma. Charlotte Delbo calls this phenomenon "living beside" rather than "living with" the Holocaust. "I live as a twofold being", she says (Delbo, 1995, p. 78). As the authors have from their own perspectives listened for years to survivors tell their stories, we too have independently come to the conclusion that extreme trauma is not truly integrated, and perhaps cannot be so without poisoning the self system. The Holocaust experience is compartmentalized in most survivors, a part of the historical self without fully being part of the present interactive self. A part of the therapeutic listener's role can be to help to round the sharp edges of the account enough that it can "fit" into personal history without shredding the survivor's sense of self. This involves finding words, as discussed earlier, and helping the survivor to respect the choices made.

The incompleteness of the integration does leave the survivor vulnerable to other life stresses in a manner that has not been drawn out in the clinical literature. Having struggled to hold back, typically with some success, the grief and pain of the Holocaust story, survivors may have unusual reactions to other episodes that would ordinarily evoke strong emotion. Holocaust survivors appeared to have greater posttraumatic stress disorder (PTSD) reactions to war-related stressors in recent combat situations (Robinson et al., 1994), and respond less well to behavioral interventions to relieve stress that have proven effective with other groups (Baider et al., 1997).

A more personal example of this phenomenon was given by Yosek K., who was describing the death of his son. He could not cry, he said, except when he was washing the dishes. (It was not unusual for survivors to tell us that they did not cry, that there were too many for whom to mourn.) At this time, however, the grief would overcome him and he would sob deeply. While he did not make the connection himself, he had told the interviewer that much of his time in camp was spent as a dishwasher. At times of great stress, and particularly in the presence of Holocaust-related imagery, the survivor may fuse past and present, and respond with a variability and depth that may seem inappropriate to the event. Moniak Z. told us, "When I came over I was thinking a lot. But then I tried to forget about all the experiences. But it comes back when I dream at night. It comes back."

Such examples encourage us to adjust our definition of "survivor" to include human reactivity to symbols of the compartmentalized trauma. The authors were deeply impressed and moved by the strength of the survivors we interviewed, and by their success in building families, businesses and new lives. To argue that Moniak or Yosek had not succeeded in "overcoming" their trauma seems again a misunderstanding of the type of life that *can* be led or even *should* be led after such a history. Moniak, Yosek, Lika, Anna, Yael and Tanya, and perhaps all of the survivors mentioned here, feel changed by their experience, and so do we from our own time spent with them. Trying to obey Rabbi Emil Fackenheim's 614th commandment not to give Hitler a posthumous victory, we urge others to listen to the survivors of the Holocaust in these final decades of their life with us. The alternative is to leave them, as Lika W. put it in her interview, "in silence but not in peace".

REFERENCES

Allen, J. & Coyne, L. (1995). Dissociation and vulnerability to psychotic experience: The Dissociative Experiences Scale and the MMPI-2. *Journal of Nervous and Mental Disease*, **183**, 615–622.

Baider, L., Peretz, T. & Kaplan-DeNour, A. (1997). The effect of behavioral intervention on the psychological distress of Holocaust survivors with cancer. *Psychotherapy and Psychosomatics*, **66**, 44–49.

Bettleheim, B. (1960). *The Informed Heart*. Glencoe, IL: Free Press.

Bryan, C. (1995) *Close Encounters of the Fourth Kind: Alien Abduction, UFOs and the Conference at M.I.T.* New York: Alfred Knopf.

Caruth, C. (1995). *Trauma: Explorations in Memory*. Baltimore, MD: Johns Hopkins University Press.

Chodoff, P. (1997). The Holocaust and its effects on survivors: An overview. *Political Psychology*, **18**, 147–157.

Coyne, J., Kessler, R., Tal, M., Turnbull, J., Wortman, C. & Greden, J. (1987). Living with a depressed person. *Journal of Consulting and Clinical Psychology*, **55**, 347–352.

Dalenberg, C. (1996a). Accuracy, timing and circumstances of disclosure in therapy of recovered and continuous memories of abuse. *Psychiatry and the Law*, **19**, 229–275.

Dalenberg, C. (1996b). Fantastic elements in child disclosures of abuse. *APSAC Advisor*, **3**, (1), 5–10.

Dalenberg, C. & Carlson, E. (in press). Ethical issues in the treatment of the recovered memory trauma victims and patients with false memories of trauma. In S. Bucky (Ed.), *Comprehensive Textbook of Ethics and Law in the Practice of Psychology*. New York: Plenum Press.

Dalenberg, C. & Jacobs, D. (1994). Attributional analyses of child sexual abuse episodes: empirical and clinical issues. *Journal of Child Sexual Abuse*, **3**, 37–50.

Dalenberg, C., Hyland, K. & Cuevas, C. (1997). *Fantastic Elements in Child Accounts of Abuse*. Paper presented at the Annual meeting of the International Society for the Study of Traumatic Stress, Montreal, Canada.

Danieli, Y. (1984). Psychotherapists' participation in the conspiracy of silence about the Holocaust. *Psychoanalytic Psychology*, **1**, 23–42.

Davies, J. & Frawley, G. (1994). *Treating the Adult Survivor of Childhood Sexual Abuse: A Psychoanalytic Perspective*. New York: Basic Books.

Delbanco, A. (1997). *Required Reading: Why our American Classics Matter Now*. New York: Farrar, Strauss, and Giroux.

Delbo, C. (1995). Voices. In L. Langer (Ed.), *Art from the Ashes* (pp. 77–92). Oxford: Oxford University Press.

Dimsdale, J. (1980). *Survivors, Victims and Perpetrators*. Washington, DC: Hemisphere.

Fine, E. (1988). The absent memory: The act of writing in post-Holocaust French literature. In B. Lang (Ed.), *Writing and the Holocaust* (pp. 26–40). New York: Holmes & Meier.

Garwood, A. (1996). The Holocaust and the power of powerlessness: Survivor guilt an unhealed wound. *British Journal of Psychotherapy*, **13**, 243–258.

Hass, A. (1995). *The Aftermath: Living with the Holocaust*. New York: Cambridge University Press.

Hedges, L. (1992). *Interpreting the Countertransference*. Northvale, NJ: Jason Aronson.

Howe, I. (1988). Writing and the Holocaust. In B. Lang (Ed.), *Writing and the Holocaust* (pp. 179–199). New York: Holmes & Meier.

Kessler, R., McLeod, J. & Wethington, E. (1985). The costs of caring: A perspective on the relationship between sex and psychological distress. In I. Sarason & B. Sarason (Eds.), *Social Support: Theory, Research, and Applications* (pp. 491–506). Dordrecht: Martinus Nyhoff.

Kogon, E. (1980). *The Theory and Practice of Hell*. New York: Berkley Books.

Kuch, K. & Cox, B. (1992). Symptoms of PTSD in 124 survivors of the Holocaust. *American Journal of Psychiatry*, **149**, 337–340.

Langer, L. (1988). Interpreting survivor testimony. In B. Lang (Ed.), *Writing and the Holocaust*. New York: Holmes & Meier.

Langer, L. (1991). *Holocaust Testimonies: The Ruins of Memory*. New Haven: Yale University Press.

Levi, P. (1976). The truce. In A. Friedlander (Ed.), *Out of the Whirlwind*. New York: Schoken Books.

Maroda, K. (1991). *The Power of Countertransference*. New York: Guilford.

Modai, I. (1994). Forgetting childhood: A defense mechanism against psychosis in a Holocaust survivor. *Clinical Gerontologist*, **14**, 67–71.

Niederland, W. (1968). Clinical observations on the survivor syndrome. *International Journal of Psychoanalysis*, **49**, 313–315.

Ofshe, R. & Watters, E. (1994). *Making Monsters: False Memories, Psychotherapy, and Sexual Hysteria*. New York: Scribner's.

Pagis, D. (1995). Written in Pencil in the Sealed Railway Car. In L. Langer (Ed.), *Art from the Ashes* (p. 588). Oxford: Oxford University Press.

Pearlman, L. & Saakvitne, K. (1995). *Trauma and the Therapist: Countertransference and Vicarious Traumatization in Psychotherapy with Incest Survivors*. New York: W.W. Norton.

Pendergrast, M. (1995). *Victims of Memory: Sex Abuse Accusations and Shattered Lives*. Hinesburg, Vermont: Upper Access Books.

Pennebaker, J., Barger, S. & Tiebout, J. (1989). Disclosure of traumas and health among Holocaust survivors. *Psychosomatic Medicine*, **51**, 577–589.

Rabkin, L. (1976). Survivor themes in the supervision of psychotherapy. *American Journal of Psychotherapy*, **30**, 593–600.

Rittner, C. & Roth, J. (1993). *Different Voices*. New York: Paragon House.

Robinson, S., Hemmendinger, J., Netanel, R., Rapaport, M., Zilberman, L. & Gal, A. (1994). Retraumatization of Holocaust survivors during the Gulf War and SCUD missile attacks on Israel. *British Journal of Medical Psychology*, **67**, 353–362.

Roiphe, A. (1988). *A Season of Healing: Reflections on the Holocaust*. New York: Summit Books.

Salamon, M. (1994). Denial and acceptance: Coping and defense mechanisms. *Clinical Gerontologist*, **14**, 17–25.

Santonastaso, P., Favaro, A., Olivotto, M. & Friederici, S. (1997). Dissociative experiences and eating disorders in a female college sample. *Psychopathology*, **30**, 170–176.

Shanon, J. & Shahar, O. (1983). Cognitive and personality functioning of Jewish Holocaust survivors during the midlife transition (45–65) in Israel. *Archives of Psychology*, **135**, 275–294

Shengold, L. (1979). Child abuse and deprivation: Soul murder. *Journal of the American Psychoanalytic Association*, **27**, 533–559.

Shortt, J. & Pennebaker, J. (1992). Talking versus hearing about Holocaust experiences. *Basic and Applied Social Psychology*, **13**, 165–179.

Silver, R., Boon, C. & Stones, M. (1983). Searching for meaning in misfortune: Making sense of incest. *Journal of Social Issues*, **39**, 81–101.

Simeon, D., Gross, S., Guralnik, O., Stein, D., Schmeidler, J. & Hollander, E. (1997). Feeling unreal: 30 cases of DSM-III-R depersonalization disorder. *American Journal of Psychiatry*, **154**, 1107–1113.

Slochower, J. (1996). *Holding and Psychoanalysis*. Hillsdale, NJ: Analytic Press.

Traue, H. & Pennebaker, J. (1993). *Emotion, Inhibition, and Health*. Seattle: Hogrefe & Huber.

van der Kolk, B., van der Hart, O. & Marmar, C. (1996). Dissociation and information processing in posttraumatic stress disorder. In B. van der Kolk, A. McFarland & Weisaeth (Eds.), *Traumatic Stress: The Effects of Overwhelming Experience on Mind, Body and Society* (pp. 303–327). New York: Guilford Press.

Weisel, E. (1993). Interview with Elie Weisel. In J. Cargas. (Ed.), *Voices from the Holocaust*. Lexington, KY: University of Kentucky Press.

Weisel, E. (1995). A plea for the dead. In L. Langer (Ed.), *Art from the Ashes* (pp. 138–152). Oxford: Oxford University Press.

Wilkomirski, B. (1996). *Fragments: Memories of a Wartime Childhood*. New York: Schoken Books.

Wolpe, D. (1992). *The Speech and the Silence*. New York: Henry Holt.

Part 2

Special Interviewing Tools

Motivational Interviewing

Ann Terry
Therapist and Research Consultant, Birmingham, UK

Motivational interviewing is a particular way of helping people to recognize and do something about a problem behaviour. It was developed in the early 1980s from work with people with alcohol problems (Miller, 1983; Miller, Sovereign & Krege, 1988). It rapidly became a major way of working in the addictions field by providing an attractive counselling method particularly useful in dealing with ambivalent or resistant drinkers. More recently the technique has been applied to other areas of behavioural change including working with patients with chronic diseases (Stott et al., 1996), smokers (Rollnick, Butler & Scott, 1997), sex offenders (Garland & Dougher, 1991) and in the field of mental health (Long & Hollin, 1995). It has also been shown to help increase the uptake of various treatments (Bien, Miller & Boroughs, 1993).

Motivational interviewing can be described as a specific interpersonal style involving the application of appropriate counselling skills to initiate the process of behavioural change. It is a way of being with the client that emphasizes a facilitatory interpersonal relationship coupled with recognition of the client's autonomy and freedom of choice. The main purpose of the approach is the resolution of the client's ambivalence to change. Motivational interviewing is defined by Rollnick and Miller (1995) as "a directive, client centred counselling style for eliciting behaviour change by helping clients to explore and resolve ambivalence".

The theoretical context for motivational interviewing will be reviewed and the salient features of the approach described. The evidence for its effectiveness is presented and the wide range of potential applications of the approach examined. For reasons of simplicity throughout the text the word counsellor or therapist is used to describe the person carrying out an intervention. However, as will be explored later, the approach can be used by a wide range of professionals in various settings.

Handbook of the Psychology of Interviewing. Edited by A. Memon and R. Bull.
© 1999 John Wiley & Sons Ltd.

THEORETICAL CONTEXT

Miller originally developed motivational interviewing intuitively from his work with problem drinkers. It draws on various schools of psychology: social, cognitive and motivational (Miller & Rollnick, 1991).

The broad strategies of the approach are directive whilst the micro elements of counselling interventions are more clearly based in Rogerian therapy. Emphasis is placed on using core counselling skills of accurate empathy, unconditional positive regard and congruence to create the optimum climate for internal change (Egan, 1982; Truax & Mitchell, 1971; Rogers, 1957). The quality of the relationship between the client and counsellor is seen as crucial to the approach.

Motivation is conceptualized as a balance of weighing up the pros and cons of changing. The person is not labelled as being unmotivated; rather the model argues that some individuals may be more strongly motivated to stay with a given behavioural pattern rather than to change. In essence, motivational interviewing is concerned with shifting the balance by creating a climate conducive to the development of intrinsic change. The main factors important in shifting the client's decisional balance include:

(a) Gaining increased awareness and understanding of the personal implications of both continuing the problem behaviour and of change.
(b) Becoming aware of the discrepancies between their present behaviour and important personal goals.
(c) Believing that change is really possible for them and desirable.

Ambivalence

One of the main tenets of motivational interviewing is the way the client's ambivalence and resistance are interpreted and managed. Rather than being seen exclusively as a type of ego defence mechanism or personality trait, resistance which develops during a consultation is seen largely as a normal psychological response influenced by interpersonal interactions. Emphasis is placed on exploring and resolving the ambivalence and "rolling" with resistance.

People entering treatment programmes for problem behaviours often have conflicting and fluctuating motives or ambivalence (Orford, 1985). Problem drinkers, smokers, repetitive offenders and illicit drug users often recognize the costs and harm of their behaviours yet are also quite attached and attracted to them. For some individuals the intensity of this struggle is so strong that it is described as an approach–avoidance psychological conflict (Miller & Rollnick, 1991). Here the person is both attracted to and repelled by a given behaviour, object or person and it is often characterized as a "love hate relationship". This can result in the person becoming stuck, see-sawing back and forth. In many cases they are unclear about what they want to do, whether to stop or to continue the problem behaviour.

A person demonstrating ambivalence is often labelled as being unmotivated or as having a difficult personality. This forms the scenario in many settings, for example in GPs' surgeries. In this situation, when faced with little time and an apparently unmotivated individual the most commonly used intervention is likely to be persuasion. However, if a person is feeling ambivalent about change, this strategy is likely to be counterproductive, with the client either defending or denying the problem. This can be recognized as the "Yes but . . ." response. In this case the counsellor has fallen into the "confrontation-denial" trap described by Miller and Rollnick (1991). A possible mechanism underlying this response is psychological reactance (Rollnick, Heather & Bell, 1992a). Psychological reactance occurs where a person perceives their freedom to be under threat. It is characterized by an assertion of autonomy in direct response to the perceived threat (Brehm & Brehm, 1981).

Ambivalence is viewed as a decisional balance with the conflicting costs and benefits of both continuing and changing behaviour needing to be explored (Janis & Mann, 1977). The goal of motivational interviewing is to explore the conflict between indulgence and restraint, encouraging the person to express their reasons for concern and arguments for change (Rollnick & Miller, 1995). Ambivalence is a complex area which will be unique to each individual. It is an area that can cause much frustration for the counsellor, as not only do the factors making up the balance for the pros and cons fluctuate over time but so does the relative importance placed on these (Orford, 1985). However, it is important to work through the ambivalence as an increase can be indicative of the person moving closer to making a behavioural change (Miller & Rollnick, 1991). Ambivalence can be resolved through careful use of micro counselling skills, in particular using active listening and reflection (Miller, Benefield & Tonigan, 1993). The counsellor does not argue in favour of restraint or change, rather helps clients to do this for themselves.

In addition to assisting the client in articulating the pros and cons of both staying and changing, the change process can also be helped by the counsellor facilitating the client in expressing self-motivational statements. Miller and Rollnick (1991) describe how these statements may relate to the cognitive (e.g. recognition), affective (e.g. concern) or behavioural (e.g. intention to act) dimensions of the commitment to change. By eliciting such self-motivational statements the balance tips further towards the direction of change.

Resistance

If ambivalence is ignored or confronted directly there is an increased potential for resistance to develop in the client. A level of resistance is quite normal within counselling but when it escalates or persists there may be an impact on the therapeutic outcome.

Increased levels of resistance have been associated with high dropout rates from therapy and poorer outcomes (Miller et al., 1993; Miller & Sovereign, 1989;

Chamberlain et al., 1984). The therapist's style has been shown to impact directly on the level of resistance seen in the client. The more confrontational the approach the higher the resistance (Miller & Sovereign, 1989; Patterson & Forgatch, 1985). Miller and Rollnick (1991) argue that confrontation should be a goal of counselling not a style and is particularly contraindicated in individuals with low self-esteem. The overall aim is to help a person confront and explore their own ambivalence rather than it being forced upon them. Increasing or persisting levels of resistance indicate that the counsellor needs to reflect on where the client is in terms of readiness to change and whether the counsellor is maintaining congruence with this.

A crucial part of any behavioural shift is making the decision to change. Often with interventions by health care workers too much emphasis is placed on how to change rather than on the crucial issues of gaining commitment to change. In reality less than 20% of smokers have arrived at the point where they have decided to change their behaviour imminently (Velicer et al., 1995). Many of the interventions for smokers that have been developed over the last 30 decades give advice on how to change rather than assisting clients with making the decision to stop. This has led to high dropout rates and high levels of resistance to various smoking interventions, and to burnout and frustration in health care workers.

The classic example of this has been the lack of success of stop smoking clinics run typically in GP surgeries or the workplace. Initially, the numbers signing up for such offers of support with giving up the habit are high but as the activity is started the numbers drop off rapidly, with less than 5% typically completing the course. Such interventions are primarily focused on the action stage, assuming that the commitment to change has already been made when the person signed up (DiClemente, 1991; Prochaska, DiClemente & Norcross, 1992). However, the crucial distinction between commitment and intention has not been made. Intention relates to the idea that in an undefined future change may take place as compared to having actually made a firm commitment and decision to change usually in the imminent future.

Transtheoretical Model

The transtheoretical model developed by Prochaska and DiClemente (1982) provides a valuable, comprehensive framework which helps in understanding how people change. It characterizes processes they go through as they make the decision and alter behaviour. It was developed as an integrative model drawing on a range of theoretical schools and through extensive review of the stages that smokers went through when successfully giving up (i.e. self-changers) (Prochaska & DiClemente, 1983; Prochaska et al., 1992). Although the model was developed initially with smokers it has been successfully applied to other areas of change (Prochaska et al., 1994b).

The model consists of five constructs (Velicer et al., 1996). There are the stages of change that an individual will move through which characterizes their readiness to change. Secondly, there is the importance of the decisional balance, i.e. the pros and cons of changing or not changing behaviour. A further construct is self-efficacy or an individual's belief in their ability to change. This is inversely related to the situational temptation experienced by the individual which relates to the temptation to resume the problem behaviour. In the early stages of change, situational temptation tends to be high and self-efficacy is low. As an individual moves through the stages of change there is a characteristic increase in self-efficacy and reduction in situational temptation. The final construct relates to the specific processes which individuals use to help move through the stages. These are either experiential or behavioural processes.

Stages of Change

The model consists of six stages that people were found to pass through when making changes. The utility of the model comes from the framework, which facilitates the therapist in doing the right thing at the right time. Typically, in the early stages of change, those who are successful employ experiential processes involving cognitive and or affective activities. By comparison, those moving through the later stages focus more on behavioural activities (Perz, DiClemente & Carbonari, 1996). Details of the processes typically used to move successfully through the different stages when giving up smoking are shown in Table 1.

Precontemplation

Clients in the first stage of change, precontemplation, are often labelled as being in denial of their problem or being resistant to change. An alternative explanation is that the person is uninformed or unconvinced of the need for change. They may have experienced few negative consequences of their behaviour or believe that they are able to self-regulate their behaviour adequately. In order to be able to move forward out of this stage precontemplators need to gain increased awareness of the impact of their problem behaviour on themselves and others (Prochaska, Norcross & DiClemente, 1994a).

Precontemplation can be one of the most difficult stages of change to manage as a therapist. Appropriate interventions in this stage typically have relatively low success rates on short-term outcome measures as compared to those found in clients in later stages of change. Action is often equated with change and there tends to be little appreciation of how much help counsellors can be by merely facilitating a client's progress through these early stages. Moving a client through this stage to contemplation can double the chance that the participant will take action on their own in the near future (Prochaska et al., 1992).

Strategies which help clients move through precontemplation include raising doubts and planting seeds for future behavioural change. It is important to note that prescriptive advice is likely to be ineffectual when a person is in this stage of change. This stage is also characterized by "more is not necessarily better". The

Table 1 Stages of change in which change processes are most emphasized

Processes	Stages				
	Precontemplation	Contemplation	Preparation	Action	Maintenance
Experiential	*Consciousness raising* (becoming informed) *Dramatic relief* (emotional awareness) *Environmental re-evaluation* (noticing how your behaviour affects others)	*Self re-evaluation* (creating a new self-image)	*Self liberation* (making the commitment to change)		
Behavioural			*Social liberation* (increasing environmental alternatives)	*Reinforcement management* (self reward) *Helping relationships* (support) *Counter conditioning* (use of substitute) *Stimulus control* (taking control)	

Adapted from: *Changing for Good* by James O. Prochaska, John C. Norcross and Carlo DiClemente. Copyright 1994 by James O. Prochaska, John C. Norcross and Carlo DiClemente. Reproduced by permission of William Morrow and Company, Inc.

more counselling interventions given the greater the chance of resistance being engendered within the client (Miller & Rollnick, 1991).

Contemplation

This stage is marked by a growing awareness of the problem and possible solutions. The client's ambivalence to change will be high. Decision-making processes are started by the person weighing up the benefits and drawbacks of change or of maintaining their current behaviour.

Clients are likely to be receptive to information at this stage, often waiting for that elusive piece of information that will finally help them make up their mind to change. For information to be effective it needs to become personally relevant for the client. The client will typically begin exploring the impact of the problem behaviour on achievement of important values and goals in their life. Typically they will be engaging in a process of self-revaluation. In helping move the clients forward through this stage it is also important to explore some of the barriers to change and to achievement of the client's goals.

The overall aim of the counselling interventions during the contemplation stage is to evoke from the client reasons for change and strengthen the client's belief in their ability to change, i.e. their self-efficacy. Put another way, the client needs to convince the therapist that they recognize their need to change (DiClemente, 1991).

Preparation

This stage is associated with a readiness to change. Characteristically there will have been several previous attempts at changing behaviour. There is likely to be a certain amount of ambivalence still present. The person is likely to be at the stage of needing to set goals and decide on their priorities for action. There is a requirement to look at self-regulatory activities.

A strong verbal commitment to change is often not sufficient and may actually indicate a paradoxically low chance of successful change. Clients may require help in making plans more concrete. It is useful to explore potentially difficult situations that may arise and effective coping strategies to manage these.

Action

This is the stage at which overt behaviour change takes place. It is the one that requires the greatest commitment of time and energy from the client. It is a time when support for the client should continue. The emphasis is placed on more behavioural and skills-based change processes including counter conditioning (changing one's reaction to stimuli), stimulus control (changing environments to minimize the occurrence of the stimuli) and contingency management (changing reinforcers and contingencies for a behaviour) to interrupt habitual patterns of behaviour (Prochaska et al., 1992). In addition, there is a need for awareness of other pitfalls that will undermine change, including ongoing ambivalence and environmental factors (Marlatt & Gordon, 1985), coupled with a need to explore strategies available to prevent lapses and slips. Helping clients increase their sense of self-efficacy is a further important task of this stage.

Maintenance

After the initial intensive period of change the person enters the maintenance stage. At this point the behaviour change is becoming more firmly established. However, ambivalence about the change may still be present. Helping relationships continue to be of importance at this stage to help reduce the risk of relapse. Strategies particularly useful in this stage include counter conditioning and stimulus control (Prochaska et al., 1992).

Termination

This is the ultimate goal for all changers. The characteristic of this stage is that the former addiction or problem behaviour no longer poses a temptation or threat. The individual has a clear self-awareness and insight into their problem behaviour. At this stage typically they have considerable confidence in their ability to cope without relapse (Prochaska et al., 1994a).

In the review of self changers and those receiving interventions (Prochaska et al., 1992) it was clear that there is not a logical progression through the stages. Individuals may recycle through the stages several times before they succeed in their efforts to change. In their early research Prochaska and DiClemente (1982) found that smokers on average gave up three to seven times before finally breaking the habit. Relapse, rather than being seen as a failure, is brought into the therapy and reframed as "some success" with lessons to be learnt to help increase the success of future attempts (Prochaska et al., 1992). This has led to the model being portrayed as a spiral rather than as a circle, as in earlier versions. The spiral model suggests that most people who relapse do not just go around in circles ending up where they began, rather the client gradually makes their way towards sustained behaviour change (Prochaska et al., 1994a).

Therapists can best influence change by understanding where the client "is" in terms of readiness to change and which activities are likely to be most effective. This can be achieved by paying attention to the subtle balance between the directive and client-centred components of the motivational approach. Use of inappropriate interventions at the wrong time may hinder change and is associated with high dropout rates (Perz et al., 1996; Prochaska, 1994). Motivational interviewing as an approach is particularly relevant to the early stages of change where ambivalence is high and the aim is to raise awareness and increase commitment to change.

Creating a Motivational Environment

Since his seminal paper in 1983 Miller's work has been taken up and modified to fit different settings and problem behaviours. What has remained core to the approach has been the importance of creating a motivational environment conducive to intrinsic change. In addition to the areas already discussed, further important conditions include: the de-emphasis of labels, a focus on individual responsibility for change, the development of discrepancy between valued goals and current behaviour, and the building of clients' self-esteem and self-efficacy (Miller et al., 1988).

In his early work with problem drinkers Miller found power in not using labels such as "alcoholic" or "problem drinker" with his clients. For some individuals the use of disease labels may help in providing a cognitive shift important in helping them recognize and acknowledge that their behaviour is causing problems. However, overall the use of labels has been shown to be a poor predictor of future change and is associated with relapse (Miller et al., 1996).

An important aspect of motivational interviewing is the development of an individual's responsibility for change. To assist this process throughout the approach it is emphasized that the client has the choice whether to decide to change or not (Rollnick & Miller, 1995). This can be useful in providing the client with space and creating an atmosphere of freedom of choice, important in reducing the risk of psychological reactance developing.

The development of internal discrepancy is particularly relevant in clients moving from contemplation to preparation. The aim is to explore how the current problem behaviour is inconsistent with or undermines important values or goals for the client (Miller et al., 1988). These inconsistencies are highlighted through exploring the pros and cons of staying with current behaviour or changing, providing of information and feedback, and through the exploration of personal goals.

Before information or feedback is given, the client's permission is sought to assess whether or not they would like the information or would find it useful. Information is provided in an objective way for the client to consider. Feedback may be given on biochemical tests such as liver function in the case of heavy drinkers, alcohol consumption in terms of units of alcohol etc. It is important that they are able to relate the information to their own situation. It is for the client to either take or leave the information. This helps in fostering the crucial element of personal choice and control whilst at the same time helping the client to consider the relevance of the information by bringing it to their attention.

In his early work on motivational interviewing Miller included the giving of advice as an important component (Miller, 1983; Miller et al., 1988; Miller & Rollnick, 1991). This has since been removed with emphasis placed on the provision of meaningful personal feedback that is compared to some normative reference (Rollnick & Miller, 1995).

Important to creating the motivational climate is ensuring that throughout the counselling process attention is paid to building a client's self-esteem through the provision of genuine empathy and an affirming atmosphere (Miller & Rollnick, 1991).

Self-efficacy

The building of client's self-efficacy has been an important component of the motivational interviewing approach. It was first described by Bandura (1977, 1982) and refers to a person's belief in their own ability to carry out and succeed at a given task. It is a good predictor of change and a good indicator of treatment outcome (DiClemente, Prochaska & Gibertini, 1985). During the contemplation stage internal discrepancy is increased and the client becomes more aware of the negative effects of their behaviour. In the absence of self-belief the risk of a defence reaction such as denial or rationalization being developed within the client is increased. Self-efficacy appears to provide a mediation role on the choice between behavioural change (risk reduction) and a cognitive defence type of response (fear avoidance) (Miller & Rollnick, 1991).

The levels of self-efficacy are seen to be increased in the later stages of change (Velicer et al., 1990; Galavotti et al., 1995). The levels are highest during the action and maintenance stages. Self efficacy can be increased by fostering the attitude that it is the client who is responsible for the change and not the therapist. Providing the client with a range of options for them to consider is also important. Even if they have had difficulties with one method, instilling the concept that there are numerous other avenues to try is important for fostering a climate of personal choice and freedom (Miller & Rollnick, 1991).

EVIDENCE FOR EFFECTIVENESS OF THE MOTIVATIONAL INTERVIEWING APPROACH

At both a conceptual and practical level motivational interviewing has much face validity. It has rapidly been taken up and used in the addictions field in many parts of the world (Saunders, Wilkinson & Phillips, 1995). This is largely because workers have found it a valuable approach which can be incorporated into their clinical practice, particularly when dealing with resistant or ambivalent clients. However, in the literature, there is a paucity of randomized controlled trials to confirm its clinical effectiveness. Where studies have been reported (e.g. Miller et al., 1988; Saunders et al., 1995) the results validate the efficacy of the approach when used on its own and in combination with other therapies. The majority of these studies are in the area of substance misuse. The effectiveness of the model for other problem behaviours is currently being evaluated (see Rollnick & Miller, 1995).

The Drinkers Check-up

To capture the essence of the brief motivational style Miller et al. (1988) developed the Drinkers Check-up. Through a newspaper, a free check-up was offered to drinkers which was billed as being unrelated to a treatment programme but would rather offer health-related information. The intervention involved two sessions with a counsellor, one for assessment and one for feedback. Key elements of the intervention were an empathic style, information relating to the client's current drinking activity, the provision of details on the range of options available for change and emphasis on the individual's personal choice and responsibility. In randomized controlled trials using this Drinkers Check-up (Miller, 1996; Miller et al., 1988) significant reductions in alcohol consumption were observed (over 50%) as compared to other interventions.

Heather et al. (1996), working with heavy drinkers identified in male hospital wards, found that clients who were in the early stages of change (i.e. were not ready to change) showed significantly improved outcome measures following use of a motivational interviewing intervention as compared to those receiving a skills-based intervention. There was no difference between the two approaches in the improvements seen in the clients who were already motivated for change. In a further study, the partners of intravenous drug users recorded reduced unprotected sexual activity three months after receiving two joint sessions of motivational interviewing designed to encourage use of safe sex practices (Gibson et al., 1989).

Further studies using a limited number of motivational interviewing sessions have demonstrated significant changes in several indices relating to behavioural change. Saunders et al. (1995) found benefits in the use of a brief motivational intervention with illicit drug users as compared to an educational programme. Those who underwent the motivational programme demonstrated greater immediate commitment to abstention, reported more positive expected outcomes for abstention and reported fewer opiate-related problems. They also complied better with the methadone programme for longer and relapsed less quickly. There were no differences, however, in the levels of drug use between the two groups. Paradoxically, Saunders et al. found that the levels of self-efficacy were actually lower in the experimental group. As one possible explanation they argue that the motivational interviewing increased the client's commitment to change without providing the required skills and knowledge in initiating or sustaining change. Saunders and Allsop (1991) found greater levels of self-efficacy in patients who received both motivational interventions and skills-based training as compared to those who received motivational interviewing alone.

Benefits of the motivational interviewing approach have been found in using it to help increase the uptake of various treatment programmes. Attendees of a substance misuse outpatient clinic who received an initial motivational intervention showed superior clinical outcomes as compared to the controls who received no such intervention (Bien et al., 1993). Improvements were seen at three months in the percentage of abstinent days and in the amount of alcohol consumed. However, the differences between the two groups were small and were lost after six months. Brown and Miller (1993) found that patients who received two sessions of motivational interviewing prior to commencing in an in-patient programme for substance abuse fared better than those who did not. They showed improved compliance and participation with treatment. The experimental group also had lower levels of alcohol consumption at three months.

By comparison a large hospital-based study of problem drinkers with gastro-intestinal disease failed to show any improved benefit of motivational interviewing over controls (Kuchipudi et al., 1990). However, there are several methodological issues worthy of consideration in this study. Firstly, during the period of the study there were three complete turnovers of the staff on the ward. The interventions applied appeared to run contrary to the basic philosophy underpinning the motivational interviewing approach. Their so-called motivational interventions appeared to consist of convincing the client of the benefits of change and of the treatments available to achieve the goal of abstinence. In addition, there was an overt emphasis on the use of the disease label of alcoholism.

One of the difficulties in drawing conclusions from reviewing these different studies is the inconsistency in chosen outcome measures. Measures include: the number of absolute alcohol-free days, continuous periods without a drink and amount of alcohol consumed during a given period. Some of these outcome measures have more to do with the accepted philosophy of the treatment programme than with individuals' personal goals, and some do not take into account relapse as being an important part of the movement through behavioural change. The relevance of these measures in testing an intervention whose main function is gaining commitment to change is questionable. The aim of the motivational interviewing approach is facilitating the decision to change rather than primarily on the action phase (DiClemente, 1991; Heather et al., 1996). The use of outcome behavioural measures is therefore not appropriate for measuring critical changes which occur, particularly during the earlier stages of change.

The main advantage of using outcome behavioural measures for studies is that they are relatively easy to measure or obtain, which probably accounts for their widespread use. By comparison, there are many factors interacting with both the processes of deciding to change and altering behaviour. Velicer et al. (1996) call for multivariate criteria measures which are more sensitive in identifying movement towards behavioural change. Based on the transtheoretical model they have developed three constructs which they have validated empirically:

- Habit strength – a combination of physical, psychological and learned behaviours
- Positive evaluative strength – positive images and beliefs about smoking, linked to the pros of the decisional balance
- Negative evaluative strength – evaluation of the importance of the negative consequences of smoking

Velicer et al. identified predictable patterns of change within the constructs and their relation to each other across the stages of change. They argue that multivariate outcome models provide sensitive, and arguably more applicable, frameworks for evaluating interventions relating to such a complex area as behaviour change when compared to short-term behavioural change outcome measures.

CLINICAL APPLICATIONS

Motivational interviewing was originally developed for use in the addictions field. The strength of the approach in working with clients who are resistant and ambivalent to a specific behaviour change has led to its recent popularity in a wide range of capacities and settings.

As an approach it still is used widely in the addictions field. Increasingly, it is being used in combination with other therapies and approaches including cognitive behavioural and skills-based interventions (Annis, Schober & Kelly, 1996; Kadden, 1995; Van Bilsen & Whitehead, 1994). It is also a useful approach in working with clients where the goal of the therapy may not be abstinence or reduced use, rather the goal may be one of harm minimization. An example of this is working with intravenous drug users where the risk of HIV infection may be high. Application of the motivational approach has been found to be particularly valuable when looking at both injecting practices and safer sex issues (Gibson et al., 1989; Baker & Dixon, 1991).

Motivational interviewing has also been applied to other areas of mental health including eating disorders (Long & Hollin, 1995), family therapy (Hoffman, 1994), compliance with medication in psychotic patients and in the development of the therapeutic alliance in child and adolescent psychotherapy (Digiuseppe et al., 1996).

Increasingly, motivational interviewing is being combined with an assessment of the client's stage of change to help the counsellor in matching the intervention strategy with the client's readiness to change (Annis et al., 1996; Rollnick et al., 1992b). Brief assessment tools for staging clients in their readiness for change have been developed (Rollnick et al., 1992b). These combined approaches have been used to help improve the management of patients with diabetes (Stott et al., 1996), smokers (Rollnick et al., 1997) and have been recommended for use in the management of clients with obesity (Rollnick, 1996).

In other settings the approach has proved valuable in working with repetitive offenders, particularly where alcohol and drugs have played a role in the offence (McMann, 1996). Further value has been found in using the approach to help engage sex offenders in treatment (Garland & Dougher, 1991).

The general applicability of the approach to different settings and problem behaviours is resulting in widespread application of the intervention in both health, social and penal settings. The original approach has been modified and adapted for use in settings where limited time is available for consultations, e.g. in GP surgeries. Initial results show that the professionals involved are receptive to the approach and have been able to apply it in practice (Stott et al., 1996), although the results of outcome studies are still awaited.

SUMMARY

Motivational interviewing provides a promising approach to working with problem behaviours in people with high levels of ambivalence to change. Key to the approach is eliciting intrinsic motivation for change by enabling the client to resolve ambivalence and through promotion of the client's self-determination and freedom in any decision-making process. The overall approach draws heavily on client-centred philosophies and aims to minimize client resistance. Studies carried out to date lend support for its use as a stand-alone therapy, in combination with other psychological interventions and in increasing the uptake and compliance with a variety of treatments. More recently it has been used in a variety of settings. This enthusiasm for motivational interviewing has occurred despite the lack of published data on its efficacy in these conditions.

REFERENCES

Annis, H.M., Schober, R. & Kelly, E. (1996). Matching addiction outpatient counselling to client readiness for change: The role of structure relapse prevention counselling, *Experimental and Clinical Psychopharmacology*, **4** (1), 37–45.

Baker, A. & Dixon, J. (1991) Motivational Interviewing for HIV Risk Reduction. In W.R. Miller & S.R. Rollnick (Eds.), *Motivational Interviewing: Preparing People to Change Addictive Behaviours* (pp. 293–302). New York: Guilford Press.

Bandura, A. (1977). Towards a unifying theory of behavioural change. *Psychological Review*, **84**, 191–215.

Bandura, A. (1982). Self-efficacy mechanism in human agency. *American Psychologist*, **37** (2), 122–147

Bien, T.H., Miller W.R. & Boroughs, J.M. (1993). Motivational interviewing for alcohol outpatients. *Behavioural and Cognitive Psychotherapy*, **21** (4), 347–356.

Brehm, S.S. & Brehm, J.W. (1981). *Psychological Reactance: A Theory of Freedom and Control*. New York: Academic Press.

Brown, J.M. & Miller, W.R. (1993). Impact of motivational interviewing on participation and outcome in residential alcoholism treatment. *Psychology of Addictive Behaviours*, **7**, 211–218.

Chamberlain, P., Patterson, G., Reid, J., Kavanagh, K. & Forgatch, M. (1984). Observation of client resistance. *Behavior Therapy*, **15**, 144–155.

DiClemente, C.C. (1991). Motivational interviewing and the stages of change. In W.R. Miller & S.R. Rollnick (Eds.), *Motivational Interviewing: Preparing People to Change Addictive Behaviors* (pp. 191–202). New York: Guilford Press.

DiClemente, C.C., Prochaska, J.O. & Gibertini, M. (1985). Self-efficacy and the stages of self-change of smoking. *Cognitive Therapy and Research*, **9** (2), 181–200.

Digiuseppe, R., Linscott, J. & Jilton, R. (1996). Developing the therapeutic alliance in child-adolescent psychotherapy. *Applied and Preventative Psychology*, **5** (2), 85–100.

Egan, G. (1982). *The Skilled Helper: A Model for Systematic Helping and Interpersonal Relating*. Monterey, CA: Brooks/Cole.

Galavotti, C., Cabral, R.J., Lansky, A., Grimley, D.M., Riley, G.E. & Prochaska J.O. (1995). Validation of measures of condom and other contraceptive use among women at high risk for HIV infection and unintended pregnancy. *Health Psychology*, **14** (6), 570–578.

Garland, R.J. & Dougher, M.J. (1991). Motivational intervention in the treatment of sex offenders. In W.R. Miller & S. Rollnick (Eds.), *Motivational Interviewing: Preparing People to Change Addictive Behaviours* (pp. 303–314). New York: Guilford Press.

Gibson, D.R., Wermuth, L., Lovelle-Drache, J., Ham, J. & Sorenson J.L. (1989). Brief counselling to reduce AIDS risk in intravenous drug users and their sexual partners: Preliminary results. *Counselling Quarterly*, **2**, 15–19.

Heather, N., Rollnick, S., Bell, A. & Richmond, R. (1996). Effects of brief counselling among male heavy drinkers identified on general hospital wards. *Drugs and Alcohol Review*, **15**, 29–38.

Hoffman, F.J. (1994). Adult children of addicted parents: Family counselling strategies. In J.A. Lewis (Ed.), *Addictions: Concepts and Strategies for Treatment*. Gaithersburg, US: Aspen Publishers.

Janis, I.L. & Mann, L. (1977). *Decision-making: A Psychological Analysis of Conflict, Choice, and Commitment*. New York: Free Press.

Kadden, R.M. (1995). Cognitive behavioural approaches to alcoholism treatment. *Alcohol Health and Research World*, **18** (4), 279–286.

Kuchipudi, V., Hobein, K., Flickinger, A. & Iber, F. (1990). Failure of a two hour motivational intervention to alter recurrent drinking behaviour in alcoholics with gastrointestinal disease. *Journal of Studies on Alcohol*, **51**, 356–360.

Long, C.G. & Hollin, C.R. (1995). Assessment and management of eating disordered patients who over-exercised: A four year follow-up of six single case studies. *Journal of Mental Health*, **4** (3), 309–316.

Marlatt, G.A. & Gordon, J.R. (Eds.). (1985) *Relapse Prevention: Maintenance Strategies in the Treatment of Addictive Behaviors* (pp. 271–314). New York: Guilford Press.

McMann, M. (1996). Alcohol, drugs and criminal behaviour. In C.R. Hollin (Ed.), *Working with Offenders: Psychological Practice in Offender Rehabilitation* (pp. 211–242). Chichester: Wiley.

Miller, W.R. (1983). Motivational interviewing with problem drinkers. *Behavioural Psychotherapy*, **1**, 147–172.

Miller, W.R. (1996). Motivational interviewing: Research, practice and puzzles. *Addictive Behaviors*, **21** (6), 835–842.

Miller, W.R. & Rollnick, S. (1991). *Motivational Interviewing: Preparing People to Change Addictive Behaviours*. New York: Guilford Press.

Miller, W.R. & Sovereign, R.G. (1989). The check-up: A model for early intervention in addictive behaviors. In T. Loberg, W.R. Miller, P.E. Nathan & G.A. Marlett (Eds.), *Addictive Behaviors: Prevention and Early Intervention* (pp. 219–231). Amsterdam: Smets and Zeitlinger.

Miller, W.R., Benefield, R.G. & Tonigan, J.S. (1993). Enhancing motivation for change in problem drinking: A controlled comparison of two therapist styles. *Journal of Consulting and Clinical Psychology*, **61**, 455–461.

Miller, W.R., Sovereign, R.G. & Krege, B. (1988). Motivational interviewing with problem drinkers: II. The drinkers check-up as a preventative intervention. *Behavioural Psychotherapy*, **16**, 251–268.

Miller W.R., Westerberg, V.S., Harris, R.J. & Tonigan, J.S. (1996). What predicts relapse? Prospective testing of antecedent models. *Addiction*, **91** (*supplement*), S155-S171.

Orford, J. (1985). *Excessive Appetites: A Psychological View of Addictions*. New York: Wiley.

Patterson, G.R. & Forgatch, M.S. (1985) Therapist behavior as a determinant for client noncompliance: A paradox for the behavior modifier. *Journal of Consulting and Clinical Psychology*, **53**, 846–851.

Perz, C.A., DiClemente, C.C. & Carbonari, J.P. (1996). Doing the right thing at the right time? The interaction of the stages and processes of change in successful smoking cessation. *Health Psychology*, **15** (6), 462–468.

Prochaska, J.O. (1994). Strong and weak principles for progressing from precontemplation to action based on twelve problem behaviours. *Health Psychology*, **13**, 47–51.

Prochaska, J.O. & DiClemente, C.C. (1982). Transtheoretical therapy: Toward a more integrative model of change. *Psychotherapy*, **20**, 161–173.

Prochaska, J.O. & DiClemente, C.C. (1983). Stages and processes of self change in smoking: Toward a more integrative model of change. *Journal of Consulting and Clinical Psychology*, **5**, 390–395.

Prochaska, J.O., DiClemente, C.C. & Norcross, J.C. (1992). In search of the structure of change. In J.D. Fisher, J.M. Chensky & A. Nadler (Eds.), *Initiating Self-changes: Social, Psychological and Clinical Perspectives* (pp. 87–114). New York: Springer-Verlag.

Prochaska, J.O., Norcross, J.C. & DiClemente, C.C. (1994a). *Changing for Good*. New York: Morrow and Company.

Prochaska, J.O., Velicer, W.F., Rossi, J.S., Goldstein, M.G., Marcus, B.H., Rakowski, W., Fiore, C., Harlow, L.L., Redding, C.A., Rosenbloom, D. & Rossi, S.R. (1994b). Stages of change and decisional balance for 12 problem behaviors. *Health Psychology*, **13** (1), 39–46.

Rogers, C.R. (1957). The necessary and sufficient conditions for therapeutic personality change. *Journal of Consulting Psychology*, **21**, 95–103.

Rollnick, S. (1996). Behaviour change in practice: Targeting individuals. *International Journal of Obesity and Related Metabolic Disorders*, **20** (Suppl 1), S22–26.

Rollnick, S. & Miller, W.R. (1995). What is motivational interviewing? *Behavioural and Cognitive Psychology*, **23**, 325–334.

Rollnick, S., Heather, N. & Bell, A. (1992a). Negotiating behaviour change in medical settings: The development of brief motivational interviewing. *Journal of Mental Health*, **1**, 25–37.

Rollnick S., Heather, N., Gold, R. & Hall, W. (1992b). Development of a short "Readiness to Change Questionnaire" for use in brief, opportunistic interventions with excessive drinkers. *British Journal of Addiction*, **87**, 743–754.

Rollnick, S., Butler, C.C. & Scott, N. (1997). Helping smokers make decisions: The enhancement of brief intervention for general medical practice. *Patient Education and Counselling*, **31** (3), 191–203.

Saunders, B. & Allsop, S. (1991). Motivational intervention with heroin users attending a methadone clinic. *Journal of Consulting and Applied Social Psychology*, **1**, 213–221.

Saunders, B., Wilkinson, C. & Phillips, M. (1995). The impact of a brief motivational intervention with opiate users attending a methadone programme. *Addiction*, **90**, 415–424.

Stott, N.C., Rees, M., Rollnick, S., Pill, R.M. & Hackett, P. (1996). Professional responses to innovation in clinical method: Diabetes care and negotiating skills. *Patient Education and Counselling*, **29** (1), 67–73.

Truax, C.B. & Mitchell, K.M. (1971). Research on certain therapist interpersonal skills in relation to process and outcome. In A.E. Bergin & S.L. Garfield (Eds.), *Handbook of Psychotherapy and Behavioural Change: An Empirical Analysis* (pp. 299–344). New York: Wiley.

Van Bilsen, H.P.J.G. & Whitehead, B. (1994). Learning controlled drug use: A case study. *Behavioural and Cognitive Psychotherapy*, **22** (1), 87–95.

Velicer, W.F., DiClemente, C.C., Rossi, J.S. & Prochaska, J.O. (1990). Relapse situations and self-efficacy: An integrative model. *Addictive Behaviours*, **15**, 271–283.

Velicer, W.F., Fava, J.L., Prochaska, J.O., Abrams, D.B., Emmons, K.M. & Pierce, J. (1995). Distribution of smokers by stage in three representative samples. *Preventative Medicine*, **24**, 401–411.

Velicer, W.F., Rossi, J.S., Prochaska, J.O. & DiClemente, C.C. (1996). A criterion measurement model for health behavior change. *Addictive Behaviors*, **21** (5), 555–584.

The Psychology of Interpersonal Skill

Owen Hargie *and* **Dennis Tourish**
University of Ulster, Northern Ireland, UK

The interview is a special type of interactive event. As the name indicates, it is an *inter view*, a forum wherein people come together in a particular type of interpersonal exchange. As with all communicative episodes, any analysis of the interview is complex, since the process itself is influenced by a large number of impinging personal and contextual factors. Indeed, many of the theoretical and conceptual perspectives which have been developed by social scientists for the analysis of interpersonal encounters *per se* can also be applied directly to the interview. Thus the interview has variously been depicted as:

- A form of *transactional analysis* (TA) in which the participants are perceived as acting and responding within one of three ego states – adult, parent or child. Interestingly, transactional analysts use their approach both as a model with which to analyse interviews and as a tool in counselling, wherein the TA format is taught to the interviewee as part of the helping process (Lapworth, Sills & Fish, 1993).
- A type of dramatic exchange, dependent upon a *cognitive performing script*, in which the overall act is composed of several major scenes (Tullar, 1989). For example, the selection interview can be divided into scenes such as opening, gathering information, inviting questions and closing. In the closing "scene" the interviewer's script includes stating that the interview is about to end, outlining what the next step will be, thanking the candidate, and effecting goodbyes. Both the interviewer and interviewee need to learn their scripts to perform at optimum level.

Handbook of the Psychology of Interviewing. Edited by A. Memon and R. Bull.
© 1999 John Wiley & Sons Ltd.

- A form of *reciprocal interaction* which involves either matching increases and decreases in the other person's verbal and non-verbal behaviour, or compensating for the lack of reciprocation (Liden & Parsons, 1989). For example, in a counselling interview the skilled counsellor will achieve synchronisation of behaviour by matching the facial expression and voice tone of a worried client. In terms of verbal communication, what has been termed the "norm of reciprocity" suggests that we are motivated to respond positively to the self-disclosures of others by initiating our own, in a process of social exchange (Tardy & Dindia, 1997). However, in the interview context it would not be appropriate for a counsellor to self-disclose at the same level as the client, since this would violate the expectations of both sides about appropriate role behaviours and relational boundaries. Rather, the counsellor will compensate for this disparity through the increased use of reward and encouragement for the disclosing client.

These are but three of many panoramas. Furthermore, within specific contexts there are particular conceptualisations. For example, in medicine the consultation between doctor and patient has been viewed *inter alia* as a purely diagnostic medical procedure; as a sociological event in which knowledge of concepts such as "roles" and "illness" is crucial; and as an anthropological phenomenon in which "illness behaviour" is compared across cultures (Pendleton et al., 1984).

Despite this array of approaches to perceiving the interview, there has been a dearth of published work on what has been shown to be a very useful and robust template for charting the nature and process of interpersonal interaction, namely that of communication as a form of skilled behaviour. Within psychology this perspective was first presented over 30 years ago (Argyle, 1967). It is based upon the view that social behaviour can be conceptualised as a form of skilled activity and can therefore be compared to sensory-motor skills such as playing tennis or operating a machine. The study of motor skill has a long tradition within psychology, dating back some 100 years to the studies by Bryan and Harter (1897) into Morse code learning. Since these early studies, the literature on sensory-motor skills has become voluminous, and sophisticated models for the identification and analysis of motor skills have been developed (Proctor & Dutta, 1995).

The analogy between social and motor skill was of particular import, in that it meant that the methods and models developed in the latter field could be applied to interpersonal performance. The key features of both sets of skills can be summarised by the acronym FRASK, in that the characteristics of skilled performance are:

*F*luency. The behaviour flows smoothly and without hesitation. Just as a skilled tennis player moves with grace and apparent ease, so a skilled counsellor will appear in control and unflustered.

*R*apidity. Someone who is skilled makes quick (and usually correct) decisions. The top ranked squash player executes very difficult shots without delay. So, too, will the skilled television interviewer respond with apposite follow-up questions to an interviewee's answers.

*A*utomaticity. The ability to respond rapidly is dependent upon learned sets of responses which become automatic. The experienced cyclist does not have to think about how to achieve and maintain balance. Likewise, an experienced employment interviewer does not have to think consciously about how to open or close the interview.

*S*imultaneity. Skill necessitates the execution of a number of behaviours conjointly. The car driver has to learn to simultaneously use a range of component parts including the steering wheel, gears, brake, mirrors, accelerator, radio, and so on. In interviews the component parts include a wide array of verbal and non-verbal behaviours which must be meshed and coordinated with other actions (such as taking notes).

*K*nowledge. Skill involves knowing what, how, when and why. The highly skilled person is aware of the best possible responses in any situation; has learned how to implement these; chooses the optimum time to execute them; and, can provide a coherent rationale for the chosen repertoire.

While there are many similarities between interpersonal and motor skill, there are also some key differences. The former by definition always involve other people whereas the latter do not (it is possible to walk, swim, operate a machine and so on in the absence of others). As a result, aspects relating to emotions and feelings, as well as to the perception of others are crucial to the effective implementation of social skill. However, in recognising these differences, Hargie (1997a, 1997b) has shown how the analogy between the two sets of skills has proved to be a most fruitful avenue of study, leading to a well developed theoretical model of interpersonal skills. This model has been applied in a diversity of fields including health care (Dickson, Hargie & Morrow, 1997), negotiation (Hughes, 1994), counselling (Irving, 1995), the priesthood (Lount & Hargie, 1997) and interviewing (Millar, Crute & Hargie, 1992).

This chapter will present a transactional model of interviewing based upon the skills paradigm. Throughout, we will integrate a consideration of the skills of interviewing within the overall model of interpersonal skill.

THE INTERPERSONAL SKILLS MODEL

Social skill has been defined as "the process whereby the individual implements a set of goal-directed, interrelated, situationally appropriate social behaviours which are learned and controlled" (Hargie, 1997b, p. 12). This definition forms the basis for the operational model of skilled performance as shown in Figure 1. Behaving in a skilled fashion involves engaging in a process which includes the adoption and pursuit of goals, devising coordinated action plans to attain these, carrying out appropriate behaviours, monitoring the responses of others and adjusting future actions accordingly. Within this, the physical and psychological features of both parties will have an impact upon the outcome, as will the context in which the encounter takes place. To understand the model it is useful to examine each of the stages in more detail.

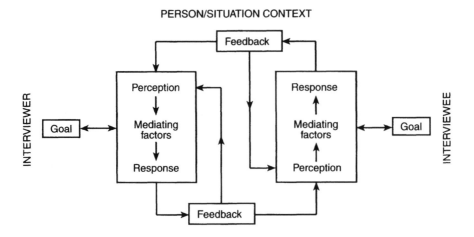

Figure 1

Goals

Both sides in interviews have goals. Indeed, goals and the motivation to pursue them are the starting point in the skills model. This is because, as noted by Slater (1997), "The presence of various goals or motivations changes the nature of affect and cognitions generated, and of subsequent behaviors" (p. 133). In other words, our goals, and their potency, direct and shape how we feel, think and act. As a consequence, they also impact upon the goals and behaviours of the other party involved in the interview.

It has been suggested (Chulef, 1993) that goals can be typically grouped into three higher-order clusters:

- Personal (e.g. intellectual and spiritual growth, happiness and enjoyment)
- Social (e.g. to be friendly, competitive or cooperative)
- Family (e.g. concerned with family, marriage, romance and sex)

It is also possible to select goals which are meaningless, which conflict with other more important goals already established, which violate the social norms of a particular organisation or wider society, and which are unrealistic (Millar et al., 1992). However, it is generally the case that people with clear goals make wiser choices and find planning for interaction much easier and more fruitful than those with less well developed goals (Egan, 1990). Given that we interpret the behaviour of others based upon what we perceive their goals to be, it is therefore also clear that an important objective during interviews is to establish commonly agreed goals between participants. The absence of such common aims has been held to be one of the most common problems during the interview process (Wicks, 1982).

Interviews can become a complex process of negotiation, fraught with difficulty and liable to break down. However, an emphasis on openly stating goals, while framing them clearly and in specific behavioural units, seems more likely to lead to success (Cormier & Cormier, 1985). For example, a client may approach a counsellor complaining of chronically low self-esteem. A general and long-term goal is obviously to improve self-esteem. However, this would be best achieved by focusing on problematic areas of the client's life (such as problems at work, with bodily self-image, or difficulties in relational maintenance) and identifying specific steps which the client can take in the short term towards improved functioning in that area. In turn, it is more likely that such goals (involving behaviour changes within specified time-frames) will contribute to improved self-esteem. Furthermore, the nature of the goals to be adopted will vary significantly from person to person. As Rigazio-DeGilio and Ivey (1997) point out: "No matter what the issue . . . no two clients will talk about their concerns in the same way" (p. 415). Thus, goal setting is not a mechanical exercise, but a dynamic process flowing from the interpersonal relationship which has been established.

Accordingly, setting goals for the immediate interview is important. In many interviews, particularly those with a focus on helping, it is also the case that a key purpose of the interview is to assist clients in developing their own ability to formulate goals for post-interview action (Locke & Latham, 1984; Culley, 1991). A distinction needs to be made here between primary and secondary goals. The former, longer-term objectives are achieved through a series of related short-term, or secondary, goals. It is the latter which guide our moment-by-moment behaviour and act as a route for the achievement of the longer-term goals. Understanding this distinction is also a useful conceptual framework for ensuring that goals remain both specific and attainable. We have already discussed the example of a counsellor working with a client suffering from low self-esteem, and who will therefore have in all interviews the primary objective of raising self-esteem. If, however, it is the case that low esteem in part flows from a chronic weight problem a secondary goal will be to assist the client to develop strategies for weight loss. It is clearly crucial for client and helper to be in agreement on such an agenda for action. To cite some of the pointers within a framework proposed by Egan (1990), this will involve setting goals which:

- Are clear and specific enough to facilitate action
- Are realistic
- Can be measured
- Can be accommodated within resources at the client's command
- Remain under the client's control, so generating a feeling of empowerment

More generally on this issue, Parks (1994) has delineated communication competence in terms of hierarchical control theory, in which more abstract principles and idealised self-concept are at the top and these guide more concrete perceptual and behavioural responses lower down. Properly formulated primary and secondary goals represent the actualisation of such theory, and their formulation is a central objective of effective interviewing processes.

Of course, people operate with varying levels of awareness of the goals which they possess. Actions may be guided by conscious or subconscious goals. During skilled performance we tend to operate at a subconscious level, since an important feature of skill is the capacity to act and react rapidly – "without thinking". Thus, skilled interviewers are not constantly and consciously aware of the goal which is guiding each of their verbal and non-verbal responses. However, the distinction made by Brody (1987) between *being aware* of what is happening, *and being aware of being aware* of what is happening, is important. Skilled interviewers perform for the most part at the former level, but if required can invoke the latter level to analyse their performance. To return to the analogy between motor skill and social skill, the process is similar to how we feel when driving a car. Typically, we are unaware of the sequence involved in changing gears (lifting our foot from the accelerator; depressing the clutch; changing gear; releasing the clutch; depressing the accelerator), but can become conscious of this when a problem develops (e.g. we cannot change gear) and we then become aware of our motor actions. Skilled interview performance requires a similar ability to "switch" in our levels of awareness. For example, a counsellor may be progressing well with a client in free-flowing exchange. But if the client suddenly becomes emotionally upset for no apparent reason, the counsellor will then have to consider consciously possible causes.

The final feature of goals worthy of note here is that interaction will flow more smoothly if the goals of interviewer and interviewee concur. A detective will find interaction much easier with a voluntary and public-spirited eyewitness to a crime than with a reluctant and recalcitrant chief suspect to the crime. Likewise, police interrogators often attempt to establish some common goals with a suspect (perhaps through claiming that they really wish to help), in order to increase their prospects of achieving their objective – in this case, a confession.

Mediating Factors

The mediation stage involves translating goals into action plans. Mediating factors refer to the internal states and processes which mediate between the goal being sought, the feedback received and the responses made. There are two main mediating factors – cognition and emotion.

Cognition has been defined as "all the processes by which the sensory input is transformed, reduced, elaborated, stored, recovered and used" (Neisser, 1967, p. 4). In other words, our cognitive processes enable us to assimilate and retain incoming information which is then used to decide future responses. Indeed, Eder (1989) has shown how, in the interview context, "cognitive factors are the essential determinants of behavior" (p. 116). Once goals have been decided, the next step in the execution of skill is the design of plans to achieve them, and here cognitions are central. Berger, Knowlton and Abrahams (1996) make a useful distinction between plans and goals. They point out that the purpose of the plan is to provide a means to a goal, but that while a plan implies a goal, a goal does not necessarily indicate a plan. For example, an employer may have the goal of appointing a new employee capable of developing a coherent marketing strategy, but lack a detailed plan (such as deciding to draw up a personnel specification) capable of achieving the goal. Meanwhile, the interviewee may have the goal of getting the job, but lack a detailed plan for self-presentation capable of making the necessary positive impression on the interviewer. Similar discrepancies abound in people's personal lives and in our relationships, giving rise to considerable frustration.

Cognitions therefore play a key role in skilled performance. As expressed by Hawkins and Daly (1988), "most, if not all communication behaviors are generated through cognition. We must think to communicate" (p. 191). In particular, social cognition, which refers to how individuals think about human interaction, is central. There is considerable evidence to show that we use conceptual schemas to evaluate people and situations and to enable appropriate responses to be implemented rapidly (Kagan, Evans & Kay, 1986). A schema is a conceptual structure which is developed as a result of continued exposure to the same situation, and which provides a reservoir of information about how to behave in that context.

This has both positive and negative implications. Positively, we must resort to some form of primitive social categorisation, on a moment-by-moment basis, to impose order and sequence on a chaotic social world (Leyens, Yzerbyt & Schadron, 1994). As Berger (1987) postulates, a primary concern in interpersonal encounters is to reduce our feeling of uncertainty about the intentions of the other. This uncertainty takes two forms (Berger & Calabrese, 1975). With predictive uncertainty we are concerned with predicting others' attitudes, feelings, values, beliefs and future behaviour. With explanatory uncertainty we are concerned with reducing our uncertainty about explanations for the behaviour of strangers. This predisposes us to reach rapid conclusions, sometimes based on flimsy evidence or simply by allocating people to categories which in turn activate the stereotypes that we have accumulated.

In the context of interviews, this suggests that interviewers may have a tendency to assign people prematurely to various social categories which are often useful, but which also may prevent them from seeing the interviewee as the unique human being that they are, and which may act as a barrier to achieving the goals of the interview. Thus, it is well known that selection interviewers often over-rate interviewees who are similar to themselves in religion, social class, educational background or a variety of other important social indicators, and that such liking obscures the person's actual suitability for the job (Greenwald, 1981). The communication skills approach discussed in this chapter should help ameliorate such problems, by enabling interviewers and interviewees to probe social reality more deeply and so test the efficacy of their interpersonal perceptions.

The second main mediating factor is *emotion*. Emotions play an important role both in determining responses and in judging the behaviour of others (Metts & Bowers, 1994). In their review of research in this field, Maule and Hockey

(1996) conclude that changes in emotion clearly affect the way people make decisions. The emotional state of the individual will influence how the world is "seen", and how the behaviour of others is interpreted and responded to. Thus, an extremely nervous candidate at an employment interview is likely to find this degree of emotional arousal dysfunctional in terms of performance. Evidence of the pervasiveness of affective state can be shown in the host of labels used to describe the vast array of emotions. Studies have shown thousands of adjectives used to describe emotional states (Hargie, 1997a). However, there would seem to be six core emotional categories – love, happiness, surprise, anger, sadness and fear – and these tend to be expressed in common fashion across cultures (Shaver et al., 1987).

There is a reciprocal relationship between cognition and emotion in that how we feel can affect how we think and vice-versa. In everyday terms, those who are "too emotional" or "too worked up" are unlikely to be able to "think straight". Conversely, it may be possible to overcome irrational emotions through the application of logical thinking. For example, an interviewer may attempt to assist a client develop a higher level of self-esteem. One approach to achieving this is through what is known as cognitive behavioural modification (Meichenbaum & Genest, 1980), in which the understanding (or cognitions) of clients is challenged and reshaped. The focus might be on getting them to identify an area of their lives where the schema they have imposed on themselves (e.g. of general incompetence) has such low validity it must even be rejected by the client. Eventually, a recognition of this reality compels an emotional readjustment to follow.

As well as cognition and emotion, other mediating factors include the attitudes, values and beliefs of those involved. Prior experiences in the specific interview setting can also influence how the situation is perceived and responded to. For example, a candidate who is unsuccessful at 20 employment interviews may begin to perceive them as a waste of time and respond accordingly. Finally, previous experience of the other person will affect goals and responses. A doctor who is always hurried, never listens and prescribes rapidly is unlikely to be sought out by the patient when emotional problems arise.

Responses

> What we think, or what we know, or what we believe is, in the end, of little consequence. The only consequence is what we do (John Ruskin 1819–1900).

When a goal has been formulated and a plan devised, the next stage in the performance of skill is to execute the plan in terms of actual responses. As the Ruskin quotation indicates, it is at this point that skill becomes manifest. Judgements about interpersonal skill are based upon the *behaviour* of the individual. It is now recognised that no one set of skills can be applied across different interview contexts. Rather, considerable strides have been made in recent years to identify the main skill determinants of different types of interview. For example,

Anderson and Shackleton (1993) applied a skills approach to selection interviewing. They stated that the six most crucial skills areas for interviewers in this field encompass rapport development, empathic listening, process management, questioning strategies, note-taking and closing down. The specific weight attached to each of these skills, and others, obviously varies between interview contexts. Thus, empathy emerges as a central skill in client-centred counselling (Rogers, 1986). Not surprisingly, therefore, researchers in this field have been particularly keen to identify specific behaviours which are said to constitute its core dynamic (e.g. Mayeroff, 1971). Similarly, a variety of core communication skills such as questioning, listening, and confronting have been identified in appraisal interviews (Gillen, 1995).

Some researchers have been particularly concerned with developing methodologies capable of identifying communication skills used in a variety of interview contexts. Thus, Hargie, Morrow and Woodman (1993) videotaped a total of 350 actual consultations between community pharmacists and patients. The tapes were then analysed by the pharmacists themselves, using a methodology termed "constitutive ethnography". This identified 11 categories (and 45 related sub-categories) of skills deemed particularly pertinent during pharmacist–patient interviews, the most important of which were rapport building, explaining, questioning, listening and advice giving. Other studies have investigated core interviewing skills used by various professional groups including nurses (MacLeod Clark, 1982), speech therapists (Saunders & Caves, 1986) and priests (Lount & Hargie, 1997). While there are general similarities across these studies, there are also situation-specific responses. For example, a priest may suggest that a prayer be said, whereas this is unlikely to be in the professional response repertoire of the community pharmacist!

As Figure 1 indicates, the responses of both parties to an interview are important. Thus, there are core interviewee skills which will determine success or failure in different interview contexts (Millar et al., 1992). Furthermore, the responses of the interviewer will help to shape interviewee behaviour and vice-versa. Interestingly, in one investigation into the communicative activities of Catholic priests, Lount and Hargie (1997) found that there were differences between what priests saw as their most important interpersonal skills and what the laity with whom they interacted perceived to be key skills. This difference in perceptions of appropriateness of responses has also been found in other interviewing fields.

Feedback

Once a response has been executed, feedback is available to enable the individual to evaluate its effectiveness and adjust future responses accordingly. Without feedback it is not possible to behave in a skilled fashion. The skilled interviewer depends upon the cues available from the interviewee and from the environment to perform at optimum level. Social feedback, in the form of the verbal and non-verbal responses of other people, is essential in interpersonal encounters. Indeed we are most disconcerted if we have to interact with someone who is mono-syllabic and static, since we are unsure about how we are "being received". It is widely recognised that a crucial skill in promoting feedback in most interview contexts is that of reflecting. Reflecting is concerned with "presenting back to the other all or part of the message which has just been received" (Dickson, 1997, p. 160). Essentially, this involves restating in the interviewer's own words the affective and/or factual content of the interviewee's utterances. The central objective is to promote a common agenda and discourage misperceptions of key interaction goals.

Social feedback is obtained from two sources – self and others (Figure 1). As well as observing the behaviour of others, skilled individuals are also high self-monitors (Snyder, 1987). They control and regulate their own responses, and adjust these to suit the needs of particular people or situations. This involves having an awareness of the ability level of those with whom one is interacting and of how they think, thereby making it more likely that common expectations will be formed for the interview process and that the communicative styles of interview participants can be matched. Successful interaction in general requires an ability to "form cognitive conceptions of the other's cognitive conceptions" (Wessler, 1984, p. 112). Additionally, the capacity for self-monitoring enables interview participants to compare their biases, stereotypes and the general social categories they initially create with the emerging reality from the interview process. In this fashion, feedback forms a crucial component of the interviewer's "communication with themselves", or what is generally defined as intrapersonal communication.

Another feature of feedback is that it is selective. In any encounter there is simply too much information to deal with from the physical and social environment – the ticking of a clock, the pressure of our arms on the chair, the temperature, what the other person is saying and every little accompanying non-verbal nuance. If attempting to monitor all of this, the person's perceptual facility would become overloaded. As a result, much of this information is filtered out and a limited amount dealt with. Thus, while there is considerable feedback available from our physical and social environment, we do not per-ceive all of it.

Perception

It is the function of the perceptual system to gather, filter and make sense of incoming information from the physical and social environment. Forgas (1985) described this as "the first crucial stage in any interaction between people. We must first perceive and interpret other people before we can meaningfully relate to them" (p. 21). Skilled interviewers will be perceptive individuals. In particu-lar, they will have high acumen in the field of person perception, which can be divided into three main parts:

- *Perception of self* – the capacity for self-monitoring
- *Perception of others* – the ability to evaluate other people objectively
- *Metaperception* – the aptitude for perceiving the perception process: here judgements are made both about how others are perceiving us, and about how they seem to think we are perceiving them

While our initial impressions of other people may not always be accurate, they do influence how we relate to them. Such social perception is often concerned with asking questions such as what qualities do other people possess? How do we explain their behaviour? How do we determine their affective state? How accurate are our perceptions? (Zebrowitz, 1990). Accordingly, there is now considerable evidence to suggest that much of social interaction is influenced by what have been termed "expectancy effects", in which the expectations which we have of others shape our perceptions of what they do and in turn help frame our own response (Darley & Oleson, 1994). For example, one review in the field of selection interviews (Dipboye, 1989) has found that pre-interview impressions are highly related to post-interview assessment. Dougherty, Turban and Callender (1994) discovered, in a study of semi-structured interviews, that when interviewers formed positive first impressions of interviewees they then:

- Engaged in more rapport-building behaviours
- Showed higher levels of positive regard
- Provided greater job information
- "Sold" the company more strongly
- Engaged in less information gathering

Others have found that positive or negative expectations in promotion interviews are often generated from application forms and then followed through in appointment decisions (Wareing & Stockdale, 1987). It has also long been known that interviewer attitude can produce corresponding distortions in the responses received from interviewees in survey research interviews (Brenner, 1981).

How expectations are managed is often crucial to the interview's success. Thus, matching styles of communication between interactors is generally regarded as a core characteristic of skilled communication (Hamilton & Parker, 1990). This means that identifying the expectations which all sides bring to the interview is a crucial prerequisite of effectiveness. The interview skills of questioning, listening and reflecting are paramount in this regard. Learning the expectations of others and acquiring the ability to formulate appropriate responses in line with the scripts of both interviewer and interviewee is in turn honed by repeated exposure to the interview situation.

Despite this, much perception often remains on a superficial level. Thus, although it is common wisdom that we should not judge books by their covers, we in fact do! When meeting people for the first time, our evaluations will be influenced by factors such as physique and physical attractiveness, dress, race, gender, accent, age, and so on. As summarised by Dipboye (1992): "Several decades of research have shown that the search for and processing of information on applicants can be influenced to an inordinate degree by the data encountered in the initial phases of the interview" (p. 120). Such reliance on initial impressions may be one explanation for the finding that, in selection interviews, attractive applicants are perceived more favourably in terms of anticipated job performance and personality, which in turn increases the likelihood that they will be recruited (Gilmore, Beehr & Love, 1986). Skilled interviewers are aware of the hazards of labelling, favouring and stereotyping interviewees. They also suspend assessment until maximum information has been obtained to enable a more informed evaluation to be effected (Millar et al., 1992).

Perception is the final central process involved in the skills model (Figure 1). However, in order to achieve a full understanding of the interactive encounter, it is necessary to take cognisance of the context in which the interview occurs.

The Person–Situation Context

All communication is embedded within a context and can only be interpreted and made sense of within that frame. What Hargie, Saunders and Dickson (1994) termed the "person–situation context" is therefore of core importance. The behaviour of interviewer and interviewee will be a function both of the types of people they are and of the situation in which the interaction takes place (Gorden, 1980).

On the person side, impinging factors include the following.

Gender

A body of evidence now exists to show that gender plays an enormous role in shaping an individual's behaviour and in determining how others are responded to. For example, one study of medication-history interviewing found that male and female pharmacists differed in their use of expressive, interactive and interrogative skills, and that success depended upon the use of different sets of skills during same-sex and opposite-sex dyads (Gettman, Ranelli & Ried, 1996).

Appearance

As mentioned earlier, the attractiveness, dress and physique of ourselves and of those with whom we interact may influence responses. Research has found that interviewers are extremely attentive to the appearance and dress codes of job interviewees, with 100% of interviewers in one study noticing when job applicants needed a haircut, 97% recognising soiled shirt cuffs and collar, and 83% being aware that the applicant needed a shave (Hamilton & Parker, 1990). It is therefore not surprising that in research studies a positive correlation has been found between interpersonal attraction and employment interview outcomes, leading Wade and Kinicki (1997) to posit that interviewers measure applicant fit as well as job skills. One caveat here is that much employment interview research has tended to use simulations rather than real world job interviews, so more work is required before definite conclusions can be reached. Racial features also influence perceptions and behaviour (see Chapter 4.3).

Personality

The disposition of both parties plays an important role in shaping behaviour. Without adopting an exclusively trait-oriented approach, it is nevertheless clear that a person's personality helps ensure that their behaviour often differs from that of other people in exactly similar circumstances (Hampson, 1988). Thus, how nervous people feel in particular interviews is not completely determined by the behaviours of the interviewer: the pre-existing disposition of the interviewee is a crucial factor in the equation. The communication skills exercised by interviewer and interviewee interact with the disposition of each to shape the progress of the interaction.

Age

The relative ages of interviewer and interviewee will influence their behaviour and their expectations of one another. For example, a fear of ageing (gerontophobia) may contribute to a morbid aversion towards elderly people, expressed in discriminatory or hostile practices during interviews (Thomas, 1988). In turn, such attitudes may encourage the elderly to act out the roles prescribed for them, thus creating a self-fulfilling prophecy (Phillipson, 1982).

Cultural background

The second part of the equation is the situation in which interaction occurs. Of relevance here is the *cultural background* of the participants. Those from similar cultures can understand one another more readily and are more likely to be attuned to the often subtle nuances which guide social encounters. Likewise, the wider the disparity of cultural identity the less common ground there will be, and hence the greater the potential for communication breakdown. Other contextual features include the *roles* of both parties and the extent to which these are mutually understood, the *rules* which govern the encounter, and the *physical environment* in terms of layout of furniture and fittings, lighting, heating, colour, etc. Overall, this analysis supports the interactionist perspective on human behaviour, which purports that behaviour is the result of continuous feedback between the person and the situation, that the person is a conscious and active factor in the process, that behaviour is to a considerable extent determined by cognitive and affective factors and that the meaning which people assign to a given situation is also a crucial determinant of eventual behaviour (Endler & Edwards, 1978).

More research is needed into all of these dimensions, since as Eder (1989) noted, "interviewers operate under a variety of situational constraints . . . Yet little is known about how the interview context affects interviewer judgement" (p. 114).

CONCLUSION

The model as described in this chapter has outlined the skills approach to our understanding of the interview. This highlights the importance of the goals of the participants, their strategies and plans for achieving these goals, related behavioural routines and associated perceptual concerns. It also takes cognisance of personal factors relating to interviewer and interviewee as well as the situated features of the actual interviewing encounter. The model provides a systematic and coherent perspective for the analysis of interviews. It has also provided a coherent system for training communication skills, and a wide range of studies have shown that such training has very positive outcomes for recipients (Hargie, 1997c; Tourish & Hargie, 1995).

Clearly, it is not possible to conclude from this analysis that a simple repertoire of predetermined communication skills can be applied generically to any interpersonal encounter capable of being labelled as an interview. Hargie (1997c) explicitly counsels against the notion that training in communication skills results in identikit patterns of behaviour by recipients – such a view is akin to anticipating that by teaching everyone to talk we will all end up saying exactly the same things! Individual differences mean that each of us applies individual skills in our own unique way. Moreover, as this chapter has suggested, we are deeply influenced by the nature of the other person that we meet. This further ensures the novelty of each interaction in which we participate. Thus, it is not the intention of the model which we have advocated to prescribe drab and uniform standards of behaviour in interview contexts. However, it is our intention to suggest that the theoretical framework outlined here is a robust means of conceptualising interview behaviours in a wide variety of contexts, and that more awareness of the skills issues delineated in this chapter will equip both interviewers and interviewees with greater communication choices at each stage of the process.

REFERENCES

Anderson, N. & Shackleton, V. (1993). *Successful Selection Interviewing*. Oxford: Blackwell.

Argyle, M. (1967). *The Psychology of Interpersonal Behaviour*. Harmondsworth: Penguin.

Berger, C. (1987). Communicating under uncertainty. In M. Roloff & G. Millar (Eds.), *Interpersonal Processes: New Directions in Communications Research* (pp. 39–62). London: Sage.

Berger, C. & Calabrese, R. (1975). Some explorations in initial interactions and beyond: toward a developmental theory of interpersonal communication, *Human Communication Research*, **1**, 99–112.

Berger, C., Knowlton, S.W. & Abrahams, M.F. (1996). The hierarchy principle in strategic communication. *Communication Theory*, **6**, 111–142.

Boreham, P. & Gibson, D. (1978). The informative process in private medical consultations: a preliminary investigation. *Social Science and Medicine*, **12**, 408–416.

Brenner, M. (1981). Skills in the research interview. In M. Argyle (Ed.), *Social Skills and Work* (pp. 28–58). London: Methuen.

Brody, N. (1987). Introduction: Some thoughts on the unconscious. *Personality and Social Psychology Bulletin*, **13**, 293–298.

Bryan, W. & Harter, N. (1897). Physiology and psychology of the telegraphic language, *Psychological Review*, **4**, 27–53.

Chulef, A. (1993). *Towards a hierarchical taxonomy of human goals*. Unpublished doctoral dissertation. Los Angeles: University of Southern California.

Cormier, W. & Cormier, L. (1985). *Interviewing Strategies for Helpers* (2nd edn). Monterey, CA: Brooks/Cole.

Culley, S. (1991). *Integrative Counseling Skills In Action*. London: Sage.

Darley, J. & Oleson, K. (1994). Introduction to research on interpersonal expectations. In P. Blanck (Ed.), *Interpersonal Expectations: Theory Research, and Applications* (pp. 45–63). Cambridge: Cambridge University Press.

Dickson, D. (1997). Reflecting. In O. Hargie (Ed.), *The Handbook of Communication Skills* (2nd edn, pp. 159–182). London: Routledge.

Dickson, D.A., Hargie, O.D.W. & Morrow, N.C. (1997). *Communication Skills Training for Health Professionals* (2nd edn). London: Chapman and Hall.

Dipboye, R. (1989). Incremental validity of interviewer judgements, in R. Eder & G. Ferris (Eds.), *The Employment Interview: Research, Theory and Practice*. Newbury Park: Sage.

Dipboye, R.L. (1992). *Selection Interviews: Process Perspectives*. Cincinnati: South-Western Publishing.

Dougherty, T., Turban, D. & Callender, J. (1994). Confirming first impressions in the employment interview: a field study of interviewer behavior. *Journal of Applied Psychology*, **79**, 659–665.

Eder, R. (1989). Contextual effects on interview decisions. In R. Eder & G. Ferris (Eds.), *The Employment Interview: Research, Theory and Practice* (pp. 113–126). Newbury Park: Sage.

Egan, G. (1990). *The Skilled Helper* (4th edn). Pacific Grove, CA: Brooks/Cole.

Endler, N. & Edwards, J. (1978). Person by treatment interactions in personality research. In L. Pervin & M. Lewis (Eds.), *Perspectives in Interactional Psychology* (pp. 141–169). New York: Plenum.

Forgas, J. (1985). *Interpersonal Behaviour*. Oxford: Pergamon.

Gettman, D.A., Ranelli, P.L. & Ried, L.D. (1996). Influence of gender on outcomes of medication-history interviewing. *Patient Education and Counseling*, **27**, 147–160.

Gillen, T. (1995). *The Appraisal Discussion*. London: Institute of Personnel and Development.

Gilmore, D., Beehr, T. & Love, K. (1986). Effects of applicant sex, applicant physical attractiveness, type of rater and type of job on interview decision. *Journal of Occupational Psychology*, **59**, 103–109.

Gorden, R. (1980). *Interviewing: Strategy, Techniques, and Tactics* (3rd edn). Homewood, IL: Dorsey Press.

Greenwald, M. (1981). The effects of physical attractiveness, experience and social performance on employee decision-making in job interviews, *Behavioral Counseling Quarterly*, **1**, 275–288.

Hamilton, C. & Parker, C. (1990). *Communicating for Results* (3rd edn). Belmont, CA: Wadsworth.

Hampson, S. (1988). *The Construction of Personality: An introduction* (2nd edn). London: Routledge.

Hargie, O. (1997a). Interpersonal communication: A theoretical framework. In O. Hargie (Ed.), *The Handbook of Communication Skills* (pp. 29–63). London: Routledge.

Hargie, O. (1997b). Communication as skilled performance. In O. Hargie (Ed.), *The Handbook of Communication Skills* (pp. 7–28). London: Routledge.

Hargie, O. (1997c). Training in communication skills: Research, theory and practice. In O. Hargie (Ed.), *The Handbook of Communication Skills* (pp. 473–482). London: Routledge.

Hargie, O., Morrow, N. & Woodman, C. (1993). *Looking into community pharmacy: Identifying effective communication skills in pharmacist–patient consultations.* Jordanstown: University of Ulster.

Hargie, O., Saunders, C. & Dickson, D. (1994). *Social Skills in Interpersonal Communication* (3rd edn). London: Routledge.

Hawkins, R.P. & Daly, J. (1988). Cognition and communication. In R.P. Hawkins, J.M. Wiemann & S. Pingree (Eds.), *Advancing Communication Science: Merging Mass and Interpersonal Processes* (pp. 191–223). Beverly Hills: Sage.

Hughes, K. (1994). *An investigation into non-verbal behaviours associated with deception/concealment during a negotiation process.* University of Ulster, Jordanstown: DPhil Thesis.

Irving, P. (1995). *A reconceptualisation of Rogerian core conditions of facilitative communication: Implications for training.* University of Ulster, Jordanstown: DPhil Thesis.

Kagan, C., Evans, J. & Kay, B. (1986). *A Manual of Interpersonal Skills for Nurses: An Experiential Approach.* London: Harper and Row.

Lapworth, P., Sills, C. & Fish, S. (1993). *Transactional Analysis Counselling.* Bicester, Oxon.: Winslow Press.

Leyens, J., Yzerbyt, V. & Schadron, G. (1994). *Stereotypes and Social Cognition.* London: Sage.

Liden, R. & Parsons, C. (1989). Understanding interpersonal behavior in the employment interview: A reciprocal interaction analysis. In R. Eder & G. Ferris (Eds.), *The Employment Interview: Research, Theory and Practice.* Newbury Park: Sage.

Locke, E. & Latham, G. (1984). *Goal Setting: A Motivational Technique That Works!* Englewood Cliffs, NJ: Prentice-Hall.

Lount, M. & Hargie, O. (1997). The priest as counsellor: an investigation of critical incidents in the pastoral work of Catholic priests. *Counselling Psychology Quarterly,* **10**, 247–259.

MacLeod Clark, J. (1982). *Nurse–patient verbal interaction: an analysis of recorded conversations from selected surgical wards.* University of London: PhD Thesis.

Maule, A.J. & Hockey, G.R. (1996). The effects of mood on risk-taking behaviour. *Psychologist,* **9**, 464–467.

Mayeroff, M. (1971). *On Caring.* New York: Harper and Row.

Mayou, R., Williamson, B. & Foster, A. (1976). Attitudes and advice after myocardial infection. *British Medical Journal,* **1**, 1577–1579.

Meichenbaum, D. & Genest, M. (1980). Cognitive behavioral modification: an integration of cognitive and behavioral methods. In F. Kanfer & A. Goldstein (Eds.), *Helping People Change: A Textbook of Methods* (2nd edn). New York: Pergamon Press.

Metts, S. & Bowers, J. (1994). Emotion in interpersonal communication. In M. Knapp & G. Miller (Eds.), *Handbook of Interpersonal Communication* (2nd edn, pp. 508–541). Thousand Oaks: Sage.

Millar, R., Crute, V. & Hargie, O. (1992). *Professional Interviewing.* London: Routledge.

Neisser, U. (1967). *Cognitive Psychology.* New York: Appleton-Century-Crofts.

Okun, B. (1992). *Effective Helping: Interviewing and Counseling Techniques* (4th edn). California: Brooks/Cole.

Parks, M.R. (1994). Communication competence and interpersonal control. In M. Knapp & G. Miller (Eds.), *Handbook of Interpersonal Communication* (2nd edn, pp. 589–620). Thousand Oaks: Sage.

Pendleton, D., Schofield, T., Tate, P. & Havelock, P. (1984). *The Consultation: An Approach to Learning and Teaching.* Oxford: Oxford University Press.

Phillipson, C. (1982). *Capitalism and the Construction of Old Age.* London: Macmillan.

Proctor, R. & Dutta, A. (1995). *Skill Acquisition and Human Performance.* Thousand Oaks: Sage.

Rigazio-DiGilio, S. & Ivey, A. (1997). The helping interview: a cognitive-developmental approach. In O. Hargie (Ed.), *The Handbook of Communication Skills* (2nd edn, pp. 409–429). London: Routledge.

Rogers, C. (1986). Reflection of feelings. *Person-Centered Review*, **2**, 375–377.

Roter, D. (1983). Physician–patient communication. *Maryland State Medical Journal*, **32**, 260–265.

Saunders, C. & Caves, R. (1986). An empirical approach to the identification of communication skills with reference to speech therapy. *Journal of Further and Higher Education*, **10**, 29–44.

Shaver, P., Schwartz, J., Kerson, D. & O'Connor, G. (1987). Emotion knowledge. Further exploration of a prototype approach. *Journal of Personality and Social Psychology*, **52**, 1061–1086.

Slater, M.D. (1997). Persuasion processes across receiver goals and message genres. *Communication Theory*, **7**, 125–148.

Snyder, M. (1987). *Public Appearances Private Realities: The Psychology of Self-monitoring*. New York: Freeman.

Tardy, C. & Dindia, K. (1997). Self-disclosure. In O. Hargie (Ed.), *The Handbook of Communication Skills* (2nd edn, pp. 213–235). London: Routledge.

Thomas, L. (1988). Images of ageing. In S. Wright (Ed.), *Nursing the Older Patient* (pp. 9–23). Cambridge: Harper and Row.

Tourish, D. & Hargie, C. (1995). Preparing students for selection interviews: a template for training and development. *Innovation and Learning in Education*, **1**, 22–27.

Tullar, W. (1989). The employment interview as a cognitive performing script. In R. Eder & G. Ferris (Eds.), *The Employment Interview: Research, Theory and Practice*. Newbury Park: Sage.

Wade, K.J. & Kinicki, A.J. (1997). Subjective applicant qualifications and interpersonal attraction as mediators within a process model of interview selection decisions. *Journal of Vocational Behavior*, **50**, 23–40.

Wareing, R. & Stockdale, J. (1987). Decision making in the promotion interview: an empirical study. *Personnel Review*, **16**, 4.

Wessler, R. (1984). Cognitive-social psychological theories and social skills: A review. In P. Trower (Ed.), *Radical Approaches to Social Skills Training* (pp. 111–141). Beckenham: Croom Helm.

Wicks, R. (1982). Interviewing: Practical aspects. In A. Chapman & A. Gale (Eds.), *Psychology and People. A Tutorial Text*. London: BPS/Macmillan.

Zebrowitz, L. (1990). *Social Perception*. Milton Keynes: Open University.

Interview in Qualitative Research

Sheila Payne
University of Southampton, UK

INTRODUCTION

The semi-structured or unstructured interview is arguably the most common method of collecting data for qualitative analysis. Interviewing, to the novice, often appears deceptively easy. It is assumed to be just a matter of talking to another person, asking a few questions and waiting to be told everything which is needed to complete the research project. It will be argued that research interviewing is a highly skilled activity which needs careful preparation. Moreover, research interviewing, like many other sorts of interviewing, requires special skills to ensure that the data elicited are suitable for the proposed method of analysis, especially since interviews generate large amounts of data. The transcription and processing of interview texts using various methods of qualitative analysis will not be the primary focus of this chapter; for more about this subject, see O'Connell and Kowal (1995).

This chapter is an overview of the process of interviewing for qualitative analysis. Research interviewing has been defined along a dimension of researcher control from unstructured to structured (Smith, 1995). This implies at one extreme that the interviewer approaches the interview with no clear agenda or list of questions but just aims to enable the person to talk generally about issues. At the other extreme the structured interview is based on the same rationale as the psychological experiment, in that there is a strict order of presentation of questions which are usually pre-coded in limited response formats. A middle position is the semi-structured interview which involves predefining a range of questions or topics to be addressed in the interview but being flexible

Handbook of the Psychology of Interviewing. Edited by A. Memon and R. Bull.
© 1999 John Wiley & Sons Ltd.

enough to allow the respondent to initiate new topics or expand on relevant issues. In addition, there are a number of specialist research interview techniques such as in feminist research (Oakley, 1981; Devault, 1990), the in-depth interview (Fielding, 1993) and the counselling interview (Colye & Wright, 1996).

The purpose of this chapter is to consider the skills necessary to conduct these types of interviews and the nature of the data generated. This chapter will make the assumption that interviews are dyadic interactions, occurring in face-to-face contexts, although a brief review of the advantages and disadvantages of telephone interviewing will be included. Group interviews and focus group discussions require somewhat different skills and will not be dealt with here (see Krueger (1988) or Morgan (1988) for more on these topics, and Chapter 2.5 Using Focus Groups in this volume). A number of important aspects of interviewing will be considered, including style of presentation, choice of questions or topics, interventions designed to elicit or respond to feelings, non-verbal behaviours and characteristics of the effective interviewer. Because good interviewing techniques often elicit highly personal data, it is relevant to consider issues of consent and confidentiality. The terms "reliability" and "validity" will be discussed in relation to interviewing and their appropriateness as concepts in qualitative research endeavours will be debated. Interviews, like any other means of collecting data, are open to various possible sources of bias. This chapter will acknowledge potential factors which may contribute to bias and what can be done to minimise or at least become aware of them. Research interviews are demanding of participants but they are also demanding of interviewers. Strategies will be suggested about how to survive being an interviewer.

There are numerous qualitative methodologies which are underpinned by differing notions about the nature and purpose of talk (Tesch, 1990). The chapter will end by discussing two different epistemological approaches to interview data; namely the ethnographic and the ethnomethodological perspectives. These will be contrasted in terms of the status afforded to the responses of participants, the implications for the inferences which may be drawn from talk, and the purpose of the analysis of discourse. Examples of research in palliative care and psychosocial oncology will be used to illustrate and illuminate the issues raised in the chapter.

IMPORTANT ASPECTS OF INTERVIEWING

The qualitative interviewer aims to establish a relationship with the respondent which allows the individual to feel comfortable enough to share their thoughts and feelings. According to Kvale (1983), the qualitative interview is centred on the interviewee's life-world. It seeks to understand the meaning of phenomena from their perspective. This section deals with the practical aspects of interviewing which to some extent may be considered to be taken for granted but I would suggest that it is helpful to itemise and reflect on each aspect before embarking on a study.

The Interview Context

Although in theory interviews can be conducted anywhere, ideally a comfortable, private and reasonably quiet location is desirable. A degree of control over the environment is more difficult to achieve when the researcher is on another person's territory; for example, it may be difficult in someone else's home to insist that the television is switched off. Yet people may feel more secure and confident in their own space, be that at their home or work place. There is often a compromise to be made between the desirable elements such as quietness and privacy, and what is possible because of financial and practical constraints. However, the researcher should be mindful that there are choices and not assume that interviews conducted in the clinic, for example, are necessarily comparable to those conducted in people's homes.

Telephone Interviewing

Telephone interviews have advantages for researchers, largely in terms of economy. Marcus and Crane (1986) indicate that using telephone interviews in public health research reduces the costs by between 50% and 75% compared to face-to-face interviews. Generally they are cheaper and faster because of the lack of travel time and travel costs incurred by the researcher and therefore it is possible to complete an increased number of interviews per working day. There is specialist equipment which allows audio-recording of telephone conversations, although ethically it is essential to obtain consent. If structured interviews are planned, computer assisted interviewing may permit direct coding of data. Telephone interviews are best for fairly structured and short interviews. They may also elicit greater frankness especially in sensitive areas such as sexual behaviour (Siemiatycki, 1979). The disadvantage is that they exclude certain sections of the population, those too poor to have a telephone, or in hostel accommodation such as students. Certain people may have functional problems in using the telephone such as deafness and difficulty in comprehension. Response rates are typically lower than face-to-face interviews but can be improved by advanced warning letters or meetings to arrange times for the interview (Worth & Tierney, 1993). It may be difficult to ask complex questions, and without access to non-verbal cues it may not be possible to pursue topics using probes to elicit more information.

The Interviewer

There are some aspects of an interviewer which are relatively unchangeable such as gender, age and ethnicity. Since the interviewer is the main research "tool" in qualitative interviewing, the presentation of self is an important factor. Simple things like appearance, the style of clothing worn or the accent used in speech, provide clear markers of social status and power. For example, a postgraduate student undertaking research with bereaved relatives of organ donors dressed smartly in red and black for her first interview only to be mortified to learn from the respondent that she could not bear the colours red and black as for her, they recalled the sight of her daughter's stained clothing following a fatal car accident (Sque, 1997). Therefore it is important to consider carefully the image you wish to convey.

Interview data need to be recorded for subsequent analysis. There are a number of options including note-taking, audio-tape recording and video recording. Each method has its advantages and disadvantages. My view is that audio-tape recording is the preferred option as it remains as a permanent record of the interaction. However, the usefulness of the data is dependent upon high quality audio recording equipment (if possible broadcast quality equipment should be used) and the environmental conditions in which the recording is made. It is not my intention to describe the technical aspects of the equipment, except to say that quality can be enhanced by using a separate microphone. It is also imperative that the researcher is completely familiar with the equipment before starting to interview, as there is nothing more annoying than conducting a good interview only to discover later that there has been a technical hitch in the recording. Becoming familiar with the equipment also helps to reassure the respondent that this is a normal part of the interview, so neither interviewer nor interviewee is overly conscious of its presence. In addition to the audio recording, I find it helpful to make brief field notes after the interview which describe contextual features. Video recording is more likely to be perceived as invasive by the respondent. However, it has the advantage of enabling non-verbal behaviour to be recorded. If video recording is to be employed then more than one camera should be used to enable recording of both interviewer and interviewee though, of course, this may increase the perceived invasiveness.

Conducting the Qualitative Interview

There are general aspects of interviewing which need to be considered before devising the actual questions or topics for a specific project. Question types have been categorised into open, closed, double or multiple choice (Bowling, 1997). None are inherently wrong but each type of question may be more effective for eliciting different types of data. For example, open questions may invite respondents to describe their situation or relate a narrative, and tend to produce more expansive responses. Closed questions are useful for checking factual details such as "How many children do you have?" and tend to produce more constrained responses. Double questions basically ask two questions at once and have the danger that only one will be answered. Multiple choice questions (like questionnaires) present respondents with a series of options, none of which may accurately reflect their views. Moreover, this type of question tends to constrain their answers but to be helpful people may select one of the options even it is inappropriate.

In preparing for an interview, investigators need to consider strategies which are likely to increase their ability to establish rapport. Colye and Wright (1996) have advocated the use of basic counselling skills especially in research on "sensitive" topics. It is difficult to define what are "sensitive" topics, although it is likely to include any issue that potentially poses a substantial threat and raises emotionally meaningful memories (Lee, 1993). Many qualitative interviews require people to recall, reflect on, and recount emotionally difficult episodes such as bereavements or other major life events. Thus skills are not only needed in eliciting feelings but acknowledging these feelings and supporting respondents through the interview experience. Drawing on counselling theory, Rogers (1951) advocated that interviewers develop the ability to be alert, interested, relaxed, warm, empathetic and genuine. Many of these attributes could be conveyed by non-verbal behaviours identified by Egan (1994) which include: positioning oneself squarely in relation to the interviewee, maintaining an open and relaxed body posture while leaning slightly towards the respondent and using eye contact to express interest.

The ability to conduct a "good" interview is not only dependent upon asking the "right" questions but involves careful listening. It may be helpful to conceptualise "listening" as an active rather than a passive process. Giving people undivided attention is likely to enhance the quality of the relationship. Displaying attention is achieved through establishing eye contact and looking at the interviewee, rather than the interview protocol. Try to maintain a natural and relaxed position which indicates interest in the person; orientate your body towards theirs. The use of natural hand and facial gestures can help to communicate interest and empathy, although the actual gestures are likely to be influenced by cultural and gender norms. Limit the number of interruptions and try to maintain the flow of the conversational topic (see also Chapter 5.6 by Memon). Signal changes in topic by acknowledging that a change to the next topic will be made.

Techniques derived from counselling can be used to elicit and respond to feelings. The following are some suggestions. At the outset, it can be appropriate to directly request self-disclosure of feelings such as "How did you feel about that?" When feelings are elicited, they should be acknowledged and may be reflected back in a summary statement. For example, following a harrowing account, the interviewer could comment on the sadness, anger or confusion experienced. Colye and Wright (1996) have argued that "fostering of the counselling attributes of empathy, genuineness and unconditional positive regard should be a constant feature" (p. 437). These attributes can be displayed by summarising the main point made by an interviewee while using their words or expressions to indicate that they have been heard. The interviewer can offer linkages between various elements of the interview, for example commenting on feelings of loneliness that were expressed following divorce, and/or a house move, and/or leaving the parental home. In this case the respondent may be asked to clarify the differences between these different types of loneliness or acknowledge their similarity. I am not suggesting that the qualitative interview is synonymous with a therapeutic counselling session or even advocating that it should be, rather I am proposing that it may be useful to acquire some counselling skills.

CONSENT AND CONFIDENTIALITY

This section discusses issues in obtaining consent and maintaining confidentiality. There are inequalities in the power relationship between interviewers and participants (Oakley, 1981) which are rarely acknowledged. Although the balance of power is likely to be weighted in favour of the interviewer, interviewees are not powerless and they may subvert the enterprise by taking control, for example, by talking endlessly about topics from their own agenda. Whilst it is vital to obtain informed consent, participants will only have full knowledge of what an interview involves after they have experienced it (Gale, 1993). The researcher may ask about feelings and experiences which are disturbing to the participant. How can participants be warned of this possibility without suggesting what are "normal" emotions or reactions? For example, in research with bereaved people there is an expectation that people will be distressed; thus behaviour which is not indicating grief might be viewed as problematic (Wortman & Silver, 1989). Even using the term "loved one" for the deceased makes an assumption that the dead person was "loved"; so it is better to use the person's name. There is a need to acknowledge and accept participants' level of adjustment. For example, during interviews with women with advanced cancer, some people could not bring themselves to explicitly use the word "cancer" (Payne, 1989). In this case, it would be inappropriate to force individuals to confront issues like a diagnosis of cancer although this might be the purpose of a therapeutic intervention.

The role played by an investigator in health care contexts may be ambiguous, especially if the respondent has already interacted with them clinically. Should research interviewing be therapeutic? Wright and Colye (1996) have argued the case that it should in the context of a study of AIDS-related bereavement among gay men. I would propose that there is a fundamental difference between research and therapeutic interviews not in the style or format of the interview but in relation to the intention of the interview and the consent given. In eliciting consent for a research interview it is important to indicate that the prime purpose is to obtain data rather than to help the individual, while a therapeutic encounter should aim primarily to help the individual although gaining information is often important for therapy. However, many research interviews are perceived to be therapeutic by interviewees even when difficult topics are addressed. In a study of bereaved organ donor relatives, participants were asked about how they perceived the interview (Sque & Payne, 1996). All except one person found the experience helpful despite the distress experienced, especially as few had previous opportunities to recount their "stories".

The qualitative interview may raise sensitive issues. How can this be effectively managed to minimise distress and at the same time produce optimal data? It is suggested that the researcher should be willing to share the agenda. This means being honest about the nature of the study and being explicit about the questions which will be asked. Many Ethical Committees now require written information to be provided, and written consent to be obtained. However, there is evidence from research on breast cancer that many information leaflets are written in language which is incomprehensible for many people (Beaver & Luker, 1997). It may also not be clear from written information what type of questions will be asked; therefore it might be helpful to share the question protocol with respondents. There is always a tension between putting participants off and thus reducing the response rate, and the need to recruit people while giving opportunities for fully informed consent. A possible strategy is to discuss the study with participants, to build a relationship and to establish boundaries before a first interview. However, this is expensive in researcher and respondent time.

During the interview, issues may be raised which are impossible or inappropriate for the researcher to deal with such as long-time effects of childhood sexual abuse, or an ongoing need for bereavement support. The investigator should anticipate that some respondents may need referral for further help and consider how this can be negotiated without violating confidentiality. Within bereavement research, Parkes (1995) has recommended that prior to starting data collection, researchers should have established referral mechanisms and offer these to all participants. For example, in the previously mentioned study of organ donor relatives (Sque & Payne, 1996), the interviewer explained that the interviews may be distressing and that tears were a normal part of expressing grief and were to be expected. She also provided participants with telephone numbers of local counselling services which they could call if they wished after the interview. She ensured that she did not leave them in a distressed state and that other family or friends were available immediately after the interview.

The ability to build rapport and trust with a participant is often a key element in successfully acquiring data (see Chapter 5.6 by Memon) and, especially in longitudinal studies, in gaining repeated access to participants. Researchers may establish strong relationships with their respondents which they find difficult to terminate. There is a dilemma between a necessary conclusion to the data collection and an abrupt dropping of informants which appears callous and uncaring. Negotiating the withdrawal of the researcher requires careful planning and a recognition of the effects on the situation (Meyer, 1993).

Qualitative studies may have relatively few participants, and the intensely personal nature of the data presents dilemmas in the use of verbatim quotes, or even in using episodes in a participant's life, as in narrative analysis. It is vital that the identities of informants are protected. This is very important when people are reporting illegal or socially unacceptable behaviours. Thus, qualitative researchers may be in the unenviable position of being unable to use some of their most meaningful and valuable data (Payne & Westwell, 1994).

INTERVIEW RELIABILITY

Reliability refers to the degree of consistency between instances which are assigned the same category label by different observers or by the same observer on different occasions (Hammersley, 1992). In relation to interviews reliability refers to the degree to which they are reproducible, although there is a question of whether that refers to the interviewer or the interviewee responses. The reliability of structured interviews is established via a number of strategies including: training of the interviewers to ensure comparability in question format and style, a formal interview schedule where questions tend to have fixed or limited choice responses, and interrater reliability correlations on the coding of responses. It is also possible to ask the same question twice within the interview to determine consistency of responding, although there is the danger that people recognise the question and are annoyed by this. There is more debate about whether qualitative interviews are replicable or even can be. Essentially the qualitative interview is a dyadic interaction which is contextually and temporally situated. The nature of the relationship established is unlikely to be exactly recreated by others. Moreover, as Kvale (1983) has argued, the qualitative interview can change participants, by getting them to think about issues or recount narratives, during which the events and feelings become reconstructed. Researchers from a narrative analysis perspective make the assumption that "stories" will change over time, as they become recounted, depending on the rhetorical stance being taken.

INTERVIEW VALIDITY

Hammersley (1990) defines validity in terms of the extent to which an account accurately represents the social phenomena to which it refers. In the quantitative paradigm, validity is taken to mean that the measure assesses what it purports to measure. Validity presents considerable problems to the qualitative researcher in the absence of a belief in an objective reality, which has led some researchers to reject the notion (Agar, 1986). Instead, Hammersley (1990) has argued for three criteria to be applied: plausibility, credibility and evidence to establish the validity or trustworthiness of qualitative research. Two strategies have been proposed to help establish validity in qualitative research, namely triangulation and respondent validation, although they have been criticised by Silverman (1993).

   Triangulation of data and methods implies that by using other techniques of data collection such as diaries, observations or questionnaires, in addition to the qualitative interview, evidence can be accumulated about phenomena of interest. However, this is often problematic because different methods of data collection may imply different epistemologies such as positivistic assumptions that underpin questionnaire construction. In addition, the researcher may be left with the difficult task of having to reconcile discrepancies and contradictions produced by the use of different methods. For example, a person asked to complete a standardised measure of anxiety may display behavioural signs of physical tension such as trembling hands and strained facial expression but in the self-report questionnaire all feelings of anxiety may be denied. The dilemma for the researcher is which method should be privileged?

Respondent validation is another strategy which draws on the expertise of the participants in validating the data by returning it to them as final arbiters of the "truthfulness" of the analysis. This has also been advocated as a means for involving participants to a greater extent in the research and therefore addresses power differentials to some extent. I have found it problematic both ethically and practically. For example, in the organ donor study (Sque & Payne, 1996), we were concerned about the ethical impact of returning full transcripts of distressing interviews to people in the post. Firstly, we had no control over when the transcript arrived or who was present (or absent) in the home to offer support. Secondly, we had grave concerns about requiring people to re-live painful experiences. At a practical level, full transcripts are bulky documents which, depending upon the transcription conventions used (O'Connell & Kowal, 1995), can be very difficult to read. We compromised by sending some respondents two page summaries of the interviews, to elicit their comments on the interpretations made, the accuracy of the summary and their perception of the experience of being interviewed. We regarded their responses as additional data.

SOURCES OF BIAS

As has been argued, the qualitative interview is a social situation in which interpersonal dynamics may influence the outcome. At a simple level, the participant may not like you, the way you dress, speak or behave. The conventions of politeness mean that they are very unlikely to tell you so explicitly. Participants may also be motivated to sabotage the research because they feel compelled to take part, for example by managers or employers. It may be helpful to reflect critically on respondents' reasons for participation which may include: seeking advice, to gain status, to elicit sympathy, to relieve boredom or to get back at superiors and managers. Simplistic notions that they are merely motivated by altruism or to support scientific endeavour are probably inappropriate. To determine, and if possible to address, their agenda may be an essential first step in obtaining good quality data. More obvious, but by no means less important, sources of bias result from poor quality questioning, such as using jargon, leading questions, not asking all the questions and making assumptions about answers. Finally, technical problems caused by poor quality recording equipment may waste everyone's time and effort.

SURVIVING AS AN INTERVIEWER

This section deals with the perspective of the interviewer. There are two major issues to be addressed, personal safety and emotional support. Personal safety when collecting data should be recognised as paramount. Undertaking interviews may involve going alone into people's homes, or visiting unfamiliar and potentially hazardous locations, perhaps during the evening or night. A few suggestions would be to leave contact names and addresses and an indication of the duration of the visit with another member of the research team or supervisor when visiting participants' homes, and to telephone in to the host department after each visit. The use of a mobile telephone may give researchers a sense of security. Careful route planning may minimise risks of getting lost and being vulnerable.

Within an interview, there are always some participants who describe experiences which are personally meaningful for the researcher. It is frequently difficult to know how to deal with personal feelings that are unleashed, often quite unexpectedly. Researchers may also experience feelings of powerlessness, especially those who have had professional roles such as in social work and are used to providing interventions to relieve distress. Despite all the best efforts the researcher may at times be unable to establish good rapport, obtain privacy and quiet, get good quality recordings or even like the respondent. It is helpful to off-load these negative experiences and feelings but there are dilemmas as to whom, because it is important to maintain the confidentiality of participants. Payne and Westwell (1994) have argued that researchers should have access to personal and emotional support from a suitably qualified professional who is not involved in the project. In the case of postgraduate students, academic supervisors are not always in the best position to provide this type of support because their primary role is in guiding the student to completion of a thesis within the deadlines of time and budget. It may be appropriate for interviewers to set up routine regular counselling support or seek stress management training prior to commencing a study.

Before undertaking research, individuals should become well informed about the topic. This means that they are knowledgeable about the issues and can recognise cues presented by participants. For example, in the organ donor study the interviewer, who was already a qualified and experienced nurse, undertook additional training in the use of counselling skills in bereavement and became familiar with specialist procedures related to organ donation such as brain stem death testing. She found this knowledge to be essential in establishing her credibility with participants and in aiding an understanding of their responses. Of course, there is a risk that formal training in whatever area will mean that researchers enter the interview with presuppositions which make it difficult to accept or really explore the interviewee's life-world. It is suggested that interviewers present themselves as interested but naive about the topic to justify asking probing questions.

CONTRASTING EPISTEMOLOGICAL PERSPECTIVES ON THE NATURE AND PURPOSE OF TALK

The final section concerns the status afforded to the responses of participants and the implications which are drawn from talk, and the purposes of the analysis of talk from differing perspectives. This section will contrast two perspectives, the ethnographic approach using methods such as grounded theory analysis (Strauss & Corbin, 1990) and the ethnomethodological approach using methods such as conversation analysis (Psathas, 1995). In the ethnographic perspective the purpose of talk is to identify what people *mean*. In comparison, the ethnomethodological perspective is concerned with identifying what people *do* with talk. Thus when undertaking a grounded theory analysis interview responses are construed as evidence of what people think and feel, how they interpret their world. These insights are assumed to have a stability over time and are inferred to be characteristic of that individual. In comparison, the ethnomethodological approach uses interview responses as evidence about how people use words to construct that particular situation at that particular time. This approach makes no assumptions about consistency of responses in other situations, no inferences about intra-psychic processes, and explains talk as representing a repertoire of ways that people have of dealing with questions, in an interview for example. In contrast, grounded theorists draw conclusions about the state of mind of individuals on the basis of their talk. They are interested in exploring the influence of previous experiences and personal understanding on the emotional and cognitive reactions displayed in talk. Thus from this perspective talk is seen as representing the contents of people's minds, whereas from an ethnomethodological stance, analysis of talk is concerned with individuals' attempts to deal with current situations (the interview).

To illustrate these differences, I will use an example taken from an interview with a woman with advanced ovarian cancer (Payne, 1989).

Interviewer: Can we start at the beginning of your treatment for cancer. How did you know that there was something wrong with you?

Interviewee: Well, last August, I went up North, went on holiday up to Yorkshire and that was the first time. I had a job to sit down with it. I was constipated and I thought it was that. And of course, naturally, I didn't go to the doctor because I thought it was because I was constipated that it was pressing on it. Anyway, this went on. And I haven't been able to sit down for quite a while, you know. If I have been sitting down in the evening, I have sat on the floor with my hands resting on the chair. Well, sitting on the side, you know, and if I have sat anywhere I have sat on my side and then, oh, when would it be about, well it was before Easter because I went to the doctor before Easter, didn't I?

Interviewer: um.

Interviewee: And I told him, you know, about this that I was constipated and that. He gave me some Isogel and he said try it for a month.

An ethnographic approach to this interview would seek to identify segments of text which could be labelled as categories. For example, it can be observed that the patient refers to a number of dates/times which locate her story in a temporal sequence, and this could generate a category called "Significance of timing" and further instances of this category could be searched for in subsequent interviews. The description of the symptoms of constipation are taken to represent a "real" account of her experiences and her feelings *at the time* before diagnosis of cancer.

An alternative ethnomethodological approach to this interview might be concerned with the interactional aspects of the situation. A caveat is that interviews are not often used in ethnomethodological research, and that the transcription style in this example is inappropriate, because a much more detailed transcription indicating overlapping speech and other performance details would be required. However, returning to this example, the researcher sets the context with the key words "beginning" "cancer" and "know". This interview draws on a taken-for-granted understanding about "medical" interviews such as the need to provide a history located in time and place, the description of (physical) symptoms and the justification of actions and non-actions. The analysis might identify how this is achieved in the interaction. For example, she justifies her actions by saying "naturally, I didn't go to the doctor because I thought it was because I was constipated". Thus the purpose of the analysis is to identify the way talk (*what* and *how*) is *used in the interview* situation to create an account; no inferences are made about underlying motives or feelings (*why*) experienced at the time.

CONCLUSIONS

The interview method is arguably the most common means of obtaining data in qualitative research. This chapter has concentrated on examining the rationale and procedures for dyadic, face-to-face interviews. It has highlighted the role of the interviewer, and emphasised the need for reflexivity, and ethical sensitivity. It has been argued that the concept of reliability as being strictly consistent may be inappropriate, as within a social constructionist framework, dyadic interactions are necessarily temporally and contextually dependent. However, interviewers should be concerned about validity, the "truthfulness" of their data, and need to be aware of strategies used to minimise bias.

This chapter has briefly reviewed the skills and attributes necessary to conduct interviews for qualitative research. These skills require preparation and practice. Since one of the strengths of qualitative analysis is the "rich data" and the opportunity to obtain respondent-centred accounts, it is important that the interviewer facilitates the generation of these insights. Therefore it is argued that investing in the development of interviewer skills is likely to be rewarded by high quality data.

REFERENCES

Agar, M. (1986). *Speaking of Ethnography*. London: Sage.

Beaver, K. & Luker, K. (1997). Readability of patient information booklets for women with breast cancer. *Patient Education and Counseling*, **31**, 95–102.

Bowling, A. (1997). *Research Methods in Health*. Buckingham: Open University Press.

Colye, A. & Wright, C. (1996). Using the counselling interview to collect research data on sensitive topics. *Journal of Health Psychology*, **1**, 431–440.

Devault, M.L. (1990). Talking and listening from women's standpoint: Feminist strategies for interviewing and analysis. *Social Problems*, **37**, 96–116.

Egan, G. (1994). *The Skilled Helper: A Problem-management Approach to Helping* (5th edn). Pacific Grove, CA: Brooks/Cole.

Fielding, N. (1993). Qualitative interviewing. In N. Gilbert (Ed.), *Researching Social Life* (pp. 135–153). London: Sage.

Gale, A. (1993). Ethical issues in psychological research. In A. Coleman (Ed.), *Companion Encyclopaedia of Psychology*. London: Routledge.

Hammersley, M. (1990). *Reading Ethnographic Research: A Critical Guide*. London: Longmans.

Hammersley, M. (1992). *What's Wrong with Ethnography: Methodological Explorations*. London: Routledge.

Krueger, R. (1988). *Focus Groups: A Practical Guide for Applied Research*. London: Sage.

Kvale, S. (1983). The qualitative research interview: A phenomenological and hermeneutical mode of understanding. *Journal of Phenomenological Research*, **14**, 171–196.

Lee, R.M. (1993). *Doing Research on Sensitive Topics*. London: Sage.

Marcus, A. & Crane, L. (1986). Telephone surveys in public health research. *Medical Care*, **24**, 97–112.

Meyer, J.E. (1993). New paradigm research in practice: The trials and tribulations of action research. *Journal of Advanced Nursing*, **18**, 1066–1072.

Morgan, D. (1988). *Focus Groups as Qualitative Research*. London: Sage.

Oakley, A. (1981). Interviewing women: A contradiction in terms. In H. Roberts (Ed.), *Doing Feminist Research* (pp. 30–61). London: Routledge and Kegan Paul.

O'Connell, D.C. & Kowal, S. (1995). Basic principles of transcription. In J.A. Smith, R. Harre & L. Van Langenhove (Eds.), *Rethinking Methods in Psychology* (pp. 9–26). London: Sage.

Parkes, C.M. (1995). Guidelines for conducting ethical bereavement research. *Death Studies*, **19**, 171–181.

Payne, S.A. (1989). *Quality of life in women with advanced cancer*. Unpublished PhD thesis, University of Exeter.

Payne, S. & Westwell, P. (1994). Issues for researchers using qualitative methods. *Health Psychology Update*, **16**, 7–9.

Psathas, G. (1995). *Conversation Analysis: the Study of Talk-in-interaction*. Thousand Oaks, CA: Sage.

Rogers, C.R. (1951). *Client-centered Therapy*. Boston, MA: Houghton Mifflin.

Siemiatycki, J. (1979). A comparison of mail, telephone and home interview strategies for household health surveys. *American Journal of Public Health*, **69**, 238–245.

Silverman, D. (1993). *Interpreting Qualitative Data*. London: Sage.

Smith, J.A. (1995). Semi-structured interviewing and qualitative analysis. In J.A. Smith, R. Harre & L. Van Langenhove (Eds.), *Rethinking Methods in Psychology*, (pp. 9–26). London: Sage.

Sque, M. (1997). *The personal impact of undertaking research involving bereaved people*. Paper presented at the Fifth Congress of the European Association of Palliative Care, 10–13 September, London.

Sque, M. & Payne, S.A. (1996). Dissonant loss: The experiences of donor relatives. *Social Science and Medicine*, **43**, 1359–1370.

Strauss, A.L. & Corbin, J.A. (1990). *Basics of Qualitative Research: Grounded Theory Procedures and Techniques*. Newbury Park, CA: Sage.

Tesch, R. (1990). *Qualitative Research: Analysis Types and Software Tools*. Basingstoke: Falmer.

Worth, A. and Tierney, A.J. (1993). Conducting research interviews with elderly people by telephone. *Journal of Advanced Nursing*, **18**, 1077–1084.

Wortman, C.B. & Silver, R.C. (1989). The myths of coping with loss. *Journal of Consulting and Clinical Psychology*, **57**, 349–357.

Wright, C. & Colye, A. (1996). Experiences of AIDS-related bereavement among gay men: implications for care. *Mortality*, **1**, 267–282.

2.4

The Survey Interview

Daniel B. Wright
University of Sussex, UK

Of all types of interviews, the most regimented is the survey interview as used in much political, market and social research. The results of these surveys inform political policies, guide marketing strategies and underlie much social and behavioural science. With its rigidity comes the myth that responses from the interviewee are basically correct and unaffected by subtle changes in question form. However, survey methodologists have identified numerous situations in which the reliability of the data is questionable. Slight alterations in question wording and question order can create substantial changes in the responses.

To understand how people answer questions, it is necessary to understand the composition of the survey interview. While many of the interviews described in this book allow the interviewee to dictate the flow and direction of the interview, with the survey interview these are dictated by the interview schedule and enforced by the interviewer. It is an artificial situation in which the interviewer asks all (or almost all) of the questions. The goal is to gain information from the person being interviewed. However, like all the interviews described in this book, the interviewees also pick up information from the situation, from the interviewer and from the actual questions. This information can affect their responses.

The aim of this chapter is to give a taster of survey methodology research which has used theories from cognitive and social psychology to help to model the survey interview in order to understand and ultimately to minimise response biases. This area is called CASM (short for *cognitive aspects of survey methodology*) and is described in more detail in several edited books (e.g., Jabine et al., 1984; Moss & Goldstein, 1979; Schwarz & Sudman, 1992, 1994; Wright & Gaskell, 1998; see also review papers by Jobe & Mingay, 1991, Jobe, Tourangeau & Smith, 1993; and the book by Sudman, Bradburn & Schwarz, 1996). I focus on research conducted with George Gaskell and Colm O'Muircheartaigh simply

Handbook of the Psychology of Interviewing. Edited by A. Memon and R. Bull.
© 1999 John Wiley & Sons Ltd.

because I know it better than other groups' research. We looked at several methodological biases that can occur in all types of interviews. Here I discuss three of these. The first concerns the choice of response alternatives for behavioural frequency questions. The second is the impact of intensifiers, words like "very" and "extremely", when used within survey questions. Finally, for several topics, there is interest in people's knowledge and how this relates to people's attitudes. We explored whether having to answer scientific knowledge questions creates a context that can alter people's expressed interest in science and what they think "science" is.

RESPONSE ALTERNATIVES

Almost every survey asks people about past behaviours and experiences. For common behaviours and experiences surveys attempt to elicit the frequency of these. Typical examples include how much television people watch, how often people have fried foods, and how many train journeys people make. There are several ways that these questions can be phrased. There are also several ways in which the response alternatives can be constructed. Answering questions presented with response alternatives is something that is usually done in surveys. Free recall is generally avoided because of coding costs and because trying to estimate an exact value can be cognitively taxing for the respondent, if done for many questions. Having response alternatives informs the interviewee which answers are appropriate (Schuman & Scott, 1987). Depending on the survey's purpose this can be an advantage.

Consider the question: "How much television do you watch on a typical weekday?" This question is of particular importance to people involved with media surveys. One common approach with behavioural frequency questions like this is to present people with a scale composed of *vague quantifiers*, phrases like "hardly any" and "quite a bit". One worry is whether these phrases have the same meaning to different people. Of particular concern is whether groups of people systematically differ from each other because this could confound substantive group comparisons. Wright, Gaskell and O'Muircheartaigh (1994) asked this question to a UK national sample ($n = 1106$) with the following response alternatives: "none at all", "hardly any", "a little", "quite a bit" and "a lot". Respondents then said how many hours this was. This allowed the numerical interpretations to be compared for people who gave the same vague quantifier response.

We were most interested in differences by social class. Much research exists showing that people from the working classes watch more television than people from the middle classes. The classification used in this survey has "AB" as the highest social class, followed by "C1", "C2" and "DE". The results are shown in Figure 1. Each line represents the mapping between the vague quantifiers and the numerical responses for one social class. These lines are (statistically) significantly different, and the differences are large in substantive terms. For example, "quite

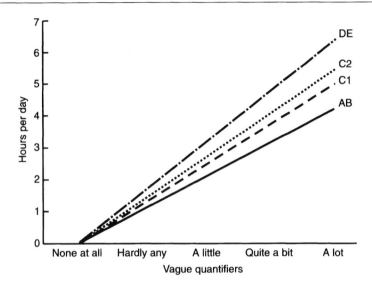

Figure 1   Different interpretations of vague quantifiers when asking about television viewing. Each line represents a social class. From Wright et al., 1994, figure 3; reproduced with permission of John Wiley & Sons Ltd

a bit" for AB respondents is about three hours a day, but it is almost five hours for the DE respondents. The groups that watch more television gave higher estimates for each vague quantifier. It is clear that researchers should be cautious when comparing responses to questions with vague quantifiers.

Given the problem with vague quantifiers, an obvious question is "Why not ask for numerical amounts?" As I said above, open-ended questions are usually avoided because of coding problems and the difficulty respondents have with them. Because of this, the respondents are often presented with a list of alternatives for different bands of amounts on what is called a "showcard".

However, Schwarz (1995) has shown that the choice of alternatives can affect responses. For this particular question, Wright et al. (1994; see also Schwarz et al., 1985) asked 1028 respondents "How many hours do you spend watching television on a typical weekday?" For one version, the time bands concentrated on *low* frequencies: less than ½ an hour, ½ an hour but less than 1 hour, 1 hour but less than 1½ hours, 1½ hours but less than 2 hours, 2 hours but less than 2½ hours, 2½ hours or more. The second version was concentrated at *high* frequencies: less than 2½ hours, 2½ hours but less than 3 hours, 3 hours but less than 3½ hours, 3½ hours but less than 4 hours, 4 hours but less than 4½ hours, 4½ hours or more. If the version does not affect the number of hours that people say they watch, then approximately the same percentage of people in the *low* condition should give one of the first five categories as people in the *high* condition giving the first category. The two are logically equivalent: less than 2½ hours. However, about 45% of the people in the *low* condition said that they watched this amount, while only 25% of the people in the *high* condition reported this. This difference is both statistically significant and large enough to be of substantial concern to survey researchers.

By understanding the processes it is possible to identify when biases are likely to occur and what effect they may have. The argument goes that the response alternatives convey information that can alter the meaning of the target behaviour. If the target behaviour is well defined, then it would be difficult to alter its meaning and therefore a response shift would not be predicted. Wright, Gaskell and O'Muircheartaigh (1997) tested this by asking a large sample (*n* = 3828) "How many cups or mugs of coffee or tea do you *usually* drink in a day" with either a response alternative set concentrating on high amounts or one concentrating on low amounts. While there are some disagreements about what is a "cup" and even what is "coffee", most people know what is being described. When collapsed into logically comparable categories, there were no significant differences on amount consumed between the conditions. However, the response alternatives did have an effect. People were also asked if they thought they drank more coffee than most, about the same as most, or less coffee than most. Those given the *high* set felt they drank less coffee than most compared with people given the *low* set of alternatives. The scale imparted information about behavioural norms.

Finally, it is worth mentioning that there are numerous other considerations for behavioural frequency questions. As these rely in some way on memory, all the problems and biases of memory can influence responses. The strategies that people use can have a profound effect on the detail and accuracy of recall. For a thorough review see Jobe, Tourangeau and Smith (1993; see also Loftus, Feinberg & Tanur, 1985; Wright & Loftus, 1998).

INTENSIFIERS IN SURVEYS

Many survey methodology papers begin by describing an area, discussing theoretical reasons for why there might be a bias, and then demonstrating the bias. O'Muircheartaigh, Gaskell and Wright (1993) thought to take this approach. Intensifiers, words like "very", are often used in surveys. There are good reasons to suppose that including these phrases alters the meanings of the phrases to which they are applied. This seems like common sense, and there is academic research supporting this (Cliff, 1959; Smith et al., 1988). The plan was simply to demonstrate that adding intensifiers altered responses in survey interviews.

Consider the following questions:

How often do you feel unsafe in the area where you live?
How often do you feel very unsafe in the area where you live?

Because anybody who feels very unsafe should also feel unsafe, and, with a few assumptions, there should be some incidents where people feel unsafe, but not very unsafe, we predicted that more people should feel unsafe than very unsafe. Another large national sample (*n* = 4404) was used so that the effect size could be accurately measured. Half of the people were asked the first question and half the second. Even with this large sample the difference was not significant.

What was the explanation for this surprising result? O'Muircheartaigh et al. (1993) ran a memory recognition study. Respondents were asked several questions, some with and some without intensifiers, and then had to decide which they had seen. Respondents had difficulty deciding between the question with and without the intensifier for the items that showed no response effect in our surveys. If respondents in our surveys were not adequately encoding the intensifiers then it is not surprising that no effects were detected for many items (several other items were also used, a couple did produce differences).

This left another problem: why were our results different from the research in cognitive psychology? There are clearly differences between survey interviews and laboratory experiments (and less regimented forms of interview). In our survey experiments, we usually use between-subjects designs. This is for reasons of *ecological validity*. The survey designer would be deciding between asking about "feeling unsafe" *or* "feeling very unsafe". In most laboratory experiments on word meaning, respondents are given several phrases to interpret. This is done to increase the power so that hundreds of respondents are not needed for every study. So, while the survey interviewee has to interpret the phrase in isolation, the laboratory participant has several, often similar, phrases to try to interpret. This means that the participants are attuned to notice differences and that they may frame their response in relation to their previous responses. When O'Muircheartaigh et al. (1993) asked people a question without an intensifier and then with one – a within-subject design – large response shifts did occur.

There are two theories for how these within-subject effects might occur. Both require that the person notices and at some adequate level processes the intensifier. The first, the "scalar theory" of intensifiers (Cliff, 1959), argues that once noticed, the intensifier effectively multiplies the value of the phrase to which it has been applied. Accordingly, "very" might have a value of 1.25 and "extremely" a value of 1.45. Suppose the word "good" has a pleasantness value of 1.16. "Very good" would be 1.45 and "extremely good" 1.68. The second theory is that people know "very good" is more good than just "good", and "extremely good" is even higher, but they do not know how much higher each one is. They understand only the ordering of the intensifiers. When responding, they simply add on an increment.

To evaluate these theories, a national UK sample were asked on how many days in the previous week they were satisfied with their life, in several different conditions (see Wright, Gaskell & O'Muircheartaigh, 1995, for details). I will consider just two conditions here. Respondents in both of these conditions were initially asked the question without an intensifier. Scores were nearly identical. Next, one group was asked how many days they were "very satisfied", and the other was asked with "extremely satisfied". The first theory predicts that responses should differ; the second does not. We found the responses were not significantly different. It could be argued that the difference between the multipliers for "very" and "extremely" may be too small to pick up the effect. If this were true, we would expect that if people in the first group were asked, after the "very" question, the "extremely" question, that their responses would not differ.

We did this and found the scores were much lower. Thus, it appears from our studies that people only understand the ordering of intensifiers.

With regard to surveys, these studies demonstrate that intensifiers often produce no effects in surveys. It is recommended that they are avoided, simply because people assume that they do have an effect and therefore results can be misleading. If several questions are used, some with and some without intensifiers, care is necessary because it appears that the way people interpret intensifiers is more impoverished than first thought.

With respect to everyday communication and possibly other forms of interview, it still seems that intensifiers *must* make a difference, sometimes. Wright, Gaskell and O'Muirheartaigh (1995) argue this occurs principally in two circumstances. The first is when the people in the dialogue have spoken enough, with and without intensifiers, across several topics, so that a within-subject situation is essentially being mimicked. The second situation is when an intensifier is grammatically inappropriate for the main meaning of the word to which it is applied. For example, in its normal usage, a person is "pregnant" or "not pregnant", is either "dead or "not dead". If you describe someone as "very pregnant", the word "pregnant" refers more to how far into the pregnancy a person is than to whether the person is pregnant or not.*

CONTEXT EFFECTS

Many researchers are interested in how knowledge about a subject is associated with interest and beliefs about that subject. Much social psychology and sociology has shown that as people increase in knowledge about a topic, they tend also to be more interested in the topic. One assumption in science education is that by teaching people more about science, they will become more interested in it. Therefore, knowledge and interest are often assessed in the same survey interview. We were concerned whether actually having to answer scientific knowledge questions could alter people's expressed interest.

Gaskell, Wright and O'Muircheartaigh (1995) examined this question by giving respondents in a national survey ($n = 2099$) one of four brief science quizzes as well as asking them about their interest in science and what "came to mind" when science was mentioned. The quizzes were either about life sciences or physical sciences, and were either relatively easy or difficult. The sample was further subdivided by whether respondents were given the quiz before or after the other questions.

There are three hypotheses for how taking the science quizzes could affect interest scores. The first is that the interest ratings may be reliable across conditions.

---

* The intensifier "very" is unique in that its sole purpose is to intensify. Others, like "really", have additional aspects that they can convey and in some cases can be used without changing or altering the definition of the word. "Really pregnant", for example, may mean that the person is not faking being pregnant, or convey that the speaker is very confident.

This would be good news for survey researchers in this field. The second is that there could be a main effect shift. When people take the quiz, they may feel that knowing minute pieces of information is not interesting. The respondents would adjust their meaning of science. We call this the *framing* hypothesis and predict, if it occurs, it will be stronger for the difficult quizzes because the interviewees are likely to dislike these the most. If true, answering the difficult quiz questions should lower reported interest. The final hypothesis predicts that respondents who get a lot of the questions right will raise their scores, but those who miss lots will lower their scores. This *consistency* explanation can be based on either Bem's (1972) self-perception theory or Festinger's (1957) cognitive dissonance theory.

For each quiz we ran a series of regressions to predict interest. First we included the number of questions the person correctly answered. As expected, this was highly significant for all quizzes; the more correct answers the higher the interest.* Whether the quiz was before the interest question was then entered as a dummy variable. This was significant for the two difficult quizzes, but not for the easy quizzes. This supports the framing hypothesis. Finally, we entered an interaction term to assess the consistency hypothesis. None of these effects were significant. Thus, we only found a main effect for order. At each level of correctness, people given the difficult quiz first report lower interest than those given the quiz after the interest question. This supports the framing hypothesis, but not the consistency hypothesis.

The framing hypothesis assumes that respondents' notion of science is altered by the quizzes. To examine this, we asked people what comes to mind when science is mentioned (Gaskell, Wright & O'Muircheartaigh, 1993). We compared people's responses depending on whether they were given the "comes to mind" question first (effectively a control group) or given one of the four quizzes first. Responses were collapsed into "physical", "life sciences", "technology", "environmental", "social sciences" and "other". The $\chi^2(20) = 55.38$ is significant, demonstrating an association. A correspondence analysis was conducted to examine this association and is shown in Figure 2. Each of the "comes to mind" responses has been shortened (phy, life, tech, envir, social, other) and is in lower case. the experimental conditions are NQ (No Quiz before answering), EP (Easy Physical sciences), EL (Easy Life sciences), HP (Hard Physical sciences) and HL (Hard Life sciences). This figure shows that the people given the physical science quizzes were more likely to think of science as physical sciences, while the control group, and the people given life science quizzes were more likely to say life sciences. There is a suggestion that the easy quizzes produce more environmental responses and the hard quizzes more technology responses. However, some caution is urged as the first dimension is accounting for a much larger proportion of variance (see Wright, 1997).

---

* It is important to note that the number of correct responses did not vary by the order of the quiz. If it had, additional statistical considerations would be necessary.

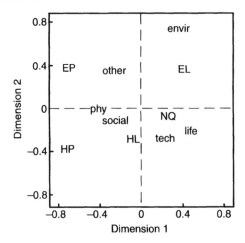

Figure 2   Correspondence analysis of experimental condition and "what comes to mind" when science is mentioned. See text for abbreviations. The data were originally described in Gaskell et al. (1993). This figure is from Wright (1997, figure 7.3); reproduced with permission of Sage Publications, Ltd

CONCLUSION

When survey interviewers knock on your door, ring you on the phone, or question you in the street, they are taught to follow the interview schedule precisely. This is necessary for reliability across interviews, but it also gives the impression that each question is without bias. The survey interview is designed to be as context free as possible. While this puts it near the opposite end to therapeutic interviews, information presented can still impact on responses. Three areas were chosen for this chapter: response alternatives, intensifiers and context effects. Here I describe why I chose these and relate the findings more broadly to other types of interview.

Survey researchers have long realised that the actual question asked can make a difference. It is less obvious that the response alternatives can affect responses, but as described here, they can. Other interviews, for example investigative interviews, have also explored the importance of response format. A child being interviewed about suspected abuse will be told to say "don't know" when he or she is unsure. Similarly, witnesses are told first to report in free recall everything they remember of an incident, rather than to answer the more restrictive yes/no questions.

The second topic was the lack of an effect of intensifiers in between-subjects survey experiments. I chose this because it stands out from the norm in survey methodology. A change was made which many people predicted would alter the response pattern but it did not. The norm in the field is the opposite. Our findings also highlight the care needed when translating from laboratory studies to other areas. It was not that the laboratory per se produced a different result.

What produced the difference was the within-subject design. This is used in many laboratory studies because of the small number of participants usually used. A between-subjects design is more ecologically valid for the survey interview. The lesson for the other types of interview is that interviewees will not use every word in every question as was intended.

The final area explored how asking questions in different orders can produce a context which affects subsequent responses. These question order effects have been well documented by survey researchers and are of most concern for survey designers. Clearly, context effects can occur in all types of surveys. Previous questions can depress clients, set up unfair expectations and suggest memories.

In summary, the survey interview is designed to be rigid and "scientific". However, research has accumulated showing where response biases exist. This "measurement error" can have profound consequences on both reliability and validity. As is true with all types of interviews, the more that is understood about the interview process, the better the quality of the resulting data.

ACKNOWLEDGEMENTS

The research described was conducted with George Gaskell and Colm O'Muircheartaigh, as part of the London School of Economics' "Cognitive Survey Laboratory", an ESRC funded project. The surveys that I describe were all conducted by British Market Research Bureau International (BMRBI) to whom I am grateful. An earlier version of this paper was delivered to the UK Department of Transport's Transport Research Laboratory at Esher Place, 15 April 1997.

REFERENCES

Bem, D.J. (1972). Self perception theory. In L. Berkowitz (Ed.), *Advances in Experimental Social Psychology* (Vol. 6, pp. 2–62). New York: Academic Press.

Cliff, N. (1959). Adverbs as multipliers. *Psychological Review*, **66**, 27–44.

Festinger, L. (1957). *A Theory of Cognitive Dissonance*. Evanston, IL: Row, Peterson.

Gaskell, G.D., Wright, D.B. & O'Muircheartaigh, C.A. (1993). Measuring scientific interest: The effect of knowledge questions on interest ratings. *Journal for the Public Understanding of Science*, **2**, 39–57.

Gaskell, G.D., Wright, D.B. & O'Muircheartaigh, C.A. (1995). Context effects in the measurement of attitudes: A comparison of the consistency and framing explanations. *British Journal of Social Psychology*, **34**, 383–393.

Jabine, T.B., Straf, M.L., Tanur, J.M. & Tourangeau, R. (Eds.) (1984). *Cognitive Aspects of Survey Methodology: Building a Bridge Between Disciplines*. Washington, DC: National Academic Press.

Jobe, J.B. & Mingay, D.J. (1991). Cognition and survey measurement: History and overview. *Applied Cognitive Psychology*, **5**, 175–192.

Jobe, J.B., Tourangeau, R. & Smith, A.F. (1993). Contributions of survey research to the understanding of memory. *Applied Cognitive Psychology*, **7**, 567–584.

Loftus, E.F., Feinberg, S. & Tanur, J. (1985). Cognitive psychology meets the national survey. *American Psychologist*, **40**, 175–180.

Moss, L. & Goldstein, H. (Eds.) (1979). *The Recall Method in Social Surveys*. London: University of London Institute of Education.

O'Muircheartaigh, C.A., Gaskell, G.D. & Wright, D.B. (1993). Intensifiers in behavioral frequency questions. *Public Opinion Quarterly*, **57**, 552–565.

Schuman, H. & Scott, J. (1987). Problems in the use of survey questions to measure public opinion. *Science*, **236**, 957–959.

Schwarz, N. (1995). What respondents learn from questionnaires: The survey interview and the logic of conversation. *International Statistical Review*, **63**, 153–177.

Schwarz, N. & Sudman, S. (Eds.) (1992). *Context Effects in Social and Psychological Research*. New York: Springer.

Schwarz, N. & Sudman, S. (Eds.) (1994). *Autobiographical Memory and Validity of Retrospective Reports*. New York: Springer.

Schwarz, N., Hippler, H.-J., Deutsch, B. & Strack, F. (1985). Response scales: Effects of category range on reported behavior and comparative judgments. *Public Opinion Quarterly*, **49**, 388–395.

Smith, E.E., Osherson, D.N., Rips, L.J. & Keane, M. (1988). Combining prototypes: A selective modification model. *Cognitive Science*, **28**, 485–527.

Sudman, S., Bradburn, N.M. & Schwarz, N. (1996). *Thinking about Answers: The Application of Cognitive Processes to Survey Methodology*. San Francisco: Jossey-Bass.

Tanur, J.M. (Ed.) (1992). *Questions about Questions: Inquiries into the Cognitive Bases of Surveys*. New York: Russell Sage Foundation.

Wright, D.B. (1997). *Understanding Statistics: An Introduction for the Social Sciences*. London: Sage Publications.

Wright, D.B. & Gaskell, G.D. (Eds.) (1998). *Surveying Memory Processes*. East Sussex: Psychology Press.

Wright, D.B. & Loftus, E.F. (1998). How memory research can benefit from CASM. *Memory*, **6**, 467–475.

Wright, D.B., Gaskell, G.D. & O'Muircheartaigh, C.A. (1994). How much is "Quite a bit"? Mapping absolute values onto vague quantifiers. *Applied Cognitive Psychology*, **8**, 479–496.

Wright, D.B., Gaskell, G.D. & O'Muircheartaigh, C.A. (1995). Testing the multiplicative hypothesis of intensifiers. *Applied Cognitive Psychology*, **9**, 167–177.

Wright, D.B., Gaskell, G.D. & O'Muircheartaigh, C.A. (1997). How response alternatives affect different kinds of behavioural frequency questions. *British Journal of Social Psychology*, **36**, 443–456.

Using Focus Groups in Social Research

Monique Hennink *and* **Ian Diamond**
University of Southampton, UK

WHAT IS A FOCUS GROUP?

A focus group is a unique method of qualitative research which involves a group of people discussing a specific set of issues, problems or research questions. Focus groups are different from other methods of qualitative research in their purpose, composition and procedure. The purpose of a focus group is to explore the range of perspectives around a particular issue and to obtain detailed qualitative data from a predetermined group of people. This is achieved through a process described in detail in this chapter.

Although focus groups have been used by social scientists since the 1930s, they were primarily developed within market research in the 1950s (Greenbaum, 1988; Krueger, 1988; Morgan, 1997). Focus group research emerged in response to the limitations of other methods of interviewing, such as the influence of an interviewer on a respondent's comments and the limitations of predetermined closed questions on enabling spontaneous responses or identifying new issues. The development of non-directive interviewing techniques, whereby the interviewer plays a minimal role in the process of information gathering, overcame these difficulties (Krueger, 1988). The emphasis in focus groups on non-directive interviewing shifted the attention from the interviewer's agenda to the interaction between group participants, which enabled issues of importance to be identified by group members rather than imposed by the researcher. Non-directive interviewing had particular appeal to social scientists and psychologists in the 1930s and 1940s. During the past four decades most applications of focus group

Handbook of the Psychology of Interviewing. Edited by A. Memon and R. Bull.
© 1999 John Wiley & Sons Ltd.

research have continued to be in market research to determine the views, preferences and behaviour of consumers (Krueger, 1988). More recently, however,
focus groups have become an increasingly popular method of qualitative data
collection and have been used to investigate a wide range of research issues in
the social sciences. Focus groups are able to provide valuable data for public
policy, health and behavioural research, evaluating social programmes, strategic
planning, needs assessments, health education and public opinion research.

A focus group may be defined as:

> a carefully planned discussion designed to obtain perceptions on a defined area of
> interest in a permissive, non-threatening environment. It is conducted with approx-
> imately seven to ten people by a skilled interviewer . . . Group members influence
> each other by responding to ideas and comments in the discussion (Krueger, 1988,
> p. 18).

Focus groups are composed of a group of individuals with similar characteristics
or experiences related to the topic of discussion. The discussion is focused on a
particular area of interest and is usually confined to a limited number of issues to
enable participants to explore each issue in detail. The group is guided by a
moderator who introduces the topics for discussion and facilitates the group
discussion. One of the key characteristics of a focus group is that it creates a
"permissive environment" which enables participants to feel comfortable to
share their views, even if they oppose those of other group members, without
fear of censure or judgement. The aim of the focus group discussion is not to
reach consensus or to find solutions to issues discussed, but rather to encourage a
range of responses which provide insights into the attitudes, perceptions, behaviour or opinions of participants about a particular area of psychological
research. A desired outcome of a focus group is to identify a range of different
perceptions about the same issue.

A focus group is *not* a group interview, whereby a moderator asks the group
questions and participants individually provide answers; it is a non-directive
interview technique which encourages discussion between participants. Interaction between participants is a key feature of a focus group, whereby the moderator plays an important but limited role in the discussion. Group discussions allow
participants to agree or disagree with each other and can provide valuable insights into how the group considers an issue, the range of issues discussed and
the decision-making process. Focus groups also allow participants to identify the
issues which they feel are relevant and important to the discussion topic rather
than the researcher imposing issues, as in other methods of interviewing such as
a survey. Focus group discussions are held with a range of groups to identify
trends and patterns in perceptions around the research issue. Careful and systematic analysis of the information provides valuable insights into participants'
views about the area of research.

The benefits and drawbacks of using focus group discussions are summarised
in Table 1. There are many advantages in using focus group research. Firstly, as
Krueger (1988) points out succinctly, focus groups are a socially oriented

Table 1   Benefits and drawbacks of using focus group discussions

Benefits	Drawbacks
Well accepted and enjoyable	Requires skilled moderator
Reflects human behaviour	Participant selection
Detailed information	Less controlled
Large volume of information	
	Participants may agree
Considered responses	Influence of social pressure
Interactive process	Requires permissive environment
Issues identified by group	Variation between groups
Used to understand decision-making	
Provides context to issues	Poor generalisability
	Not suitable for individual data
Exploratory, explanatory, evaluative research	Data analysis difficult
Generates hypotheses/new ideas	Time-consuming
Flexible	Costly
Utilises "props"	
Identifies feelings/behaviour	
Complementary to quantitative research	

research procedure in which people are placed in a setting which reflects social interaction in daily life, rather than in an experimental environment which is often created in quantitative research. They are therefore generally well accepted by participants.

Secondly, the group environment of focus groups offers several advantages. On a practical level it enables a large volume of detailed information to be captured at once and is suitable for participants who have literacy difficulties. The group environment also provides a dynamic and interactive environment, which enables the expression of a range of views and leads to participants providing considered responses after discussion within the group. This type of social moderation of views is not present in individual interviews. As groups are composed of a number of individuals, the discussion will often identify a wide range of varying responses to a single issue, which is not possible in other research methods. The group dynamics and progress of discussion enable the process of decision-making to be identified and uncovers factors which influence the views and attitudes of participants, providing detailed contextual information around the views expressed about each issue.

Thirdly, the flexible nature of focus group discussions enables the researcher to explore a research topic about which little is known. It is therefore suitable for exploratory research about a new field, explanatory research which identifies motivations behind behaviour and evaluative research which assesses a service, product or idea. This flexibility also allows issues which were not anticipated by the researcher to be identified by the participants. It also enables participants to identify issues which are important to them rather than the researcher assuming the importance of certain issues. This enables the generation of hypotheses and new ideas. The flexible format of focus group discussions also enables the use of "props" such as products, posters or video material to gauge participants' reactions or opinions. This has been particularly valuable when working in the promotion of sexual health (Cooper et al., 1992; Pearson et al., 1996). See also Chapter 3.1 by Ingham, Vanwesenbeeck and Kirkland.

As with all research methods there are also drawbacks in using focus group discussions which need to be considered in deciding whether to use this method. Firstly, the technique requires an experienced moderator who can facilitate the group discussion. The flexibility of focus group discussions, which enable participants to contribute openly to the discussion, requires skill and experience on the part of the moderator to facilitate effective discussion and gain useful responses. The less controlled environment of a focus group discussion can easily lead to a large amount of redundant data if the moderator allows the discussion to diverge too far from the issues of interest. Moderators need to be trained to facilitate group discussions using techniques to encourage contributions by participants; they also need to create an atmosphere that is conducive to open participation. Researchers conducting focus group research need experience in constructing a question route which is free from bias and in selecting participants to create an atmosphere which is conducive to discussion.

Secondly, difficulties may arise due to group dynamics. Participants may simply agree with one another (for different reasons), they may be influenced by social pressure within the group to express socially acceptable responses, or a hierarchy may be evident within the group due to poor selection of participants which will inhibit open responses. Each group varies; therefore enough groups need to be conducted to capture the full extent of this variation. This can become costly and time-consuming.

Thirdly, focus group data have their drawbacks. Focus groups are designed to identify a range of responses from participants. They are not designed to be representative; therefore the results are not generalisable across a population. Data analysis is also difficult and time-consuming. Comments from participants need to be analysed within the context of the group discussion as participants may change their views during the course of discussion. The group nature of a focus group means that it is not suitable for data on individuals, as their responses may be influenced by the group discussion.

When to Use Focus Groups

Focus groups are a very effective method for exploring many aspects of people's beliefs, attitudes, opinions or behaviour. However, they give little indication of how general these issues are in the community. Therefore, focus groups are not suitable for research which requires identifying the prevalence of an issue in the community. Focus group research allows participants to identify issues of importance to group members. Therefore, they are most suitable for exploratory, evaluative and explanatory research.

Firstly, focus groups may be used for exploratory research which involves investigating an area about which the issues are unknown or unclear. For example, focus groups may provide baseline information before developing a specific social programme (e.g. health, education, recreation). Focus groups can be used to generate information prior to the development of a questionnaire to enable questions to become more focused, to identify categories to design closed questions, to investigate appropriate language or terminology or to identify sensitive or political issues to avoid. Focus groups may be used to conduct needs assessments for community programmes. They are useful for testing new ideas about a service, product or proposal and how acceptable these may be. They may also provide information to decision-makers about new opportunities. Focus groups may be used to provide valuable insights into the factors or considerations that influence decision-making, which can be useful for the launching of a new service.

Secondly, focus groups are useful in evaluative research which involves investigating the effectiveness of a service or product in the community. Focus groups can investigate the positive and negative aspects, the characteristics which are valued or the image portrayed to the community. Focus groups can also identify the characteristics of non-users and how best to recruit them.

Thirdly, focus groups can contribute to explanatory research which seeks to understand particular behaviour or specific problems and provide explanations. For example, focus groups may be used to explain the success or failure of a particular programme, to investigate the influence of a company's image on consumers or to examine specific problems within an existing programme. Focus groups can also be used to elaborate on the findings of a questionnaire and explain, clarify or validate the outcomes of quantitative research.

PLANNING FOCUS GROUP RESEARCH

Planning focus group research involves defining the research objectives and the study population, identifying who can best provide the information required and considering the desired outcome of the research and the resources available.

Defining the Research Problem

The first task in focus group research involves carefully defining the objectives of the research, identifying the areas to be investigated and constructing detailed research questions. This forms the basis for the *focus* of the group discussion and allows respondents to identify issues within these areas. It is important to have clear objectives even if the research is exploratory. It is worthwhile considering the following questions to bring clarity and precision to the research objectives. Why is the study being conducted? What types of information will be required? Who is the study being conducted for? Who will use the results?

It is also necessary to identify the study population clearly. This will generally be guided by the research objectives. It is worthwhile identifying previous research or secondary sources of information which will provide some information about the nature of the study population, identify key issues which may influence the research issue or identify terms and vocabulary used by the study population which will assist in the development of research and discussion questions.

Considering Research Outcomes

Consideration needs to be given to how the information from focus groups will be used. For example, is the intention to feed the information into the development of a questionnaire, or to use the information in its own right? Is the research intended to solve a problem within an existing programme or to carry out a needs assessment for a new programme? Answering these types of questions will help to develop the discussion questions and guide the data analysis. Finally, consideration must be given to the resources (time, skills and money) and the time-frame available for the research process.

PARTICIPANTS IN A FOCUS GROUP

Participants are the central component of focus groups. Careful consideration needs to be given to the selection of participants and the composition of focus groups to enable the focus group discussion to be conducted effectively and to produce valid results. It is important to identify the target group of the research as precisely as possible to assist in participant selection and group composition. To a large extent the purpose of the study and the issues to be discussed will dictate the degree of specification of the participants; for example, whether a study of young people needs to focus on teenagers or a study of the community needs to be defined as the working population. It is possible, in defining the target population, that more than one target group becomes apparent. In this case it is advisable to conduct different focus groups with each target group.

Group Composition

It is vital that the environment created within a focus group is "open" and non-judgemental. This will enable participants to feel comfortable in revealing their true feelings, attitudes or behaviour without fear of judgement or reprimand by the moderator or other participants. The importance of this environment needs to be stressed, as without it participants may not be willing to disclose their true feelings about the issues discussed. This will reduce the quality and validity of the information provided. The permissive environment of a focus group is created through the composition of the group members and the role of the moderator. The role of the moderator will be discussed in detail later.

To create a permissive environment researchers need to consider two aspects of group composition: (a) that groups are generally composed of people who are strangers to one another, and (b) that the characteristics of group members are largely homogeneous. Wherever possible focus group participants should not have met before the focus group. Familiarity with other participants tends to inhibit disclosure due to fears that comments will be judged by those familiar individuals, particularly if there is likely to be contact between participants in another context after the group discussion (Krueger, 1988). Similarly, familiarity between the moderator and participants should be avoided as the interviewer may be identified with a particular point of view which may influence participants' comments. Care also needs to be taken in conducting focus groups within organisations where participants work together or have regular contact. If participants are reluctant to reveal their true feelings this will jeopardise the quality of results in the analysis stage as the researcher will be unable to distinguish whether participants' comments were influenced by the composition of the group and fears of disclosure or by their actual views in the issue discussed. In reality, however, it may be difficult to compose a group of total strangers who meet the target criteria (Morgan, 1997). In these circumstances the researchers must decide whether acquaintance between group members is likely to affect their ability to discuss the topic. Many successful focus groups have, in fact, been conducted with individuals who are acquaintances (Jarrett, 1993; Morgan & Krueger, 1993; Kitzinger, 1994).

The characteristics of focus group participants should be homogeneous in such areas as age, sex, education or level of experience with the topic under discussion, yet there should be sufficient variation between participants to allow for contrasting opinions (Krueger, 1988). Jourard (1964, p. 15) states that "subjects tended to disclose more about themselves to people who resembled them in various ways than to people who differ from them". People will be reluctant to reveal information about themselves or their feelings and beliefs if they perceive others to be more knowledgeable, influential or to have a higher status than themselves. It is unwise, for example, to compose a group of employees and managers or people from different socio-economic groups, where this is likely to influence their views on the topic of discussion (e.g. property ownership). Care needs to be taken when mixing people from different life stages (i.e. professionals and home-makers), as they are likely to have less common ground for discussion. Mixing the sexes in a focus group may also not be advisable, particularly if the topic of discussion may be viewed differently between the sexes. Krueger (1988) states that males may dominate the discussion or behave differently in front of women than if they were in a single sex group. In these situations it is best to have separate groups for men and women, professionals and non-professionals. Wherever possible groups should comprise individuals who are alike in characteristics. Group homogeneity can be reinforced by the moderator telling participants that they were selected because they have *similar* characteristics. The nature of group homogeneity will be determined by the nature of the study and by the information which is available about participants prior to the group discussion. The moderator must also ensure that they are themselves not considered as experts on the topic under discussion, which may equally inhibit discussion. It is good practice to match the characteristics of the group with that of the moderator (e.g. female group, female moderator), so as not to create barriers which may inhibit discussion.

Participant Selection

Quantitative research aims at randomisation in selecting participants so that the results can be used to describe characteristics across an entire population. Focus group results cannot be used to describe an entire population; therefore the types of sampling techniques which require random selection of respondents are not necessary or appropriate. The intent of a focus group is "not to infer but to understand, not to generalize but to determine the range and not to make statements about the population but to provide insights about how people perceive a situation" (Krueger, 1988, p. 96). Therefore, randomisation is not the primary factor in participant selection although it may be implicitly achieved. The researcher must, however, be aware of the possible bias in how participants are recruited. Participant selection will be largely determined by the purpose of the research and the types of participants required.

There are a number of methods to recruit focus group participants. Firstly, purposive or convenience sampling, which ensures that only participants with the required characteristics or experience are selected for the focus group discussion. One method to achieve purposive selection of participants is to develop a sift questionnaire, which is a series of brief questions to determine an individual's suitability for inclusion in the group discussion and filters out those who are not suitable. For example, to identify the target population for a study on reproductive health a sift questionnaire was used to select respondents who were 15–24-year-old females and 15–30-year-old males. The brief filter questions (shown in Figure 1) discarded people who were not in the age categories required. Those who did meet the required criteria were invited to an interview and given additional information about the research. In inviting participants it should be stressed that the individual has special experience or knowledge which is of value to the study. Sift questionnaires are a very useful tool to identify focus group participants.

A second method of participant selection is to identify a list of individuals or service users who meet the characteristics of the target population (e.g. GP registers, antenatal care users, domiciliary care recipients) and then take a systematic or random sample of the names. A systematic sample involves dividing the number of people required by the number of people on the list and then selecting every *nth* name on the list. For example, if 10 participants are required from a list of 250 (250/10 = 25), every 25th person on the list will be selected. Alternatively, names can be chosen randomly using random number tables.

Area (Cluster) _____

Hello, I am conducting some interviews as part of a research project on reproductive health and behaviour of young people. This survey is being carried out by researchers at the University of Malawi. Would you spare me a few minutes to answer a few questions?

1. Sex (fill in) . . . .

2. Would you tell me how old you are?
   (a) Under 15   → *Thank you very much (terminate interview)*
   (b) 15–19
   (c) 20–24
   (d) Female over 25/Male over 30   → *Thank you very much (terminate interview)*

3. How best would you describe your current marital status?
   (a) Married and Living with Partner
   (b) Living with a Partner
   (c) In a Steady Relationship but not Living with Partner
   (d) Not in a Steady Relationship
   (e) Divorced/Separated

4. Do you have any children?
   (a) Yes   How Many? . . . .
   (b) No

5. What is your usual occupation?
   (a) In School (on holiday)
   (b) Employed (include self employed, farmers)
   (c) Unemployed

That is all I have to ask you for now. The researchers are holding a discussion group at *(venue)* at *(time)*. This will be a confidential, informal discussion amongst 8 to 10 young men/women like yourself and will focus on issues concerning reproductive health and behaviour of young people in your local area. Participants will be given some refreshments. Would you like to take part in this discussion group? I stress that it will be confidential and that no knowledge is needed. Please do not feel as though you have nothing to contribute as we are interested in your experiences and opinions.
   If respondent agrees:

Would you tell me your name? . . . .

Contact details . . . .

Figure 1   Example of a sift questionnaire for focus group discussions

A third possible method of participant selection is to identify whether there are any professional organisations to which participants belong and to identify whether a membership list is available. Participants may then be selected from the list as described above. Researchers must consider whether members of such organisations are likely to be familiar with each other, which will influence group dynamics and the quality of information, as described earlier. With very large professional organisations, such as the British Psychological Society, this may not be a problem. Some professional organisations may be reluctant to release the names and addresses of their members. Cooperation is likely to increase if the research is of benefit to the members in some way and if the holders of the list are assured that the list is not required for a marketing exercise.

Fourthly, if participants need to meet very specific criteria (e.g. unmarried Chinese women), selection will be more difficult. Krueger (1988) suggests that participants in focus groups can be asked for names of others who meet the necessary characteristics. This can be effective if focus groups are scheduled with an adequate time delay to contact the new participants.

It may be tempting to conduct a focus group with existing groups (e.g. boards of directors, sports groups). However, the danger in using pre-existing groups is that these groups will often have a pre-existing structure and group dynamics of their own and have formal or informal ways of relating to each other which can influence their response in a focus group discussion. Their contributions may also be inhibited by the fact that they will continue to function as a group after the focus group, which *ad hoc* participants do not (Walker, 1985). Using existing groups is therefore not ideal.

There are also some logistical issues to consider in the process of participant selection. It is usually necessary to over-recruit participants to anticipate some non-attendance, so a rule of thumb is to recruit ten participants and expect eight to attend. Recruitment of participants generally takes place one week before the focus group discussion. If there is a long time gap between recruitment and the focus group people may forget to attend and if it is scheduled too soon after recruitment people may have other commitments. Researchers may telephone participants the day before the focus group to remind them and to determine their intention to attend. Researchers should be aware of the seasonal timetable of participants so that recruitment does not take place at times when participants will be too busy to attend (e.g. term time for teachers, harvest time for farmers). It is worth considering providing incentives to participants, for example money or gifts. This will, however, depend on the community under study and the topic of discussion. However, payment may impress on participants the importance of the research and of their contribution.

Group Size

Usually focus groups comprise seven to ten people who share similar characteristics. The group needs to be small enough to give everyone the opportunity to share their views, yet large enough to provide diversity of perceptions and stimulus for discussion. A group of four to six participants may have a smaller pool of ideas, which can restrict discussion. If a group has more than ten participants there is a tendency for fragmentation and it becomes difficult for the moderator to control the discussion. Participants may find they are unable to contribute due to the large size of the group and may therefore begin to whisper comments to those seated around them. This is a clear sign that the group is too large.

Often the nature of the research topic will indicate the most suitable group size. For example, if participants are likely to have had intense or lengthy experience of an issue, such as bereavement or cancer, smaller groups are more appropriate, whereas for topics where the researcher wants to discover a range of perceptions in more general terms (e.g. the influences on home ownership) larger groups can be used.

Occasionally, too many people will turn up for a group or unexpected people, such as spouses, may want to participate. In this instance it is useful to have a pre-prepared questionnaire to give to these people, tell them that some participants are being asked to complete the questionnaire, thank them and tell them they are free to leave. This makes them feel that they have contributed in some way and that their time was not wasted. It also enables the moderator to avoid having to run a group which is too large, or composed of people who are acquainted.

Number of Groups

The aim of focus group research is to identify the diversity of perceptions around a particular issue. Therefore, enough focus groups need to be conducted which cover the range of issues expressed by the study population. Once focus groups cease to provide new information there is no benefit in continuing with more groups. At this stage the research has reached what Glaser and Strauss (1967) termed "saturation", the point at which additional data collected generates no new information of understanding. Typically the first two or three groups will provide a considerable amount of new information, later groups contribute fewer new ideas. It is worthwhile conducting groups with different types of participants (e.g. rural/urban women, young/older women) according to factors which may influence participants and facilitate homogeneity within groups. However, care must be taken not to separate groups by too many variables as this can lead to a vast number of groups. As a general rule, it is good practice to schedule at least three groups per type of participant, but be prepared to arrange more or fewer depending on the information obtained. A few practice sessions may also need to be scheduled for researchers new to focus group research, which may not provide data of the required quality.

Group Location

The physical location of the focus group as well as the internal environment needs to be given careful consideration. The venue where the focus group will be held must be easy to find, accessible by public transport and central for participant access. Transport may need to be provided to the venue, especially if the focus group is held in the evening. The focus group should be held in a quiet location to assist in tape recording the session and where participants will not be interrupted. The location should be neutral and non-threatening. The room must be free from visual or audio distractions, for example a large window with passing pedestrians or a television screen in the background, which may distract participants' attention from the issue of discussion. Seating needs to be arranged so that participants can face each other, generally in a circle with or without a central table. A lecture theatre is not suitable: a casual seating arrangement is preferable to a formal meeting atmosphere.

DEVELOPING THE QUESTION ROUTE

Much of the success of a focus group depends on the quality of the questions and the forethought given to the question route (as a focus group "questionnaire" is normally called). The question route is the research tool which will guide the discussion and, if well developed, will elicit the types of responses to meet the research objectives. The question route is a pre-prepared series of questions that is used to guide the group discussion. It may be a list of general topics to be explored with participants or, more often, a list of questions for discussion with probes under each. The question route needs to be flexible enough to allow the group to direct the discussion towards the issues which they view as important, yet must have enough structure to prevent the group from diverging too far from the topic of interest. The moderator should use the question route as a guide rather than as a rigid format. This enables him/her to change the order of topics if they are spontaneously introduced by participants and explore issues not considered by the researchers but considered important to participants.

The series of questions on a question route may look deceptively simple. Those inexperienced in qualitative research may be tempted to include too many or too complex questions in the question route. It must always be remembered that the questions will always be asked of a *group* of people, and in order for everyone to express their views and for the group to discuss related issues discussion about a single issue may take some time. Responses by participants are likely to spark new ideas or invite controversy from other participants which will inevitably lengthen the discussion time. Therefore, the question route needs to be limited to two or three main areas to allow sufficient time to explore each issue in detail. Including too many questions will lead to only superficial coverage of all the issues and will overlook other areas that could be developed. One example of a question route is shown in the appendix at the end of the chapter. A question route should ideally be designed for a discussion of no more than two hours (although many focus group researchers prefer 90 minutes). After this time participants will become tired or lose interest and the value of information given will decline.

The first step in developing the question route is to list the most obvious questions and then to examine the questions for clarity, bias, ambiguity, length

---

Welcome and thank participants for attending.
Introduce the observer (if appropriate).
Explain the project in general terms.
Tell participants why they were chosen and the importance of their contribution.
Explain why the session is being tape recorded.
Assure participants of confidentiality.
Explain the "rules" of a focus group discussion.
Tell participants the expected length of the session.

Figure 2   Points to include in the introductory statement

and types of response evoked. Focus groups are part of an interactive research process. Researchers should expect to rewrite the question route several times to capture new issues and to achieve clarity, precision and brevity in the questions. New information from early groups can be incorporated into the question route to explore in later groups. This allows participants greater influence on the research process and enables the researcher to focus the question route on the main issues of the investigation. Qualitative research is often an iterative process which involves feedback of information during the research process in redefining research issues.

The question route should include an introductory statement which should cover the main points shown in Figure 2. The introduction should not be read to participants but used by the moderator as a checklist to make sure all the points have been made. It should be introduced naturally rather than as a formal set of rules. An example of an introductory statement is shown in Figure 3.

During the introduction participants should be welcomed and thanked for attending. The purpose of the research should be explained in general terms, but not the objectives or the research questions. For example, *We are researching perceptions of physical fitness, and are interested in the views of community members*. Participants should be told in the introduction why they were selected and the importance of their contribution. It is particularly important that the moderator assures participants of the confidentiality of their responses and explains why the session is being tape recorded, as this will help to create the

---

Good evening everyone. I would like to thank you all for coming tonight. I am . . . . and I have been asked by the University of Southampton to moderate this group tonight. I will start by giving you a little information about the background of this group discussion. The project is being done by the University of Southampton for the Department of Health in the Wessex Region. As many of you are probably aware, there are a lot of changes going on at present in the Health Service and one of these is to find out how best to improve the family planning services that are available to everyone. So it was decided the best way to find out was to actually talk to people who use these facilities. During the course of the next few weeks we are talking to similar groups like yourself, but of various ages and both male and female, so that we can find out as much as possible about your knowledge of what is available, your experiences of using family planning services, whether you use a family planning clinic or your own doctor, or maybe you don't use any of these facilities. We would also like to talk tonight about how these facilities can be improved in the future. I do hope that none of you will feel that you have little knowledge on the subject, as any opinion you have will be helpful to future planning. We are using a tape recorder, so that we don't miss anything that is said, but I want to assure you that anything you say here tonight will be completely confidential. We will only use first names in our discussion, and there will be no way of identifying any individual in the report of this research. Because we don't want to miss anything it is important only one person talks at a time, and that you share everything you have to say with the group rather than just the person next to you. Remember we want to hear as may different points of view as possible, so feel free to disagree with everyone else.

Let us start by you introducing yourselves and telling the group a little about your background . . .

Source: Adapted from original research instrument used by Cooper et al. (1992).

Figure 3   Example of an introductory statement

permissive atmosphere within the group, described earlier. It is important to define the "rules" of the group discussion, in particular that they should use first names only; that one person talks at a time to assist in recording quality; that all views are important and that everyone be allowed to express their opinion; that all participants should feel free to express different opinions; and that the conversation should be confined to the group rather than individuals participating in a sub-discussion with people seated next to them. Finally tell participants how long the session is expected to last.

The first question asked in a focus group should be very general. It should be a simple question and one that everyone is able to make a contribution to. This will act as an icebreaker in the "warm-up" stage of the discussion.

Question Design

The questions used in a focus group are different from those used in a survey, which is aimed at gaining precise, direct and often factual information. Focus groups, however, investigate new areas or explore people's attitudes, opinions or behaviour and the range of responses to focus group questions are often unknown. Therefore questions used in focus groups need to reflect the exploratory, flexible nature of qualitative research. They also need to encourage group discussion and to make participants feel comfortable in expressing their views openly.

Questions used in focus group discussions are open-ended and non-directive. An open question is one in which no response categories are given, and a non-directive question gives the respondent no indication of the type of answer the researcher expects. For example, *What do you think of the local youth club?* is an open, non-directive question as it allows participants to determine the direction of the answer and provides them with the opportunity to answer from a variety of dimensions. It allows participants to identify both positive and negative aspects and encourages individuals to respond according to their experience or situation. Open questions also encourage detailed responses (see Chapter 5.6 by Memon). What participants choose to discuss indicates what is important to them. Focus group questions usually progress from very general to more specific. Open, non-directive questions are most suitable at the beginning of the discussion to identify the range of issues or views. As the discussion continues it may be necessary to limit the types of responses and focus the discussion on particular issues by asking more directed questions. This has been termed a "funnel strategy" (Morgan, 1997). For example, *What do you think about the opening times of the local youth club?* Extreme care must be taken not to change directed questions into loaded or leading questions, for example, *What do you think about the **poor** opening times of the local youth club?* This forces participants to believe that the opening times are poor when they may think otherwise. Directing the discussion towards more specific issues may also be achieved through probing participants to comment about particular aspects of a topic; for example, *What* *do you think about the opening times/location/parking*, etc. Care must be taken not to force participants to discuss aspects of only minor importance to them.

Avoid dichotomous questions in a focus group. These are questions which, for example, elicit a yes/no response. This type of question does not evoke the desired group discussion and may attract ambiguous responses. Questions or probes must not be judgemental or loaded with social morals so that participants feel guilty or embarrassed to admit to particular behaviour or attitudes. Questions must be able to be clearly understood by participants. They should be short, use simple language and ask about only one issue. Questions with several parts should be avoided as they may invite different responses from different participants and lead to confused discussion. It is better to have several short, precise questions.

It is better to avoid too many "why" questions in focus groups. These questions assume people have given detailed thought to motivations which explain their behaviour, but participants may only give superficial answers or instant rationalisations. "Why" questions may also have overtones of interrogation and trigger defence barriers which elicit only socially acceptable responses. Lazarfeld (1986) states the "why" questions can typically be answered on two levels, (a) according to what influences behaviour, and (b) according to desirable attributes. For example, the question *Why did you go to this university?* may invite the responses, *because my parents encouraged me* or *because the physics labs were well equipped*. It is better to break "why" questions into attributes (e.g. *What influenced you to . . . /What features of . . .*).

Pre-testing (or piloting) the question route is an essential part of question design. It is difficult to know how people will respond to questions until they are asked. Ideally the question route should be tested on people with similar characteristics to the participants before any focus groups are conducted. If this is not possible then the first focus group may act as a pilot. However, if major changes to the question route are made the results of this focus group should not be used in the analysis. After the pilot, researchers should reflect on the wording, sequencing, types of responses given and the timing of responses. The first draft of a question route is rarely problem free and will often have to be revised and retested several times.

ROLES OF THE FOCUS GROUP TEAM

A focus group team generally consists of a moderator, an observer and, optionally, a housekeeper. Each member of the team needs to be clear and confident about their role. Confusion during the focus group session will make participants feel uneasy, which may affect data quality. The emphasis for all members of the team is on creating a friendly, warm and comfortable environment for participants. Serving refreshments prior to and during the focus group session can aid social cohesion.

The role of the observer is primarily to take notes during the focus group discussion. The observer's notes should identify the key issues discussed and should be complete enough to provide a coverage of the main responses of the group if the tape recorder should fail. Other factors which may influence the interpretation of information during analysis should also be included in the observer's summary, such as non-verbal messages and body language which may indicate how the group is feeling about the topic under discussion. Observers should be aware that body language and facial expressions may have different meanings amongst different cultural groups. The observer's notes should include a summary of what was actually said; care must be taken not to make judgements or interpretations about the comments. The observer should not be especially obvious to the group; he/she should not take part in the discussion or questioning and should avoid making eye contact with participants. The observer may assist the moderator after the session to identify any areas that were not well explored, questions missed or areas worth following up in later groups. The observer is also responsible for dealing with unexpected intrusions (e.g. latecomers, background noise), controlling environmental conditions (e.g. lighting, seating, heating). Observers should try to write up their notes in full within 24 hours of the group session and certainly before the next group, otherwise information from the groups may be confused.

The housekeeper, when used, is not present during the discussion but attends to organisational matters, leaving the moderator and observer free to concentrate on the discussion. The housekeeper's role includes welcoming participants and making them feel at ease, issuing name tags, organising refreshments and paying expenses after the session. Occasionally the housekeeper may be called upon to look after children.

The moderator's role is critically important. A moderator needs to create an open and permissive atmosphere within the group as well as to manage the group discussion. The moderator's role is to introduce topics, encourage discussion and keep the discussion focused so that all the issues of interest are addressed. The discussion flows as a result of the careful nurturing of the moderator. Moderators need to be familiar with the study objectives to enable them to make on-the-spot decisions about whether issues raised by participants are worthy of further exploration or whether they are marginal to the research objectives. One of the skills of a moderator is flexibility in modifying the question route during the session to anticipate the flow of discussion. Moderators must also have a good sense of timing, not only to pace the group through the question route, but also to sense whether a group is ready to move on to the next topic or whether more general discussion will make respondents feel more comfortable. This is particularly important when discussing more sensitive issues. Moderators need to have good listening and leadership skills; they need simultaneously to be listening carefully to participants, monitoring the respondents' reactions, remembering earlier comments, anticipating the next questions, bearing in mind the overall study objectives and ensuring that enough time is devoted to each issue on the question route – the moderator's role is not easy! Moderators also usually control the tape recorder as they are able to do this with the least disruption to the group discussion.

The Moderator's Tasks

Arrival of Participants

It is advisable for the focus group team to arrive at the venue early enough to arrange seating, check equipment *in situ* and greet early arrivals. Upon arrival, participants may be given a brief questionnaire which collects demographic and other background information that will be helpful in later analysis. Although it is important to make participants feel at ease by making small talk and serving refreshments at this time, the research team should avoid any discussion about the issues which will be covered by the group discussion. Participants will probably only want to raise their issues once and if they have done this with the moderator before the group discussion they may be reluctant to repeat their comments in the group discussion and their comments will no longer be spontaneous.

The time when participants are arriving is a crucial time to identify participants who are likely to be talkative or quiet and to arrange seating to accommodate them in the group discussion. Seating can be controlled with the placement of place names after identification of participant characteristics. Quiet participants are best placed directly opposite the moderator to facilitate maximum eye contact, while talkative participants are best seated at the moderator's side.

Starting the Session

During the first few moments of the focus group the moderator must create an open, comfortable and permissive atmosphere, introduce the discussion topic and set the "rules" for the focus group discussion. Excessive formality and rigidity at this stage can stifle discussion, whilst too much humour can result in participants not considering the issues seriously. The moderator should introduce the discussion and ask questions in natural, informal language consistent with the tone of the discussion. The moderator should cover all the points shown in Figure 2 in his/her introductory comments.

During the introduction the moderator should provide participants with enough information about the study (but not questions or objectives) to enable participants to understand what is required of them as focus group participants. This ensures that respondents have *cognition*, a necessary condition to enable them to know what type of information is required of them and ensure that they understand what is expected of their participation (May, 1993). Without *cognition* respondents may feel uncomfortable or confused about their role, which may affect data quality. A moderator must also generate *motivation* amongst participants so that they feel that their participation and responses are valued and that their cooperation is fundamental for the research.

Participants should be asked to introduce themselves. This gets everyone involved straight away and helps the transcriber to identify each speaker. The first question should be very general so that everyone will be able to contribute.

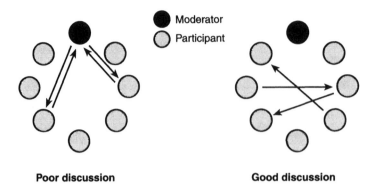

Poor discussion   **Good discussion**

Figure 4 Diagrammatic representation of good and poor focus group discussion

It can take 10–15 minutes of general discussion before the group is comfortable to move onto the central issues for discussion.

Moderating Techniques

Encouraging group discussion is one of the key roles of the moderator. Focus groups should never be a question-and-answer session between participants and the moderator, but a discussion between participants, as depicted in Figure 4. A focus group is working well when the moderator has only little to contribute, but he/she must remain in control and ensure that all group members are involved.

A moderator should try to avoid obtaining the *deference effect*, whereby participants tell the moderator what they think the moderator wants to know (Bernard, 1994). This can be corrected by instilling in participants, early in the discussion, the value of their personal views, encouraging all comments both positive and negative, encouraging differences of opinion, sometimes saying that negative comments may be the most helpful. The deference effect may also be avoided if the moderator does not express his/her own personal viewpoints about issues, as participants may want to agree with this.

"Pause and probe" are useful techniques for soliciting additional information from participants. A well placed five second pause may encourage a speaker to expand further or another speaker to contribute spontaneously. This is particularly effective when coupled with eye contact from the moderator. However, pauses need to be used carefully as a pause which is too long can cause discomfort amongst participants and have the opposite effect. An extended pause may also be risky because respondents may genuinely have nothing more to say and be waiting for the moderator's guidance (Bernard, 1994)

A probe is a question which seeks to gain additional information or clarification about an issue. For example, *Would you like to explain further? Is there anything else? Can you describe what you mean?* It is best to use probes generously early in the discussion to introduce the idea of precision of responses. Although it is possible or sometimes necessary to use several probes to clarify some issues, the moderator must take care not to over-probe as respondents may feel that they have not yet provided the answer that the moderator wanted.

In general, longer questions tend to elicit longer, more detailed answers. It can be helpful to rephrase the question or expand on the question if the group finds it difficult to respond; this also gives them more time to consider their responses. Also, the question may be repeated after a period of discussion to elicit any further comments. Hypothetical questions may also be used to probe the discussion.

It is important for the moderator to keep the discussion focused. Due to the flexible nature of the question route participants are free to introduce topics themselves. However, the moderator should prevent the discussion from deviating too far from the research questions. If the moderator decides not to pursue an issue they can say *OK, let's hold off on that for now* and revert back to the question route. Sometimes topics may be introduced spontaneously in a different order from the question route and discussion moves on too quickly before previous issues are discussed fully. The moderator can control this situation by saying *Can we come back to that in a minute?* and restating the current topic. This should not be done too often as the discussion will lose its spontaneity.

The moderator also needs to be aware of the non-verbal signals given to participants through their own body language. Head nodding may be seen as approval for a given view and discourage opposite points of view. Short verbal responses also need to be kept in check; many of these are acceptable such as *OK, Yes, Ah-ha*, but some to be avoided include *Great, That's good, Excellent*, as they imply a judgement about the quality of the comment (Krueger, 1988).

Managing the Group

The moderator's role involves managing group dynamics to ensure a balance between the contributions of dominant and more passive participants. Body language and verbal cues can be used to encourage or discourage individual participants.

Quiet participants have an equally important contribution to make to discussion as other participants but they may need some encouragement. These participants need to feel that their comments are wanted and valued; this may be achieved by using open body posture, making frequent eye contact, smiling or gentle probing for contributions. Try not to put these participants on the spot as this can further inhibit a shy person. However, if all else fails the moderator can call on them by name. It is good to legitimise the contribution of a quiet member to stop them feeling swamped or threatened (Walker, 1985). The moderator can state that he/she has heard the same idea expressed in other groups, or that it is a valid or important issue and ask the rest of the group for their views.

Dominant participants can make useful contributions to the group discussion but the moderator must ensure that they do not monopolise the discussion. A moderator can discourage them by using non-verbal messages such as turning slightly away or avoiding eye contact. Verbal cut offs should be tactful and kind as harsh comments may deter other participants. For example, *Thank you Barry. Does anyone feel any differently?* or with a smile, *OK we've heard quite a lot from Barry. What about the rest of you?* or *That's one point of view, does anyone have another?* It is important to emphasise that *all* group members have an important contribution. Dominant participants can be useful to stimulate discussion and can be used by the moderator by picking up their points and asking other participants' views on them.

"Expert" participants may consider themselves more knowledgeable than other participants because they have experience in the area under discussion, have participated in a focus group before or may hold a high social or community position. The difficulty with these participants in focus group discussions is that they may inhibit other participants who may perceive that they have little to contribute due to their lack of experience. The best way to handle this is to emphasise that *everyone* is an expert and the researchers are interested in the opinions and experiences of all group members.

Rambling participants feel comfortable in a focus group environment and give long-winded accounts that are often only of marginal relevance. The moderator should try body language to discourage a lengthy monologue, discontinue eye contact after 30 seconds, look at the question route but avoid looking at the rambler. As soon as the rambler pauses, the moderator should repeat the question to the rest of the group or introduce a new topic. With only a limited amount of time for discussion it is important to keep these people under control!

Post Session Questionnaire

It is often useful to give participants a brief questionnaire at the end of the session. This may ask about more sensitive issues which were not suitable for group discussion but are important to the research objectives, or it may simply collect demographic and other background information about participants. A post session questionnaire may sometimes be preferred to the pre session questionnaire, described earlier, because the questions asked may lead participants to answer in a particular way if they feel they know the issues which interest the researchers. An example of a post session questionnaire is shown in the appendix.

Using Stimulus Material

It is sometimes useful to introduce stimulus material during the discussion to provoke reactions and stimulate responses. This may include product samples, packaging, leaflets, posters, advertising or short video material. One study (Cooper et al., 1992) used examples of contraceptives to assess knowledge of different methods of contraception in a study of family planning provision. Another study (Pearson et al., 1996) used examples of posters which promoted family planning services to assess their appeal to young people.

Debriefing Meeting

Immediately after the focus group session the moderator and observer should have a debriefing meeting. The purpose of the debrief is for the moderator and observer to compare their initial impressions of the session, to identify the main themes to come from the discussion and identify any difficulties with the group, equipment or location. It is useful for the moderator to complete a short summary report immediately after the session has ended, which comments on the moderator's impressions of group dynamics, location, seating and any difficulties encountered. An example of such a report is shown in Figure 5. The debriefing session, moderator's report and observer's notes are important for identifying any revisions required to the question route, moderator's technique, location or group composition.

DATA MANAGEMENT

Focus groups are typically recorded in two ways, by a tape recording of the discussion and/or by notes taken by the observer. Tape recording the discussion is highly recommended: it gives a full account of the session, reduces the influence of the observer and greatly increases data quality. Data analysis can also be carried out more fully with verbatim information from the discussion. Tape recording group discussions is difficult. Recording often picks up background noise rather than softly spoken participants. Microphones which are built into the tape recorder have limited sensitivity; an omni-directional remote microphone is the best option to pick up group discussion and it can be placed in the middle of the table. Hidden recording equipment is not advisable as it suggests secrecy and may inhibit discussion if discovered. In selecting cassette tapes, try to avoid using C120 cassettes, as they are thin and may break during the constant stopping and rewinding during transcription (Bernard, 1994).

Tape recorded sessions need to be transcribed to provide a written account of the discussion. Transcription should be carried out as soon after the session as possible. The moderator and observer should edit the transcripts while listening to the tapes as they may be able to recall much of the discussion and fill in the gaps the transcriber could not understand. Confidentiality of participants should be protected. The names of all participants should be replaced with speaker identifiers or numbers and the names of other individuals mentioned (e.g. doctors, teachers) should be deleted during the editing process.

The use of a video recorder during focus group discussions needs to be considered carefully. Using a video camera will enable researchers to identify participants' actions, such as body language and facial expressions in addition to verbal messages. However, a continuing concern is that video cameras are intrusive, they may change the focus group environment and participant spontaneity (Krueger, 1998). Researchers must consider these influences and whether or not data quality will be significantly improved by using a video camera.

Focus Group Report

Date: Friday 2nd December 1994

Place: [. . . .] School

Participants: Five male 18 year olds

Moderator: [. . . .]

Length: One hour, 33 minutes (start 9.27am, finish 11.00am)

Participant Selection:
Participants were asked to volunteer by a form tutor to take part in a discussion group. They were not told the subject to be discussed. Approximately ten students were asked to volunteer, the students who did not turn up were reported to be too busy or doing other things.

Setting:
Office of Headmistress (she was not present that day). Comfortable seating, warm, well lit. Quiet, no interruptions during group.

Group Dynamics:
The group seemed to know each other quite well. They seemed at ease talking about personal things with each other. A lot of cross-participant conversation took place. One participant [R2] took a slightly more dominant role within the group – his mother worked at the local family planning clinic and the participant was obviously used to talking about relationships and contraception. The other participants spoke about equally, although one [R5] was slightly quieter than the others.

Comments and Feedback:
At the end (not recorded on tape) the participants reported that the group had gone well and that a lot of material had been covered, more than they had expected. They also reported that they often talk about these issues anyway so felt at ease talking in this situation.

Seating Sketch:

M = Moderator
P = Participant
* = Microphone

Source: Pearson et al. (1996)

Figure 5   Example of a moderator's report

ANALYSIS OF FOCUS GROUP DATA

Qualitative data analysis is complex, time-consuming and involves managing a large volume of textual data. The difficulties in analysis stem from the features which make focus group research unique, that is, its flexibility, spontaneity and the interactive process of discussion. Analysis of focus group data poses difficulties on two levels (Walker, 1985). Firstly, there are practical difficulties in determining how to cope with the large volume of data and how to segment the data into manageable parts for analysis. Secondly, there are interpretive problems in extracting the meaning of the data and how this can address research objectives. Particular difficulties which arise in analysing data from a *group* discussion include: determining whether frequently made comments reflect the views of the group or of individual participants, and monitoring the influence of group interaction on the changing opinions of participants.

Analysis is often an ongoing process that begins with fieldwork and continues until the final report is written. However, analysis of the transcripts is the most formal process. Early analysis of the group sessions enables the study to focus quickly on the main issues so this can be fed back into later groups to explore issues more fully. It also enables methods to be checked so that the focus group is conducted in the best possible way to obtain results which are able to meet the research objectives. Debriefing after every focus group is an important part of the analysis process. Analysis is conducted by all members of the research team. The moderator, in particular, can provide valuable insights about group comments. All data are used in the analysis including secondary data, notes taken in the field, the observer's notes from the discussion, the summary of the debriefing session or information collected from participants via the pre-group questionnaire.

Process of Analysis

Analysis of focus group data can be performed at a range of levels depending on how the information will be used and on the time, skills and resources available. The process of analysis generally involves reading the data and segmenting the data in some way to provide a structure for investigation into specific topics, areas or themes. It is a systematic process of reading, examining, categorising and tabulating the information.

Data cleaning is an important initial task. This involves listening to the tapes for transcription errors. The omission of one small word can change the whole meaning of a comment. Poorly recorded or transcribed areas, where the information is unclear or where many people are speaking at once, should be deleted from the transcripts. Similarly, areas where the moderator has clearly asked a leading or a biased question should also be deleted.

The first stage in analysing the transcripts is descriptive and involves reading them as a whole and noting down general impressions, trends, patterns, the range of issues, common issues, opinions and attitudes expressed across groups. At this stage the variety of responses as well as the consistency of responses across groups should be noted. Opinions expressed only once may not be important to the overall research objectives. The second stage involves re-reading the transcripts but this time focusing on more specific issues, themes or research topics and attaching some meaning and interpretation to the data. The question route may be used as a guide to broad issues. It is often easier to examine one research issue at a time and to undertake detailed investigation. This interpretation often goes beyond the transcripts and includes field notes and other data as well as considering the intensity and consistency of comments and the specificity of examples. The issues may be put into categories or along a continuum. At this stage it is useful to consider the types of respondents who hold particular views or raise specific issues, by dividing the data into different groups of respondents. Responses may differ, for example, between groups held with male or female participants, old or young participants, those with more or less experience of the issue. These observations will be important research findings.

During the reading process it may be useful to identify the frequency of comments about a particular issue within each focus group and across all groups (Knodel, 1993; Morgan, 1997). This procedure is useful to identify both the frequency and consistency of comments and eliminates the problem whereby one individual participant makes the same comment several times giving the impression that it may be a group response. This process involves descriptive counting and can be done by constructing a tally chart of responses for each code or comment (see Table 2). This involves listing comments or issues down the left margin and the number of focus groups across the top of each column. Each time a comment on the list is mentioned a tally mark is made corresponding to the focus group in which it was mentioned. The totals in the last two columns indicate the number of participants who made the comment (frequency) and the total number of groups in which the comment was made (consistency). Comments which are made in many groups carry more importance than comments made by many participants in one group as it may be that participants are simply agreeing with one another. This process enables what Morgan (1997, p. 63) terms "group-to-group validation", which measures the importance of issues according to the number of individuals who mentioned the issue, the number of groups in which the issue was mentioned and the level of enthusiasm generated by the issue.

The third stage of data analysis generally involves developing a coding scheme by dividing the data into segments, categories or themes to facilitate data retrieval for further analysis or manipulation (Walker, 1985; Appleton, 1995; Siedel, Friese & Leonard, 1995; Mason, 1996). Coding the data provides a framework for analysis and gives analytical "handles" on the data to focus analysis and make comparisons and connections between the data. Coding

Table 2   Grid of frequency and consistency of comments

Code: features of a Family planning clinic	FG 1	FG 2	FG 3	Total no. participants	Total no. focus groups
1. Staff attitude	1	1		2	2
2. Anonymity/ Confidentiality	1	11	111	6	3
3. Length of consultation		1	1	2	2
4. Female staff	111	11	11	7	3
5. Expertise/ specialist staff		1		1	1
6. Location	1	11		3	2
7. Image of clinic	1		1	2	3

data involves identifying a uniform set of key themes, issues or areas and indexing the whole data set according to these categories. For example, the code *Type of Illness* may be given to all comments which identify respondents' illnesses, and the code *Treatment* given to all comments about health care sought. Coding is an interactive process whereby the range of codes will emerge from the data itself and from the research objectives, rather than the researcher imposing a coding framework upon the data. This enables the issues identified by the respondents to guide the analysis and results. The level of detail of the coding scheme will depend on the specificity of the data required. Coding data is essential if one is planning to use computer packages in the analysis. There are now many computer packages to assist in the analysis of qualitative data (e.g. *The Ethnograph, NUDIST, QualPro, Atlas-ti*). Before embarking on this process, researchers must consider the value that more in-depth analysis will bring to meeting the research objectives and whether they have the resources to carry this out.

Throughout the analysis there are a number of issues which need continually to be considered; these have been identified by Krueger (1988).

1. Consider the context of comments and whether they were made with or without prompting from the moderator, or whether they were triggered by a response from another participant.
2. Internal consistency may be influenced if participants change their views as a result of the group discussion. Researchers may need to identify the trigger for this change if examining decision-making behaviour.
3. Specificity of responses will indicate the value to be attached to particular comments. Responses based on personal experience should be given more weight than those which are vague and impersonal.
4. Identify the major themes in the whole study. It is easy to become absorbed in sub-themes and miss the wider issues.
5. Continually revisit the research objectives to guide the process of analysis.

REPORTING FOCUS GROUP FINDINGS

Focus groups produce an enormous amount of textual data and it is often difficult to determine what should be reported. In focusing the research report it is necessary to consider the audience of the report and whether this is a public audience, policy makers or service providers. Secondly, the research team needs to decide which results are important enough to include in the report. Although different findings may be appropriate for different target audiences, there are often a range of key findings which emerge from the research. The structure of the report may be determined by these main results.

Numbers and percentages are not relevant to focus group research and should be avoided in the report. Numbers suggest that results can be extrapolated to the population and this is not the aim of qualitative research. Instead, adjectival phrases are a common way of expressing the frequency of particular issues or the importance of some issues to participants. For example, *The majority of particip-ants stated . . .* or *Participants strongly felt that . . .* or *Many participants . . .*

It is very common to use verbatim quotations in reports of qualitative re-search. Verbatim extracts from the discussion often convey the richness, quality and nature of the results better than the researcher's descriptions. They help to validate the points made in the report and make the report more interesting. Deciding which extracts to include in a report presents a problem to many qualitative researchers. The selection of quotations should be guided by the research objectives or the part of the objectives being analysed. Quotations should be used to support the findings of the research, whether these are positive or negative, to illustrate a particular issue or demonstrate the variety of opposing points of view expressed by participants. If the objective is to identify common or typical comments or repeating themes then quotations used should reflect this, while if the objective is to demonstrate the range and diversity of responses on issues then several quotations should be used to reflect these extremes. "The goal of connecting the reader and the original participants through 'well chosen' quotations requires a match between the importance of the topic and richness of the example" (Morgan, 1997, p. 64).

REFERENCES

Appleton, J. (1995). Analysing qualitative interview data: Addressing issues of validity and reliability. *Journal of Advanced Nursing*, **22**, 993–997.

Bernard, H.R. (1994). *Research Methods in Anthropology: Qualitative and Quantitative Approaches* (2nd edn). Beverly Hills, CA: Sage.

Cooper, P., Diamond, I., Gould, C., High, S. and Partridge, J. (1992). *Choosing and using contraceptives: Consumers experiences in Wessex.* University of Southampton, Depart-ment of Social Statistics. Report to the Wessex RHA Quality Measures in Family Planning Steering Group, November.

Glaser, B.G. & Strauss, A.L. (1967). *The Discovery of Grounded Theory.* Chicago: Aldine.

Greenbaum, T. (1988). *The Practical Handbook and Guide to Focus Group Research.* Mass.: Lexington Books, D.C. Heath & Co.

Jarrett, R.L. (1993). Focus group interviewing with low income, minority populations: A research experience. In D.L. Morgan (Ed.), *Successful Focus Groups: Advancing the State of the Art* (pp. 184–281). Newbury Park, CA: Sage.

Jourard, S.M. (1964). *The Transparent Self.* Princeton, NJ: D. Van Nostrand.

Kitzinger, J. (1994). The methodology of focus groups: the importance of interaction between research participants. *Sociology of Health and Illness*, **16**, 103–121.

Knodel, J. (1993). The design and analysis of focus group studies: A practical approach. In D.L. Morgan (Ed.), *Successful focus groups: Advancing the State of the Art* (pp. 35–50). Newbury Park, CA: Sage.

Krueger, R.A. (1988). *Focus Groups: A Practical Guide for Applied Research.* London: Sage.

Krueger, R.A. (1998). Analysing and reporting focus group results. In *Focus Group Kit.* Thousand Oaks: Sage.

Lazarfeld, P. (1986). *The Art of Asking Why.* New York: The Advertising Research Foundation.

Mason, J. (1996). *Qualitative Researching*. London: Sage.

May, T. (1993). *Social Research: Issues, Methods and Process*. Buckingham, England: Open University Press.

Morgan, D.L. (1997). *Focus Groups as Qualitative Research* (2nd edn). Qualitative Research Methods Series 16. London: Sage.

Morgan, D.L. & Krueger, R.A. (1993). When to use focus groups and why. In D.L. Morgan (Ed.), *Successful Focus Groups: Advancing the State of the Art* (pp. 3–19). Newbury Park, CA: Sage.

Pearson, S., Cornah, D., Diamond, I., Ingham, R., Peckham, S. & Hyde, M. (1996). *Promoting Young People's Sexual Health Services*. Report Commissioned by the Health Education Authority.

Seidel, J., Friese, S. & Leonard, C. (1995). *The Ethnograph v4.0, A Users Guide: A Program for the Analysis of Text based Data*. Amherst, MA: Qualis Research Associates.

Walker, R. (Ed.) (1985). *Applied Qualitative Research*. Aldershot, UK: Gower.

APPENDIX

Question Route for Focus Group Discussions

Unmarried Youth

Introduction
I would like to thank you all for coming today. My name is . . . . and I am conducting some interviews as part of a research project on reproductive health and behaviour of young people. This survey is being carried out by researchers at the University of Malawi. We feel that by talking to people like you we can best find out about activities, opinions and feelings about these issues. There are no right or wrong answers, we are interested in your views, so please feel comfortable to say what you honestly feel. I have a list of topics I would like us to talk about but please feel free to bring up any other issues you feel are relevant. During the discussion . . . . will be taking notes and keeping track of what has been covered, and to remind me if I forget to ask certain things. However, so that s/he does not have to worry about getting every word down on paper, we will also be recording the whole session. Please, do not let that worry you, our discussion will remain completely confidential. Regarding the language, we want you to feel comfortable throughout the discussion, so please just use the language (terminology) that you use when you chat with friends. Finally, please try to let everyone have a turn at saying something, all your views are important, and please try to keep the talk within the group rather than just with the people sitting around you. Are there any questions before we begin?

Ice breaker
Perhaps we could go around the room and let each person tell us their first name and their usual occupation, whether you are in school or perhaps you are unemployed at the moment . . .

Social Environment of the Young People
1. How do people such as yourselves spend their leisure time in this area?
   (probe: with whom, males and females together)
2. What types of entertainment are popular in this area?
   (probe: film, dances, what time of day, why is this entertainment popular)
3. Do a lot of your peers have boy/girlfriends?
4. What do you think it means to have a boy/girlfriend?
   (probe: someone you feel comfortable with, have sex with, exchange gifts with)

5. What do you think of boys/girls who have boy/girlfriends?
   (probe: they are cool, naughty)
6. What is your opinion on getting married?
7. What is your opinion on having children?

Knowledge
8. How do people like yourselves know about issues concerning sex, contraception, sexually transmitted disease, HIV/AIDS?
   (probe: friends, parents, teachers, radio, print media)
9. Do you talk about sexual issues with anyone?
   (probe: friends, parents, teachers, relatives, medical personnel)
10. Do you find it easy or difficult to talk about these issues with the people you mentioned?
11. Do you think the information you get from them is useful?
12. (a) Do young people in this area go through initiation ceremonies?
    (b) Which kinds are popular?
    (c) At what stage in their life do they go through each ceremony?

Services
13. What would you advise a friend to do if . . .
    (probe: in each case who would be consulted and why)
    (a) They wanted to know more about the "facts of life".
    (b) They were experiencing pressure to have sex (prompt: peers/partner).
    (c) They wanted to have sex for the first time.
    (d) They thought they/their partner was pregnant.
    (e) They thought they had caught something from having sex (prompt: STD or HIV).
    (f) They wanted to discuss how to avoid getting pregnant.
14. How best can reproductive health messages be passed on to people such as yourselves?
    (prompt: radio advertising, newspapers, posters, interpersonal communication, e.g. peer network, one-to-one counselling, group discussion, initiation, etc.)

Conclusion
We are reaching the end of the discussion. Does anyone have anything to add before we conclude the session?

Just before you go, could you fill in this short questionnaire as we have some questions we would like to ask you all individually. This gives us some basic information on who takes part in these discussions. We do not need to know your name as it is anonymous and confidential. Thanks again for your contributions today.

Questionnaire to be Completed by Participant at the End of the Focus Group

Please note: This questionnaire is for research purposes only. You do not need to put your name on it and anything you write will be strictly confidential.

AGE: . . . . Years   . . . . .Months

SEX: Male   Female

I AM: At School/College
            Working (please state occupation) . . . .
            Looking for Work
            Other (please specify) . . . .

Section One – Services you may have used
(Please circle the answer that applies to you, and fill in the spaces)

1. Have you ever visited/used a family planning clinic? YES/NO
2. Have you ever obtained contraceptives from a GP (doctor)? YES/NO

   If **YES**: Was it your own GP (doctor) or another one? OWN/OTHER
3. Have you ever visited a Brook Advisory Centre? YES/NO
4. Have you ever used a youth advisory or counselling service? YES/NO

   If **YES**: Which one? ....

Section Two – Your Sexual Experience
(This section is optional; however, all answers are anonymous and strictly confidential)

5. Have you ever had sex? YES/NO

   If **YES**: How old were you when you first had sex?

   .... years   .... months
6. How many people have you had sex with? ....
7. Do you usually use some form of contraception? YES/NO

   If **YES**: What type of contraception do you usually use?

   ....

   If YES: Where is it usually obtained? (e.g. doctor, clinic, chemist, vending machine, etc)

   ....
8. Have you ever had sex without using some form of contraception? YES/NO

THANK YOU FOR COMPLETING THIS QUESTIONNAIRE AND FOR TAKING PART IN THE FOCUS GROUP

Source: Pearson et al. (1996).

Part 3

Sensitive Interviewing

Interviewing on Sensitive Topics

Roger Ingham
University of Southampton, UK
Ine Vanwesenbeeck
*Department of Women's Studies Tilburg University
and NISSO, Utrecht, the Netherlands*
Denise Kirkland
University of Southampton, UK

INTRODUCTION

This chapter raises some issues relating to interviewing on sensitive topics; sexual conduct is used as an illustration, drawing on the authors' research over many years exploring this complex and enigmatic behaviour amongst young people in the UK and the Netherlands. In many ways, interviewing on sensitive topics is not markedly different from interviewing on any other topic, but there may be some issues which need particular attention and care over and above those required for less sensitive and personal topics. The chapter provides a very brief background of the area of research into sexual conduct, and then considers a number of relevant issues over and above the actual interview process itself. These include sampling and obtaining participants, the selection and training of interviewers, the design of protocols, and the interview process itself. The handling and analysis of data are not dealt with in this chapter. Obviously, coverage of each of these will need to be brief but they are included since we believe they are all relevant to the completion of a successful research project. We are assuming a relatively large-scale research project with sufficient funding, although we hope that the various matters raised will also be relevant to those conducting smaller projects.

Handbook of the Psychology of Interviewing. Edited by A. Memon and R. Bull.
© 1999 John Wiley & Sons Ltd.

Background

The large increase in the level of research into sexual conduct which followed the awareness of the threats posed by HIV and AIDS in the early/mid 1980s was vitally necessary in the context of the lack of reliable knowledge prior to this time. It was (and, indeed, remains so) extremely important to attempt to understand the factors which influence behavioural outcomes, in particular the use of safer sexual practices in order to minimise the probability of HIV transmission and of unplanned conception, and to use such understanding to devise interventions aimed at risk reduction.

What characterised many of the early, questionnaire-based, projects was a serious lack of prior experience on which to build. Some of these studies were theoretically based on health psychology notions from other domains of disease or harm, whilst others aimed simply to collect baseline data on levels of sexual activity amongst particular samples. In hindsight, it can be seen that there was little basis regarding best practice concerning the construction of suitable items for questionnaires, how to avoid the ambiguities in the language used to describe sexual encounters (e.g. see Coxon, 1988), which theoretical approaches were suitable, and so on. For these, and other, reasons, some of these earlier studies produced very variable results in terms of reported levels of sexual activity amongst young people, even within geographically close regions (Ford & Bowie, 1989; Ford & Morgan, 1989; Ford, 1990; Breakwell & Fife-Schaw, 1992; Fife-Schaw & Breakwell, 1992).

Survey data are potentially invaluable in providing information on patterns of activity, levels of risk behaviour, demographic predictors and correlates of outcome measures, and so on. They are also potentially useful for enabling any changes – as a result of targeted interventions, or socio-cultural changes over time, for example – to be monitored. They do have limitations, however, in explaining *why*, and often *how*, such patterns of conduct occur, and so need to be supplemented by more intensive research approaches.

THEORETICAL APPROACHES

This then raises the question as to the most appropriate theoretical model(s) with which to inform research designed to account for variation obtained (over and above demographic variables). With the lack of previous research into sexual conduct on which to base their studies, many investigators used existing theoretical approaches to social and health issues to inform their studies. These approaches (e.g. the Theory of Reasoned Action (Ajzen & Fishbein, 1980), or the Health Belief Model (Rosenstock, 1974)) rely on quantifiable self-report measures of various dimensions which are held to predict behavioural intentions and, thus, health behaviour outcomes. They have been to some extent successful in previous research into other aspects of social life, but there is some controversy regarding their applicability to complex areas such as sexual conduct.

Criticisms have included drawing attention to the difficulties involved in selecting the appropriate terminology, the relative lack of consideration given in these models to the role of wider social contexts, the reduction of complex behaviours to a series of seven point scales, the emphasis on individual decision-making, and the assumption within these models that individuals behave in a rational manner. This is not the appropriate place to dwell on such criticisms at length; they have been more fully articulated elsewhere (Ingham, Woodcock & Stenner, 1992; Kippax & Crawford, 1993; Ingham, 1994; Ingham & van Zessen, 1997).

QUALITATIVE APPROACHES

Alongside questionnaire-based studies, attention has also been paid to the use of qualitative research approaches to the study of sexual conduct. Through the use of focus group discussions and, more prominently, individual interviews, considerable data have been collected on the ways in which people perceive the nature of the threat of HIV and AIDS, their own vulnerability, their reactions to the advice received through national campaigns and other forms of intervention, the ways in which they negotiate their wishes with actual and/or potential sexual partners, and so on.

It is important to stress that such a methodological approach does not intend to provide fully representative data on the population under consideration. Rather, the aim is to understand the range of interpretations and meanings amongst young people, to explore the importance of social contexts (for example, the impact of peers, subcultures, etc.), the various overt and covert influences on sexual conduct, the importance of understanding the discourses within which sexual conduct is located, and other dynamic processes which may help to account for and explain (rather than simply to describe) patterns of sexual activity and outcomes. Such data, when considered alongside those obtained from studies based on much larger samples using survey methods, enable a much richer understanding than data based solely on one or other approach.

A key feature of qualitative or interpretative research is that different sampling techniques pertain than the formal criteria concerning representative samples required for survey-based research. Qualitative research is focused on the identification of the possible *range* of behavioural patterns, opinions, justifications and explanations. Explaining behaviour is not expressed in terms of explained variance but in terms of understanding the underlying processes that lead to *specific* behavioural outcomes of *specific* individuals in *specific* contexts. An understanding of the various individual patterns and solutions precedes the formulation of theoretical relations that can be verified across the sample, as opposed to the traditional positivist paradigm where theory precedes the instrument and the interpretation of the participants' answers. The emphasis on the individual participant's or actor's perspective in the qualitative paradigm has important implications for the sampling procedures, the instrument and the way it is used in the interview situation.

The sample should be drawn in a way that maximises the likelihood of covering a sufficiently broad range of behaviours or explanations. The interviewer should enable and encourage the participant to present his or her personal experience and perspective, yet do so in such a way that allows for systematic analysis of the transcribed interviews.

SAMPLING ISSUES

Theoretical Sampling

The definition of the desired sample is, in qualitative research, not guided by the need for representativeness or generalisability. "Theoretical sampling" is an often used term to describe the process of obtaining a qualitative sample. In its most open form, theoretical sampling is guided by the outcomes of the analysis itself. Analysis of interviews starts as soon as the first transcripts are available, and the outcomes of the preliminary analyses are used to adapt the sampling procedures. When a certain category of participants or behaviours appears to be "saturated", the sampling of that type of participants can stop. Saturation occurs when the researcher feels that adding more interviews with a certain type of participant will not add more variation or new information.

Furthermore, certain types of participants may not help address the questions at hand. For instance, interviewing young women with little sexual experience and a steady partner can turn out to provide little information on the role of interactional competency in HIV-preventive behaviour. Consequently, the sampling process should focus more on older and/or more experienced women in order to provide contrasts. Another outcome from analysis could be to draw attention to categories that seem to be missing; when the current sample gets filled with participants with very high education or income, or with a remarkably happy childhood, *and* there appears to be a relation between these characteristics and the key outcomes that are studied, it might be useful to search actively for the missing categories. In this way, the sampling frame can be adapted several times during the fieldwork phase.

A more structured form of theoretical sampling is to pre-define certain categories that one wants to be present in the final sample, based on expectations of the possible interconnections between these categories and the key outcomes under study.

Theoretical sampling requires some form of screening before a potential participant is actually interviewed, with an increasing chance of rejection of volunteers as the sampling progresses. Screening can be informal, via the telephone for instance, or via a more or less elaborate screening questionnaire.

The definition of the sample, or the adaptations to the sampling procedures during fieldwork, should be directly related to the core research questions. In much of our research, we have been mainly interested in the HIV-preventive behaviour (especially condom use) of young people. This has led to entry criteria for age (16–30 years) and, in some cases, to criteria concerning levels of safety adopted. For example, in a comparative study of young people in the UK and the Netherlands, we adopted selection criteria of having had two or more new sexual partners during the previous 12 months, being within the age range 16 to 30, and having varying levels of reported condom use.

When the researcher's interest lies in other areas, for instance, when contraceptive use during first intercourse is the main outcome behaviour, the sample definition and sampling criteria will have to be modified accordingly. The key issue remains identical; the research question guides the (theoretical) sampling.

Sampling Sites

The choice of a sampling site can have a profound effect on the outcomes of the study. Specific interests of the researcher or the funding bodies may require that a specific regional area, social stratum, holiday resort or neighbourhood is designated as the sampling site. In cases where the research question does not require specific sites, convenience can have priority; all participants are usable as long as they fit the entry criteria. When confinement to a specific site is unavoidable, a certain youth club for instance, a general principle should be to maximise heterogeneity in order to include as much variation as possible within the target population, which may in itself be quite homogeneous, since visitors to the same place tend to have many socioeconomic and other attributes in common, as well as sharing discourses about the appropriateness and meaning of particular behaviours.

Sampling Methods

The quest for participant heterogeneity implies that it is undesirable to rely on one sampling method that is likely to target a specific kind of participant, although clearly this issue is dependent on the nature of the research to be conducted. Limiting sampling to advertising in one paper or magazine, to only addressing psychology students, or to advertising on the Internet is bound to produce a restricted sample. Instead, it is better to use varied methods in combination. Theoretically, the ideal situation would be to find a large sample (several hundred participants), administer a screening questionnaire, and select an interesting subsample for in-depth interviews. This might be feasible in circumstances where the qualitative study can be attached to an existing large-scale survey or census study. In a previous qualitative survey in the Netherlands (Rademakers et al., 1992), participants from the population national survey on sexual behaviour and HIV risks (van Zessen & Sandfort, 1991) were reapproached for qualitative interviewing. In many instances, however, no such pool of participants will be available.

Which method will be successful will be strongly dependent on time, place and the target population chosen, and also on the available budget. Drawing a sample from population registers gives good control over age, gender and living area, but may be expensive, especially when a certain minimum number of sexual partners is used as an entry criterion since people with multiple sexual partners over a short time period are relatively scarce, even among young adults.

In the field testing phases, we have tried a large array of methods to find participants, with varying degrees of success and at varying costs in terms of labour and money. In various studies, we have used the following – local college health fairs, advertisements in local and national newspapers and magazines, notices in university magazines, local TV and radio broadcasts, national TV (teletext), local colleges and secondary schools, posters at universities, advertisements in shop windows, e-mail, advertisements on Internet, student welcome parties, GUM (genito-urinary medicine) – or STD (sexually transmitted disease) clinics, personal invitations handed out at dance parties ("raves") and in queues for clubs and cinemas.

Snowballing, finding new participants via people already interviewed, can be effective and time-efficient, but carries the risk of decreased variation in the sample. People found via snowballing tend to share many background characteristics, social networks and leisure activities, especially amongst the young. For this reason, we advise that this method is used sparingly, by, for example, limiting to one the number of new participants that each participant can recruit; thus, participants who are themselves recruited via the snowball technique should not be asked to come up with new names.

The effectiveness of these and other methods will vary with the setting. Nevertheless, unless a pool of potential participants is available, sufficient time should be reserved for recruitment and the logistics should not be underestimated.

Approaching Participants

Young people have various reasons and motives for participating in a study on sexual behaviour. Motives may range from feelings of guilt over one's sexual behaviour, a need for information or referral to sexual health services, a need to confess, to altruistic reasons or scientific interest. Consequently, there is no single argument that will convince all young people in all locations to participate. It is necessary to acknowledge this diversity and have a range of arguments available when recruiting. Some issues that deserve to be emphasised are that the study is serious and has a scientific and/or health-related purpose, that the anonymity of the participants will always be protected, and that the study is not the initiative of a particular individual, but of a university or research institute. It is vitally important to distance the study from the not uncommon use of sexual surveys in popular newspapers and magazines.

Some participants will be approached in person (via snowball, researcher or key informant), which gives more opportunity to explain about the study and interview, whilst others will respond to advertisements or other sources in the media. We find it useful to have a telephone number available in order to give information in person, note down names and addresses and send an information pack containing a screening questionnaire. When personal contact was not possible, for instance because internetters provided their address by e-mail, the return rate of screening questionnaires was very low (a few per cent). However, even in cases where the potential participant spoke to a researcher, the return rate of completed screening questionnaires never exceeded 50% and many of these did not fit the criteria, despite the information pack. People may have been put off by the information, had second thoughts or simply forgot to fill in the form.

It will be dependent on local circumstances whether the researcher decides to be very specific as to the goal of the study, or choose a more general formulation in the advertisements. In some countries, referring directly to an interview about sexuality may be too explicit, and then phrases like "relationships and health" or "improving health/sex education" might be more apt. When having multiple partners is an entry criterion, one could try to convey this in the initial advertisements, otherwise the loss as a result of participants not fitting the criteria will be immense. On the other hand, if it is thought that the invitation to participate will be read by people in the company of their regular partner (in a cinema queue, for example) then any mention in the flyer of other partners might be counter-productive!

The use of incentives (cash, vouchers, compact discs, etc.) can make recruitment a lot easier, but is not the custom in all countries or research institutes for reasons of ethics, or for fear of appearing to "blackmail" people into participation, or because being interviewed for money might influence participant self-selection and/or the content of the answers. We generally take care to be moderate in the value of the incentives.

In some countries, legal rules require the researcher to ask permission from parents or guardians to have young people interviewed (this is dependent on age); researchers should, of course, be aware of and obey these local rules. Matters related to privacy, the need to inform the potential participant explicitly about the content and purpose of the interview, the need for written informed consent, the ways anonymity is guarded, and so on, are in many countries regulated by law or custom. As studies into sex are particularly vulnerable (as may be the participants), it is essential to be very precise in these respects. A further issue relates to other forms of legislation (for example, the 1996 UK Children Act), under which it may be obligatory to report to the Social Services any case in which one suspects that a young person under the age of 16 years is "at risk". Thus, learning during the course of an interview with a 14-year-old that he or she is being sexually abused by, for example, a step-father, may place the researcher in a position of needing to break a prior assurance of confidentiality. For this reason, many studies solely interview people over the age of 16 years; although this is not ideal, since memory for earlier sexual events may be clouded, it avoids some possible serious dilemmas.

Even when people ask for information packs, fill them in and return the screening questionnaire, additional arguments might be needed to have them follow through with participation. As mentioned above, motives vary amongst individuals. We found that, for some people, the prospect of participating in a European study, with young people being interviewed in many countries, was appealing. Some, with perhaps more personal motives, were persuaded by explaining that it can be very useful to talk about one's sex life with an experienced, anonymous interviewer. Others were motivated by the thought of improving the AIDS prevention campaigns, or in having a forum to criticise such campaigns or to evaluate their own sex and sexuality education. Again, the researcher involved in the recruitment should be aware of, and honour, this motivational diversity.

Sample Size

There is no simple advice on how to plan the "right" sample size. Theoretically and ideally, the proper sample size can only be determined as the fieldwork and conceptual analyses proceed; namely, when the researcher feels that the data collected are conceptually dense enough or saturated, and that the research questions can be answered. Researchers interested in the linguistics of negotiating condom use, may be satisfied with an intensive analysis of ten transcripts. For other purposes, a sample of 200 might be more appropriate. In the field testing of a European protocol, we interviewed roughly 100 individuals in each of two countries (the UK and the Netherlands) and a further ten or so interviews were carried out in a range of other countries to ensure the acceptability and suitability of the protocol for different contexts (Ingham et al., 1996).

Based on that experience and earlier, similar studies conducted in the UK and the Netherlands, a sample size between 80 and 120 is probably sufficient for most purposes. It should be noted that the first series of approximately 20 interviews is usually disproportionately more time-consuming in terms of analyses than later interviews. On the other hand, the informative value of individual interviews decreases substantially after the 50th or so interview (except when new categories of participant or topic are introduced), while at the same time the costs of data collection and analysis continue. It is sometimes possible to check the resulting sample against larger data sets based on survey techniques to ensure that the final sample selected is not too atypical of the wider population (in terms of demographic structure, timing and levels of sexual activity, or whatever), although there are grounds why one would not expect it to be completely similar if some selective entry criteria have been used.

SELECTION AND TRAINING OF INTERVIEWERS

Interviewer Selection

It is not hard to define a list of criteria that would describe the ideal interviewer. He or she should be stable and experienced, empathic yet intrusive when necessary, non-directive yet structured and systematic, know about the joys and pains of sex, sexual lifestyles and variations, be sensitive to the spoken and unspoken word, be aware of his or her gender roles and values, be aware of the effect he or she has on participants of the same or other sex, be genuinely interested in what the particip- ants say, be completely non-judgemental and accepting, and so forth. Kinsey's (Kinsey, Pomeroy & Martin, 1948, 1953) descriptions of the good interviewer and good interviewing are, in many ways, still valid today. However, finding such interviewers is far from easy, and one often has to rely on relatively inexperienced, recently graduated interviewers, a restriction that emphasises the importance of adequate training and preparation.

In-depth interviewing is a complex skill and people differ strongly in this respect. The worth of (even) one good interviewer for a qualitative research project cannot be overestimated, because he or she will provide the analysts with rich descriptive material. A good description usually explains more than a whole set of intelligent interpretations or advanced statistical analyses. Investing in the selection and training of interviewers is therefore essential. There are some key issues concerning interview skills that might be useful for the training and monitoring of the interviewers.

Qualitative researchers (but also psychotherapists, for instance) have strong, often intuitive, beliefs about the way participants and interviewers should match, boys should be interviewed by young men, homosexual women by homosexual women, and so on. In our experience, there is no evidence to assume that the perfect match can be defined by variables like gender, age, ethnicity or sexual orientation. Instead, we strongly believe that a good interviewer does the best job, with *good* meaning not only technically good, but also being able to tune in to the perspective of the person in front of them. Individual participants might have a preference for a same or opposite sex interviewer, and it is advisable to check this during the recruitment phase and to offer a choice. Our experience is that the vast majority of people do not have a specific preference; however, of those that do, both men and women normally request a female interviewer. It is therefore probably most convenient to have at least one male, and several female interviewers available.

When interviewer skill is more important than age, colour or sex per se, it might be useful to explore the possibility of hiring interviewers with experience of sexual counselling, sex education or health education, since they are already accustomed to discussing matters of relationships and health with young people. One risk with this strategy, however, is that they might use the interviews – especially those that contain information about high levels of risk behaviour – as a forum for intervention rather than for data collection; they will need careful monitoring. A further risk is that they may be particularly effective in relation to their own areas of expertise, but not so effective at covering the whole range of topics needing to be covered.

The number of interviewers required is dependent on available time and budgets, sample size, availability of potential interviewers, and so on. If time allows, the researchers could do the interviews themselves. This has several advantages: data collection and data analysis are much more closely intertwined, and the analyst gets a better understanding of the subject since substantial information is lost when one only sees the transcripts and never the participants *in vito*. We recommend that all researchers involved in analysis perform at least some real interviews to experience this difference between the live interview and the paper transcript.

Interviewer Training

The level, and nature, of training required will depend on the scale and purpose of the study. For large studies, we recommend a training course of at least two, or preferably three, days, even for experienced interviewers. The training should have multiple functions, including learning to conduct this specific interview, acquiring general in-depth interview techniques, learning about sexual issues related to the research topic, developing awareness of own sexual norms and limitations, creating commitment to the research project and each other, understanding the purpose of the data that are going to be collected (analysis, dissemination) as well as the purpose of the study as a whole (publications, policy, prevention practice, cross-national comparison), understanding the strengths and weaknesses of qualitative research and, for the researcher, to assess the qualities and weaknesses of the potential interviewers.

Prior to the training, the researcher(s) and eventual trainer(s) should have tested the protocol on each other (although this will be restricted by issues of confidentiality) as well as real trial participants to develop a feel for the flow of the interview, the time needed for the various sections, and so on. These trial interviews should preferably be video- and/or audio-taped and discussed amongst the research team. Parts that illustrate good or not-so-good types of interviewing will be useful to show in the subsequent training. The researcher(s) should be confident about the contents of the protocol; it is very disturbing to the training when problems of order or content come up and decisions need to be made on the spot (although not all eventualities can be anticipated). All this can be prevented by adequate field testing prior to the training.

Ideally, and if time allows, training should include role play and practice, and sufficient opportunity for direct feedback, the extent of this depending on the previous experience of the interviewers. Following the training, test interviews should be conducted, either on "real" participants or on the researchers or trainers. The latter is preferable when there is doubt concerning the interviewers' skills. All test interviews should be taped and assessed, and the interviewers should receive feedback and advice as soon as possible.

It is particularly useful to arrange the topics to be covered in the interviews into thematic blocks; this provides the interviewer with some "constrained freedom": the requirement to tap into the perspective of the participant and follow the flow of his or her life story, and yet, at the same time, to control the time taken and to ensure adequate coverage of all the blocks. It is helpful to develop the blocks so that they contain a limited set of starting questions followed by a series of probes; this means that the interviewers should be informed in detail on the purpose of each separate block, as well as on the combination of the blocks as a whole.

We recommend that a minimum training programme should cover the following topics:

Introduction to the study, including the purpose of the research project, the general layout of the interview, which general topics are covered and why they are there, who is going to be interviewed, why it is feasible to ask people these questions, who is going to use the material, what is needed for qualitative analysis, how a qualitative interview differs from a questionnaire, and what the role of the interviewer is.

Introduction to each block in turn, including detailed explanations of each block, the relation between each block and the whole interview, why there are starting questions, how to develop the interview from these, how to probe without steering, and how to summarise before moving on to the next block. There should be practice of each block – in dyads or in front of the group – and the trainers should improve the confidence of the interviewers yet be very critical of errors.

General interviewing techniques, including time management, how to interrupt participants, how to change the subject so that a new topic is introduced, how to probe and ask for clarification, how to seek justifications for behaviours, how to ask for participants' reactions to, and evaluations of, events, how to summarise and recap, and so on.

Difficult dilemmas, including how to manage time and yet give sufficient room to the participant, how to proceed if it is felt that the participant is hiding something, how to react if the participant makes erotic overtures, or if he or she gets emotional, frightened or angry, how to cope if the interviewer gets angry or emotional, how to react if the participant asks for information, reassurance or professional help, and what sorts of difficulties the interviewers foresee or fear.

Practical issues, including how to make appointments, how to handle privacy, how to introduce and obtain permission to tape the interviews, how to ensure interviewer safety, how to refer to aftercare, how to obtain extra training or support, and issues relating to money, travel and space should be dealt with. The absolute importance of informed consent and confidentiality must be stressed.

Once the fieldwork is started, it is recommended that the first series of interviews is monitored closely by the researcher(s). Contact by telephone following the first interviews, and/or a feedback meeting after the first few interviews, are useful options. "Weak" interviewers should be given the option of additional training and practice, or taken off the project. It is, in our experience, better to lose the investment in training than to have to work with transcripts of poor quality. Personal support for staff will also be needed when the content of the interviews may be particularly disturbing.

Interviewer Feedback

When working according to the principles of grounded theory (where data collection and analysis are intertwined; see Glaser and Strauss, 1967) researchers could brief the interviewers regularly about the proceedings of the conceptual analyses; this should be not so much about the outcomes and arising explanations, but on what proves to be usable material. This increases commitment to the project, and might sensitise interviewers to relevant areas and encourage them to explore these more deeply in subsequent interviews. As a result of interviewing experiences or analyses, the content or order of the blocks may be adapted during fieldwork. Regular feedback sessions are usually appreciated by interviewers and will improve data quality. There is, however, a concomitant risk that interviewers will "steer" the participants into certain directions suggested by the results of the initial analyses; this should be carefully monitored.

THE INTERVIEW PROCESS

Working with Blocks

Good interview formats consist of a number of blocks, each block covering a theme. Although it is theoretically possible to decide to change the order of blocks in a specific interview, the interviewers are generally advised to stick to the order given (following, for example, a life course chronology). Working with the blocks needs a balance between exploring the participants' perspectives and guarding the timing and sequence of thematic blocks. Each block contains a number of starting questions and specific issues that must be covered, but the main challenge for the interviewer is to get the participant to talk in his or her own words about the theme involved. The interviewer should be an empathic conversation partner, asking for clarification and combining parts of information ("how does this relate to what you told me earlier about . . . ?"). A block is not finished when the "core" questions have been asked, but when the interviewer feels that the picture is complete and clear enough for future analysis. This means that the same block can take ten minutes to complete with one participant, but 45 or more with someone else. During training and feedback sessions, the interviewers should be sensitised to monitor continuously whether an area is sufficiently covered.

Inconsistencies and Barriers

It sometimes occurs that an interviewer suspects that a story is inconsistent, or that the interviewee is hiding something. Interviewers should be encouraged not to finish a block before exploring this hunch further, by asking for clarification or, if that does not solve the issue, explaining their feeling that the participant might be hesitant – which, they should add immediately, is completely acceptable. It is better to bring the issue into the open and have the participant clarify his or her boundaries than to leave topics unfinished.

In general, it is good practice to teach interviewers that one effective way of guarding the flow and content of the interview is to be explicit when they feel a barrier has appeared. This barrier may be hesitant behaviour from the participant, or sexual overtures, the feeling that the participant is avoiding talking about (certain) emotions or experiences, and so forth. Ignoring the barrier is possibly ignoring an important message from the interviewee. Bringing it into the open creates an opportunity for the participants legitimately to acknowledge that they do not want to discuss this issue in that context.

Being open gives the interviewer the opportunity to bring up the question as to whether it is useful to continue the interview; this might, for instance, be the case when a male interviewee is making sexually suggestive remarks. This might not only be traditional male impression behaviour, it might also cover the fact that he is scared to talk about his emotions or insecurities. Explicitly raising the topic of his behaviour (instead of ignoring it or ending the interview abruptly) might give way to a fruitful interview. An interesting question that a skilled interviewer would ask him is whether this type of behaviour was common in his interactions with girls and women. Skilled interviewers are thus able to turn barriers and conflict into productive data collection. There will, however, be cases where a participant simply does not want to discuss a particularly traumatic experience (such as, for example, having been raped) and this must be respected by the interviewer.

Emotions

Interviewers often fear the emotional reactions of participants in response, for example, to questions on masturbation or negative sexual experiences. This fear needs to be addressed during training, as it may provoke the interviewer to ignore certain topics and thus protect the participant (although, in fact, it is the interviewer who is being protected). Of course, the aim of the interview is to gather information and not to elicit (negative) emotions in the participant. On the other hand, a good interview without the emotional layer being addressed is hard to imagine. Emotions do occur, and the essential lesson is that the interviewer need not fear these. In a recent sexual biography study (van Zessen, 1995), apparently neutral questions about the emotional relationship between and with the parents turned out to arouse strong emotions in a lot of interviewees (much more so than with the "sexual" questions). The interviewer should acknowledge and, if necessary, try to verbalise the emotions (for example, "does this make you sad?"), but never ignore them. Sometimes it is useful to suggest a short break, have a cup of coffee or tea, and ask whether the participant wishes to continue. In our experience with hundreds of in-depth interviews, it is more useful for the participants to finish the interview than to break it off – and usually this is also what they themselves prefer. Interviewers should be extremely careful with participants' emotions, but it is important to emphasise that emotions of whatever colour or intensity are an essential part of people's (sexual) lives and, in that sense, are informative and useful to know about.

Interviewers who themselves get emotional during an interview – be it sadness or confusion or being attracted to the participant – should decide whether it is better to postpone the interview and/or arrange another interviewer. The potential for interviewers' emotional reactions, and a strategy for dealing with them, should have been addressed in the training sessions.

Interviewing about Sex

A prerequisite for an open and frank interview about sexuality is an open-minded and accepting interviewer. Especially with insecure or embarrassed participants, every insecurity or uneasiness on the part of the interviewer will translate into an uneasy and uninviting atmosphere. Although some European cultures may appear very open and permissive where sex is concerned, talking about private sexual experiences and emotions is often difficult. More than with other sensitive topics, interviewing about sex requires that an interviewer is able to be specific in his or her questioning since many participants will find it hard to bring up their private thoughts or actions spontaneously. By being open and specific about sex, and non-judgemental at the same time, an interviewer can, so to speak, *give permission* to bring up these matters. The use of language is important; the interviewer must understand the terms of the participants, and decide on a type of sexual language to use in his or her questions (vernacular, the participants' terms, medical jargon). It is the interviewer's task to ensure that both understand each other. An important part of interviewer training is to avoid ambiguous or euphemistic sex talk.

A word of comfort may be that experienced sex interviewers know that it is usually remarkably easy to get people to talk very frankly about their intimate life, although this does, of course, depend on cultural backgrounds (although assumptions in this regard should not be made; we have found that people from traditionally "closed" cultures sometimes welcome the opportunity to talk with an interested and supportive interviewer). Experienced interviewers also know that it pays to be curious, to probe and ask specific questions, both in the quality of data and in the *rapport* with the participant. Many interviewees have told interviewers in our research that they never revealed so much of their sexual life to anyone, including close friends and partners. They found the interview a useful and enjoyable experience – an outcome that we can use to motivate others to participate in similar studies.

Despite the traumas of having to convince ethical committees of the value of the research, we have found that many participants actually end the interview by thanking us for taking the time to listen to them! Nevertheless, it must always be remembered that talking about these issues may induce fear and concern amongst some participants – either at the time or subsequently – so we routinely provide a contact list of telephone numbers (for example, the local AIDS Helpline, health promotion department, and, sometimes, the interviewer's).

Using the Interviewer's Observations

Especially in cases where the researcher is not an interviewer, a lot of information may get lost because the transcription (or even the audiotape) does not convey the non-verbal information or the atmosphere during the interview. Based on previous studies, we find it useful to collect information on the impressions of the interviewer. This can be in the form of a post-interview report that needs to be completed directly after the interview. It should try to capture the essentials of the atmosphere and interviewer–participant interaction. Often, this information does not add to the analysis of the transcript, but sometimes it will. For instance, when a participant appears very composed and rational in the transcript, whereas the interviewer noted that the participant was extremely tense and had tears in his or her eyes for most of the interview, this might prompt the analyst to regard the apparent absence of emotions in the transcripts from another perspective.

Co-presence

Sometimes participants want a friend or partner to be present during the interview. We strongly recommend that no other people than the participant and interviewer are in the same room, but in cases where this is not possible, the interview should be postponed to another time and/or location. Hennink and Diamond (Chapter 2.5) discuss the risks posed by the presence of others to levels of honesty, "showing off" and other possibilities.

PRACTICAL MATTERS

Location

Asking participants to come to a central location (research institute, university) and be interviewed there may shorten the data collection phase and make more efficient use of interviewers' time. Travel costs of participants should be reimbursed and an incentive may motivate them to make the trip. Further, interviewer safety is easier to ensure when the interviews are held centrally, especially if it can be arranged that a colleague is in a nearby room in the building.

Safety

In cases where a central location is not feasible, or where participants are reluctant or unable to travel, it is essential to have a safety protocol available that prescribes precautions that interviewers have to take. Obvious precautions are to inform the fieldwork coordinator or a friend of the time and place of the interview, promise to call at a given moment, and have the interviewer carry a portable phone during fieldwork; we normally recommend that such phone calls be made in the presence of the participant so that they are aware of the precautions being taken. In cases where the interviewer feels threatened when seeing the participant, we advise them to reflect whether they feel safe enough to continue, or try to arrange another appointment at a different time, place or with a different interviewer. In our experience, such occurrences are uncommon, but may be more likely to occur when certain subpopulations are targeted. Despite their relative infrequency, however, comprehensive coping strategies should be devised during the training before these situations arise.

Recording and Storing

It may seem obvious, but an important practical matter is to ensure that all recording equipment is in good working order, and that interviewers carry spare batteries, adapters and tapes. We recommend using the best quality tape-recorders that can be afforded within the project resources, since some people talk about potentially embarrassing events very quietly indeed. It is extremely frustrating to discover, after a particularly rich and informative interview, that much of the speech has been lost.

It is essential to ask permission to tape the interview; this can be justified by explaining how it is impossible to write down everything the participant says and that it would be a waste not to make full use of the time and effort going into the interview. It is also important to inform participants about the storing and destruction of the tapes, and the ways that the anonymity of, and access to, the material will be guarded. In privacy laws and regulations, there is usually a time period described after which the data can be destroyed. When the data are to be transferred to the public domain after a certain period, it is obviously essential to prevent identification of the participants. This can be a time-consuming operation, as it is absolutely unacceptable simply to remove names and addresses from the top of the interview; the whole transcript needs to be scanned for referrals to living area, type of education and profession, names of parents, partners or friends, meeting places and other factors that may identify the individual person, or even the neighbourhood. For the same reason, it is essential to be careful in the presentation and choice of quotes when preparing reports.

Resources

Great care needs to be taken in costing research proposals properly. Sufficient time needs to be allocated to selection of interviewers, training, developing interviewer skills, conducting test interviews, developing the protocol, finding participants, carrying out the interviews, analysis and report writing. In our experience, a full-time interviewer may conduct ten interviews per week at a maximum, but only when recruitment and fieldwork coordination work are at an optimum. In practice, the number of interviews per interviewer is substantially lower. Conducting more than two per day is very difficult, and often leads to loss of data quality as well as fatigue.

In some kinds of research, a short and intense data collection period will be an advantage, or even a prerequisite (for instance, when the impact of a national AIDS prevention campaign has to be evaluated, it is desirable that all participants are interviewed as closely as possible to prevent time lag effects). On the other hand, it may be an advantage to spread the data collection over a longer time period; starting slowly with fieldwork offers the opportunity of intense feedback to, and between, the interviewers. Conducting in-depth interviewing is no easy task, and data quality certainly profits from a longer learning period. Further, a slow inflow of new transcripts makes a thorough analysis of the first interviews possible and offers the opportunity to use the outcomes in adaptations of the protocol, its use in practice, the sampling criteria, or the recruitment channels. Unless there are practical and/or financial reasons to have the data collected in a condensed period, we advise reserving one year for recruitment, interviewing and transcription, although this will obviously depend on the desired sample size and resource constraints. The major and most time-consuming part of the conceptual analysis can then be almost complete at the same time as the fieldwork is finished. In preparing costings for this type of work, and in addition to payments for staff, travel, office costs, and so on, it is essential to make sufficient allowance for the costs of transcription of the material. We use a rough guide of seven or eight hours of transcription time needed for each one hour of taped material; what this means in practice is that more than one transcriber might be needed if the interviews are being conducted close to each other, so as to avoid a long lag in obtaining the typed transcripts. More detailed transcribing (for example, where pauses and speech errors are to be fully notated) requires substantially more transcribing time; some researchers allow one week per interview for this level of detail.

SUMMARY

In our experience, the key to effective interviewing on sensitive topics is adequate and comprehensive preparation. Through careful selection and training of suitable interviewers, through anticipating possible problems that might arise, through ensuring that the participants find the experience worthwhile and non-threatening, and through ensuring that sight is never lost of the original aims of the research, the process should run smoothly and efficiently. A great deal has been learned about young people's sexual conduct in a relatively short period of time. It is interesting that when we started out on our own various research projects, we were told by some others that we were wasting our time, and that we would never get people to talk honestly and openly about their sexual lives and experiences. We believe that these sceptics' fears were unfounded, and that we are getting more able to explore this important domain. Given the diversity of experience between and within different cultures and subcultures, however, there is still much to be done.

REFERENCES

Ajzen, I. & Fishbein, M. (1980). *Understanding Attitudes and Predicting Social Behavior.* Englewood Cliffs, NJ: Prentice-Hall.

Breakwell, G. & Fife-Schaw, C. (1992). Sexual activities and preferences in a UK sample of 16–20 year olds. *Archives of Sexual Behaviour,* **21**, 271–293.

Coxon, A. (1988). The numbers game – gay lifestyles, epidemiology of AIDS and social science. In P. Aggleton & H. Homans (Eds.), *Social Aspects of AIDS.* Lewes: Falmer Press.

Fife-Schaw, C. & Breakwell, G. (1992). Estimating sexual behaviour parameters in the light of AIDS: a review of recent UK studies of young people. *AIDS Care,* **4**(2): 187–201.

Ford, N. (1990). *AIDS Awareness and Socio-sexual Lifestyles of Young People in Torbay and District.* Institute of Population Studies, University of Exeter.

Ford, N. & Bowie, C. (1989), Urban–rural variation in the level of heterosexual activity of young people. *Area,* **21**(3): 237–248.

Ford, N. & Morgan, K. (1989). Heterosexual lifestyles of young people in an English city. *Journal of Population and Social Studies,* **1**(2), 167–185.

Glaser, B.G. & Strauss, A. (1967). *The Discovery of Grounded Theory.* Chicago, IL: Aldine.

Ingham, R. (1994). Some speculations on the concept of rationality. In Albrecht, G. (Ed.), *Advances in Medical Sociology, vol IV: A Reconsideration of Models of Health Behavior Change* (pp. 89–111). Greenwich, CN: JAI Press.

Ingham, R., Woodcock, A. & Stenner, K. (1992). The limitations of rational decision making models as applied to young people's sexual behaviour. In P. Aggleton, P. Davies & G. Hart (Eds.), *AIDS: Rights, Risk and Reason.* London: Falmer Press.

Ingham, R., Jaramazovic, E., Stevens, D., Vanwesenbeeck, I. & van Zessen, G. (1996). *Protocol for Comparative Qualitative Studies on Sexual Conduct and HIV Risks.* Deliverable Seven submitted to European Commission Biomed Concerted Action, BMHI-CT94–1338.

Ingham, R. & van Zessen, G. (1997). From individual properties to interactional processes. In L. Van Campenhoudt, M. Cohen, G. Guizzardi & D. Hausser (Eds.), *Sexual Interactions and HIV Risk; New Conceptual Perspectives in European Research,* London: Taylor and Francis.

Kinsey, A. C., Pomeroy, W. & Martin, C. (1948). *Sexual Behavior in the Human Male.* Philadelphia, PA: Saunders.

Kinsey, A. C., Pomeroy, W. & Martin, C. (1953). *Sexual Behavior in the Human Female.* Philadelphia, PA: Saunders.

Kippax, S. & Crawford, J. (1993). Flaws in the theory of reasoned action. In D. Terry, C. Gallois & M. McCamish (Eds.), *The Theory of Reasoned Action; its Application to AIDS-preventive Behaviour.* Oxford: Pergamon Press.

Rademakers, J., Luijkx, J.B., van Zessen, G., Zijlmans, W., Straver, C. & Van der Rijt, G. (1992). *AIDS-preventie in heteroseksuele contacten. (AIDS-prevention in heterosexual contacts)*. Amsterdam: Swets and Zeitlinger.

Rosenstock, I.M. (1974). The Health Belief Model and preventive health behaviour. *Health Education Monographs*, **2**, 354–386.

van Zessen, G. (1995). *Wisseland Contact; Seksuele Levensverhalen van Mensen met Veel Partners*. Leiden: DSWO Press.

van Zessen, G. & Sandfort, Th. (1991). *Seksualiteit in Nederland* (Sexuality in the Netherlands). Amsterdam: Swets and Zeitlinger.

Interviewing Children with Learning Disabilities

Rebecca Milne
University of Portsmouth, UK

INTRODUCTION

This chapter examines the interviewing of a vulnerable population, namely children with learning disabilities. The chapter will firstly explain what learning disabilities are and will then examine how children with learning disabilities are treated within the criminal justice system. The third subsection of this chapter will outline what psychologists know about the memory capabilities of this population and then will discuss the best ways to elicit accurate information from this group for legal purposes. An examination of the efficacy of the cognitive interview for this group will be made and the chapter will end with a discussion concerning a "special" group of children – those who use facilitated communication devices.

WHAT IS MEANT BY LEARNING DISABILITIES?

Terminology

It is necessary first to give a brief description of terminology. This chapter will use the term "children with learning disabilities", which is the preferred term for this population in the UK. However, in the USA the preferred term for this same group of individuals appears to be "children with mental retardation". The term "intellectual disability" is also used. The one common theme which exists on

Handbook of the Psychology of Interviewing. Edited by A. Memon and R. Bull.
© 1999 John Wiley & Sons Ltd.

both sides of the Atlantic is "people first" language, where it is rightly said that an individual with learning disabilities is a person first and foremost and that their disability is a side issue (Fernald, 1995). Other terms which are seen throughout this literature, especially in relation to policing and the law, are "mental handicap" and "mental disorder". The former is yet another term for people with learning disabilities while the latter term is more wide-ranging and also includes people with mental illness and other vulnerable groups. Finally, with regard to children with learning disability, the British educational system currently refers to this group as "children with learning difficulties" (Brown & Turk, 1992).

Definitions

The term learning disability encompasses a wide variety of cognitive deficits and a wide range of abilities and disabilities. Despite considerable research effort and many attempts at a definition there is still no generally accepted operational definition of what constitutes learning disability. This is because learning disabilities are a heterogeneous group of difficulties (Hooper & Willis, 1989). Thus, the definition differs somewhat depending on the domain (legal or educational, for example) from which it arises.

The Legal Definition

The Mental Health Act, section 1 (1983) defines mental impairment as "a state of arrested or incomplete development of mind which includes significant impairment of intelligence and social functioning" and severe mental impairment as "a state of arrested or incomplete development of mind which includes severe impairment of intelligence and social functioning". This legislation thus mentions three characteristics: development of the mind, and impairment of intellectual and social functioning. Only the latter two categories are open to meaningful operational definition, whereas the former category can be defined but its specification can be subject to interpretation (Bull & Cullen, 1992). The ascertainment of levels of intellectual and social functioning may be carried out by appropriate psychometric and formal testing. Intellectual functioning is most commonly measured with intelligence tests, e.g. Wechsler Adult Intelligence Scale (WAIS), which gives an intelligence quotient (IQ), though a single IQ figure is now rarely used; instead it is much more valid to use confidence limits. The British Psychological Society (BPS) recommends (see Bull & Cullen, 1992) that IQs between 55 and 69 equate with significant impairment of intelligence and IQs below 54 equate with severe impairment. The World Health Organisation classification (WHO, 1982) further subdivides people with learning disabilities into one of four categories; mild (IQ of 50–70), moderate (IQ of 36–49), severe (IQ of 20–35) and profound (IQ of below 20).

The measure for social and behavioural functioning is less precise but there do exist well recognised and standardised instruments. Relevant dimensions are a person's skills and abilities to provide independently for their own eating and drinking needs and to keep themselves clean/warm and clothed appropriately. The BPS recommends that a person who needs partial help in these areas has significant impairment and a person who requires continual assistance in meeting these needs has severe impairment. Measures assessing social and behavioural functioning also examine areas such as domestic skills, educational abilities and socialisation. Groups who are interested in the welfare of people with learning disabilities are moving towards a definition which does not label people according to mild, moderate, severe and profound learning disability based on IQ but are instead looking at the intensity and pattern of changing supports needed by an individual over a lifetime.

Educational Definition (Children)

The Education Act 1981, section 156 (2)(a) and (b) defines learning difficulty as "A condition which exists if a child has significantly greater difficulty in learning than the majority of children of his age or a disability which either prevents or hinders him from making use of educational facilities generally provided for children of his age in schools within the area of the local education authority". The presence of a learning difficulty, if not already identified, is usually observed at school (Lyall et al., 1995) and the Report of the Committee of Enquiry into the Education of Handicapped Children and Young People (Warnock, 1978; The Warnock Report) concluded that in Britain at any one time about one child in six is likely to require some form of special educational provision. These figures include both temporary learning difficulty (e.g. having problems learning to read) and more persistent long-term learning difficulties. Learning difficulties have been subdivided into mild, moderate, severe and specific learning difficulties (e.g. particular problem in reading) and there still exist separate schools for children with learning difficulties (though the new governmental policy of integration may diminish the numbers of these special schools) and these fall into one of three types: schools for children with mild/moderate learning difficulties (MLD schools), schools for children with severe learning difficulties (SLD schools) and schools for children with emotional or behavioural problems (EBD schools).

CHILDREN WITH LEARNING DISABILITIES AND THE CRIMINAL JUSTICE SYSTEM

How then are children with learning disabilities treated within the criminal justice system? This section will first examine the victimisation of this population.

Victimisation of Children with Learning Disabilities and Children with Learning Disabilities as Witnesses: The Statistics

People with learning disabilities because of their vulnerability are more often victimised (e.g. Endicott, 1992; Turk & Brown, 1992; Westcott & Cross, 1996), more often solicited for crime and more often apprehended than others (Conley, Luckasson & Bouthilet, 1992; Gudjonsson et al., 1993). Furthermore, people with learning disabilities are often the only witnesses to crimes against other people with learning disabilities; for example, because of living in residential homes. Further, children with learning disabilities are also more likely to live in inner cities (Ramey, Campbell & Finkelstein, 1984) where there is a greater chance of witnessing a crime (Dent, 1992). Nevertheless, society has a responsibility to investigate such matters (Bull, 1995). There is a problem when examining the prevalence of abuse in this population in that it is estimated that as many as one in ten children with learning disabilities may have become impaired as a direct result of physical assault or neglect (Groce, 1988). Research into the direct causal relationship between sexual abuse and learning disabilities has, however, yet to be conducted, although it is well documented that developmental delays are an important sequelae of the abuse itself (e.g. Sinason, 1986). Children with learning disabilities are therefore in a "double jeopardy" in that an individual's disability may provoke or make the individual more susceptible to abuse, but at the same time abuse may exacerbate or even bring about the disabling condition in the first place (Gelles, 1973). Abuse as a causative factor to learning disabilities, though, is less likely to be recognised compared to disability as a risk factor for abuse (Brown & Turk, 1992; Camblin, 1982). This is because indicators of abuse may be attributed to the disability rather than to the abuse itself. Furthermore, information pertaining to abuse is almost always partial, usually uncorroborated and sometimes conflicting (Sobsey & Varnhagen, 1989) and allegations, suspicions, reports or disclosures may all be recorded together, thus making research into the incidence of abuse even more difficult.

Are children with learning disabilities at more risk of abuse? Westcott (1991) seems to think the answer to this question is "yes". In her review of over twenty studies examining this issue, she concluded that disabled children are at an increased risk of abuse. However, because of the large differences in populations used and definitions adopted by the various authors she believed that it is impossible to give an accurate incidence figure. Similar findings have been found in the USA (e.g. National Resource Center on Child Sexual Abuse, 1993). There are approximately 360 000 children with disabilities (aged 16 and under) in the UK (Office of Population and Census Surveys (OPCS), 1989) (that is, about 3% of the child population). Approximately 5500 of these children live in residential care and of these living in care 15% are known to have been abused (OPCS, 1989).

Characteristics said to make children with learning disabilities more vulnerable to abuse include: dependency on others for basic and social needs (Tharinger, Horton & Millea, 1990; Muccigrosso, 1991; Russell, 1993;

Womendez & Schneiderman, 1991); lack of control or choice over their own lives (Russell, 1993); compliance and obedience instilled as good behaviour (Craft & Hitching, 1989; Russell, 1993; Trevelyan, 1988); lack of knowledge about sex and misunderstandings about sexual advances (Russell, 1993); isolation and rejection by others which increases responsiveness to attention and affection (accompanied by an increased desire to please) (Muccigrosso, 1991; Sobsey & Mansell, 1990; Tharinger et al., 1990); inability to communicate experiences and lacking the language to avoid the abuse in the first place (Wertheimer, Bargh & Russell, 1994); an inability to differentiate between different types of touching (Brown & Craft, 1989); having multi-carers and residing in social service run environments (Ammerman, Lubetsky & Drudy, 1991; Sobsey & Doe, 1991; Westcott & Clément, 1992).

Sullivan, Vernon and Scanlan (1987) contend that children with learning disabilities are assumed to be "less human" and thus abuse is "not that inhumane", i.e. a licence to abuse disabled children because in society they are repeatedly stigmatised (Gabarino, 1987). Furthermore, society holds myths that no-one could or would abuse a disabled child (Marchant, 1991). However, far from protecting the child a disability would seem to protect the abuser (Kennedy, 1990). It is society's response to people with learning disabilities that may lead to their increased abuse more than the disability itself or any other attribute of the abuse victim (Middleton, 1992; Muccigrosso, 1991; Sobsey & Varnhagen, 1989; Waxman, 1991). Sobsey & Doe (1991; Doe, 1991) suggested that an ecological model of abuse is necessary to understand the abuse of children (and adults) who have learning disabilities. Interacting factors at three different levels are considered (Bronfenbrenner, 1977): the microsystem which includes the perpetrator–victim interaction (abuse), the macrosystem, which is the social context in which the abuse takes place, and the exosystem, which is the broader societal context, and includes those social and cultural beliefs which interact with the other two levels (see Westcott and Cross, 1996 for more on the theoretical nature of abuse and victimisation).

Thus, for many reasons children with learning disabilities may be at greater risk of abuse and of being witnesses to crimes, especially those committed against other children with learning disabilities.

Interviewing of Children with Learning Disabilities: Current Guidelines

In England and Wales the guidelines for interviewing child witnesses/victims with a view to possible criminal proceedings that Child Protection Unit (police officers and social workers) interviewers have, i.e. the Memorandum of Good Practice (MOGP, Home Office and Department of Health, 1992), does not in any sense cater for children with learning disabilities (Marchant & Page, 1997; Westcott & Cross, 1996). (The reason for this is that so little work had been published on this topic at the time of publication of these guidelines). The

MOGP does briefly mention children with special needs, in essence by telling interviewers that they should develop strategies to minimise the effect of the child's learning disability. However, the strategies which the MOGP suggests for use with ordinary children have not been researched to examine the reliability and validity of such procedures for use with this special group of children. Thus, professionals who are dealing with victims who have a learning disability have no guidance on how to interview this population, save for a document written for the Scottish legal system (Bull & Cullen, 1992, 1993) and a brief book chapter (Bull, 1995). Very little detailed guidance is available about ways to interview children with learning disabilities.

These professionals are becoming increasingly aware of their lack of expertise in assisting children with learning disabilities to give accounts of what has happened to them (Baladerian, 1993; Brennan & Brennan, 1994; Sayers, 1994; Westcott & Cross, 1996) and they are interested in developing their skills in order to interview children with learning disabilities appropriately (Brown, 1993). Furthermore, police officers and social workers who are trained in child protection issues may have limited experience of learning disabilities. Social workers with this experience may have limited experience of criminal investigations (Kennedy, 1990; Marchant & Page, 1997; Temkin, 1994). Indeed, this is exactly what Endicott (1992) noted in a Technical Report to the Canadian Department of Justice; "The essential barriers and gaps in accommodating the special needs of witnesses with communication disabilities are a function of the lack of adequate training of sufficient numbers of personnel for such highly specialised work" (p. 55).

Thus, many researchers and practitioners alike have recommended that training for the relevant practitioners is essential, which should include knowledge about different disabilities, how to *interview* this population and to increase the awareness of how social prejudice against people with learning disabilities may compound the effects of abuse (e.g. Baladerian, 1993; Davies et al., 1994; Russell, 1993; Sinason, 1992; Westcott, 1993). However, what should this interviewing training consist of?

MEMORY CAPABILITIES OF PEOPLE WITH LEARNING DISABILITIES, SUGGESTIBILITY AND APPROPRIATE QUESTIONING STRATEGIES

Historically people with learning disabilities have been regarded as unreliable witnesses because it is believed that their memory systems are inherently defective; therefore it is assumed that they are susceptible to suggestion and lack the skills accurately to report events (Dent, 1986; Perlman et al., 1994). Indeed, Sayers (1994) interviewed professionals involved in child protection investigations and in general found that the "adults viewed the children's (with learning disabilities) statements as unreliable products of 'a vivid imagination'" (p. 76).

However, there is an urgent need for research into the veracity of these percep-tions, as this population is over-represented in reported cases of sexual abuse (e.g. Westcott & Cross, 1996) and there is seldom witness or physical evidence available to corroborate the testimony of sexual abuse victims. Thus cases be-come a word-against-word issue in which the credibility of the victim is pitted against that of the perpetrator (Mann, 1985). Three primary questions should be asked:

1. Do children with learning disabilities have the functional memory capacity to report events accurately and adequately?
2. Can certain questioning formats be used to aid their accurate reporting of events?
3. Are such children especially prone to suggestion?

Each of these questions will be considered in turn. However, it must be noted that the amount of research and the degree of professional expertise on these three topics is very limited (Bull, 1995).

Memory Capabilities of Children with Learning Disabilities

Children with learning disabilities have particular cognitive and communication difficulties which affect the way in which they recount what has happened to them. These include poor memory, a limited vocabulary and difficulty in under-standing sentences. It must be noted, however, that there is a great heterogeneity in the learning disability population; thus not all children with learning dis-abilities will possess all the characteristics which will be discussed in the follow-ing sections. Indeed some of the abilities of some interviewees with learning disabilities will exceed those that would be expected from a child of average intelligence, and learning disability does not necessarily equate with a complete inability to remember, or with a complete inability to communicate a to-be-remembered (TBR) event. Some learning disabilities do not lead to memory problems; for example, children with autism often have very good recall capa-cities (Jordon & Powell, 1992).

The free recall of children with learning disabilities has been found to be sparse, and prompting has been found to be necessary (Westcott, 1991). One reason for this is that children with learning disabilities tend to rely on others to take the lead and they have a lack of confidence and self-esteem (Temkin, 1994). For legal purposes, however, questions need to be asked in order to elicit more detail, but questioning can also increase the probability of inaccurate informa-tion being reported.

Poor memory performance characterises children with learning disabilities (Dockrill & McShane, 1993). All the memory stores and memory systems have been thought to be deficient to a greater or lesser extent in children with learning disabilities (Detterman, 1979). Ellis (1963) proposed one of the first explanations of memory deficit in such children by suggesting that memory traces decay more rapidly. However, in general, recent research does not support this view (Kail, 1990). While children with mild and moderate learning disability remember less well than do their peers, the rate of forgetting appears to be similar in both groups. Variations in the use of mnemonic strategies also contribute to performance differences among children with learning disabilities on many kinds of memory tasks (Torgesen, Kistner & Morgan, 1987). Strategic problems have been identified both at encoding and retrieval (Butterfield & Ferretti, 1987). Children with mild learning disabilities, however, can be taught to use mnemonic strategies and enhanced performance can be obtained and maintained for appreciable time periods (Brown, Campione & Murphy, 1974). Thus, interviewing techniques which help children to access information by providing retrieval strategies should enhance recall.

Appropriate Interviewing Strategies

Researchers have recommended the use of the phased approach of interviewing and for "special care" to be taken when interviewing such a population of interviewees (e.g. Brennan & Brennan, 1994; Bull, 1995; Bull & Cullen, 1992). However, there are limitations in this method of interviewing for children with learning disabilities, especially for those children who normally use facilitated communication techniques. For example, as free report is often limited this leaves little for the interviewer to go on in terms of follow-up questioning (see Marchant and Page, 1992, 1993 for a more in-depth view of the criticisms of the MOGP interview for this group of children). As the phased approach of interviewing is described in detail in the MOGP only additional strategies which have been identified for use with children with learning disabilities will be outlined here. However, "very little prior research has been conducted on how best to interview people with learning disabilities, e.g. there has been virtually no attention given to establishing the reliability and validity of answers given by mentally retarded persons" (Sigelman et al., 1981, p. 348). There is still a dearth of literature on this topic, there being few studies which have examined how much more information can be elicited from children with learning disabilities if questioned appropriately, i.e. little practical information is available concerning optimal interviewing techniques (Dent, 1986).

Interview Duration

The Canadian Law Reform Commission consultations proposed that interviewers could make the process of interviewing less overwhelming if the interviewers just slowed down their pace of conversation a little and thus lengthened the duration of the interviews. Indeed people with learning disabilities themselves have recommended "talking to you not too fast" (Brennan & Brennan, 1994, p. 143). Furthermore, children with learning disabilities often have shorter attention spans and thus may need regular and frequent breaks (Bull, 1995).

Interview Setting

Children with learning disabilities lack adaptability to unusual situations and thus police stations and court, which are unusual to most people, are likely to be harder for children with learning disabilities to cope with (Bull, 1995). Poor adaptation has a deleterious effect on memory and communication and increases stress levels. Furthermore, the interview room should be free of distractions, a particular problem with children with learning disabilities (Baladerian, 1992).

Rapport

Children with learning disabilities may need extra time spent on getting to know a person; thus, rapport is imperative for a successful interview (Bull, 1995). Indeed, professionals working within this sphere have noted that 30–40 minutes of rapport building is not unusual (Marchant & Page, 1997). Children with learning disabilities also differ extensively from one another in their level of social, emotional and cognitive development, communication skills, degree of understanding and particular needs; thus these levels of ability can be assessed in this phase of the interview. Brennan and Brennan (1994) strongly advocated that interviewers of people with learning disabilities should adopt a very interactive model of questioning, which requires interviewers to take on a lot more responsibility for the acquisition of accurate information. These researchers emphasised a need to match the demands of the interview and questioning format to the communication ability of the interviewee. As a consequence, interviewers need to modify their interviewing style. For example, children with learning disabilities often adapt common words and phrases and ascribe unusual meanings to them. Rapport can therefore help to identify language abilities and help the interviewer also assess the likely competence of the witness.

Free Report (see also section on memory capabilities above)

In summary, children with learning disabilities provide accurate but incomplete free narrative accounts of a TBR event; thus questioning is required to elicit specific detail for legal purposes (Bull, 1995; Sigelman et al., 1981). However, the classic work of Loftus (e.g. 1979) has demonstrated that particular wording of questions can affect the later recall of adults in the general population. Thus, if children with learning disabilities are relying more heavily on external cues for more complete recall, more care is needed not to influence their recall by careless interviewing techniques (Bull, 1995). Furthermore, since children with learning disabilities, not unlike the general population, do not usually appreciate the interviewer's need for full details, this should be explicitly stated (Bull, 1995). Also interviewees should be explicitly told that the interviewer does not know what has occurred, as some children with learning disabilities may assume that the interviewer is somehow privy to what happened to them (Bull, 1995).

Questioning

Questions should be kept as simple and concrete as possible and abstract concepts and double negatives should not be used (Baladerian, 1992). As stated by people with learning disabilities, "Law people . . . don't (shouldn't) use big words, police should keep things simple" (Brennan & Brennan, 1994, p. 143). Interviewers should tailor the lengths of their sentences to those of the interviewees and use plain English (Baladerian, 1992). Furthermore, the interviewee should be asked to repeat back in their own words what was said to them to ensure that they have understood (Bull, 1995). Children with learning disabilities have difficulty with time (Malin, 1980); thus care should be taken with regard to this detail.

What types of questions should be used with children with learning disabilities? Pear and Wyatt (1914) found that the free recall of children with learning disabilities was as reliable as that of children without learning disabilities. However, their prompted recall was much less reliable, with 50% of their answers to questions being inaccurate. Dent (1986) examined the effects of three types of questioning for use with children with mild learning disabilities (8–11 years of age): free recall, general questions and specific questions. Specific questions were found to produce the most information, followed by general questions, with free recall producing the least information. However, information produced in response to specific questions was the least accurate with more than 30% of it being incorrect. The information in response to general questions was the most accurate (10% being incorrect). Thus, Dent (1986) concluded that "general, open-ended questions would appear to be optimal for use with mildly mentally handicapped children" (p. 17).

Dent (1992) also conducted research comparing children with and without learning disabilities and adults from the general population using the same three questioning styles as outlined above (Dent, 1986). Again, general questions consistently elicited the best blend of completeness and accuracy for all three population groups. However, free report consistently produced the most accurate reports. Specific questions produced a large increase in quantity of detail but at the expense of accuracy, particularly for the two groups of children. However, specific questions need not involve biasing as was suggested by Dent (1986, 1992). More research is necessary which examines the various types of specific questions which exist (Bull, 1995). It is important to note though that children of all abilities were as reliable as adults from the general population when questioned appropriately. However, "more research is needed on how to reduce errors of omission in children's recall without increasing errors of commission" (Dent, 1992, pp. 11–12).

The disadvantages of people with learning disabilities (sometimes at least) are not insurmountable. Complete, accurate and clear accounts can be obtained from children with learning disabilities as long as the interviewing methods used are non-biasing.

Inappropriate Interviewing Strategies: Suggestibility Issues

Since children without learning disabilities are believed by some to be susceptible to suggestive questioning compared to older children and adults, are children with learning disabilities yet more suggestible? The overview papers concerning children's suggestibility (e.g. Ceci & Bruck, 1993) mention very little on this topic and one would therefore assume that there is little research examining these issues. A few studies have suggested that people with learning disabilities are particularly susceptible to suggestion (e.g. Pear & Wyatt, 1914). Lorsbach, Melendez and Carroll-Maher (1991), and Lorsbach and Ewing (1995), examined the development of source monitoring in children with learning disabilities and concluded that such children were deficient in monitoring the source of event memories. Children with learning disabilities had a selective deficit in remembering the origin of their verbal memories. As a result of encoding deficits, children with learning disabilities may fail to incorporate contextual information that would enable them to identify the origin of the particular memory. Given their reported problems with memory retrieval (e.g. Howe, Brainerd & Kingma, 1985) children with learning disabilities may also experience difficulty gaining access to the source of the information that was stored with a specific event memory. Thus, children with learning disabilities may be more likely to base their answers on information that was obtained from a misleading or unreliable source (i.e. are more suggestible).

It is very important to ascertain how suggestible children with learning disabilities are to leading/misleading questions. The MOGP suggests the careful use of these question types, but only as a last resort at the end of the interview. Moreover, some researchers believe it necessary to use such questions to elicit information concerning abuse from children with learning disabilities (Temkin, 1994). Thus, research needs to examine how suggestible children with learning disabilities are, especially to such questions. Milne and Bull (1996) examined the relative levels of susceptibility to suggestion of children with and without learning disabilities of the same chronological ages. It was found that children with learning disabilities (of between 7 and 11 years of age) were significantly more likely to go along with misleading questions (i.e. questions which lead the child to the wrong answer). Indeed, children with learning disabilities were led by 63% of the questions whereas their "mainstream" counterparts were led by 41% of these types of questions.

THE EFFECTIVENESS OF THE CI FOR CHILDREN WITH LEARNING DISABILITIES

The cognitive interview (CI) was developed in the USA by Geiselman and Fisher (see Fisher & Geiselman, 1992 for a description of the CI) and aims to increase the quantity and quality of recall elicited from cooperative witnesses and victims, and possibly suspects of crime. The CI consists of techniques which aim to improve memory retrieval and dyadic communication. The CI has been found to increase the recall of correct information by approximately 35–45% for adult witnesses (see Köhnken et al., in press, for a meta-analysis) and is now recommended (Köhnken et al., in press) for use with children from the age of seven years and above (with the exception of the change perspective technique). As the CI aims to enhance recall through the use of non-biasing retrieval techniques it should increase the recall of children with learning disabilities. Milne and Bull (1996) therefore examined the effectiveness of the CI for use with this group of children and found that the CI enhanced the recall of correct information (83 correct facts recalled with the CI compared to 61 with the control interview) without any concomitant in incorrect (i.e. information which is discrepant with the event) or confabulated (i.e. information reported which did not exist in the event) details. Indeed, those interviewed with the CI reported information which was 79% accurate (compared to 76% accurate with the control interview). This is important as the control interview used in this study was similar to the MOGP interview. A similar study conducted by Price (1997) also found that while children with mild learning disabilities recalled less than ordinary children, the CI enhanced the recall of correct information for children with mild learning disabilities (almost double the amount compared to a MOGP control interview). Furthermore, it was found that the CI helped inoculate children (with and without learning disabilities) against subsequent misleading questions. This is another important finding as the MOGP recommends the careful use of such questions as a last resort (see also Milne et al., 1995). Thus, the CI could well be a useful technique for such children and further research is warranted.

FACILITATED COMMUNICATION

There are some children with whom we do not yet know how to communicate in ways which would be seen as evidentially safe, for example children with severe learning disabilities. However, there are a group of children who can be heard but through mediums other than the spoken word. These are children who use facilitated communication systems. Such non-verbal systems vary in their degree of sophistication, from the British Sign Language (a language in its own right – European Community, 1988) to Makaton (a much simpler system which has a core vocabulary of a limited number of signs – Westcott and Cross, 1996). Few professionals in social work or police forces have the ability to communicate using the child's preferred alternative method of communication and thus they will need to seek the advice of a human aid to communication (Westcott & Cross, 1996). Special planning and preparation is needed when such an interview is to be conducted. As yet, the criminal justice system has not opened its arms or addressed the many difficulties that exist when such communication techniques are used. (See Kennedy, 1992 for a fuller description of the problems that these groups of children face within the criminal justice system.)

CONCLUSION

This chapter it is hoped will leave the reader the message that children with learning disabilities, if questioned appropriately, can produce accurate reports of events that have occurred. However, what is urgently needed is the development of techniques which enhance such accounts. The cognitive interview could be one such technique. Future research should also address those who require facilitated communication techniques to aid in their reporting of events. Judicial procedures are not offering justice to these children. This is rendering them vulnerable to gross victimisation. Justice must be done regardless of people's disabilities.

REFERENCES

Ammerman, R.J., Lubetsky, M.J. & Drudy, K.F. (1991). Maltreatment of handicapped children. In R.T. Ammerman & M. Hersen (Eds.), *Case Studies in Family Violence*. New York: Plenum Press.

Baladerian, N.J. (1992). *Interviewing Skills to Use with Abuse Victims who have Developmental Disabilities*. Washington, DC: NARCEA.

Baladerian, N.J. (1993). Comment. In *Responding to Sexual Abuse of Children with Disabilities: Prevention, Investigation and Treatment*. Huntsville, AL: National Resource Center on Child Sexual Abuse.

Brennan, M. & Brennan, R. (1994). *Cleartalk: Police Responding to Intellectual Disability*. Wagga Wagga: School of Education, Charles Stuart University, Australia.

Bronfenbrenner, U. (1977). Toward an experimental ecology of human development. *American Psychologist*, **32**, 513–531.

Brown, A.L., Campione, J.C. & Murphy, M.D. (1974). Keeping track of changing variables: Long-term retention of a trained rehearsal strategy by retarded adolescents. *American Journal of Mental Deficiency*, **78**, 446–453.

Brown, H. (1993). Report on the Kent study. *NAPSAC Newsletter*, **3**, 3–6.

Brown, H. & Craft, A. (1989). *Thinking the Unthinkable: Papers on Sexual Abuse and People with Learning Difficulties*. London: FPA Education Unit.

Brown, H. & Turk, V. (1992). Defining sexual abuse as it affects adults with learning disabilities. *Mental Handicap*, **20**, 44–55.

Bull, R. (1995). Interviewing witnesses with communicative disability. In R. Bull & D. Carson (Eds.), *Handbook of Psychology in Legal Contexts*. Chichester: Wiley.

Bull, R. & Cullen, C. (1992). *Witnesses who have mental handicaps*. Document prepared for The Crown Office, Edinburgh.

Bull, R. & Cullen, C. (1993). Interviewing the mentally handicapped. *Policing*, **9**, 88–100.

Butterfield, E.C. & Ferretti, R.F. (1987). Toward a theoretical integration of cognitive hypotheses about intellectual differences among children. In J.G. Borkowski & J.D. Day (Eds.), *Cognition in Special Children: Comparative Approaches to Retardation, Learning Disabilities and Giftedness*. Norwood, NJ: Ablex.

Camblin, L.D. (1982). A survey of state efforts in gathering information on child abuse and neglect in handicapped populations. *Child Abuse and Neglect*, **6**, 465–472.

Ceci, S.J. & Bruck, M. (1993). Suggestibility of the child witness: A historical review and synthesis. *Psychological Bulletin*, **113**, 403–439.

Conley, R.W., Luckasson, R. & Bouthilet, G.N. (1992). *The Criminal Justice System and Mental Retardation*. Baltimore, MD: Paul. H. Brookes.

Craft, A. & Hitching, G.M. (1989). Keeping safe: Sex education and assertiveness skills. In H. Brown & A. Craft (Eds.), *Thinking the Unthinkable: Papers on Sexual Abuse and People with Learning difficulties*. London: FPA Education Unit.

Davies, G.M., Wilson, C., Mitchell, R. & Milsom, J. (1994). *Videotaping Children's Evidence: An Evaluation*. London: HMSO.

Dent, H. (1986). An experimental study of the effectiveness of different techniques of questioning mentally handicapped child witnesses. *British Journal of Clinical Psychology*, **25**, 13–17.

Dent, H. (1992). The effects of age and intelligence on eyewitnessing ability. In H. Dent and R. Flin (Eds.), *Children as Witnesses*. Chichester: Wiley.

Detterman, D.K. (1979). Memory in the mentally retarded. In N.R. Ellis (Ed.), *Handbook of Mental Deficiency, Psychological Theory and Research*. Hillsdale, NJ: Erlbaum.

Dockrill, J. & McShane, J. (1993). *Children's Learning Difficulties: A Cognitive Approach*. Oxford: Blackwell.

Doe, T. (1991). Towards an understanding: An ecological model of abuse. *Developmental Disabilities Bulletin*, **18**, 13–20.

Ellis, N.R. (1963). The stimulus trace and behavioral inadequacy. In N.R. Ellis (Ed.), *Handbook of Mental Deficiency*. New York: McGraw-Hill.

Endicott, E. (1992). *The impact of Bill C-15 on persons with communication disabilities*. Technical report to the Department of Justice, Canada.

Fernald, C.D. (1995). When in London . . .: Differences in disability language preferences among English-speaking countries. *Mental Retardation*, **33**, 99–103.

Fisher, R.P. & Geiselman, R.E. (1992). *Memory-enhancing Techniques for Investigative Interviewing: The Cognitive Interview*. Springfield, IL: Charles Thomas.

Gabarino, J. (1987). The abuse and neglect of special children: An introduction to the issues. In J. Gabarino, P.E. Brookhauser & J. Authier (Eds.), *Special Children – special risks. The Maltreatment of Children with Disabilities*. New York: De Gruyter.

Gelles, R. (1973). Child abuse as psychopathology: A sociological critique and reformulation. *American Journal of Orthopsychiatry*, **43**, 611–621.

Groce, N. (1988). Special groups at risk of abuse: The disabled. In M. Strauss (Ed.), *Abuse and Victimisation Across the Lifespan*. New York: Johns Hopkins University Press.

Gudjonsson, G., Clare, I., Rutter, S. & Pearse, J. (1993). Persons at risk during interviews in police custody: The identification of vulnerabilities. *Research Study No. 12. The Royal Commission on Criminal Justice*. HMSO: London.

Home Office and Department of Health. (1992). *Memorandum of Good Practice for Video Recorded Interviews with Child Witnesses for Criminal Proceedings*. London: Her Majesty's Stationery Office.

Hooper, S.R. & Willis, W.G. (1989). *Learning Disability Subtyping: Neuropsychological Foundations, Conceptual Models and Issues in Clinical Differentiation*. New York: Springer-Verlag.

Howe, M.L., Brainerd, C.J. & Kingma, J. (1985). Storage-retrieval processes of normal and learning disabled children: A stages-of-learning analysis of picture-word effects. *Child Development*, **56**, 1120–1133.

Jordon, R. & Powell, S. (1992). *Investigating memory processing in children with autism*. Paper presented at the BPS Conference, London.

Kail, R. (1990). *The Development of Memory in Children*. New York: Freeman.

Kennedy, M. (1990). The deaf child who is sexually abused – is there a need for a dual specialist? *Child Abuse Review*, **4**, 3–6.

Kennedy, M. (1992). Not the only way to communicate: A challenge to voice in child protection work. *Child Abuse Review*, **1**, 169–178.

Köhnken, G., Milne, R., Bull, R. & Memon, A. (in press). The cognitive interview: A meta-analysis. *Psychology, Crime and Law*.

Loftus, E.F. (1979). *Eyewitness Testimony*. Cambridge, MA: Harvard University Press.

Lorsbach, T.C. & Ewing, R.H. (1995). Source monitoring in children with learning disabilities. *International Journal of Disability, Development and Education*, **42**, 241–257.

Lorsbach, T.C., Melendez, D.M. & Carroll-Maher, A. (1991). Memory for source information in children with learning disabilities. *Learning and Individual Differences*, **3**, 135–147.

Lyall, I., Holland, A.J., Collins, S. & Styles, P. (1995). Incidence of persons with a learning disability detained in police custody. A needs assessment for service development. *Medical, Science and Law*, **35**, 61–71.

Malin, N. (1980). *Group homes for mentally handicapped adults. E.R.G. Report No. 9.* University of Sheffield.

Mann, E. (1985). The assessment of credibility of sexually abused children in criminal court cases. *American Journal of Forensic Psychiatry*, **6**, 9–15.

Marchant, R. (1991). Myths and facts about sexual abuse and children with disabilities. *Child Abuse Review*, **5**, 22–24.

Marchant, R. & Page, M. (1992). Bridging the gap: Investigating the abuse of children with multiple disabilities. *Child Abuse Review*, **1**, 179–183.

Marchant, R. & Page, M. (1993). *Bridging the Gap: Child Protection Work with Children with Multiple Disabilities.* London: NSPCC.

Marchant, R. & Page, M. (1997). The memorandum and disabled children. In H. Westcott and J. Jones (Eds.), *Perspectives on the Memorandum: Policy, Practice and Research in Investigative Interviewing.* Aldershot: Arena.

Middleton, L. (1992). *Children First: Working with Children and Disability.* London: Venture Press.

Milne, R. & Bull, R. (1996). Interviewing children with mild learning disability with the cognitive interview. In N.K. Clark & G.M. Stephenson (Eds.), *Investigative and Forensic Decision Making: Issues in Criminological Psychology*, No. 26. Leicester: British Psychological Society.

Milne, R., Bull, R., Köhnken, G. & Memon, A. (1995). The cognitive interview and suggestibility. In N.K. Clark & G.M. Stephenson (Eds.), *Criminal behaviour: Perceptions, Attributions and Rationality Issues in Criminological Psychology, No. 22.* Leicester: British Psychological Society.

Muccigrosso, L. (1991). Sexual abuse prevention strategies and programs for persons with developmental disabilities. *Sexuality and Disability*, **9**, 261–271.

National Resource Center on Child Sexual Abuse. (1993). *Responding to sexual abuse of children with disabilities: Prevention, investigation and treatment.* Huntsville, AL: National Resource Center on Child Sexual Abuse.

Office of Population and Census Surveys. (1989). *OPCS Surveys of Disability in the UK.* London: HMSO.

Pear, T.H. & Wyatt, S. (1914). The testimony of normal and mentally defective children. *British Journal of Psychology*, **6**, 388–419.

Perlman, N.B., Ericson, K.I., Esses, V.M. & Isaacs, B.J. (1994). The developmentally handicapped witness: Competency as a function of question format. *Law and Human Behavior*, **18**, 171–187.

Price, E. (1997). *Assessing the cognitive interview: How effective is it for use with children with mild learning disabilities?* Unpublished MSc dissertation, University of Portsmouth.

Ramey, C., Campbell, F. & Finkelstein, N. (1984). Course and structure of intellectual development in children with high risk for developmental retardation. In P. Brookes, R. Sperber & C. McCauley (Eds.), *Learning and Cognition in the Mentally Retarded.* New York: Lawrence Erlbaum.

Russell, P. (1993). Children with disabilities – a Challenge for child protection procedures. In H. Owen and J. Pritchard (Eds.), *Good Practice in Child Protection: A Manual for Professionals.* London: Jessica Kingsley Publishers.

Sayers, L. (1994). Objects without voices: An exploration of the experiences of parents and professionals who have been involved in an investigation of the abuse of a child with disabilities. Unpublished MA dissertation. In H. Westcott & M. Cross (1996). *This Far and no Further: Towards Ending the Abuse of Disabled Children.* Birmingham: Venture Press.

Sigelman, C.K., Budd, E.C., Spanhel, C.L. & Schoenrock, C.J. (1981). When in doubt say yes: Acquiescence in interviews with mentally retarded persons. *Mental Retardation, April*, 53–58.

Sinason, V. (1986). Secondary mental handicap and its relationship to trauma. *Psychoanalytic Psychotherapy*, **2**, 131–154.

Sinason, V. (1992). *Mental Handicap and the Human Condition: New Approaches*. London: Free Association Books.

Sobsey, D. & Doe, T. (1991). Patterns of sexual abuse and assault. *Sexuality and Disability*, **9**, 243–259.

Sobsey, D. & Mansell, S. (1990). The prevention of abuse of people with developmental disabilities. *Developmental Disabilities Bulletin*, **18**, 51–66.

Sobsey, D. & Varnhagen, C. (1989). Sexual abuse and exploitation of people with disabilities: Towards prevention and treatment. In M. Wapo and L. Gougen (Eds.), *Special Education across Canada*. Vancouver: Centre for Human Development and Research.

Sullivan, P.M., Vernon, M. & Scanlan, J.M. (1987). Sexual abuse of deaf youth. *American Annals of the Deaf*, **3**, 256–262.

Temkin, J. (1994). Disability, child abuse and criminal justice. *The Modern Law Review*, **57**, 402–418.

Tharinger, D., Horton, C.B. & Millea, S. (1990). Sexual abuse and exploitation of children and adults with mental retardation and other handicaps. *Child Abuse and Neglect*, **14**, 301–312.

Torgesen, J.K., Kistner, J. & Morgan, S. (1987). Component processes in working memory. In J.G. Borkowski & J.D. Day (Eds.), *Cognition in Special Children: Comparative Approaches to Retardation, Learning Disabilities and Giftedness*. Norwood, NJ: Ablex.

Trevelyan, J. (1988). When it's difficult to say no. *Nursing Times*, **84**, 16–17.

Turk, V. & Brown, H. (1992). Sexual abuse and adults with learning disabilities: Preliminary communication of survey results. *Mental Handicap*, **20**, 56–58.

Warnock, H.M. (1978). *Special Educational Needs: Report of the Committee of Enquiry into the Education of Handicapped Children and Young People*. London: HMSO.

Waxman, B.F. (1991). Patterns of sexual abuse and assault. *Sexuality and Disability*, **9**, 243–259.

Wertheimer, A., Bargh, J. & Russell, P. (1994). *Something to Say*. London: National Children's Bureau.

Westcott, H.L. (1991). The abuse of disabled children: A review of the literature. *Child: Care, Health and Development*, **17**, 243–258.

Westcott, H.L. (1993). *Abuse of Children and Adults with Disabilities*. London: NSPCC.

Westcott, H.L. & Clément, M. (1992). *NSPCC Experience of Child Abuse in Residential Care and Educational Placements: Results of a Survey*. London: NSPCC.

Westcott, H. & Cross, M. (1996). *This Far and no Further: Towards Ending the Abuse of Disabled Children*. Birmingham: Venture Press.

Womendez, C. & Schneiderman, K. (1991). Escaping from abuse: Unique issues for women with disabilities. *Sexuality and Disabilities*, **9**, 273–279.

World Health Organisation (1982). *International Classification of Impairments, Disabilities and Handicaps*. Geneva: WHO.

Interviewing Spine Surgery Candidates: Presurgical Psychological Screening

Cynthia Pladziewicz *and* Andrew R. Block
Texas Back Institute, Plano, USA

At some point in their lives most people will experience back pain (Fordyce, Brockway & Spengler, 1986). In over 80% of these cases, the pain subsides within six weeks regardless of treatment (Spengler et al., 1986). For those whose pain lingers, surgery may be considered. Unfortunately, the results of spine surgery are quite inconsistent and patients may find themselves with no pain reduction or even an increase in pain after the operation. Moreover, spine surgery is expensive, with estimated physician, hospital and rehabilitation costs ranging from $18 000 to over $40 000 per case (Block, 1996). The medical community has addressed this inconsistency in a number of ways, including refining diagnostic procedures, improving surgical techniques and instrumentation, and identifying any medical risk factors for spine surgical candidacy. Nevertheless, much of the variance in surgical outcomes remains unexplained by medical data. Psychological research suggests that personality and psychosocial factors may best answer the question of why two people with seemingly identical physical pathology may have vastly different surgical outcomes. This chapter provides an overview of a presurgical psychological screening (PPS) interview designed to assess potential surgical candidates for psychological and medical risk factors. In a chapter of this type it is impossible to cover the PPS process at the level needed for full implementation in a clinical setting. (The reader is referred to Block's 1996 *Guide* for a detailed explanation of the procedures, theory, and forms.)

Handbook of the Psychology of Interviewing. Edited by A. Memon and R. Bull.
© 1999 John Wiley & Sons Ltd.

WHAT IS PPS?

PPS is a technique that combines a clinical interview and psychological testing to assist surgeons in deciding whether a patient is an appropriate candidate for elective surgery for pain reduction. The PPS process starts with an interview by a trained clinician. The purpose of the interview is to gather information from the patient regarding demonstrated psychological and medical risk factors for poor surgical outcome. This information is then combined with psychological test data to determine the patient's probable surgical outcome: good, fair, or poor. In addition, the surgeon and patient are provided with a treatment plan that is designed to augment surgical outcome. Alternatively, if the patient is not a good surgical candidate, recommendations are provided for non-surgical alternatives to enhance pain control and functioning.

When is PPS Appropriate?

PPS is an appropriate prerequisite for elective surgeries with variable outcomes that are influenced by personality and psychosocial factors. Our work has focused primarily on candidates for spine surgery and that procedure is emphasized in this chapter. Presurgical screening has been extended, however, to other surgical procedures such as surgeries to relieve chronic pelvic pain and temporal mandibular joint dysfunction.

COMPONENTS OF PPS

The PPS consists of seven components:

1. Review of medical records.
2. Interview to identify surgical risk factors.
3. Observation of pain-related and other behaviors.
4. Psychological testing.
5. Determination of surgical prognosis.
6. Suggestions to facilitate surgical outcome or alternative treatment plan.
7. Preparation of the PPS report (Block, 1996).

REVIEWING MEDICAL RECORDS

Medical records form the basis for gathering information related to medical risk factors. For example, spine surgery risks are increased by chronicity of the illness, number of prior spine surgeries, degree of invasiveness, non-organic signs of pain, non-spine medical problems, smoking and obesity (Junge, Dvorak &

Ahrens, 1995; Finneson & Cooper, 1979). By first reviewing the medical records, the interviewer is better prepared to determine the presence of these risk factors during the interview. When the PPS interview is conducted on-site at the surgeon's office, medical records generally are readily available for review. If the interview is conducted at the clinician's office or at another off-site facility, the interviewer will need to pre-arrange for records to be made available.

CONDUCTING THE INTERVIEW

As previously mentioned, the PPS interview has two goals, identification of surgical risk and formulation of treatment recommendations. A patient generally attends the PPS interview because the physician has told the patient that the interview is a requirement for proceeding with surgery. Patients who have been referred for PPS often do not understand how the referral relates to the surgery or is relevant to their pain. Often, they believe the referral indicates the doctor views the pain as being "all in their head". Thus, the first task of the interviewer is to explain the purposes and goals of the interview and to assure the patient that the referral is routine. We typically start the interview by telling the patient that we are aware of the many problems created by spine pain, including marital conflict, loss of income, and uncertainty about the future. We explain that the purpose of the interview is to learn more about how the patient has been impacted by pain, how the patient will be affected by surgery, and how the surgeon can best treat the patient.

Rapport

Rapport is best developed by empathetically listening to the patient's description of the injury and symptoms. At the onset of the interview, most patients are more comfortable discussing the level of pain and the circumstances of injury rather than deeper emotional issues. However, the patient often opens the door to psychological inquiries through the use of emotionally charged language ("I feel", "stress"), vague references to intense feelings ("let's not go into that"), and body or facial expressions of negative affect. It is not uncommon for patients to become teary during the interview, especially if psychosocial stressors are significant. Even though initially apprehensive, many patients leave the interview feeling better emotionally and with a better understanding of how to meet the challenges presented by surgery and rehabilitation.

Interview Format

During the information-gathering phase of the interview, we recommend adhering to a semi-structured interview format. While a flexible, non-mechanical approach is helpful in establishing rapport, the PPS requires the gathering of a large amount of information in a short period of time. The interviewer may have only one opportunity to see the patient prior to the scheduled surgery so efficiency is of the essence. Basing the interview upon a written format insures that all relevant information is obtained. The format should list each of the surgical risk factors to be determined during the interview and may also list questions designed to elicit these risk factors. In addition, the format should include relevant demographic information to be obtained (name, date of injury, marital status), an area for rating of pain behaviors, and a listing of possible treatment recommendations. Allowing deviation from the order of the format enables the development of rapport and exploration of issues that may later prove relevant to treatment planning.

Identification of Risk Factors

Medical Risk Factors

As mentioned previously, we examine seven "medical" risk factors associated with reduced surgical results. These are: chronicity of the pain and injury, number of previous spine surgeries, destructiveness of the surgery, signs of non-organic pain, excessive non-spine medical utilization, smoking and obesity. The research underlying these risk factors is discussed at length in the *Guide*. Although medical records should be reviewed, they may be unavailable at the time of the interview or may provide insufficient information to assess all of the medical risks. The interview provides an opportunity to clarify and assess medical risk factors with the patient. During the interview, we assess obesity and non-organic pain primarily by observation. An extensive discussion of non-organic pain assessment follows below. The remaining medical risk factors are addressed directly with the patient in the interview.

Questions

When were you first injured or when did you first become aware of your pain? Have you had any previous spine surgeries? What type of surgery is your doctor planning? Do you smoke? How much? Do you have any other health problems not related to your back? What types of treatments have you had for these? Do you take any medications for these conditions?

Financial Factors

A patient who stands to gain monetarily from remaining ill may be at greater risk for poor surgical outcome. Monetary gain issues are present when the patient has a legal action pending to collect damages for the injury, a pending disability claim, or a worker's compensation claim. For example, Haddad (1987) found that workers' compensation claimants not represented by an attorney were eight times more likely to be working than their counterparts who were represented by counsel. Similarly, Junge et al. (1995) found that patients who were applying for disability were less likely to have a positive spine surgery outcome. These results should not be interpreted to suggest that patients with financial gain issues malinger. Rather, the better explanation for the influence of financial gain on outcomes is that these patients are more sensitive to pain signals at an unconscious level (Chapman, 1978).

Questions

Have you applied for worker's compensation or disability payments? Have you retained an attorney in connection with your injury?

Vocational Factors

A patient who expresses a high level of job dissatisfaction is 2.5 times more likely to sustain a work-related injury than is a satisfied worker (Bigos et al., 1991). Patients who have physically demanding jobs also present surgical risks. Patients who lift more than 50 pounds frequently are less likely to be surgically successful. Such patients are especially fearful about returning to the job. Not only are they keenly aware that they will be "put to the test" when they return, they may have no skills transferable to lighter work. We often use this part of the interview to introduce the topic of rehabilitative services. We assure the patient that there are opportunities for education and work training in the event they cannot return to the pre-injury job. The name of the local rehabilitative representative can be provided. If the client is especially fearful about post-surgical employment, it can also be helpful to share stories of positive outcomes, e.g. patients who have successfully trained for better jobs.

Questions

What type of work were you doing at the time of your injury? What are the physical requirements for that job? What are your plans for work in the future?

Alcohol and Drug Abuse

Patients with back pain often rely on narcotic medication for pain relief. The minority of spine patients who abuse medication or who abuse alcohol or street drugs should be considered at increased risk for poor outcome. (Spengler et al., 1980; Uomoto, Turner & Herron, 1988.) Abuse of narcotic medication is identified when the patient has increasing tolerance for the medication, evidences withdrawal symptoms, takes medication in larger amounts and over longer periods than prescribed, is persistently unsuccessful in efforts to reduce the medication, spends a great deal of time and energy obtaining the medication or continues medication use even though the patient knows it is causing additional physical or mental problems (DSM-IV, Criteria for Substance Dependence, American Psychiatric Association, 1994).

Substance abuse can also be evaluated in terms of the patient's behavior during the interview. Since patient reports are not always reliable, behavioral observation is a useful adjunct to patient self-report. The interviewer should be alert for signs of opioid intoxication during the interview. Sleepiness, slurred speech and slowed thought processes may reflect intoxication. Similarly, some patients may present with the smell of alcohol on their breath. A second consideration is how medication is impacting patient functioning. If the patient reports taking medication prior to the interview, yet displays high levels of pain behavior, the question arises as to whether the patient is using medication appropriately. Finally, the patient may display medication-seeking behavior during the interview. Overuse of medication may be indicated when the patient requests the interviewer to assist in obtaining additional pain medication.

Questions

What types of medication do you take for your pain? (Often patients have the medications with them during the interview and can show you the bottles. Some even carry a list of medications and dosages.) How often do you take these medications? Do you ever need to take more than prescribed for the pain? Have your dosages increased since starting the medications? About how much alcohol do you drink? Have you ever had problems with alcohol in the past?

Abuse History

Schofferman et al. (1992) studied the impact on spine surgical outcome of five categories of abuse: sexual abuse, physical abuse, parental substance abuse, abandonment and emotional abuse. Patients who experienced at least three of the five types of abuse were 17 times more likely to have unsuccessful surgeries than patients reporting no abuse history.

Questions

Have you ever been abused physically, sexually, or emotionally, either as an adult or as a child? (*If the patient hesitates*) The reason I ask is that sometimes when you have been injured, the pain can remind you of prior times that you felt hurt.

Prior Psychological Treatment

Psychological problems are common among people with back pain (Kinney et al., 1993). It is unclear whether psychopathology predates, or results from, the pain (Gamsa, 1994; Polatin et al., 1993). What is clearer is that patients with a history of past psychological treatment are at increased risk for poor recovery from spine surgery (Polatin et al., 1993).

Questions

Prior to meeting me have you ever met with a psychologist, psychiatrist or counselor? What caused you to seek treatment? Were you ever hospitalized for this condition?

Marital Interaction

Pain affects both the patient and the patient's family. Family members can encourage or discourage pain behaviors both directly and indirectly through their responses to the patient's expressions of pain. For example, the family may directly encourage pain behavior by encouraging the patient to rest and to take additional medication when the patient expresses pain. In a study by Block, Kremer and Gaylor (1980), patients whose spouses were solicitous to pain reported higher pain levels when their spouses were present than when they were absent. Patients whose spouses were not solicitous to pain expressions rated their pain as lower when their spouses were present. Pain behavior can also be indirectly encouraged if the patient avoids family chores or undesired sexual activity by expressing pain.

Spouses of patients with back pain are more likely than spouses generally to be highly dissatisfied with their marriages and to be themselves depressed (Romano, Turner & Clancy, 1989; Schwartz et al., 1991). Dissatisfied spouses are more likely to be pessimistic and to view the patient's pain as purely psychological (Block & Boyer, 1984). Dissatisfied spouses also have poorer expectations for treatment (Block, Boyer & Silbert, 1985) and commonly experience sexual difficulties (Muruta & Osborne, 1978). Based on this research, it is our assumption that dissatisfied spouses are less able to support and encourage the patient appropriately and should be considered as a risk factor for surgical outcome.

Questions

I know that an injury can put stress on a family. How has your family handled your injury? How has the injury affected your marriage? Does your spouse understand what you are going through?

OBSERVING PAIN BEHAVIORS

Inconsistency between physical manifestations of pain ("pain behaviors") and tissue damage have long been used to assess back pain patients. Waddell et al. (1980) first developed a series of symptom magnification tests to measure this discrepancy more objectively. During a spine patient's physical examination, physicians frequently perform Waddell's tests to determine the presence of non-organic physical signs of pain. The Waddell tests examine five signs of non-organic pain:

1. Tenderness, as evidenced by pain in response to a light pinch of the skin (superficial tenderness) or by deep tenderness distributed over an area too wide to be localized to one source; distraction; regional disturbances, and overreaction (non-anatomic tenderness).
2. Stimulation, as evidenced by low back pain when pressing on the patient's head (axial loading) or by low back pain when rotating shoulders and pelvis (rotation).
3. Distraction, as evidenced by pain experienced when tested formally by straight leg raising but not when tested with distraction.
4. Regional disturbances, as evidenced by "giving away" of muscles that cannot be explained on a localized neurological basis (weakness) or by diminished sensation to a pinprick or light touch in a non-neurological pattern (sensory).
5. Overreaction, as evidenced by excessive verbalization, facial expression, or other overtly dramatic behaviors.

The discrepancy between tissue damage and pain perception is often attributable to a greatly exaggerated or distorted perception of the pain (Block et al., 1996). For patients with excessive pain sensitivity, repairing damaged tissues may be ineffective in providing pain relief.

The critical issue in assessing pain behavior of spine surgery candidates is the degree of consistency between the patient's reported level of pain and the behaviors exhibited. When experiencing pain, a patient often is unable to comfortably sit, stand or walk. This discomfort is evidenced by observable behaviors. Inconsistency indicates an increased risk for surgical recovery. During the interview, we ask the patient to rate pain. "I'm going to ask you to rate your current level of pain on a scale of zero to ten. Zero means you have no pain at all and ten means you are experiencing the worst pain you can possibly imagine." These ratings are then compared to the patient's pain behaviors as observed by the interviewer.

We observe and rate five behaviors quantified by Keefe and Block (1982):

1. Guarding – stiff, interrupted movement.
2. Bracing – using a limb abnormally to support weight.
3. Rubbing – touching the affected area.
4. Grimacing – a facial expression of pain.
5. Sighing – exaggerated exhalation of breath.

Observations should be made under as many circumstances as possible. The patient's behaviors can be observed in the waiting room, walking to the interview room, during testing, and while completing registration forms. The interviewer should observe pain behaviors from three perspectives. First, are the behaviors consistent with the patient's self-reported ratings? Second, do pain behaviors increase as expected during pain-generating activities such as walking, sitting for an extended period or bending. Third, do the behaviors intensify when the patient is aware that the behaviors are being observed? For example, does the patient display more behaviors in the presence of the interviewer than are exhibited while completing psychological testing?

The patient's medical records can also provide information relevant to the assessment of inconsistent pain. For example, spine surgery patients may have completed diagnostic testing such as a discogram, facet injection, or differential spinal block, designed to locate the "pain generator". When medical test results are inconsistent, the tissue damage to be repaired by the surgery may not be the actual pain generator, rendering the surgery ineffective. Although a lengthy discussion of these tests is beyond the scope of this chapter, the interviewer must remain abreast of current medical testing procedures and integrate these results into the PPS.

PSYCHOLOGICAL TESTING

The usefulness of psychological testing in predicting surgical outcome is well documented. Test results offer objective information regarding the patient's personality, cognitive processes and behaviors. Test data serve as a check on the clinician's subjective perceptions. Finally, testing may offer information relevant to treatment planning. For these reasons, we highly recommend the integration of psychometric testing into the PPS decision-making process.

The best-researched psychometric predictor of spine surgery outcome is the Minnesota Multiphasic Personality Inventory (MMPI) (Dahlstrom, Welsh & Dahlstrom, 1975; Keller & Butcher, 1991). The MMPI and its successor, the MMPI-2, yield ten clinical scales results. Research consistently has demonstrated that individuals with elevations on scale 1 Hy (hysteria) and scale 3 Hs (hypochondriasis) are at higher risk for poor surgical outcome. These findings make sense intuitively since these scales were designed to measure increased propensity for physical complaints (Graham, 1990). Patients with elevated Hs and Hy scales are likely to exhibit excessive pain sensitivity. That is they experience pain well in excess of that expected from the tissue damage sustained (Block et al., 1996).

Research also supports associations between diminished surgical results and elevations of MMPI scales 2 (depression), 4 (anti-social) and 6 (anxiety). Elevations on scale 2 (depression) are seen in up to 85% of chronic pain patients (Lindsay & Wyckoff, 1981) and are associated with poor surgical outcome (Cashion & Lynch, 1979; Dvorak et al., 1988). Although pain can precipitate depression, for many patients the depression is chronic and predates the injury (Polatin et al., 1993). We consider chronic depression predating the injury to reflect a greater surgical risk. Patients with pre-existing depression are more likely to retain depressive symptoms after the surgery. These depressive symptoms in turn may impede recovery of functioning.

Patients with elevations on MMPI scale 4 tend to be rebellious, hostile and aggressive (Graham, 1990). Anger has been demonstrated to adversely affect recovery from injury (DeGood & Kiernan, 1996) and is common in patients with chronic pain (Turk & Fernandez, 1995). At least five studies have found an association between scale 4 elevations and poor surgical outcome (Dvorak et al., 1988; Herron et al., 1992; Long, 1981; Sorenson & Mors, 1988; Spengler et al., 1990).

Psychometric testing is also helpful in identifying cognitive risk factors for surgical outcome. Cognitive testing identifies how the patient thinks about and copes with pain. Two cognitive attributes, the patient's level of self-reliance and the patient's beliefs regarding pain control, are particularly relevant to assessment of surgical risk (Jenson, Turner & Romano, 1991; Gross, 1986). Although a number of questionnaires have been designed to assess coping and pain-related beliefs, we recommend using the Coping Strategies Questionnaire ("CSQ") (Rosensteil & Keefe, 1983) for PPS evaluations. The CSQ has been extensively researched with chronic pain populations and is the only coping assessment instrument that has been demonstrated effectively to assess surgical outcome (Gross, 1986). Low self-reliance and poor pain control as assessed by the CSQ should be considered risk factors for poor surgical outcome.

DEFINING A "SUCCESSFUL" OR "UNSUCCESSFUL" SURGICAL OUTCOME

Surgical outcomes generally are measured in terms of improvement in the patient's pain experience, decreases in pain medication use, and improvement in the patient's level of functioning (Stauffer & Coventry, 1972; Turner et al., 1992). Pain experience typically is defined by the patient's self-report. Does the patient subjectively feel less pain following the surgery? Functioning can be measured more objectively in terms of decreased physical restrictions and increased ability to work. Measuring improvement as opposed to absolute outcomes is critical. Each surgical candidate presents with varying levels of physical and emotional symptoms. For a patient with significant physical or psychological pathology presurgery, a successful outcome may mean a return to an improved level of well-being, although not one that is free of problems.

Based on Stauffer and Coventry's criteria (as revised by Turner et al., 1992), we define an outcome to be "good" if pain is absent or mild, the patient is able to work, and the patient has minimal or no restrictions on activity. A "fair" outcome is defined as one in which the patient continues to experience persistent mild pain or occasional moderate pain. The patient is able to work and perform most normal activities; however, some physical restrictions are present. "Poor" outcome occurs when the patient continues to experience persistent moderate pain or occasional severe pain, the surgery has provided little or no pain relief, or activities are severely restricted.

Determining whether a patient's predicted outcome is good, fair or poor requires a balancing of medical and psychological risk factors gathered through the review of medical records, interview, testing, and observation of pain behaviors. When both medical and psychological risk factors are low, we expect the patient to respond well to the surgery. This patient is assigned a prognosis or expected outcome of "good". When the medical and psychological risk factors vary (low medical risk/high psychological risk or high medical risk/low psychological risk) the patient's prognosis is expected to be "fair". If both medical and psychological risk factors are high the prognosis is "poor". Clinical judgment becomes most important when medical or psychological risk factors fall in the moderate range. For a thorough discussion of risk factor cutoff scores, suggested numerical weightings, and further guidelines for risk determination, the reader is referred to the *Guide*.

PROVIDING FEEDBACK TO THE PATIENT

Timing of Feedback

Feedback regarding the interview results is best provided at a separate follow-up session. Often the interviewer needs time to assess results or to discuss the case with the referring physician prior to finalizing recommendations. Additional reference to medical records may be needed. Nevertheless, at times the surgery is scheduled within a day or two of the interview, leaving no time for a separate follow-up feedback session. In such cases, interview feedback can be provided at the end of the interview.

Approach to Feedback

Telling the patient that results are tentative and subject to further evaluation should preface feedback. It is helpful to acknowledge the problems the patient has encountered and the positive ways in which the patient has responded to these problems. For example, if the patient has used medication appropriately or made good use of social support, these accomplishments should be noted. The interviewer can then examine with the patient the risk factors for the surgery and how each should be addressed. If the risk factors are within the patient's control, e.g. smoking, the interviewer should include a plan for minimizing the risk factor. A patient who smokes could be offered training in self-hypnosis and other strategies for smoking cessation following the surgery. Risk factors should be presented in a non-judgmental manner, emphasizing that the risks are not the patient's fault and, in fact, may be common in spine patients. However, certain problems make surgical success less likely. The interviewer should express care and concern for the patient. It is important to convey that the interviewer's goal is to minimize the patient's overall risk of poor outcome, whether through non-surgical interventions or through modifications to be made as a condition to surgery.

Reporting Surgical Prognosis

The feedback report should include the surgical prognosis: good, fair or poor. This part of the feedback is best preceded by an explanation of the rationale for the prognosis. Advise the patient that the prognosis is based on the interview, medical records review and test data. Make sure the patient understands that ultimately the surgeon will decide whether the surgery should proceed. The PPS merely provides recommendations. The interviewer should help the patient understand how each of the identified risk factors impact outcome. For example: "One risk factor you have is a history of abuse. Research shows that patients with a history of abuse have a higher surgical risk. We do not fully understand why this is and it certainly is not your fault. In fact, the way you have moved on with your life following this trauma is a true accomplishment. It may be that trauma impacts the brain's reaction to pain sensations or that these new pains bring up memories of prior injuries. We do not know precisely the connection. However, what we do know is that this factor, in combination with other risk factors, makes you more vulnerable to an unsuccessful surgery. So, this is something that you, I, and your doctor need to consider carefully prior to going ahead with a surgery".

It is important to help the patient understand that the PPS surgical prognosis will provide helpful information in determining a successful course of treatment for the patient, regardless of whether the prognosis is good, fair, or poor. A good prognosis can provide the patient with assurance that he or she has a good surgical risk profile. Even though spine surgery results are quite variable, this patient can be more confident approaching surgery. For the patient with a fair prognosis, a plan for enhancing surgical outcome can be created. Taking the steps outlined in the plan may mean the difference between a successful and an unsuccessful surgery. Even for the patient with a poor surgical prognosis, the PPS has provided a benefit. Had this patient proceeded with surgery, a poor result likely would have followed. In fact, the patient might have undertaken a long course of spine surgeries with poor results. The PPS offers the opportunity to formulate a non-surgical course of treatment with a much greater likelihood of success.

Formulating a Plan

A key element of a successful patient feedback session is the formulation of a plan to enhance the patient's recovery. For purposes of treatment planning we generally identify five patient categories:

1. Patients cleared for surgery without need of psychological treatment. These patients need little professional help and can be referred to community resources or readings for additional information relevant to their circumstances.
2. Patients cleared for surgery with need for postoperative psychotherapy. For these patients feedback should help the patient to identify problem areas and possible solutions.
3. Patients placed on hold pending the outcome of psychological intervention. In this category, a more directive approach is recommended. Feedback should clearly identify risk factors and specific steps needed to obtain a favorable surgical recommendation. For example, if the patient is suffering from depression, an antidepressant medication trial coupled with consistent attendance at cognitive therapy sessions might be required prior to surgical clearance. The patient should clearly understand that failure to adhere to the treatment plan will result in the patient's not being cleared for surgery.
4. Patients with poor prognosis who should be treated with non-surgical care only. Patients in this category often are unhappy with the decision against surgical clearance. Some patients view surgery as the only answer to solving their pain problem. The challenge in providing feedback to such patients is to gain their understanding of the prognosis determination and to instill hope that recovery is none the less possible through interdisciplinary treatment.
5. Patients with poor prognosis who should be discharged from treatment immediately. Patients in this group generally have not found pain relief despite numerous medical and psychological interventions. Often, such patients share the interviewer's assessment that further treatment is unlikely to yield successful results. The feedback session offers an opportunity for acceptance of the patient's situation and for developing a plan of action outside the medical system. We often use this opportunity to recommend self-help groups and community resources.

REPORTING RESULTS

PPS reports should be timely, succinct and tactful. Surgeries often are scheduled well in advance of the proposed surgery date. If the patient is not a surgical candidate, the surgeon may need to move another patient from a waiting list. Unfortunately, in many cases, the referral has come only days before the scheduled surgery. For these reasons, we generally call the surgeon with verbal feedback as soon as the PPS assessment is completed. In addition, a brief summary of risk factors and prognosis may be faxed or delivered to the surgeon's office. Of course, the initial feedback should be followed by a more comprehensive report. Because the comprehensive report serves a limited purpose and will be utilized by the surgeon and the insurer, it should be organized, readable, free of jargon, and relevant to the referral questions. Suggested report formats are available in the *Guide*.

CONCLUSION

Surgery is often considered for patients with chronic pain problems; yet surgical results are variable. For many patients, costly surgeries do little to reduce pain or increase physical functioning. The PPS interview provides an organized, research-based approach for assessing surgical risks. By using the PPS as a basis for treatment planning, the clinician can enhance surgical outcome or provide more effective, less costly alternatives to surgery for high-risk surgical candidates.

REFERENCES

American Psychiatric Association (1994). *Diagnostic and Statistical Manual of Mental Disorders* (4th edn). Washington DC: APA.

Bigos, S.J., Battie, M.C., Spengler, D.M., Fisher, L.D., Fordyce, W.E., Hansson, T., Nachemson, A.L. & Worthly, M.D. (1991). A prospective study of work perceptions and psychosocial factors affecting the report of back injury. *Spine*, 16, 1–6.

Block A.R. (1996). *Presurgical Psychological Screening in Chronic Pain Syndromes: A Guide for the Behavioral Health Practitioner*. Mahwah, New Jersey: Lawrence Erlbaum Associates.

Block, A.R. & Boyer, S.L. (1984). The spouse's adjustment to chronic pain: Cognitive and emotional factors. *Social Science Medicine*, 19, 1313–1317.

Block, A.R., Boyer, S.L. & Silbert, R.V. (1985). Spouse's perception of the chronic pain patient: Estimates of exercise tolerance. In H.L. Fields, R. Dubner & F. Cervero (Eds.), *Advances in Pain Research and Therapy* (Vol. 9, pp. 897–904). New York: Raven Press.

Block, A.R., Kremer, E.F. & Gaylor, M. (1980). Behavioral treatment of chronic pain: The spouse as a discriminative cue for pain behavior. *Pain*, 9, 243–252.

Block, A.R., Vanharanta, H., Ohnmeiss, D. & Guyer, R.D. (1996). Discographic pain report: Influence of psychological factors. *Spine*, 21, 334–338.

Cashion, E.L. & Lynch, W.J. (1979). Personality factors and results of lumbar disc surgery. *Neurosurgery*, 4, 141–145.

Chapman, R.C. (1978). Pain: The perception of noxious events. In R.A. Sternbach (Ed.), *The Psychology of Pain* (pp. 169–202). New York: Raven Press.

Dahlstrom, W.G., Welsh, G.S. & Dahlstrom, L.E. (1975). *An MMPI Handbook*, volume 2, Minneapolis: University of Minnesota Press.

DeGood, D.E. & Kiernan, B. (1996). Perception of fault in patients with chronic pain. *Pain*, 64, 153–159.

Dvorak, J., Valach, L., Fuhrimann, P. & Heim, E. (1988). The outcome of surgery for lumbar disc herniation. II. A 4–17 years' follow-up with emphasis on psychosocial aspects. *Spine*, 13(12), 1423–1427.

Finneson, B.E. & Cooper, V.R. (1979), A lumbar disc predictive score card: A retrospective evaluation. *Spine*, 4, 141–144.

Fordyce, W.E., Brockway, J.A. & Spengler, D. (1986). Acute back pain: A control group comparison of behavioral versus traditional management models. *Journal of Behavioral Medicine*, 4, 127.

Gamsa, A. (1994). The role of psychological factors in chronic pain. II. A critical appraisal. *Pain*, 57, 17–29.

Graham, J.R. (1990). *The MMPI-2: Assessing Personality and Psychopathology*. New York: Oxford University Press.

Gross, A.R. (1986). The effect of coping strategies on the relief of pain following surgical intervention for lower back pain. *Psychosomatic Medicine*, **48**, 229–238.

Haddad, G.H. (1987). Analysis of 2932 workers' compensation back injury cases: The impact of the cost to the system. *Spine*, **12** (8), 765–771.

Herron, L., Turner, J.A., Ersek, M. & Weiner, P. (1992). Does the Millon Behavioral Health Inventory (MBHI) predict lumbar laminectomy outcome? A comparison with the Minnesota Multiphasic Personality Inventory (MMPI). *Journal of Spinal Disorders*, **5**(2), 188–192.

Jenson, M.P., Turner, J.A., Romano, J.M. (1991). Self-efficacy and outcome expectancies: relationship to chronic pain coping strategies and adjustment. *Pain*, **44**, 263–269.

Junge, A., Dvorak, J. & Ahrens, S. (1995). Predictors of bad and good outcomes of lumbar disc surgery: A prospective clinical study with recommendations for screening to avoid bad outcomes. *Spine*, **20**(4), 460–468.

Keefe, F.J. & Block, A. (1982). Development of an observation method for assessing pain behavior in chronic low back pain patients. *Behavioral Therapy*, **13**, 636–675.

Keller, L.S. & Butcher, J.N. (1991). *Assessment of Chronic Pain Patients with the MMPI-2 [MMPI-2 Monographs]* (Vol. 2). Minneapolis: University of Minnesota Press.

Kinney, R.K., Gatchel, R.J., Polatin, P.B., Fogarty, W.T. & Mayer, T.G. (1993). Prevalence of psychopathology in acute and chronic low back pain patients. *Journal of Occupational Rehabilitation*, **3**(2), 95–103.

Lindsay, P. & Wyckoff, M. (1981). The depression-pain and its response to antidepressants. *Psychosomatics*, **22**, 571–577.

Long, C. (1981). The relationship between surgical outcome and MMPI profiles in chronic pain patients. *Journal of Clinical Psychology*, **37**, 744–749.

Muruta, T. & Osborne, D. (1978). Sexual activity in chronic pain patients, *Psychosomatics*, **19**, 531.

Polatin, P.B., Kinney, R.K., Gatchel, R.J., Lillo, E. & Mayer. T. (1993). Psychiatric illness and chronic low-back pain. The mind and the spine – which goes first? *Spine*, **18**, 66–71.

Romano, J.M., Turner, J.A. & Clancy, S.L. (1989). Sex differences in the relationship of pain patient dysfunction to spouse adjustment. *Pain*, **39**, 289–296.

Rosensteil, A.K. & Keefe, F.J. (1983). The use of coping strategies in chronic low back pain patients: Relationship to patient characteristics and current adjustment. *Pain*, **17**, 33–44.

Schofferman, J., Anderson, D., Hinds, R., Smith, G. & White, A. (1992). Childhood psychological trauma correlates with unsuccessful lumbar spine surgery. *Spine*, **17** (Suppl. 6), S138–S144.

Schwartz, L., Slater, M.A., Birchler, G.R. & Atkinson, J.H. (1991). Depression in spouses of chronic pain patients: The role of patient pain and anger, and marital satisfaction. *Pain*, **44**, 61–68.

Sorenson, L.V. & Mors, O. (1988). Presentation of a new MMPI scale to predict outcome after first lumbar diskectomy. *Pain*, **34**, 191–194.

Spengler, D.M., Bigos, S.J., Martin, N.A., Zeh, J., Fischer, L., Nachemson, A. (1986). Back pain in industry: A retrospective study. *Spine*, **11**, 241.

Spengler, D.M., Freeman, C., Westbrook, R. & Miller, J.W. (1980). Low-back pain following multiple lumbar spine procedures: Failure of initial selection? *Spine*, **4**(4), 356–360.

Spengler, D.M., Ouelette, E.A., Battie, M. & Zeb, J. (1990). Elective discectomy for herniation of a lumbar disc. *Journal of Bone and Joint Surgery (America)*, **12**, 230–237.

Stauffer, R.N. & Coventry, M.B. (1972). Anterior interbody lumbar spine fusion: Analysis of Mayo clinic series. *Journal of Bone and Joint Surgery (America)*, **54**, 756–789.

Turk, D.C. & Fernandez, E. (1995). Personality assessment and the Minnesota Multiphasic Personality Inventory in chronic pain: Underdeveloped and overexposed. *Pain Forum*, **4**(2), 104–107.

Turner, J.A., Ersek, M., Herron, L., Haselkorn, J., Kent, D., Ciol, M.A., Marcia, A. & Deyo, R. (1992). Patient outcomes after lumbar spinal fusions. *Journal of the American Medical Association*, **268**(7), 907–911.

Uomoto, J.M., Turner, J.A. & Herron, L.D. (1988). Use of the MMPI and MCMI in predicting outcome of lumbar laminectomy. *Journal of Clinical Psychology*, **44**, 191–197.
Waddell, G., McCulloch, J.A., Kummel, E. & Venner, R.M. (1980). Nonorganic physical signs in low-back pain. *Spine*, **5**(2), 117–125.

Ethics of Qualitative Interviewing in Grieving Families

Paul C. Rosenblatt
University of Minnesota, St Paul, USA

Abstract

Qualitative research interviews in grieving families provide the researcher with helpful information for making ethical decisions and for evaluating the outcomes of those decisions. At the same time, this type of research faces the researcher with many ethical challenges. Illustrations from the author's study of farm families who have lost a family member in a fatal farm accident are used to illuminate some of the ethical challenges in qualitative bereavement research. Included in these challenges are the ethics of recruiting people to be interviewed, the ethics of causing pain, the ethics of informed consent, ethical issues at the boundary between research and therapy, ethical problems in supporting family dysfunction, and the ethics of revealing family members to one another.

ETHICAL ADVANTAGES OF QUALITATIVE INTERVIEW RESEARCH

Researchers function in many ethical communities, including that of their research institution, their disciplinary colleagues, their current families, their friendship group, and so on. They also enter a new ethical community with each new relationship. Thus, a research encounter sets up a new ethical community

Handbook of the Psychology of Interviewing. Edited by A. Memon and R. Bull.
© 1999 John Wiley & Sons Ltd.

with fresh necessity of socially constructing ethical understandings. One may enter such a situation trying to apply certain ethical principles, but inevitably there will be matters on which the people being interviewed will have their own ethical perspectives. If one wants to be sensitive to the ethics of the people studied and to work with them toward what both they and one might consider ethically acceptable, give-and-take interaction is necessary. Qualitative interviewing can provide such interaction.

People who do not value qualitative interview research may consider it less ethical than quantitative research. If one does not value the outcomes of qualitative interview research, there is no point to causing people who are being interviewed discomfort or inconvenience. Moreover, if a qualitative researcher cannot specify in advance what will come up in the research, it is impossible to provide fully informed consent in advance of people's participation in the research (LaRossa, Bennett & Gelles, 1981). I think, however, that researchers carrying out intensive qualitative interviews are better positioned than people carrying out other kinds of research to recognize ethical issues, to acquire information that could help in making ethical decisions, and to engage in a genuine give-and-take about ethical issues with people participating in the research. During in-depth qualitative interviews one can learn people's understandings (of the research, of their relationship with the researcher, of the questions they are asked), their shoulds, their perceptions of the shoulds of people around them, their ethical dilemmas, and the ways they prefer to resolve those dilemmas. They may also, by sharing more about themselves and by being partners in interaction, engage more of the researcher's ethical complexity. In fact, I experience a special moral involvement from the intimacy that can come with interviews dealing with loss. That the moral involvement is not one-sided is suggested by the fact that I and other researchers carrying out qualitative loss interviews are often told at the end of an interview that the person(s) being interviewed have never revealed to others major parts of what they said in the interview.

In my experience with qualitative interview research, people will inevitably volunteer information about ethical matters, and they can also help the researcher to understand where they are ethically by answering questions on various ethical issues and by their reactions to what the researcher says and does. I have wrestled with ethical issues when I could not interact with the people providing data (particularly when I studied nineteenth century diaries – Rosenblatt, 1983, pp. 165–169). I feel on much firmer ground having the people who are providing data speak directly to ethical issues. Interviews not only give additional input but also, if one is not governed by a rigid interview script, free one to behave more ethically by the standards of the people being interviewed and by one's own standards.

In what follows, I use interviews carried out for a study of farm families in which there had been a fatal farm accident (Rosenblatt, 1993a, 1993b; Rosenblatt & Karis, 1993, 1993–1994) to provide illustrations for this chapter. In the farm accident study, as in all other research in which I engage, I abided by the mandates and constraints of my University's Institutional Review Board (IRB).

But there is so much more to being ethical than that. In what follows I discuss what I experienced as the most intense ethical challenges in the study of family aftermaths of fatal farm accidents.

COMMON ETHICAL CHALLENGES

Recruiting People to be Interviewed

As approved by my university's Institutional Review Board, the approach used in recruiting most of the people who were interviewed in the farm accident study involved advertising for volunteers. That model may seem quite straightforward ethically. One might think that as long as the advertisement does not contain any coercive or deceptive elements (and it did not, according to the IRB review), there should be no ethical problems in recruiting. However, it did not take much conversation with potential or actual interviewees to realize that people were being coerced into the study.

Some people were "recruited" by a member of their own family. People who would not, on their own, have volunteered to participate were drawn into the study because a spouse, parent or offspring was interested in participating. They did not say "no" to the family member or to me, but they might not have said "yes" had they not been pressed by a family member.

One example of what I consider coercion by a family member began when a woman whom I was going to interview told another about the study. The latter woman and her husband had lost a child in a farm accident a few years before. She called me while I was interviewing her neighbors and asked me to visit after I finished with the neighbors. I came to her farm as soon as I was free, and as we walked to the barn where her husband was milking, she told me he had never talked about the accident. I entered the barn, she told him a bit about my research, and then left it to her husband to talk with me and to decide whether he wanted to schedule an interview. (She said she couldn't stay because of allergies to the cows.) I followed the husband from cow to cow, telling him the things the advertisement of the study said and answering his questions. He was obviously hurting as we talked, using jokes and laughter to hold back tears, but he said he would do it, and I arranged an appointment for a couple interview. So this was a couple in which the woman volunteered, but the man seemed somewhat coerced by his wife's pressure to take me and the research seriously. He was also coerced in that he lacked the distance that other potential interviewees had from me as they read the advertisement. Our face-to-face contact may have meant that I persuaded him to volunteer even though I was trying not to persuade him but only to answer his questions. Perhaps the ethical thing to do would have been not to visit and not to try to recruit him face-to-face. Was it ethical for me to interview this couple?

Several weeks later, as we went through the interview, the husband and wife repeatedly, and with intense emotion, talked of their grief, their difficulties

communicating with each other, and their different memories and understandings of the accident. I am sure that for them this was a session of healing far more
than it was a way to help a researcher.

> *She*: We haven't really talked about it. It's a, it's, the few times that we have
>   brought it up, it's such a hurt that we just haven't gotten into it, you know.
> *He*: More or less start crying, the two of us, and then hug each other.
> *She*: Umhm.
> *He*: and just [he laughs]. We just loved him that much that [pause].
> *She*: . . . I think [very loud], there's times I feel like there's a wall between us since
>   then, maybe partly because we have not sat down and really talked about it and
>   let our feelings out on certain things, you know, the accident, because we really
>   have not, the two of us. So it's [long pause], you know, it, to me it has put up a
>   wall between us, but not to the point where, you know, we'd leave each other. It's
>   just there.

Had I violated my agreement with the university's Institutional Review Board by
allowing the wife to use me to get her husband to talk? Had he been coerced? I
gave him room to say "no" to an interview and "no" to any or all interview
questions. But he was not exactly a volunteer. On the other hand, perhaps the
most ethical thing I could have done was what I did, to allow the interview to be
used by the wife (and I think the husband) as a catalyst for their healing.

Causing Pain

Like other researchers seeking approval for research on grief (Cook, 1995),
sometimes when I propose a study of grief a reviewer for my university's Institutional Review Board has strong reservations about the study, reservations that
have to do with the ethics of my choice of topic. Some reviewers question the
right to carry out a study that causes people to feel emotional pain. From the
perspective of the cost–benefits analysis that is at the heart of most IRB reviews,
some reviewers consider that the grief that people may experience during a loss
interview such a high cost that it is difficult to justify the research.

I am not eager to cause people pain. I question the ethics of my carrying out
research on loss whenever somebody I interview seems to experience pain while
talking with me about a loss. However, I also believe, perhaps from my own
experience as much as from the large bereavement literature on the importance
of knowing and expressing feelings, that hurting may be part of healing. I think
that bereaved people may gain enormously from talking with someone who
takes their stories seriously and witnesses and acknowledges their pain. I have
done enough loss interviews to know that people who cry, fight back tears, or
express grief in other ways often seem afterwards to be glad to have had a chance
to talk about the issues that brought them to those feelings. So I do not think that
it is a cost, or only a cost, to people to experience pain during an interview about
loss. I also do not think I or an IRB reviewer can decide, in advance of a research
interview, what will or will not be very costly for a person being interviewed. I

need to rely on the words and nonverbal communications of the people being interviewed, and often they seem to me to communicate that it is ethically right for me to do what I am doing, even if they are hurting.

However, there are interviews where I am sure I am doing wrong, that I am causing or helping to cause pain that is too intense or that seems not to have any healing elements. I think most of the time when that happens either the death is very recent or previous grieving has been very limited. There are also family interviews where I think family members say destructive things to each other. So even though I disagree with people who seem to believe that experiencing grief during an interview is necessarily a bad thing, I think sometimes my bringing people to places where they hurt is the wrong thing to do.

When I believe that an interview is causing pain that is wrong to cause, I will try to move the interview away from the painful matters. I might, for example, skip questions that could be especially painful, or I might move to an abbreviated and more upbeat interview. For example, in the farm accident study, one elderly couple who volunteered to be interviewed had lost an adult son less than a year before the interview and had many issues surrounding his death still unresolved, including who would farm their farm, how they would retire, how to deal with a complicated lawsuit concerning the death, and their future relationship with the son's widow. Early in the interview it became clear to me that the couple were hurting more than they had bargained for or consented to (see the discussion of informed consent later in this chapter). The couple did not take me up on my offer to stop or my repeated suggestions that they could decline to answer a question, but I moved into a mode of interviewing that omitted many questions I might have asked and emphasized questions I hoped would be more benign. I think it was easy to recognize that this was an interview that should be cut short. The man was putting enormous energy into fighting back tears. Both he and his wife were often silent (or very terse) after my questions, as though they were shocked by the question, shocked by what they found inside of themselves, or struggling to find words that would be true but not cause them to lose control.

Sometimes it is not so clear what is right. Sometimes a person seems to be hurting horribly as a result of my questions but also seems convinced that this path of questions and answers is the right path to travel. I had interviewed a mother for perhaps two hours when her 18-year-old son entered the kitchen where we were talking. I did not think he wanted to be interviewed and did not intend to interview him, and his mother did not tell him to answer my questions or tell me to ask them, but somehow he and I found ourselves facing each other, an unwilling question asker and quite possibly an unwilling question answerer. However, he may have been curious about what I was doing and may have found himself, as the interaction developed, wanting to say things to his mother that he never had said before. In the following, I am P, D is the 18-year-old, whom I call here David, and M is the mother.

> *P*:   Would it be appropriate to ask you questions about [your sister's] being killed? Or if you don't want to talk, that's OK too.

D: Some I don't mind. Like what?

P: Well, like, you know, she was closest to you in age, and my guess is she was your playmate. Do you have memories of missing her as a playmate?

D: Oh, yeah. Not good ones. Wrong question.

P: Wrong question.

D: Yeah.

P: All right, with your parents grieving, do you remember feeling like maybe your parents were gone too?

D: No. I don't really remember like that age, 'cause I was too young then yet, so. Now it hurts, but back then it never really bothered me. I was only seven years old, so . . .

P: What would be a good question to ask you?

D: I don't know.

P: If I wanted to write things for families that had kids who were around the age you were when it happened, to help them deal with their problems or the things that might affect their kid . . .

D: [interrupting] Oh, it's more of a problem for them later than it is when it first happens. Tell them that right now. They think more, more of it when they get older [starting to cry] than they ever did when they were young [voice shaking].

P: Could I ask when, when it hits you?

D: Right about 15, 16. At 16.

P: What do you think made it start cooking for you?

D: Uh, I met a lot of girls and people that were her age, became really good friends of mine, so [voice shaking]. Yeah. [He hammers the wall with his fist and strides out of the kitchen to his bedroom]. [long, long pause].

P: I'm sorry. I should have backed off. I couldn't tell until that last . . .

M: I didn't either until then.

P: I don't know. I'd like to apologize to him, but I . . .

M: Well, just tell him you're sorry. He'll understand.

P: Should I go over there and tell him I'm sorry? I don't know. Or will he show up again?

M: Yeah, he has to go to work. [long pause].

P: Oomph! [long pause]. [sound of door opening and closing].

M: Say, that's one thing I didn't even, you know, realize.

P: That it's been cooking more with him?

M: And he does hang around with, or talk a lot with the girls that are younger than him. And she was about a year younger than him. [sound of door opening, D walks into the kitchen].

P: I'm sorry.

D: Oh, that's no big deal. Not like the first time.

P: I'll back off. I'm sorry.

D: You can ask questions.

P: Uh, I won't, but if you want to say things I'll, I'll be glad to hear them.

M: He just wants to write pamphlets on . . .

D: Yeah, I know.

M: What may, you know, if they were to help people, how they would help them.

D: I'll tell you that right now. What I said before. It doesn't really bother them when they're a little kid [voice shaking]. It's when they get older. And they can really start to feel.

M: To understand the finality of it. Yeah, because I remember when it happened, David was little that time, and . . .

D: I remember too. I was asleep. They come and wake me up. They go, "[Your sister's] dead." And I went back to sleep. I think that's such a *bad* memory. A little kid, and you think when you're older, "Gee, they woke you up. You went

> back to sleep. Your sister's dead." That's why I said I really don't want to talk about memories 'cause [crying] you only remember the bad. [long pause].

I thought I had pushed him to more pain than he wanted to feel or had bargained for, but then he came back and volunteered more. My initial on-the-spot cost–benefit analysis was that we had entered an area of great pain without any great benefit to him, his mother, other members of his family, or humanity. But since he came back for more, he may have been benefitting more than I thought initially. On the other hand, his mother seemed to have decided at that point that it was time to derail the conversation.

> *M*: You want some pie, David?
> *D*: Un un. [long pause].
> *M*: I didn't know how hot it would get today. I fired up [the furnace] this morning, and I think it's too hot in here. I shouldn't have fired up [she laughs].

At that point I recognized my cue and started talking with M about wood furnaces. David didn't say anything else until he left for work, and then only a goodbye. His mother told me after he left that she was delighted to hear what he had to say, that he had never talked with her about his feelings and experiences. I still do not feel good about how things had gone. I did not make the effort to frame my questions and the interview for David so as to build up to the painful matters and to couch them in terms of more benign meanings already laid out by David. And I did not get a chance, after the blast of pain, to talk with David in a way that would get him (and me, I confess) to feeling less agonized about the matters that hurt so much. Nor am I sure that going along with his mother's derailing of the conversation was the right thing to do for David, though it was the right thing to do for her.

Informed Consent

A qualitative interviewer can never give full information to which people can consent before the research begins (LaRossa et al., 1981). Qualitative interviews have an unpredictable, unfolding quality that makes it impossible to warn people fully of what will occur. I think also that it is impossible to inform people fully about what they might experience during a qualitative interview because they cannot truly understand all that they read or are told, because they can only be told abstractly about what they will have to deal with, and because nobody can fully anticipate their reactions in the research situation.

Because of this, I try to supplement the consent procedure that occurs before the research begins with "processual consent" (Ramos, 1989; Thorne, 1980). That involves repeatedly giving people opportunities to stop me or at least to slide by a particularly difficult question. Here are a few examples of processual consent things I said in my interview with the couple whose son had been killed less than a year before the interview.

I don't know if that's an appropriate question to ask or not . . .
I feel like maybe all these questions are too personal. You can tell me to shut up
anytime you want . . .
Could I ask you . . .?

I use the last question at transitions into what I think might be heavy for people
or when they seem to be hurting, holding back tears, feeling miserable, or having
regrets about participating.

Crossing the Boundary Between Therapy and Research

The boundary metaphor can be useful, but it can make trouble as well (Rosenblatt, 1994, ch. 4). I do not think there is a distinct boundary between therapy
and most human activities. Almost anything can draw one out of depression,
help one to reframe experiences, reflect oneself back to oneself, give one words
for things that before could not be conceptualized clearly, provide healing or
soothing or distraction, give one new reasons to go on, or suggest valuable new
meanings for events. Therapeutic benefits may come from cooking, shopping,
scraping one's knee, playing with a puppy, hearing a piece of music, swimming,
an overheard conversation, a brief chat, or almost anything else. That said, one
can still have great concern that with people who are hurting, needy, or stuck, a
visiting researcher might attempt a therapeutic intervention.

I am interested in carrying out research, not therapy. I am prohibited by my
university's IRB from carrying out therapy with people I research, though I am
encouraged to carry out the beginning of an intervention in the form of offering
people a referral to counseling agencies if they seem to want or need it.
However, even if not engaged in therapeutic intervention, I think a researcher
talking to people about loss and grief must have therapist-like skills in listening,
acknowledging, avoiding being judgmental, supporting, knowing when to back
off, and catching on that something has been misunderstood.

I am not a therapist. However, I am strongly inclined to provide appropriately
human support to anyone with whom I interact. I have no qualms about moving
outside the frame of research interactions to speak to someone's pain or confusion. Depending on what a person I am interviewing seems to think is appropriate, I can offer sympathy, allow myself to be fully emotional, talk about
experiences of my own that are similar, or acknowledge someone's pain. But I do
not see that as crossing a line into therapy. In fact, I see that as entirely consistent
with the principle that the needs of a distressed respondent take priority over the
needs of research (Parkes, 1995). But even here, the boundaries are unclear.
Good research interviewing, particularly about emotionally charged topics, usually requires excellent listening and a great deal of empathy and human warmth.

At the same time, there is certainly reason to believe that a loss interview can
be therapeutic (Cook & Bosley, 1995; Parkes, 1995). Asking for feelings, nudg-
ing people to know their own feelings, asking that a name be put on a feeling, or
asking for clarity about feeling statements may often be a part of grief therapy.

Also, research interviews focused on loss typically ask a person to tell the story of the loss, and in that narrating there can be integration, crystallization, naming, and the healing that comes with telling a story (Worden, 1991). Healing can occur as the narrator organizes events and goes along a linear route toward some kind of ending. Thus, although I am not trying to do therapy, I am not surprised when people tell me that they have experienced a research interview as having benefitted them therapeutically.

I often interview the same person more than once, or at least make additional contact by phone or mail. I return to people to get clarity about matters previously addressed in the research interview, to talk with family members who were not present before, to strengthen the aspects of my research dealing with change over time, or to check in on people about whom I have particularly great concern. With renewed contact it is easier to know whether there was some kind of therapeutic affect to an earlier contact. For example, a woman whom I had interviewed about the death of her father when she was an infant had talked during the first interview about her hope for some sort of therapeutic benefit from the interview:

> I feel like I've come a long way, because I'm not on the edge of something . . . When I talk to [my husband] about this [interview], he said, "Oh, good, this will be good for you." I said, "Yeah, I know." I didn't know quite how, but I guess it feels validating to me to be able to tell the story I feel proud to be able to tell.

When I interviewed her a second time, two years later, she told me that the first interview had been therapeutic.

> Probably it took three days or so for anything to get to consciousness, and then [I experienced] . . . big grieving type of things . . . I even wrote a story about it . . . It was as though the information [was] on a new level for me . . . , because I had never had it asked of me at one time . . . To have it all be focused, it was both a huge relief and it . . . took me down to a deeper level of [pause] grief . . . But as I [thought about it] it was as though I let it end. It got easier . . . [My brother] came out this summer and I . . . talked about [the interview] then . . . because it was amazing to me. I was telling various awarenesses that I had, and he said, "How, how did you put this together?" I said . . . this interview was a big part of it.

Any interaction about a loss has the potential to provide new awareness, integration and feelings of healing. So even though the woman reported experiences from the first interview that seem like the effect of therapy, I believe she could have reached those experiences in many other ways. Indeed, one can make the case, given what she said in the first interview, that she was ready for the changes that happened and might well have made them whether or not she talked with me. Janice W. Nadeau (personal communication) has suggested that it is useful to distinguish between therapy and therapeutic experiences. Some of my interviews may, like the first interview of the woman quoted immediately above, provide therapeutic experiences, transformative or growth-producing moments, but none provides therapy in the sense of interaction focused on growth or healing.

With couple or family interviews there are additional therapeutic possibilities. Family members say things during family research interviews that they have never said to each other, even things they had no intention of saying. In the couple or family interview situation, people may confront their differences, identify their similarities, and co-construct for the first time stories or parts of stories concerning the loss and their grieving, as did the first couple quoted in this article. So with couple or family interviews there is additional opportunity for researchers to cross the imaginary line into therapy and to do harm or, at the very least, to do something that people had not bargained for and that the researcher has no right to do. If interviewing individuals about loss calls for great ethical sensitivity, couple or family interviewing about loss calls for even greater ethical sensitivity.

Supporting Family Dysfunction

For me, another ethical challenge of carrying out qualitative interviews with nonclinical families is what to do about what seems to me to be family dysfunction. At times I see families with what I would label as communication cutoffs, patterns of not talking about major issues or not talking about almost anything. I also see families with verbal abuse, emotional undermining, bullying, exploitation, insensitivity to major needs, emotional neglect, emotional cutoffs and reports of wife abuse. Every time I am with such a family I wonder what is ethical for me to do. Should I comment on what I see? Should I suggest a therapeutic referral? Will people experience an offer of a referral as an attack rather than as helpful? Do I have any right to offer an opinion or referral if uninvited? These people did not bargain for an evaluation. Even if a family member seems to ask me for help or an opinion, is that a rhetorical question? Is that family member asking for anything like what I would say or offer? If I try to answer that question, will I endanger the person who seems to ask for help?

I think part of dealing with the ethics of what seems to be family dysfunction is to question whether it is appropriate for me to make judgments about family dysfunction. Who am I to say that a family is dysfunctional? The idea implies that people could do better. But maybe they do not want things to be different. Maybe what they are doing is right by their standards. Maybe they do not want to pay the costs of changing. Maybe they get good things out of the bad – for example, more time for valued activities because they are cutoff from certain family members. Maybe they are "normal" in the sense of being like their peers and families of origin, and the change I would hope to see would make them strange and unwelcome in their own social circles. Maybe I misperceive them, or maybe they are only the way I see them when I am present to interview them.

In the farm accident study I saw and heard instances of what I considered to be family dysfunction. I was never sure what was true and what was ethical. In a few cases I talked with family members about counseling that might be helpful in dealing with problems stemming from the loss. But I never spoke with family members about what looked to me like family dysfunction, and I remain unsure of what the moral thing is to do.

Revealing Family Members to One Another

In some bereaved families there seems only a narrow range of talk about the meaning of a death (Nadeau, 1998). There also seems, in some bereaved families, to be little said about individual feelings, experiences and memories regarding the death. Thus, the interviewer, even without intending to do so, may ask family members to say, in front of other family members, things that are far outside the usual range of what they say to each other. In the farm accident study, I saw people taken aback by another family member's disclosure or disappointed, and I saw people being guarded about what they said in front of another family member. Perhaps the greatest risk of negative consequences from self-disclosure to another family member came in an interview carried out by my collaborator, Terri Karis. In that interview a woman disagreed with her husband on a matter about which he felt very strongly. She seemed quite apprehensive while disagreeing with her husband (in a very diplomatic and careful way) about the allocation of responsibility for the accident that killed their daughter. We never made contact again with that couple, but I wonder whether her self-disclosure in the interview made trouble for her.

I also worry about revealing family members to one another through anything I commit to print. I have a vivid memory from my undergraduate days at the University of Chicago. In my dormitory there were two young men who had been patients at Bruno Bettleheim's residential treatment facility. I remember the two of them poring through a new Bettleheim book, finding descriptions of a number of patients they had known. Perhaps identities were not disguised well enough in that book, but perhaps one can never disguise identities well enough from people who know the players well. I worry about my efforts to disguise identities, particularly when anecdotes I relate have a real possibility of getting back to the players in those anecdotes or to their family members. I think there are ethical issues whenever one quotes or paraphrases qualitative bereavement interviews, including issues of invasion of privacy, of revealing family members to one another, and of defining people in ways that could be hurtful to them.

CONCLUSION

There are many more ethical issues in qualitative research on loss than those I have discussed – including the ethics of accepting other people's realities when your own is different, letting people misunderstand self-help literature they have read, carrying out research interviews that are emotionally connected to one's own losses, and what the researcher owes ethically to self and to own family in doing loss research. I think it is in the nature of qualitative bereavement inter-viewing to recurrently wonder if one is doing the right thing.

With regard to Cook's (1995) discussion of whether bereaved people can make rational choices in consenting to research, I think rationality is not the issue. Rather, I think it is the feelings, thoughts and experiences they will get to and how they feel about those things. With losses not processed very much or with lots of energy going into emotional control, they might need effective processual consent. I think it is often impossible (or not very helpful) to be rational about a loss interview before one is in the midst of it. However, I agree wholeheartedly with Cook (1995) that meeting an Institutional Review Board's standards is only the beginning, that we must be ethically sensitive at all times. In that regard, I still think that carrying out qualitative interview research puts me in a much better position to make ethical choices than if I had done research that was more closed to the realities of the people being studied. Qualitative research prevents me from having the ethical self-delusions that can arise when I have little contact with the individuals I am studying. It gives me the opportunity to co-construct ethical realities with the people studied, rather than simply impos-ing my own on them.

It might be helpful to conclude by offering the reader ethical guidelines about the issues discussed in this chapter. I agree with Parkes (1995) and Cook (1995) that training and supervision in dealing with people who are bereaved are essen-tial. I am all for giving people maximum freedom not to serve in a bereavement study or to stop at any time, to have informed consent prior to engaging in a study and processual consent during it, for researchers to avoid providing thera-peutic intervention and to be very attentive to the needs and realities of the people being studied. But as with the shoulds of the IRB, there is much more to doing ethical interview research than the ethical principles I have endorsed here. I do not think that there is a trustworthy ethical formula that one can bring to a qualitative research interview. If anything, one must be open to co-constructing a set of ethical guidelines as the interview unfolds.

ACKNOWLEDGEMENTS

This chapter is a revision of Rosenblatt (1995), reproduced by permission of Taylor & Francis, publishers. My thanks to Anna Hagemeister for library explorations and to her, Janice Nadeau, Ramona Oswald, David Balk, Alicia Cook, and two anonymous reviewers for *Death Studies* for a critical reading of an earlier draft of this chapter.

REFERENCES

Cook, A.S. (1995). Ethical issues in bereavement research: An overview. *Death Studies*, **19**, 103–122.
Cook, A.S. & Bosley, G. (1995). The experience of participating in bereavement research: Stressful or therapeutic? *Death Studies*, **19**, 157–170.

LaRossa, R., Bennett, L.A. & Gelles, R.J. (1981). Ethical dilemmas in qualitative family research. *Journal of Marriage and the Family*, **43**, 303–313.

Nadeau, J.W. (1998). *Families Making Sense of Death*. Thousand Oaks, CA: Sage.

Parkes, C.M. (1995). Guidelines for conducting ethical bereavement research. *Death Studies*, **19**, 171–181.

Ramos, M.C. (1989). Some ethical implications of qualitative research. *Research in Nursing and Health*, **12**, 57–63.

Rosenblatt, P.C. (1983). *Bitter, Bitter Tears: Nineteenth Century Diarists and Twentieth Century Grief Theories*. Minneapolis: University of Minnesota Press.

Rosenblatt, P.C. (1993a). *Coping with Losing a Family Member in a Farm Accident* (publication #FO-6205-B). St Paul, MN: Minnesota Extension Service.

Rosenblatt, P.C. (1993b). *Helping Someone Who Has Lost a Family Member in a Farm Accident* (publication #FO-6204-B). St Paul, MN: Minnesota Extension Service.

Rosenblatt, P.C. (1994). *Metaphors of Family Systems Theory: Toward New Constructions*. New York: Guilford.

Rosenblatt, P.C. (1995). Ethics of qualitative interviewing in grieving families. *Death Studies*, **19**, 139–155.

Rosenblatt, P.C. & Karis, T.A. (1993). Economics and family bereavement following a fatal farm accident. *Journal of Rural Community Psychology*, **12**(2), 37–51.

Rosenblatt, P.C., & Karis, T.A. (1993–1994). Family distancing following a fatal farm accident. *Omega*, **28**, 183–200.

Thorne, B. (1980). "You still takin' notes?" Fieldwork and problems of informed consent. *Social Problems*, **27**, 284–297.

Worden, J.W. (1991). *Grief Counseling and Grief Therapy: A Handbook for the Mental Health Practitioner* (2nd edn). New York: Springer.

Part 4

Interviewing in Organisational Contexts

The Employment Interview

Deborah L. Whetzel
US Postal Service
and
Michael A. McDaniel
University of Akron, Ohio, USA

Employment interviews are face-to-face interactions between an interviewer (or an interview board) and an applicant for a job. The interview is designed to acquire information concerning past, present and future behavior, beliefs, opinions or attitudes of interviewees. Information about individuals' previous experience, education and vocational aspirations reported during the interview, and behavior observed during the interview are considered the content of the interview. The content of the interview is usually determined using job analysis data (e.g. critical incidents). The extent to which the interview questions and responses are specified in advance are considered the structure of the interview. There are several levels of structure which will be described later in this chapter. Both the content and structure of the interview are thought to affect validity of the interview for predicting job performance.

This chapter will describe the psychometric characteristics of the employment interview, including reliability, validity and the incremental validity of the interview beyond cognitive ability tests. Then, we will discuss issues that have been shown to impact on the validity of the interview, including interview content and structure. We will then discuss issues regarding person–organization fit and describe supporting research. Finally, we will describe several issues that can impact on decisions made by interviewers, such as impression management and unfavorable information.

Handbook of the Psychology of Interviewing. Edited by A. Memon and R. Bull.
© 1999 John Wiley & Sons Ltd.

RELIABILITY

One of the most prevalent criticisms of the interview is its lack of reliability. That is, different interviewers independently interviewing the same candidate often disagree about the candidate's suitability for employment (Valenzi & Andrews, 1973). There are several likely causes for the lack of reliability among interviewers. First, the unstructured interview does not guide the interviewing procedure in any way to ensure that common questions are asked and that the interviewers are thereby provided with a common basis for assessment (Webster, 1964). Another problem with unstructured interviews is that they fail to standardize the way in which the obtained information is to be interpreted or weighted. For example, one interviewer may value interpersonal skills more than past experience while another interviewer may think past experience is more important than interpersonal skills. Still another interviewer may think that the way an applicant dresses is important. Differences in how interviewers weight relevant variables and whether they consider potentially irrelevant variables are likely to result in different overall evaluations of the same applicant.

Several early reviews of the literature on employment interviews suggested that interviewing applicants for jobs was unreliable, and therefore, lacking in validity (Mayfield, 1964; Ulrich & Trumbo, 1965; Wagner, 1949). Mayfield suggested that typical unstructured interviews with no prior data on interviewees were inconsistent in their coverage. He indicated that interview validities were low, even in studies that reported moderate reliabilities. He reasoned that while interviewers may be consistent in their approach to interviewees, they are inconsistent in their interpretation of data. Several researchers have made suggestions about methods for improving the reliability of employment interviews, thereby increasing their potential validity. After reviewing the literature, Landy (1985) stated that higher degrees of structure appear to increase interviewers' agreement on their overall evaluations or predictions. In addition, asking questions that tap specific job requirements increases interrater agreement.

The effect on reliability of interview structure and of using job analysis to determine interview content was addressed by Conway, Jako and Goodman (1995). They conducted a meta-analysis using 111 interrater reliability coefficients and found that the overall mean and variance were 0.70 and 0.035, respectively, and that the 90% confidence interval for the mean was 0.39 to 1.00. Since the interval did not include zero, the reliability of interviews was considered to generalize across situations. However, they uncovered a number of variables that moderated interview reliability. They found that standardization of questions, standardization of response evaluation, use of job analysis to determine interview content, and interviewer training moderated (increased) reliability. Given the levels of reliability they found, the authors estimated that the upper limits of validity were 0.67 for highly structured interviews and 0.34 for unstructured interviews.

In sum, contrary to previous reviews, recent research on the reliability of employment interviews suggests that the interview can be a reliable tool for assessment and prediction. Its reliability can be enhanced by: (1) using job analysis to define the content of the interview, (2) using a structured set of questions for all applicants, and (3) standardizing response evaluation.

VALIDITY

There have been several quantitative reviews of the validity of interviews (in which the mean validity was calculated) that appear to substantiate Mayfield's (1964) pessimistic findings. Hunter and Hunter's (1984) analysis, including 27 coefficients, found that the validity of the interview for predicting supervisor ratings was low (0.14). Reilly and Chao (1982) obtained a higher validity (0.19) for predicting training and job performance, but they only had 12 coefficients available. Dunnette, Arvey and Arnold's (1971) analysis used 30 coefficients in which the criterion was supervisor ratings, and they obtained an average validity of 0.16.

However, four relatively recent meta-analytic reviews suggest that, contrary to previous results, the interview method has at least moderate validity (Huffcutt & Arthur, 1994; McDaniel et al., 1994; Wiesner & Cronshaw, 1988; Wright, Lichtenfels & Pursell, 1989).

Wright et al. (1989) found that after correcting for criterion unreliability, the mean validity of the interview, using 13 coefficients, was 0.37. Placing the 95% confidence interval around this mean suggested that the true validity fell between –0.07 and 0.77. Since this interval included zero, they could not conclude that the interview was valid for all jobs. However, after eliminating one study that reported a negative validity coefficient (–0.22; Kennedy, 1986) with a very large sample size, the mean corrected validity was 0.39 with a 95% confidence interval of 0.27 to 0.49.

Wiesner and Cronshaw (1988) investigated interview validity using 150 coefficients in which 15 459 individuals were studied. They investigated validity as a function of interview format (individual vs. board) and degree of structure (structured vs. unstructured). They found that structured interviews, in which the questions and various levels of response were specified in advance, yielded a much higher mean corrected validity than unstructured interviews (0.63 vs. 0.20) and that structured board interviews using consensus ratings had the highest corrected validity (0.64). They also found that validity increased as a function of whether a job analysis was conducted. However, because their analysis combined validities computed using criteria such as job performance, training performance, and tenure, additional investigation was warranted.

Huffcutt and Arthur (1994) conducted a meta-analysis using 114 validity coefficients, in which 18 652 individuals were studied. They examined the level of interview structure as a moderating variable. They classified interviews in terms of standardization of interview questions and response scoring procedures. They found that: (1) structure moderated interview validity; (2) interviews, particularly when structured, can reach levels of validity that are comparable to those of mental ability tests (0.37); and (3) although validity does increase through much of the range of structure, there is a point at which additional structure essentially yields no incremental validity, thus suggesting a ceiling effect for structure.

McDaniel et al. (1994) cumulated 245 validity coefficients in which 86 311 individuals were studied. They compared different kinds of interview content (situational, job-related and psychological), different methods for conducting interviews (structured and unstructured; board and individual), and used different criteria (job performance, training performance and tenure) collected for different purposes (research criteria, administrative criteria). For the prediction of job performance criteria, situational interviews had a higher mean validity (0.50) than job-related interviews (0.39), which had a higher mean validity than psychological interviews (0.29). They found that if the interview were structured, it was more valid than previously believed (0.44). In fact, even unstructured interviews appeared to be more valid than previously believed (0.33).

Whereas these meta-analytic reviews combined several kinds of structured interviews, Pulakos and Schmitt (1995) reviewed the validity of experience-based questions (asking individuals how they had handled situations in the past requiring skills and abilities necessary for effective performance) and situational questions (asking individuals how they would respond if they were confronted with particular problems in the future). They found that experience-based interview questions yielded higher levels of validity than situational questions (0.32 vs. –0.02).

In sum, although previous quantitative reviews have suggested that the employment interview is not a good predictor of job performance, relatively recent meta-analytic studies, with greater numbers of coefficients, show that the interview does predict job performance, especially if the interview is structured and the questions and response rating scales are based on job analysis results as described later in this chapter.

INCREMENTAL VALIDITY BEYOND COGNITIVE ABILITY

There is considerable research showing that the best predictor of job performance is cognitive ability (Hunter & Hunter, 1984). However, given the relatively large differences between minorities' and nonminorities' scores on such tests (Gottfredson, 1986), identifying valid predictors, to supplement prediction beyond cognitive ability and reduce subgroup differences, is an important concern. Results from several studies (e.g. Campion, Pursell & Brown, 1988) have led to the conclusion that the interview operates like an "orally administered cognitive ability test". However, in the Campion et al. (1988) study, the interview included questions about reading, mathematics, and mechanical knowledge. In contrast, Campion, Campion and Hudson (1994) used the interview to predict constructs such as teamwork, self-management, commitment and other social attributes not typically viewed as cognitive ability. They found that the interview showed substantial correlations with the cognitive ability tests, but still had meaningful incremental validity for predicting both cognitive and noncognitive performance criteria. Pulakos and Schmitt (1995) examined the incremental validity of experience-based interviews over cognitive ability tests (the Air Force Officer Qualification Test). The correlation between the interview and a composite performance rating was 0.38; the correlation between cognitive ability and performance was 0.17. The correlation between the interview and cognitive ability was very low (0.09). Concerning incremental validity, they found that the interview explained additional variance in the performance measure beyond that explained by the cognitive test.

Huffcutt, Roth and McDaniel (1996) investigated the extent to which cognitive ability is assessed in employment interviews. Their meta-analysis of 49 studies showed that the average correlation between interview ratings and cognitive ability test scores was 0.25, which increased to 0.40 after correcting for artifacts. They also looked at potential moderating variables and found that the correlation between interview scores and ability tended to decrease as the level of structure increased and that the correlation was higher for low-complexity jobs.

In sum, these studies suggest that the correlation between cognitive ability and interview ratings is low (0.09; Pulakos & Schmitt, 1995) or moderate (0.40; Huffcutt et al., 1996). The incremental validity evidence is ambiguous, with some studies finding incremental validity (Campion et al., 1994; Pulakos & Schmitt, 1995) and others finding no evidence of incremental validity (Campion et al., 1988; Delery et al., 1994; Walters, Miller & Ree, 1993). These discrepant findings might be explained by the variability in correlations between interviews and cognitive ability. Interviews can be built to have varying levels of correlations with cognitive ability. For example, interviews emphasizing problem solving would likely have higher correlations with cognitive ability than interviews focusing on the ability to get along with others. It would be reasonable to argue that interviews with higher correlations with cognitive ability should show less incremental validity than interviews with lower correlations with cognitive ability. Future research in the area of incremental validity should consider the constructs assessed by the interview and the correlation between these constructs and cognitive ability.

Now that we have described several psychometric characteristics of the interview, we now turn to characteristics of the interview that may have an impact on validity and reliability. These include interview content and structure.

INTERVIEW CONTENT

Interview content has been described in several ways. Some interviews focus on the individual's ability to project what his or her behavior would be in a given situation that might occur on the job in the future (e.g. situational interviews

(Latham et al., 1980)). In these kinds of interviews, applicants are asked, "Given a particular situation, what would you do?" Applicants are presented with a situation and asked for a description of the actions he/she would take in that scenario.

In contrast, interviews can focus on past behaviors and job-related experience. The underlying assumption of such interviews is that future behavior is predicted by past behavior and to the extent that individuals have relevant experience in an area, they will be able to perform the duties of the job for which they are interviewing. Examples of these kinds of interviews include the structured behavioral interview (Motowidlo et al., 1992), experience-based interviews (Pulakos & Schmitt, 1995), and patterned behavior description interviews (Janz, 1982, 1989).

The important issue concerning these kinds of interviews is that the questions should be based on job analysis. Job analysis is required for developing and validating selection procedures (including interviews) according to both professional (Society for Industrial and Organizational Psychology, 1987) and legal (Equal Employment Opportunity Commission, Civil Service Commission, Department of Labor & Department of Justice, 1978) testing guidelines. The critical incident technique is a useful method of job analysis that can be used to develop interview questions. A critical incident report typically includes three pieces of information: (1) a description of the situation that led to the incident, (2) the actions or behaviors of the focal person in the incident, and (3) the results, or outcome of those actions. Given these three pieces of information, an interpretation as to the effectiveness of the actions can be made. The situations can be used as questions and the effectiveness of various responses can be determined by gathering several critical incidents of similar situations and determining the effectiveness of various responses.

Campion, Palmer and Campion (1997) discuss two other kinds of interview questions: (1) background questions that focus on work experience, education and other qualifications (e.g. What experience have you had with sales and marketing?), and (2) job knowledge questions which ask the applicant to describe their knowledge of the job (e.g. What steps would you follow in developing a training curriculum?). As with the first two kinds of questions described above, job analysis is necessary to develop these kinds of items as well.

Several narrative reviews of the validity of interviews have shown that using job analysis results improves validity (Arvey & Campion, 1982; Harris, 1989; Schmitt, 1976). Meta-analytic reviews also have provided evidence concerning the use of job analysis to improve the validity of interviews (McDaniel et al., 1994; Weisner & Cronshaw, 1988).

INTERVIEW STRUCTURE

Interviews can be differentiated by their level of structure. Huffcutt (1992) defined structure as the reduction in procedural variability across applicants, which can translate into the degree of discretion an interviewer is allowed when conducting the interview. In unstructured interviews, the interviewer typically asks the interviewee to "tell me about yourself" and the interviewee can describe a wide range of behavior including hobbies and/or experience performing duties similar to those likely to be performed on the job. In these kinds of interviews, the interviewer can ask follow-up questions, but is not required to do so. The interviewer has a great deal of discretion in terms of what questions are asked of each interviewee.

In structured interviews, on the other hand, there are predetermined rules for eliciting, observing and evaluating responses. This often includes specifying the questions in advance and rating the responses for appropriateness of content. The structured interview limits interviewers' discretion by stipulating the kinds of issues they are to ask about when questioning applicants about their behavior. Huffcutt (1992) identified two dimensions of structure related to the degree of discretion in the conduct of the interview, namely, standardization of (1) interview questions and (b) response scoring.

Huffcutt (1992) reviewed the literature on interview structure and described four progressively higher levels of structure. Level 1 was the typical unstructured interview characterized by the lack of constraints on the questions. Level 2 called for limited constraints by specifying the topics to be covered by the questions. Level 3 required the prespecification of questions, although applicants were not asked precisely the same questions because different interview forms were used or interviewers were allowed to choose among alternative questions and to probe responses to the specified questions (e.g. Janz, 1982). Level 4 involved asking applicants precisely the same questions with no deviation or follow-up probes (e.g. Latham et al., 1980).

Huffcutt's review suggested that the standardization of response scoring could be described by three progressively higher levels of structure. Level 1 was characterized by the formation of a single overall evaluation based on total interview information (e.g. Ghiselli, 1966). Level 2 involved the formation of multiple evaluations along pre-established criteria, such as job dimensions or traits (e.g. Janz, 1982, 1989). Finally, Level 3 was distinguished by the evaluation of applicant responses to each individual question according to preestablished benchmark answers (e.g. Latham et al., 1980).

In sum, there are several narrative and meta-analytic reviews that suggest that asking the same questions of all interviewees increases the validity of the interview, perhaps because it reduces contamination by preventing discussion of irrelevant topics and other biasing influences (Dipboye & Gaugler, 1993) or it reduces cognitive overload of the interviewer by focusing attention on a limited number of specific questions (Dipboye & Gaugler, 1993; Maurer & Fay, 1988).

Now that we have described issues that affect the overall reliability and validity of the interview, we will discuss issues that can impact on employment decisions made by both the employer and the prospective employee. Many of these issues are described in the person–environment fit literature. Some of that research is described below.

PERSON–ENVIRONMENT FIT

The history of person–environment fit research comes largely from Schneider's attraction–selection–attrition (ASA) model (Schneider, 1987; Schneider, Goldstein & Smith, 1995). The model is based on the premise that it is the collective characteristics of people which define an organization, rather than the organization setting the climate and people reacting to it. Further, over time, organizations become defined by the persons in them as an outcome of the attraction–selection–attrition cycle. The attraction process refers to the idea that people's preferences for particular organizations are based on an implicit estimate of the similarity of their own personal characteristics and values and the goals of the organization. The selection process is used by organizations to recruit and hire individuals with the attributes deemed desirable by the organization. Last, the attrition process refers to the notion that the people will leave an organization in which they do not fit. This cycle typically results in organizations with people who have distinct personalities and it is those distinct personalities that are responsible for the structures, processes and cultures that characterize organizations (Schneider et al., 1995).

The selection method that is probably most critical to assessments of person–organization fit is the employment interview (Chatman, 1991; Judge & Ferris, 1992). The interview allows applicants and organizations to interact to determine if the other demonstrates congruent values and interests (Bowen, Ledford & Nathan, 1991). Research has examined the relationship between person–organization fit and organizational hiring decisions. Rynes and Gerhart (1990) investigated general employability, in which characteristics of the ideal candidate included leadership, motivation, enthusiasm, creativity and analytic ability (or what they call "apple pie" attributes) versus a more tailored method of assessing person–organization fit. They found that person–organization fit is a separate construct from general employability and the interviewers evaluate person–organization fit according to their organization's values, not just their own personal preferences. They also found that applicants' interpersonal attributes (e.g. leadership) were related to interviewers' fit assessments.

Another aspect of interviews that have been examined with regard to person–organization fit is the congruence of work values. Adkins, Russell and Werbel (1994) examined work value congruence between applicants and organizations and found that work value congruence between the applicant and the recruiter was found to be related to judgments of general employability and organization-specific fit. However, congruence between the applicant and the organization (as perceived by the recruiter) was not related to judgments of employability and organization-specific fit. Although these studies appear to yield different conclusions, they were asking different questions. Rynes and Gerhart (1990) examined perceived congruence (i.e. similarity between an interviewer's perceptions of an applicant's and their organization's values), whereas Adkins et al. (1994) examined actual congruence (similarity between an applicant's attributes and an organization's attributes as reported by each). Another recent study on person–

organization fit and values congruence was conducted by Cable and Judge (1997). They found that interviewers can accurately assess applicant–organization values congruence and that interviewers compare their perceptions of applicants' values with their organization's values to assess person–organization fit. They concluded that values congruence affects interviewers' person–organization fit perceptions, but it is perceived, rather than actual, congruence that best predicts fit judgments. They reconciled previous conflicting findings by concluding that the comparatively weak effect of actual congruence is moderated by three other variables: perceived congruence, subjective fit perceptions, and recommendation to hire. Therefore, actual congruence is a relatively distal influence. Now that we have discussed broad issues surrounding person–organization fit, we will discuss specific issues that impact on employment decisions, including impression management and unfavorable information.

IMPRESSION MANAGEMENT

Impression management concerns the use of tactics to induce positive reactions among interviewers (Jones & Pittman, 1982; Schlenker, 1980). Specifically, the term refers to changes individuals make to manage aspects of their behavior in order to create a positive impression on others (Baron, 1989). Tedschi and Melburg (1984) constructed a 2×2 taxonomy of impression management behaviors. The first continuum consists of assertive and defensive self-presentations. Assertive behaviors include self-promotion used to enhance one's image. Defensive behaviors include making excuses or offering explanations to maintain a positive image. The other continuum consists of tactical and strategic behaviors. Tactical behaviors are directed at immediate, short-term issues; strategic behaviors are those directed toward long-term interests and establishing one's reputation. Interviewee behaviors can be classified into any of the four quadrants. For example, assertive tactical behaviors include claiming responsibility for positive events and promoting one's accomplishments. Both of these behaviors serve the short-term goal of influencing the interviewer. Assertive strategic behaviors that establish one's reputation are very important, but are more difficult to change during the interview itself. The quality of an applicant's background, accomplishments and credibility are difficult to manipulate during an interview. Providing information in the form of an application blank or resumé can be viewed as an assertive strategic approach. Defensive tactical behaviors, including making apologies or excuses typically occur when an applicant perceives him/herself to be in a dilemma. Defensive strategic behaviors that include long-term adjustments to failures are usually avoided by applicants who wish to make a favorable impression on an interviewer. These last two kinds of impression management behaviors are typically used when an applicant is in trouble and should certainly be avoided if possible.

Another assertive tactical technique includes appearing to have beliefs and attitudes similar to those of the interviewer (Schmitt, 1976). Research shows that

applicants who listen carefully to interviewers' opinions or who have prior knowledge of an organization can express opinions consistent with that information
and can appear to fit in with the prevailing culture. For example, if it is known
that teamwork is valued in an organization, an applicant could use tactical impression management to describe group activities in which he/she participated,
rather than individual projects for which he/she was solely responsible.

Other impression management techniques include personal appearance and
nonverbal communication. Several studies have shown that interviewers' reactions to job candidates are strongly influenced by style of dress and grooming.
Persons judged to be attractive, or appropriately groomed or attired, received
higher ratings than those judged to be inappropriately dressed or unattractive
(Cash, 1985; Forsythe, Drake & Cox, 1985). Studies also have indicated that the
use of positive nonverbal cues (e.g. leaning forward and maintaining eye contact)
can enhance ratings of applicants by interviewers (Imada & Hakel, 1977;
Rasmussen, 1984). Such tactics are likely to generate positive affect which, in
turn, increases interviewer ratings (Cardy & Dobbins, 1986).

In sum, there are several techniques applicants can use to sway an interviewer's opinions in a favorable light. These include assertive tactical maneuvers
such as promoting one's own accomplishments or taking credit for achievements.
They also include defensive strategies such as making excuses or apologizing for
actions. These defensive strategies are typically only used when a candidate
perceives that he/she is in a predicament during the interview. Other strategies
include nonbehavioral methods, such as dress and grooming and nonverbal behavior. Next, we describe the impact of unfavorable information.

UNFAVORABLE INFORMATION EFFECTS

Several studies have investigated the impact of unfavorable information (e.g.
having been fired by a previous employer) on interviewer decisions. Bolster and
Springbett (1961) found that, on average, 8.8 items of favorable information
were required to change an initially unfavorable impression, but only 3.8 items of
unfavorable information were required to change an initially favorable impression. Carlson and Mayfield (1967) reported that unfavorable information was
weighted about twice as heavily as favorable information. These studies suggest
that unfavorable information is more highly weighted than favorable information. Springbett (1958) and Rowe (1984, 1989) provided a plausible explanation
for this effect. In an organization, decision-makers are doing the jobs expected of
them by hiring appropriate applicants and not hiring inappropriate applicants.
Positive feedback or rewards for correct hiring decisions are relatively rare.
However, accepting a candidate who lacks the necessary abilities and skills for
the job has more serious consequences for the decision-maker, in terms of negative feedback and decreased productivity. On the other hand, rejecting good
candidates is likely to go unnoticed and therefore unpunished. As a result, the
costs of false positives are greater than the costs of false negatives. It is not

surprising that interviewers develop an attitude of caution and a high degree of sensitivity to negative evidence in an attempt to avoid hiring poor candidates, especially if they have had a bad experience after hiring such an applicant.

Another negative information model of interviewer behavior uses a positive test strategy (Rowe, 1989). In a selection situation, interviewers may test whether the applicant is a good applicant (i.e. a positive hypothesis test) or whether the applicant is a potentially incompetent worker (i.e. a negative hypothesis test). In the first case, favorable information supports the hypothesis, but is not conclusive as to whether the applicant is actually a good candidate, while unfavorable information, which indicates that the applicant does not meet minimum standards for the job, proves the hypothesis false. Therefore, positive information provides evidence, but is not conclusive, whereas negative information disconfirms the hypothesis. With the negative hypothesis test, the applicant is hypothesized as not fitting in with the group of competent applicants and probably would not be interviewed.

In conclusion, rather than the interview being a search for negative information, as originally proposed by Springbett (1958), it may be a search for confirmation of a positive hypothesis. When an interviewer encounters negative information, it is much more important than positive information because it disconfirms the hypothesis, which may change the decision.

SUMMARY

This chapter described the psychometric characteristics of the employment interview, including reliability, validity and the incremental validity of the interview beyond cognitive ability tests. Interview content and structure were discussed as they impact on the validity of the interview. Issues regarding person–organization fit and supporting research were then described. Finally, we described factors that can impact on decisions made by interviewers, such as impression management and unfavorable information.

REFERENCES

Adkins, C.L., Russell, C.J. & Werbel, J.D. (1994). Judgments of fit in the selection process: The role of work-value congruence. *Personnel Psychology*, **47**, 605–623.

Arvey, R.D. & Campion, J.E. (1982). The employment interview: A summary and review of recent research. *Personnel Psychology*, **35**, 281–322.

Baron, R.A. (1989). Impression management by applicants during employment interviews: The "too much of a good thing" effect. In R.W. Eder & G.R. Ferris (Eds.), *The Employment Interview: Theory, Research and Practice*, (pp. 204–215), Newbury Park, CA: Sage.

Bolster, B.I. & Springbett, B.J. (1961). The reaction of interviewers to favorable and unfavorable information. *Journal of Applied Psychology*, **67**, 3–9.

Bowen, D.E., Ledford, G.E., Jr & Nathan, B.R. (1991). Hiring for the organization not for the job. *Academy of Management Executive*, **5**, 35–51.

Cable, D.M. & Judge, T.A. (1997). Interviewers' perceptions of person–organization fit and organizational selection decisions. *Journal of Applied Psychology*, **82**, 546–561.

Campion, M.A., Campion, J.E. & Hudson, J.P., Jr (1994). Structured interviewing: A note on incremental validity and alternative question types. *Journal of Applied Psychology*, **79**, 998–1002.

Campion, M.A., Palmer, D.K. & Campion, J.E. (1997). A review of structure in the selection interview. *Personnel Psychology*, **50**, 655–702.

Campion, M.A., Pursell, E.D. & Brown, B.K. (1988). Structured interviewing: Raising the psychometric properties of the employment interview. *Personnel Psychology*, **41**, 25–42.

Cardy, R.L. & Dobbins, G.H. (1986). Affect and appraisal accuracy: Liking as an integral dimension in evaluating performance. *Journal of Applied Psychology*, **71**, 672–678.

Carlson, R.E. & Mayfield, E.C. (1967). Evaluating interview and employment application data. *Personnel Psychology*, **20**, 441–460.

Cash, T.F. (1985). The impact of grooming style on the evaluation of women in management. In M. Soloman (Ed.), *The Psychology of Fashion*. New York: Lexington Press.

Chatman, J. (1991). Matching people and organizations: Selection and socialization in public accounting firms. *Administrative Science Quarterly*, **36**, 459–484.

Conway, J.M., Jako, R.A. & Goodman, D.F. (1995). A meta-analysis of interrater and internal consistency reliability of selection interviews. *Journal of Applied Psychology*, **80**, 565–579.

Delery, J.E., Wright, P.M., McArthur, K. & Anderson, D.C. (1994). Cognitive ability tests and the situational interview: A test of incremental validity. *International Journal of Selection and Assessment*, **2**, 53–58.

Dipboye, R.L. & Gaugler, B.B. (1993). Cognitive and behavioral processes in the selection interview. In Schmitt, N., Borman, W.C., Associates (Eds.), *Personnel Selection in Organizations* (pp. 135–170). San Francisco: Jossey-Bass.

Dunnette, M.D., Arvey, R.D. & Arnold, J.A. (1971). *Validity Study Results for Jobs Relevant to the Petroleum Refining Industry*. Minneapolis: Personnel Decisions, Inc. also published as American Petroleum Institute Report No. 754.

Equal Employment Opportunity Commission, Civil Service Commission, Department of Labor & Department of Justice. (1978). Adoption by four agencies of uniform guidelines on employee selection procedures. *Federal Register*, **43**, 38290–38315.

Forsythe, S., Drake, M.F. & Cox, C.E. (1985). Influence of applicant's dress on interviewer's selection decisions. *Journal of Applied Psychology*, **70**, 374–378.

Ghiselli, E.E. (1966). The validity of a personnel interview. *Personnel Psychology*, **19**, 389–394.

Gottfredson, L.S. (1986). The g factor in employment [Special Issue]. *Journal of Vocational Behavior*, **29**(3).

Harris, M.M. (1989). Reconsidering the employment interview: A review of recent literature and suggestions for future research. *Personnel Psychology*, **42**, 691–726.

Huffcutt, A.I. (1992). *An empirical investigation of the relationship between multidimensional degree of structure and the validity of the employment interview*. Unpublished doctoral dissertation, Texas A&M University, College Station.

Huffcutt, A.I. & Arthur, W. (1994). Hunter and Hunter (1984) revisited: Interview validity for entry-level jobs. *Journal of Applied Psychology*, **79**, 184–190.

Huffcutt, A.I., Roth, R.L. & McDaniel, M.A. (1996). A meta-analytic investigation of cognitive ability in employment interview evaluations: Moderating characteristics and implications for incremental validity. *Journal of Applied Psychology*, **81,** 459–473.

Hunter, J.E. & Hunter, R.F. (1984). The validity and utility of alternative predictors of job performance. *Psychological Bulletin*, **96**, 72–98.

Imada, A.S. & Hakel, M.D. (1977). Influence of nonverbal communication and rater proximity on impression and decisions in simulated employment interviews. *Journal of Applied Psychology*, **62**, 295–300.

Janz, T. (1982). Initial comparisons of patterned behavior description interviews versus unstructured interviews. *Journal of Applied Psychology*, **67**, 577–580.

Janz, T. (1989). The patterned behavior description interview: The best prophet of the future is the past. In R.W. Eder & G.R. Ferris (Eds.), *The Employment Interview: Theory, Research and Practice*. (pp. 158–168), Newbury Park, CA: Sage.

Jones, E.E., & Pittman, T.S. (1982). Toward a general theory of strategic self-presentation. In J. Suls (Ed.), *Psychological perspectives on the self*. Hillsdale, NJ: Lawrence Erlbaum.

Judge, T.A. & Ferris, G.R. (1992). The elusive criterion of fit in human resource staffing decisions. *Human Resource Planning*, **15**, 47–67.

Kennedy, R. (1986). *An investigation of criterion-related validity for the structured interview*. Masters thesis, East Carolina University.

Landy, F. (1985). *The Psychology of Work Behavior*. Homewood, IL: The Dorsey Press.

Latham, G.P., Saari, L.M., Pursell, E.D. & Campion, M.A. (1980). The situational interview. *Journal of Applied Psychology*, **65**, 422–427.

Maurer, S.D. & Fay, C. (1988). Effect of situational interviews, conventional structured interviews, and training on interview rating agreement: An experimental analysis. *Personnel Psychology*, **41**, 329–344.

Mayfield, E.C. (1964). The selection interview: A reevaluation of published research. *Personnel Psychology*, **17**, 239–260.

McDaniel, M.A., Whetzel, D.L., Schmidt, F.L. & Maurer, S. (1994). The validity of employment interviews: A comprehensive review and meta-analysis. *Journal of Applied Psychology*, **79**, 599–616.

Motowidlo, S.J., Carter, G.W., Dunnette, M.D., Tippins, N., Werner, S., Burnett, J.R. & Vaughan, M.J. (1992). Studies of the structured behavioral interview. *Journal of Applied Psychology*, **77**, 571–587.

Pulakos, E.D. & Schmitt, N. (1995). Experience-based and situational interview questions: Studies of validity. *Personnel Psychology*, **48**, 289–308.

Rasmussen, K.G. (1984). Nonverbal behavior, verbal behavior, resumé credentials, and selection interview outcomes. *Journal of Applied Psychology*, **69**, 551–556.

Reilly, R.A. & Chao, G.T. (1982). Validity and fairness of some alternative employee selection procedures. *Personnel Psychology*, **35**, 1–62.

Rowe, P.M. (1963). Individual differences in selection decisions. *Journal of Applied Psychology*, **47**, 304–307.

Rowe, P.M. (1984). Decision processes in personnel selection. *Canadian Journal of Behavioural Science*, **16**, 325–337.

Rowe, P.M. (1989). Unfavorable information and interview decisions. In R.W. Eder & G.R. Ferris (Eds.), *The Employment Interview: Theory, Research and Practice*. (pp. 75–110), Newbury Park, CA: Sage.

Rynes, S.L. & Gerhart, B. (1990). Interviewer assessments of applicant "fit:" An exploratory investigation. *Personnel Psychology*, **43**, 13–35.

Schlenker, B.R. (1980). *Impression Management: The Self-Concept, Social Identity, and Interpersonal Relations*. Monterey, CA: Brooks/Cole.

Schmitt, N. (1976). Social and situation determinants of interview decisions: Implications for the employment interview. *Personnel Psychology*, **29**, 79–101.

Schneider, B. (1987). The people make the place. *Personnel Psychology*, **40**, 437–453.

Schneider, B., Goldstein, H.W. & Smith, D.B. (1995). The ASA framework: An update, *Personnel Psychology*, **48**, 747–773.

Society for Industrial and Organizational Psychology. (1987). *Principles for the Validation and Use of Personnel Selection Procedures* (3rd edn). College Park, MD: Author.

Springbett, B.M. (1958). Factors affecting the final decision in the employment interview. *Canadian Journal of Psychology*, **12**, 13–22.

Tedschi, J.T. & Melburg, V. (1984). Impression management and influence in the organization. In S. Bacharach & E.J. Lawler (Eds.), *Research in the Sociology of Organizations* (Vol. 3, pp. 31–58). Greenwich, CT: JAI.

Ulrich, L. & Trumbo, D. (1965). The selection interview since 1949. *Psychological Bulletin*, **63**, 100–116.

Valenzi, E. & Andrews, I.R. (1973). Individual differences in the decision processes of employment interviews. *Journal of Applied Psychology*, **58**, 49–53.

Wagner, R. (1949). The employment interview: A critical summary. *Personnel Psychology*, **2**, 17–46.

Walters, L.C., Miller, M.R. & Ree, M.J. (1993). Structured interviews for pilot selection: No incremental validity. *International Journal of Aviation Psychology*, **3**, 25–38.

Webster, E.C. (1964). *Decision Making in the Employment Interview*. Montreal: Industrial Relations Centre, McGill University.

Wiesner, W.H. & Cronshaw, S.F. (1988). The moderating impact of interview format and degree of structure on the validity of the employment interview. *Journal of Occupational Psychology*, **61**, 275–290.

Wright, P.M., Lichtenfels, P.A. & Pursell, E.D. (1989). The structured interview: Additional studies and a meta-analysis. *Journal of Occupational Psychology*, **62**, 191–199.

The Interview as a Usability Tool

Mark S. Young *and* **Neville A. Stanton**
Brunel University, UK

INTRODUCTION

The interview is a highly flexible and adaptable tool. That fact is highlighted and exploited in this chapter, which looks at how the interview may be used to improve usability in the design of consumer products.

Many techniques have been developed for the express purpose of conducting usability evaluations, each with its own agenda and each directed at different aspects of usability. However, rather than constantly develop new devices, some researchers have applied more basic methods to the assessment of usability. These have included heuristics (e.g. Nielsen & Molich, 1990), observation (e.g. Drury, 1990), checklists (e.g. Ravden & Johnson, 1989), and questionnaires (e.g. Brooke, 1996), in addition to the interview.

One way of applying the interview to usability evaluations is described by Christie, Scane and Collyer (1990), that of "cooperative evaluation". A potential end user is given a prototype product and is asked to carry out specific tasks with it. He or she is then interviewed by a member of the design team for information on usability, problems encountered, and possible design improvements. The interaction is allowed to flow freely with few constraints, such that the user feels comfortable enough to air his/her criticisms about the product.

The research described in this chapter follows this precedent, using a similar approach to apply the interview to a specific consumer product. The chapter begins with a discussion of the concept of usability, and how the interview may be applied to usability evaluations. This is followed by details of our own study investigating reliability and validity of the interview in a usability setting. These

Handbook of the Psychology of Interviewing. Edited by A. Memon and R. Bull.
© 1999 John Wiley & Sons Ltd.

results are from a larger project which examined reliability and validity of 12 usability evaluation techniques, including the interview (see Stanton & Young, 1998, for details of the other methods). Finally, some suggestions and recommendations are made for the practitioner who wishes to adopt the interview as a usability tool.

USABILITY IN DESIGN

The concept of usability has attracted an increasing amount of attention over recent years, as designers of consumer products begin to recognise it as an important factor in customer satisfaction. Indeed, the term "ergonomically designed" is now a familiar sight on marketing material, although the validity of such claims is often questionable. Furthermore, usability can have a bearing on safety if the product in question is part of a more complex system (e.g. in-car devices). There is an increasing argument that safety in cars actually increases sales (Faith, 1996).

As such, there has been a parallel increase in psychological and human factors research directed at defining and improving usability. In a nutshell, usability is equivalent to ease-of-use. Although many researchers concentrate on the physical and anthropometric side of this, it should also include cognitive aspects. In more detail, usability may be assessed against the LEAF criteria (Shackel, 1981):

- Learnability (users reach an acceptable performance within a specified time)
- Effectiveness (criterion performance is achieved by a defined proportion of the population across different tasks and environments)
- Attitude (user satisfaction, fatigue, stress), and
- Flexibility (the product is usable beyond the tasks first specified for it)

Usability is often assessed only when a product reaches the marketplace, and customer feedback is used in designing the next generation product. If, however, it should become possible to assess usability much earlier in the design life-cycle of a product, this process of testing and refining products could be largely circumvented. Releasing a product which has already been subject to a usability evaluation, and had its design altered accordingly, would save both time and money for manufacturers. Indeed, usability information is increasingly valuable the earlier in the design cycle it is available, for it is both simple and inexpensive to change a blueprint of a product, but this situation changes dramatically when the device goes into mass production. Such was the inspiration for many human factors researchers when they devised predictive techniques for providing usability information as early as the concept stage of design (although realistically many of the methods are best applied around the prototyping stage). Stanton and Baber (1992, 1996) detail the plethora of techniques available for evaluating usability, which range from general methods such as the interview, through to techniques specially designed to tap more specific aspects of usability, such as Task Analysis For Error Identification (TAFEI; Baber & Stanton, 1994).

There are also a number of texts devoted to discussing these methods (e.g. Corlett & Clarke, 1995; Diaper, 1989; Jordan et al., 1996; Kirwan, 1994; Kirwan & Ainsworth, 1992; Wilson & Corlett, 1990), indicating a great deal of interest in measuring usability, for there are currently in excess of 60 methods available. Unfortunately, there has not been a comparable amount of research concerned with the effectiveness of such methods. Reliability, validity and even usability of the methods themselves are basic concepts which have not received just treatment in the literature. As a usability evaluation tool, the interview is no less guilty of this. The present study attempts to rectify this state of affairs.

APPLYING THE INTERVIEW TO USABILITY EVALUATIONS

Interviews are general information-gathering exercises, in this context intended to elicit users' or designers' views about a particular task or system. They are truly multi-purpose – applications include task analysis for human reliability assessment (Kirwan, 1990), pre-design information gathering (Christie & Gardiner, 1990), and collecting data on product assessment after a user trial (McClelland, 1990).

One major advantage of interviews is the high degree of ecological validity: if you want to find out what a person thinks of a device you simply ask them. Researchers agree that the flexibility of the interview is also a great asset (Kirwan & Ainsworth, 1992; Sinclair, 1990), in that particular lines of inquiry may be pursued if desired. Furthermore, the interview technique is very well documented, with an abundance of literature on this method. Finally, the main advantage of an interview is its familiarity to the respondent as a technique and this, combined with the face-to-face nature, is likely to elicit more information, and probably more accurate information.

Whilst the popular assumption may be to use interviews in market research, they can also be exploited at any stage in the design process. In usability evaluations a user trial is implied before carrying out an interview; thus at least a partial prototype should be available.

The research presented here uses a similar approach to the "cooperative evaluation" technique cited by Christie et al. (1990), which is described above. Instead of charging a user with a list of tasks to carry out on a prototype product, two members of the design team collaborate, one acting as the user and one acting as the interviewer. The "user" performs the series of tasks on the device and is then interviewed about the usability issues involved. The aim of this was to determine whether the more efficient method of interviewing another designer, rather than asking actual users for their thoughts, would provide reliable and valid output regarding usability.

Interviewing takes many forms, from the completely unstructured interview to the formally-planned, structured interview. For the current study, a semi-structured interview format was settled upon, as it has proved effective in other domains, such as personnel selection (see e.g. Wright, Lichtenfels & Pursell, 1989). The structure was based on the Ravden & Johnson (1989) checklist. This is a checklist originally devised for users to assess human–computer interfaces. The checklist is structured into 11 sections, each directed at different elements of usability, such as visual clarity, feedback and compatibility. In its original form, the section headings are followed by specific questions which are responded to in a four-point Likert manner. There is space for further comments by the user, and a "general" section at the end to capture anything which may not have fallen into the other categories. With some adaptation, it was thought that the Ravden and Johnson checklist could be applied to devices outside the realms of human–computer interaction. By using the sections of the checklist as a scaffold for the interview, one can maintain flexibility whilst ensuring thoroughness in covering all aspects of usability. Each section title is presented in turn, and relevant questions about the device under scrutiny are posed. The structure is less rigid than the original checklist, in that the interviewer is not restricted to asking the specific questions of the checklist, but rather uses these as prompts to investigate interesting avenues. The checklist is really used as a protocol for the interview, forcing the interviewer to consider all the relevant areas.

AN EMPIRICAL TEST OF THE USABILITY INTERVIEW IN AN APPLIED SETTING

The present study was intended to assess the reliability, validity and usability of the interview when applied to a typical consumer product – a car radio-cassette.

A pilot interview was performed to determine the feasibility of the structure in assessing the car radio. From this, the most striking aspect about the interview was its speed of administration – the whole process lasted around 30 minutes. As its structure was based on the sections of the checklist, we can be quite confident that it thoroughly covered all aspects of device interaction. Admittedly, some aspects of the checklist were simply inapplicable to a car radio, but this just affirmed one advantage of the interview – its flexibility in adapting to changing scenarios.

The output of the interview was on the whole unsurprising, given the structure of the checklist and the fact that it is wholly subjective, information was elicited on general issues of usability and design (Table 1). With this in mind, the interview still proved to have advantages over a mere heuristic assessment, and even over other dedicated usability analysis techniques. As an expert in the field of usability in design was present, it was possible to relate the responses to psychological issues of design (e.g. cognitive compatibility). It could be argued that the subjective responses of the interviewee, combined with the professional knowledge of the interviewer, make the interview a very strong technique for usability evaluations. It has the flexibility of a heuristic analysis, yet retains the rigour of

Table 1 Example output from pilot usability interview assessing a car radio. Section headings and suggested content (in italics) are taken from the Ravden and Johnson (1989) checklist

---

SECTION 1: VISUAL CLARITY
Information displayed on the screen should be clear, well-organised and easy to read.
- There is a certain amount of visual clutter on the LCD
- Writing (labelling) is small but readable
- Ambiguous abbreviations (e.g. DX/LO; ASPM ME-SCAN)

SECTION 2: CONSISTENCY
The way the system looks and works should be consistent at all times
- Tuning buttons (especially Scan and Seek functions) present inconsistent labelling
- Moded functions create problems in knowing how to initiate the function

SECTION 3: COMPATIBILITY
The way the system looks and works should be compatible with user expectations
- Four functions on "On/Off" switch make it somewhat incompatible
- Auto-reverse function could cause cognitive compatibility problems

SECTION 4: INFORMATIVE FEEDBACK
Users should be given clear, informative feedback on where they are in the system
- Tactile feedback is poor, particularly for the "On/Off" switch
- Operational feedback poor when programming a preset station

SECTION 5: EXPLICITNESS
The way the system works and is structured should be clear to the user
- Novice users may not understand station programming without instruction
- Resuming normal cassette playback after FF or RWD is not clear

SECTION 6: APPROPRIATE FUNCTIONALITY
The system should meet the needs and requirements of users when carrying out tasks
- Rotating dial is not appropriate for front/rear fader control
- Prompts for task steps may be useful when programming stations

SECTION 7: FLEXIBILITY AND CONTROL
The interface should be sufficiently flexible in structure, information presentation and in terms of what the user can do, to suit the needs and requirements of all users
- Users with larger fingers may find controls fiddly
- Radio is inaudible whilst winding cassette – this is inflexible

SECTION 8: ERROR PREVENTION AND CORRECTION
The system should be designed to minimise the possibility of user error, users should be able to check their inputs and to correct errors
- There is no "undo" function for stored stations
- Separate functions would be better initiated from separate buttons

SECTION 9: USER GUIDANCE AND SUPPORT
Informative, easy-to-use and relevant guidance and support should be provided
- Manual is not well structured, relevant sections are difficult to find
- Instructions in the manual are matched to the task

SECTION 10: SYSTEM USABILITY PROBLEMS
- Minor problems in understanding function of two or three buttons
- Treble and bass controls are tiny

SECTION 11: GENERAL SYSTEM USABILITY
- Best aspect: This radio is *not* mode-dependent
- Worst aspect: Ambiguity in button labelling
- Common mistakes: Adjusting balance instead of volume
- Recommended changes: Substitute pushbutton operation for "On/Off" control

---

the more objective methods. As an example of this, one aspect which emerged from the interview which can be missed by other evaluation techniques was the usability of the instruction manual for the car radio. Other techniques, in their specificity, tend not to consider anything outside system operation. The operating manual is just as important as any other component of the device, so should be just as easy to use. Of the 12 techniques scrutinised by Stanton and Young (1998), only the interview covered the manual within its ordinary remit.

With the applicability of the interview in no doubt, then, a more detailed study was conducted to assess its efficacy. The aim was to determine whether the interview could produce valid results when in the hands of trained, though otherwise novice, analysts. If so, then the output could be used in predicting potential usability problems, thereby improving design.

Method

A sample of eight engineering students, chosen for their relevance in the design process (i.e. the technique will ultimately be used by engineers and designers), were recruited as participants in this study.

The first stage involved these participants attending a training session run by the authors in applying the interview to a usability evaluation. Content of the session was directed towards using the Ravden and Johnson (1989) checklist as a pro forma for the semi-structured interview. The session began with a lecture covering the basics of interviews, and how they may be applied to assessing usability in the design of consumer products. As most participants were familiar with interviews in some form, the emphasis of the lecture was given to explaining the Ravden and Johnson (1989) checklist, and to ensuring everyone was familiar with interviewing techniques. This involved an explanation of open, probe, and closed questions, and teaching how to exploit them. Following this, a worked example of an interview was described. This example was centred around a different device to that which the participants would eventually be working on, and provided samples of the types of questions and responses which can arise in this context. In actual fact, the worked example provided was based on the pilot interview previously conducted and described above. Finally there was an opportunity to conduct a practice interview. For this, the participants paired up and interviewed each other about a mutually familiar device. This situation was a little contrived, as participants had to work from memory rather than having the device in front of them, but served the purpose of practising the interview technique. Total time for the whole session, including lecture, worked example and practice, was approximately 100 minutes.

The following week, the participants returned and were asked to conduct an interview analysis on a previously unseen car radio-cassette. Each participant had exclusive access to a working device, all assessed the same version of the device, and as before, the participants paired up to interview each other. The procedure was therefore akin to performing a user trial with a follow-up interview. Interviewers recorded all responses and time taken for the interview process was also noted. At the end of the interview, each interviewer completed a brief questionnaire, indicating on 7-point Likert scales their opinions on the interview as a usability tool. These scales were based on Kirwan's (1992) seven criteria for assessing such techniques.

To assess reliability, all of the participants returned again after a two week delay and repeated the entire procedure.

Validity of the interview output was assessed by comparing the results of the engineers with that provided by participants under "real" driving conditions. A further sample of 30 participants was asked to perform a typical driving task in the Southampton Driving Simulator. During the simulation, they were periodically asked to carry out tasks on the same radio the engineers had previously analysed. The radio was fitted into the simulator in the appropriate position on the instrument panel. After this, these participants were interviewed by the first author as to their thoughts on the usability of the radio. The interview structure was similar to that which the engineers had been trained to use, utilising all 11 sections of the Ravden and Johnson (1989) checklist.

Results

Regarding the engineers' interview sessions, average execution time increased non-significantly on the second session compared to the first (average execution time in session 1 = 60.78 minutes; session 2 = 71.88 minutes). Both times are in excess of that anticipated by the pilot study. However, it must be borne in mind that the engineers were relative novices with the technique.

Subjective evaluation of the interview by the engineers did not differ across test sessions. Average ratings along each of the seven criteria are summarised in Figure 1.

As for reliability and validity of the interview, some more complex statistics had to be performed. Predictive validity refers to how accurate the engineers' responses were when compared to those of the participants in the driving simulator. This was assessed using signal detection theory. By examining the hit ratio (percentage of predictions which were actually observed) and the false alarm ratio (percentage of predictions which were not observed), it is possible to arrive at a single figure which essentially represents how accurate the predictions were. A statistic of 0.5 indicates the hit ratio and false alarm ratio are equal, greater than 0.5 means the hit ratio exceeds the false alarm ratio. A result of 1.0 is perfect accuracy.

Predictive validity of the engineers' output on their first attempt rated 0.488. This did not improve on their second attempt two weeks later, when the score was 0.466. On the basis of these results, then, validity of the interview as a usability tool is rather disappointing.

Reliability was assessed in two ways. Intra-rater reliability refers to consistency of a single analyst across the two week time gap. Inter-rater reliability, on the other hand, is how consistent the eight engineers were to each other.

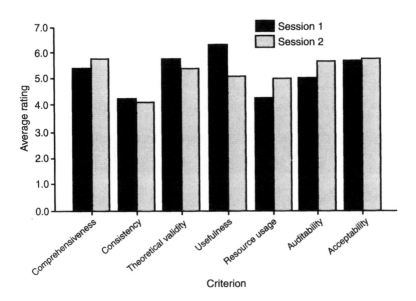

Figure 1 Average subjective ratings of the usability interview against Kirwan's (1992) seven criteria

Intra-rater reliability was measured by simple correlation coefficients. Again, a disappointing result of 0.449 which failed to reach significance leads to the conclusion that interviewers are not consistent over time in eliciting responses from their participants.

Inter-rater reliability was assessed using the Kurtosis statistic. Being a numerical measure of the shape of a distribution, the Kurtosis statistic gives an indication of how tightly grouped the responses were. A result of zero means a perfect normal distribution, greater than zero indicates less spread, less than zero means a flatter distribution. Good inter-rater reliability, then, will be reflected in a high positive value of the Kurtosis statistic.

On the first test session, the Kurtosis statistic turned out to be –1.66. For session two, this improved to 0.362. Once again, these results are less than encouraging for the fate of the interview as a usability tool.

Discussion

The apparent lack of validity and reliability of the interview as a usability tool in the current study is somewhat revelationary considering its widespread use. However, the surprise is lessened when the broad scope of the output is taken into account. Interviews cover all aspects of usability and design, and are thus subject to great variability in their responses. Other techniques which concentrate on a single aspect of usability are less prone to such variation and are consequently more accurate. In addition, there are potential flaws in the experimental design as presented here which raise the possibility that in a different situation, an entirely different set of results may emerge. The most obvious criticism of this study lies in the training regime. It can be argued that what essentially amounts to a morning's work is far from enough for training potential interviewers to an acceptable standard. More skilled interviewers could elicit different, potentially more accurate responses. This approach was adopted to reflect practical constraints in the field, in that potential designers who may wish to apply the interview to usability evaluations do not have the time or resources to spend on a full training programme. More designers are likely to try using the technique if such aspects can be economised on whilst retaining the accuracy of the method. Unfortunately, as we have found, this does not seem to be the case.

So although the usability interview as presented here might seem less than worthwhile, it is nonetheless quite probable that some useful information may be gleaned. Indeed, the mere process of conducting the interview can provide the designer with some insight into the usability of his/her product which may not have been thought of previously. It is certainly worth attempting an interview rather than not carrying out any usability evaluation at all. Thus the interview is still a realistic alternative in usability evaluations. To that end, we have compiled some notes on conducting an effective usability interview.

RECOMMENDATIONS

Although the current study sought to economise by using potential designers as interviewees *and* interviewers, it seems this strategy may not have paid off. Therefore, if the interviewer(s) have access to potential end-users of the product (i.e. customers), then the output might be more revealing by using these people as interviewees. Moreover, it is likely that a more thorough training session will produce a better interview and possibly results which more accurately predict what will happen when the product is commissioned.

For the analysis of consumer products, particularly with untrained interviewers, it is probably wise to adopt the semi-structured interview format. The Ravden and Johnson (1989) checklist served a useful purpose in providing the structure for a usability interview.

The interviewee should be granted an exhaustive user trial with the device under analysis, then interviewed for their thoughts. Each section title of the checklist should be used as a prompt for asking questions (e.g. "Let's talk about visual clarity – did you think information was clear and well organised?", etc.). It should be noted that the structure is just the bones for building an interview around – it is by no means fixed and should not be viewed as a script for asking questions. It is more of an agenda to ensure all aspects are covered. The interviewer should direct the questioning from open questions ("What did you think of this aspect?") through probing questions ("Why do you think that?") to more closed ones ("Is this a good thing?"). It may be useful to keep a protocol sheet to

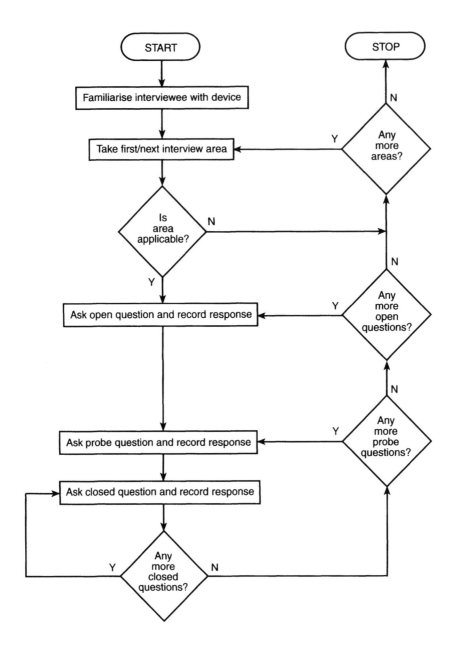

Figure 2   Flowchart of the usability interview process

hand as a prompt for this (the flowchart in Figure 2 would serve this purpose). The idea is that the interviewer opens a line of inquiry with an open question, then follows it up. When it is exhausted, he or she moves to another line of inquiry. By doing this for every aspect of the device, one can be sure of having conducted a thorough interview. It is helpful to have prepared a data sheet for filling in responses during the interview.

Interviews are of course adaptive by nature, and if the interviewer feels that any particular section is irrelevant to the particular device they are studying, they are free to exclude it. The professional wisdom of the interviewer can be an advantage for this technique.

GENERAL CONCLUSIONS

The semi-structured interview, as it was applied in the present experiment, did not score well on any of the ratings of reliability or validity. However, it does not take long to learn or apply and thus has potential in a resource-limited environment. This is reflected in the moderately good reception it received by the participants in this study. Attempts to reduce further the drain on resources by using engineers as interviewees apparently failed, so potential analysts are well-advised to target end-users for their views.

Although in its present form the interview was intended for an existing product, it can easily be adapted for application at any stage in the design process. This ranges from asking people what they want in a device to eliciting opinions about an existing design. Output is typically not limited to issues of interface design, but can extend to other aspects such as functionality.

By conducting the interview in a consistent and thorough manner, it is still possible to obtain useful results from it, despite the outcome of the study described here. That is to say, even though the interview produced more false alarms than hits in the predictive analysis, the fact that the hit rate was not zero is useful. Improving usability in just one aspect of a device can potentially enhance user satisfaction, increase sales and even improve safety. This can also save costs in the longer term by minimising necessary retooling for second generation devices. Any feedback from potential end-users about the state of a product can be used in design, and the interview is one way of eliciting such feedback. Applying the knowledge gained from the interview to changing the design of a product is essentially correcting faults before they have arisen, ensuring products are as usable as possible when they go on the market. The advice provided in this chapter should assist in achieving these goals.

ACKNOWLEDGEMENT

The research reported in this chapter was supported by the EPSRC under LINK Transport Infrastructure and Operations Programme.

REFERENCES

Baber, C. & Stanton, N.A. (1994). Task analysis for error identification: a methodology for designing error-tolerant consumer products. *Ergonomics*, **37**, 1923–1941.

Brooke, J. (1996). SUS: a "quick and dirty" usability scale. In P.W. Jordan, B. Thomas, B.A. Weerdmeester & I.L. McClelland (Eds.), *Usability Evaluation in industry* (pp. 189–194). London: Taylor & Francis.

Christie, B. & Gardiner, M.M. (1990). Evaluation of the human–computer interface. In J.R. Wilson & E.N. Corlett (Eds.), *Evaluation of Human Work: A Practical Ergonomics Methodology* (pp. 271–320). London: Taylor & Francis.

Christie, B., Scane, R. & Collyer, J. (1990). Evaluation of human–computer interaction at the user interface to advanced IT systems. In J.R. Wilson & E.N. Corlett (Eds.), *Evaluation of Human Work: A Practical Ergonomics Methodology* (2nd edn, pp. 310–356). London: Taylor & Francis.

Corlett, E.N. & Clarke, T.S. (1995). *The Ergonomics of Workspaces and Machines* (2nd edn). London: Taylor & Francis.

Diaper, D. (1989). *Task Analysis in Human Computer Interaction*. Chichester: Ellis Horwood.

Drury, C.G. (1990). Methods for direct observation of performance. In J.R. Wilson & E.N. Corlett (Eds.), *Evaluation of Human Work – a Practical Ergonomics Methodology* (2nd edn, pp. 45–68). London: Taylor & Francis.

Faith, N. (1996). *Black Box: Why Air Safety is No Accident*. London: Boxtree.

Jordan, P.W., Thomas, B., Weerdmeester, B.A. & McClelland, I.L. (Eds.) (1996). *Usability Evaluation in Industry*. London: Taylor & Francis.

Kirwan, B. (1990). Human reliability assessment. In J.R. Wilson & E.N. Corlett (Eds.), *Evaluation of Human Work: A Practical Ergonomics Methodology* (2nd edn, pp. 921–968). London: Taylor & Francis.

Kirwan, B. (1992). Human error identification in human reliability assessment. Part 2: Detailed comparison of techniques. *Applied Ergonomics*, **23**, 371–381.

Kirwan, B. (1994). *A Guide to Practical Human Reliability Assessment*. London: Taylor & Francis.

Kirwan, B. & Ainsworth, L. (1992). *A Guide to Task Analysis*. London: Taylor & Francis.

McClelland, I. (1990). Product assessment and user trials. In J.R. Wilson & E.N. Corlett (Eds.), *Evaluation of Human Work: A Practical Ergonomics Methodology* (2nd edn, pp. 249–284). London: Taylor & Francis.

Nielsen, J. & Molich, R. (1990). Heuristic evaluation of user interfaces. In J.C. Chew & J. Whiteside (Eds.), *Empowering People: CHI '90 Conference Proceedings* (pp. 249–256). Monterey, CA: ACM Press.

Ravden, S.J. & Johnson, G.I. (1989). *Evaluating Usability of Human–Computer Interfaces: A Practical Method*. Chichester: Ellis Horwood.

Shackel, B. (1981). The concept of usability. *Proceedings of the IBM Software and Information Usability Symposium* (pp. 1–30). New York: IBM.

Sinclair, M.A. (1990). Subjective assessment. In J.R. Wilson & E.N. Corlett (Eds.), *Evaluation of Human Work: A Practical Ergonomics Methodology* (2nd edn, pp. 69–100). London: Taylor & Francis.

Stanton, N.A. & Baber, C. (1992). Usability and EC directive 90/270. *Displays*, **13**, 151–160.

Stanton, N.A. & Baber, C. (1996). Factors affecting the selection of methods and techniques prior to conducting a usability evaluation. In P.W. Jordan, B. Thomas, B.A. Weerdmeester & I.L. McClelland (Eds.), *Usability Evaluation in Industry* (pp. 39–48). London: Taylor & Francis.

Stanton, N.A. & Young, M. (1998). Is utility in the mind of the beholder? A review of ergonomics methods. *Applied Ergonomics*, **29**, 41–54.

Wilson, J.R. & Corlett, E.N. (1990). *Evaluation of Human Work: A Practical Ergonomics Methodology* (2nd edn). London: Taylor & Francis.

Wright, P.M., Lichtenfels, P.A. & Pursell, E.D. (1989). The structured interview: Additional studies and a meta-analysis. *Journal of Occupational Psychology*, **62**, 191–199.

4.3

The Employment Interview and Race: A Review

Amelia J. Prewett-Livingston
Southern Natural Gas, Birmingham, Alabama, USA
and
Hubert S. Feild
Auburn University, Alabama, USA

The employment interview is probably the most widely used selection tool (Schneider & Schmitt, 1986); thus, it deserves particular attention and study by human resource specialists. The employment interview has received attention for many years. For example, Wagner (1949) cited a study on the employment interview published as early as 1915 by Scott. Studies early in the century, as well as many studies in the more recent past, have focused on the reliability and validity of the selection interview as well as process models to explain mechanisms working in the interview (see Chapter 4.1 by Whetzel and McDaniel). It was not until after the passage of Title VII of the US Civil Rights Act of 1964 (1964), however, that fairness among different applicant groups became an important issue in employee selection, including the use of the employment interview. Title VII prohibits discrimination in employment opportunities on the basis of gender, race, color, religion or national origin. Because each protected group is faced with unique challenges, facets of interview reliability, validity, and process models should be evaluated separately for each group. In this chapter, we focus on the employment interview and one of the group characteristics protected by Title VII of the US Civil Rights Act of 1964, i.e. interviewee race. Results of related research, practical guidelines for implementing the employment interview in light of the issue of race, and future research avenues are included in the discussion.

Handbook of the Psychology of Interviewing. Edited by A. Memon and R. Bull.
© 1999 John Wiley & Sons Ltd.

Researchers must first determine that there is a phenomenon to study. Are there differences in employment interview ratings of Black and White candidates? The results have been mixed. Of studies where results were reported for race separately, some results favored Blacks (e.g. Cesare, Dalessio & Tannenbaum, 1988; Lin, Dobbins & Farh, 1992; Mullins, 1982). Other researchers reported no race differences (e.g. Grove, 1981; Haefner, 1977; Motowidlo et al., 1992; Rand & Wexley, 1975; Webber & Orcutt, 1984; Wexley & Nemeroff, 1974; Wing, 1981). Finally, some researchers found differences in interview ratings in favor of Whites (e.g., Barr & Hitt, 1986; Huffcutt & Roth, 1997; Motowidlo et al. 1992; Parsons & Liden, 1984; Pulakos & Schmitt, 1995). However, even when differences were found, they were generally small (e.g., Barr & Hitt, 1986; Cesare et al., 1988; Lin et al., 1992; Motowidlo et al., 1992; Mullins, 1982; Parsons & Liden, 1984; Pulakos & Schmitt, 1995). A meta-analysis performed on 31 studies by Huffcutt and Roth (1997) estimated both Black and Hispanic interview scores as being about a quarter of a standard deviation below scores for Whites. This is a much smaller difference than the one standard deviation difference commonly estimated for cognitive ability tests that are frequently used for employee selection (e.g. Hunter & Hunter, 1984). In summary, small and inconsistent differences among racial groups in ratings of interview performance have been reported when the employment interview has been used for selection.

Given that the differences are generally small, when they exist, we might ask are these small racial differences worth studying? It is possible that the reason(s) for the differences are interesting and important from a scientific perspective. It is also possible for small differences in interview scores to have a substantial practical impact. When only a few positions are available, even small score differences may result in significant adverse impact against a group. A small difference between two scores may mean getting selected for the position, or not. Additionally, Wing (1981) reported a common situation where even though there were no mean differences in interview scores between racial groups, the standard deviation of Blacks' scores was smaller than that of Whites. Because there was a group difference in the standard deviations in scores, the top nine candidates were White with only five positions available. Thus, any type of difference in ratings between racial groups may have a significant practical impact. Socially, ensuring fairness is the right thing to do, and the 1964 Civil Rights Act (1964) requires this fairness, so small differences with potential impact are worth investigating.

INCORPORATING STRUCTURE IN THE EMPLOYMENT INTERVIEW

A lot of what we have learned through research points to different methods of structuring interviews. Even in the first review of the literature regarding the employment interview by Wagner (1949), standardization, or interview structure, was encouraged. It has since been demonstrated by many researchers that only structured employment interviews consistently show validity (e.g. Cronshaw & Wiesner, 1989; see also Chapter 4.1 by Whetzel and McDaniel). Further, it is possible that structure can work to reduce potential bias in ratings (Williamson et al., 1997). Therefore, the following review is organized around different means of incorporating structure into the employment interview including (a) basing interview questions and scoring standards on job requirements, (b) implementing standardized questions with detailed anchors, (c) using multiple interviewers, and (d) providing interviewer training. A few of the mechanisms that have been or are being studied as moderating or mediating variables with race in the interview process, such as stereotyping, will also be mentioned within this context as they may apply to interview structure.

Basing Interview Questions and Scoring Standards on Job Requirements

Basing interview questions and scoring standards on job requirements has been proposed by many to increase the legal defensibility of the employment interview (Arvey & Faley, 1988; Campion & Arvey, 1989; Gollub & Campion, 1991; Schmitt, 1976; Webster, 1982). Legal defensibility is likely to increase because the most efficient way to influence validity and reduce bias in an interview is to take a content validation approach and base the questions on the requirements of the job (Campion, Palmer & Campion, 1997; Dipboye, 1994; Siegfried, 1982). Research on stereotyping, i.e. attributing characteristics commonly associated with a racial group to an individual based on racial group membership, has suggested that people are more likely to access stereotypes when they have little information from which to form an opinion (McDonald & Hakel, 1985). As suggested by Kraiger and Ford (1985), the access of job relevant information lessens the need to use race as a factor in selection. Literature about the "Similar-to-Me" phenomenon based on Byrne's (1961) social psychological model of interpersonal attraction indicated that interviewers tend to base their ratings on how similar the candidate is to them (e.g. Rand & Wexley, 1975). It has been proposed that race, being an observable difference between an interviewer and candidate, may have an effect on interviewer ratings (e.g. Rand & Wexley, 1975); however, tying the interview to job content may ameliorate any effect. Dalessio and Imada (1984) conducted a study where they provided interviewers with a description of an ideal applicant that reflected job requirements. They found that final decisions were related more to the ideal applicant than to the similarities between the interviewers and the candidates. Basing the interview on job requirements appears to provide the appropriate comparison and reduce the tendency for interviewers to base evaluations on factors that are not related to the job.

An interesting point to note is that the type of job itself may have an effect on ratings based on race. One such job-related variable that may have an effect on ratings and race is the status and complexity of the job, assuming higher-status jobs are more complex. One study reported no interaction between ethnicity and job status (Singer & Eder, 1988). The investigators manipulated race by using selection interview videotapes with a Maori, Chinese or Dutch applicant and manipulated job status by providing a job description for department manager or filing clerk. Other researchers, however, have found interactions. Hopper and Williams (1973) and Kalin and Rayko (1978) studied the interaction between race and job status by using speech characteristics on an audiotape to cue employers to an applicant's race. Hopper and Williams (1973) found that for executive positions those who spoke standard English were preferred, but for manual labor jobs speech characteristics were not predictive. Kalin and Rayko (1978) showed that those with foreign accents were rated lower for high status jobs, but higher for low status jobs. Tepstra and Larsen (1980) indicated race on a resumé of the candidate's qualifications and found results similar to those of Kalin and Rayko. Blacks received higher ratings than Whites for Black-typed jobs (lower status), while they received lower ratings than Whites for White-typed jobs (higher status). Huffcutt and Roth (1997) reviewed the effect of job complexity in a meta-analysis. Interestingly, the meta-analysis results were the opposite of those reported by Hopper and Williams (1973). Huffcutt and Roth found that the greatest differences in ratings were for low complexity jobs (e.g. custodian, paper mill worker) with Blacks and Hispanics being rated lower than Whites. However, in high complexity jobs (e.g. technical manager, nurse) Blacks and Hispanics were actually rated slightly higher than Whites. They suggested that their results may be due to the more select applicant pool in higher complexity jobs, or because minorities are fewer in number and more salient and sought after in high complexity jobs. Differences between Hopper and Williams' (1973) and Huffcutt and Roth's (1997) results could be due to changes in society over the years. Research is needed to identify the effects of job complexity and race as they relate to the employment interview today.

Providing specific job information may help evaluators focus on true aspects of the job, rather than the characteristics of those who have historically held those jobs. The participants in the studies described above were not given detailed job information, they were only provided job categories such as clerical, sales and executive. Specificity of job information may be another variable to study in relation to the interaction between ratings based on race and job type.

Implementing Standardized Questions with Detailed Anchors

The need for interview questions and response standards to be based on job requirements has already been mentioned. Structure of the questions and response standards is further discussed here. First, it is suggested that a standard set of questions be developed for use in the interview. Standardization of questions is the most basic means of structuring an interview (e.g. Campion, Palmer & Campion, 1997). Standardizing questions prevents interviewers from delving into areas that are not job related, and potentially biased (e.g. Dipboye & Gaugler, 1993). To support this notion, Huffcutt and Roth (1997) found that interview structure slightly reduced group differences in ratings. Asking a structured set of questions is also related to court outcomes, supporting the use of the interview in employee selection (Gollub & Campion, 1991). Huffcutt and Arthur (1994) concluded that the optimal level of structure of interview questions is having a standard set of questions while allowing interviewers to probe those topics more thoroughly (see Chapter 4.1 in this book, for more detailed information on levels of question structure). Their meta-analysis showed that further structuring the interview by not letting interviewers probe provided no additional value to validity or reliability. In fact, it has been suggested by Campion et al. (1997) that allowing interviewers to probe may increase validity by providing the opportunity to clarify candidates' answers or more thoroughly discuss topics linked to job requirements, provided the interviewers do not prompt candidates in a leading fashion.

Assuming that the same questions are asked of candidates, possible differences in ratings may occur based on the type of questions asked. The two types of interview questions that appear to have the most research supporting their usefulness are behavior description questions and situational questions (see also Chapter 4.1 in this book for a discussion of behavior and situational interview questions). The biggest difference between these two types of questions is their time orientation. Behavior description questions ask candidates to describe how they have handled similar circumstances in the past. For example, a behavior description question may start out, "Tell me about a time when you . . ." Situational questions, in contrast, ask candidates to describe how they would intend to handle a specific situation proposed in the question. A situational question may start like this, "Say you find yourself in this situation, . . . how would you handle it?"

Campion, Pursell and Brown (1988) demonstrated successful use of situational questions; Pulakos and Schmitt (1995) found the behavior description questions to be valid, but not situational questions; and Huffcutt and Roth (1997) found that group differences were lower with behavior description questions than with situational questions. A number of authors have noted that the context of the interview should help determine what type of question to use. If candidates have job-related experience, then behavior description questions may be more appropriate. If candidates do not have much experience, then behavior description interviews may discriminate against those with the least experience who are likely to be women, minorities and youth (e.g. Campion, Campion & Hudson, 1994; Latham et al., 1980).

Having a standard set of questions is a start, but it is not enough if interviewers are allowed to infer anything they wish from the answers to those questions. The development of specific, behavioral anchors on rating scales based on job requirements for each interview question can help provide the needed structure. Rating scale anchors provide more objectivity to the interview ratings and subsequently should reduce bias in ratings (Arvey & Faley, 1988). Additionally, Campion et al. (1997) concluded that the use of anchored rating scales may reduce the cognitive load on the interviewers, which in turn could enhance their ability to rate accurately. Gollub and Campion (1991) also found that the use of job-related, specific, behavioral anchors was associated with positive court outcomes. Latham et al. (1980) provided a good description of the development of interview questions and job-based rating scale anchors.

Finally, the length of the interview is an important, but often overlooked aspect of structure (Campion et al., 1997). Campion et al. (1997) suggested that brief interviews may not be very reliable, but lengthy interviews may prove too taxing on both the interviewer and candidate. Of the studies they reviewed where the length of the interview was reported, two-thirds of them lasted between half an hour and an hour, and half contained between 15 to 20 questions. They recommended limiting interviews to an hour to avoid fatigue but ensuring that the interviews are long enough to obtain reliable information.

Campion et al. (1997) focused on the psychometric effects of interview length, with longer interviews increasing reliability. A longer interview may also show a benefit based on conclusions from the literature on stereotyping. If it is true that interviewers are more likely to base ratings on stereotypes when there is a lack of information to draw from, a longer interview may decrease the tendency to rate based on stereotypes.

Using Multiple Interviewers

Employing multiple interviewers may affect potential rating bias in a number of ways, particularly if interviewers are required to discuss their ratings and come to a consensus judgment. First, psychometrically, combining multiple ratings is likely to reduce the effects of random biases among interviewers (e.g. Campion et al., 1997, 1988; Hakel, 1982). Second, interviewers who are required to discuss ratings are likely to bring to others' attention any ratings seemingly based on information or characteristics that are not job related (e.g. Arvey & Campion, 1982; Campion et al., 1997). Third, from a legal perspective, Gollub and Campion (1991) found that a review of interviewer ratings, which occurs when panel interviewers review and discuss ratings, was related to court outcomes, supporting the use of the interview in employee selection. Review of ratings among interviewers provides a distributed accountability on the parts of all interviewers.

Interviewer accountability may have a number of positive effects. For example, Motowidlo, Mero and DeGroot (1995) manipulated interviewer accountability and found that interviewers who were held accountable for their ratings provided more valid ratings than those who were not held accountable. Also, Forret and Turban (1996) proposed a model of the employment interview based on Petty and Cacioppo's (1986) Elaboration Likelihood Model (ELM), a model describing factors that affect or are affected by the extent to which a person actively processes information. Forret and Turban suggested that interviewers under high accountability elaborate on information in an interview more than interviewers who are less accountable. They suggested that interviewers who do not elaborate as much will be affected more by perceived similarity to the candidate. Similarly, Fiske (1993) theorized that forcing evaluators to attend to information, akin to elaboration, will result in less stereotyping. Having multiple interviewers increases accountability, which increases attention (elaboration), which, in turn, increases the extent to which ratings are based on job-related factors, and decreases the extent to which ratings are based on stereotypes or similarity to the evaluator. The application of multiple interviewers is proposed to result in outcomes that are based more on job-related characteristics and less on characteristics that are not related to job requirements.

As pointed out by Hakel (1982), use of multiple interviewers provides the opportunity to have representatives of the different gender and racial groups, which is likely to be perceived as more fair. Further, Ledvinka (1971) reported that Black interviewers elicited more information from Black candidates than White interviewers. His finding indicates that perceptions of fairness may not be the only variable affected when different gender and racial groups are represented on an interview panel; interviewer questioning and ratings and/or candidate performance may be affected as well.

Care must be taken to form interview panels representative of gender and race whenever possible (Lin, Dobbins & Farh, 1992; Prewett-Livingston et al., 1996). Lin et al. (1992) suggested using at least one different-race interviewer on a panel based on their findings that panels made up of two Black interviewers or two Hispanic interviewers produced ratings favoring interviewees of similar racial background whereas racially mixed panels, or panels composed of interviewers dissimilar to the candidate, or panels of White interviewers, did not produce ratings that were significantly affected by candidate race.

Prewett-Livingston et al. (1996) conducted a similar study but reported a slightly different result. They found a trend where the majority race on an interview panel affected ratings favoring candidates of a similar racial background. In other words, when the panel was composed of three White and one Black interviewer, all panel members rated White candidates higher; when the panel was composed of three Black and one White interviewer, all panel members rated Black candidates higher (although this difference was not statistically significant). The panels that were racially balanced did not result in different ratings based on candidate race. Prewett-Livingston et al. suggested, at a minimum, having all panels similar to each other in racial composition, and further having the panels racially balanced. Future research is needed to determine how the racial composition of interview panels affects ratings of interview performance, but it is possible that the results of Lin et al. and Prewett-Livingston et al. converge. Given that there were two interviewers in the panels studied by Lin et al., their results suggested that the presence of at least one different-race interviewer produces a balanced panel. That is, had there been more interviewers on the panels in the Lin et al. study, they may have found that balanced panels were preferable rather than the addition of one different-race interviewer. If only to influence perceptions of fairness and candidate comfort, panels representative of gender and racial groups should be used. Further research, however, needs to be conducted to identify the requisite gender and racial representation of panel members to enhance validity and decrease potential bias in ratings of interview performance.

Providing Interviewer Training

When interviewers were trained or experienced interviewers were used, the use of the interview in employee selection was easier to defend in a United States court of law (Gollub & Campion, 1991). Campion et al. (1997) noted that Vance, Kuhnert and Farr (1978) found that brief training on rater accuracy had no effect on rater accuracy; however, Dougherty, Ebert and Callender (1986) and Pulakos and Schmitt (1995) reported that more extensive training increased the accuracy and validity of ratings. Regarding the content of an extensive training program, Campion et al. (1997) noted that legal rights, potentially biased types of interview questions, and the means by which bias can enter interview ratings are generally covered in addition to practice and feedback in conducting interviews. It is further suggested that job content be an interviewer training topic. As noted earlier, Dalessio and Imada (1984) found that when interviewers were informed of the characteristics of an ideal applicant based on job-related criteria, ratings were related more to the ideal applicant than to similarities or differences between the interviewer and candidates.

Possible cognitive effects of interviewer training are suggested by Forret and Turban (1996) who proposed that trained raters are more likely to elaborate information heard in an interview than untrained interviewers. It is also possible that interviewer training may reduce the cognitive load on interviewers as they become familiar with the interview questions and standards. Therefore, they can better attend to job-related details discussed during the interview. Though the mechanisms acting through interviewer training to increase validity of ratings need further investigation, current findings indicating that training enhances rating validity strongly support the application of extensive interviewer training.

FUTURE RESEARCH NEEDS

Of the multitudes of studies published regarding the employment interview, surprisingly few investigators have reported results separately by race. Further, very few studies have actually focused on the mechanisms that may affect ratings and decisions in the employment interview based on race. The lack of studies reporting results separately for race could be for a number of reasons. At least two are particularly important. First, for many years, there was not an emphasis on potential interviewee differences in the employment interview. The same process mechanisms were assumed to work similarly for all; thus, only one model was sought. Second, many studies, particularly field studies, have not had enough minority candidates to provide the statistical power needed to produce meaningful results when analyzing racial groups separately, let alone the statistical power to perform a microanalysis of specific mechanisms interacting in an employment interview setting.

As noted by Pulakos and Schmitt (1995), even though a few studies report subgroup means, even fewer examine the fairness (intercept differences) of the interview. This could be due to small subgroup sample sizes, as noted above.

Additionally, it could be due to the lack of a good measure of job performance, or any measure of job performance at all. A number of researchers have observed differences between racial groups on measures of job performance (e.g. Ford, Kraiger & Schectman, 1986; Pulakos et al., 1989; Pulakos & Schmitt, 1995). For example Ford et al. (1986) reported a 0.3 to 0.4 standard deviation difference for both subjective (e.g. Likert scale ratings) and objective (e.g. sales volume) measures of job performance. If both the interview ratings and job performance measure are biased in the same direction, then it is possible the interview would be deemed as fair when in fact it was not. Future research needs to be conducted to examine factors affecting differences in measures of job performance, so more accurate criterion measures can be obtained. Then, perhaps, it will be possible to perform more conclusive research on racial fairness in the interview.

Another interesting current research need focuses on the construct(s) that are being measured in employment interviews. For example, many researchers have studied whether the interview was measuring cognitive ability (e.g. Campion et al., 1994, 1988; Motowidlo et al., 1992; Walters, Miller & Ree, 1993; see also Chapter 4.1 in this book. Two of their four studies found incremental validity of the interview beyond cognitive ability tests (Campion et al., 1994; Motowidlo et al., 1992), and the other two did not. This has been an important issue, because cognitive ability tests generally result in greater adverse impact than interviews. If cognitive ability tests and employment interviews measured the same construct, then the interview would have been considered an equally valid predictor with less potential adverse impact. What is being measured by the interview remains an important issue for future research. Further, as fairness (intercept differences) of the interview is measured more, future research should examine whether any intercept differences are due to the interview process measuring different constructs for individuals from different racial groups.

The concept of racial prejudice and how it relates to interview ratings is complex and deserving of additional research. Dutton (1976) provided some subjects with a means of monitoring their behavior toward majority and minority group members. He found that when subjects could monitor their behavior, egalitarianism resulted. However, when they did not monitor their behavior, they rated the minority group higher, resulting in reverse discrimination. Wexley and Nemeroff (1974) reported that prejudiced interviewers rated both Black and White applicants lower than unprejudiced interviewers. Mullins (1982) found that subjects highly prejudiced against Blacks rated Black applicants higher than White applicants. Future research is needed to investigate these different results and the variables interacting with prejudice in interviewers. It is possible that future interviewers could be screened on these and other variables that impact accuracy in ratings.

A number of additional future research areas were mentioned in the discussion of interview structure and are reiterated here. What are the effects of the specificity of job information given to an interviewer in relation to the type of job (traditionally Black or White job)? What are the effects of cognitive elaboration on interview ratings? Does cognitive elaboration promote less stereotyping or comparisons to self? Does holding interviewers accountable have any specific effects, such as increasing cognitive elaboration? Does rater training decrease the cognitive load and increase cognitive elaboration? What is the best racial composition of an interview panel to reduce the potential for bias and increase the accuracy of ratings? As can be seen, there is much to be learned about the employment interview and effects of race.

CONCLUSIONS

Structured interviews have been shown to be valid predictors of performance and have resulted in less adverse impact than other selection instruments. Although there is much to be studied on the employment interview and the effects of candidate and interviewer race, there are many steps we can take to reduce the potential for racial bias in ratings. Structuring the interview in such a way to increase its job relatedness is the first step. This includes identifying job requirements, ensuring that structured questions and response standards are derived directly from those job requirements, and ensuring interviewers have a good grasp of the job requirements and response standards on which to base ratings. Using multiple interviewers is also a good idea to increase the perceptions of fairness, and actually affect fairness by having interviewers hold each other accountable for evaluating candidates accurately. As research continues, it is hoped that additional methods related to the development and administration of employment interviews will be discovered that act to increase accuracy and decrease any potential interviewer biases.

REFERENCES

Arvey, R.D. & Campion, J.E. (1982). The employment interview: A summary and review of recent research. *Personnel Psychology*, **35**, 281–322.

Arvey, R.D. & Faley, R.H. (1988). *Fairness in Selecting Employees* (2nd edn.). Reading, MA: Addison-Wesley.

Barr, S.H. & Hitt, M.A. (1986). A comparison of selection decision models in manager versus student samples. *Personnel Psychology*, **39**, 599–617.

Byrne, D. (1961). Interpersonal attraction and attitude similarity. *Journal of Abnormal and Social Psychology*, **62**, 713–715.

Campion, J.E. & Arvey, R.D. (1989). Unfair discrimination in the interview. In R.W. Eder & G.R. Ferris (Eds.), *The Employment Interview: Theory, Research, and Practice* (pp. 61–73). Newbury Park, CA: Sage.

Campion, M.A., Campion, J.E. & Hudson, J.P. (1994). Structured interviewing: A note on incremental validity and alternative question types. *Journal of Applied Psychology*, **79**, 998–1002.

Campion, M.A., Palmer, D.K. & Campion, J.E. (1997). A review of structure in the selection interview. *Personnel Psychology*, **50**, 1–46.

Campion, M.A., Pursell, E.D. & Brown, B.K. (1988). Structured interviewing: Raising the psychometric properties of the employment interview. *Personnel Psychology*, **41**, 25–42.

Cesare, S.J., Dalessio, A. & Tannenbaum, R.J. (1988). Contrast effects for Black, White, male, and female interviewees. *Journal of Applied Social Psychology*, **18**, 1261–1273.

Cronshaw, S.F. & Wiesner, W.H. (1989). The validity of the employment interview: Models for research and practice. In R.W. Eder & G.R. Ferris (Eds.), *The Employment Interview: Theory, Research, and Practice* (pp. 269–281). Beverly Hills: Sage.

Dalessio, A. & Imada, A.S. (1984). Relationships between interview selection decisions and perceptions of applicant similarity to an ideal employee and self: A field study. *Human Relations*, **37**, 67–80.

Dipboye, R.L. (1994). Structured and unstructured selection interviews: Beyond the job-fit mode. In G.R. Ferris (Ed.), *Research in Personnel and Human Resources Management* (Vol. 12, pp. 79–123). Greenwich, CT: JAI Press.

Dipboye, R.L. & Gaugler, B.B. (1993). Cognitive and behavioral processes in the selection interview. In N. Schmitt, W.C. Borman, Associates (Eds.), *Personal Selection in Organizations* (pp. 135–170). San Francisco: Jossey-Bass.

Dougherty, T.W., Ebert, R.J. & Callender, J.C. (1986). Policy capturing in the employment interview. *Journal of Applied Psychology*, **71**, 9–15.

Dutton, D.G. (1976). Tokenism, reverse discrimination, and egalitarianism in interracial behavior. *Journal of Social Issues*, **32**, 93–107.

Fiske, S.T. (1993). Controlling other people: The impact of power on stereotyping. *American Psychologist*, **48**, 621–628.

Ford, J.K., Kraiger, K. & Schectman, S.L. (1986). Study of race effects in objective indices and subjective evaluation of performance: A meta-analysis of performance criteria. *Psychological Bulletin*, **99**, 330–337.

Forret, M.L. & Turban, D.B. (1996). Implications of the elaboration likelihood model for interviewer decision processes. *Journal of Business and Psychology*, **10**, 415–428.

Gollub, L.R. & Campion, J.E. (1991). *The employment interview on trial*. Paper presented at the annual conference of the Society of Industrial and Organizational Psychology, St Louis, MO.

Grove, D.A. (1981). A behavioral consistency approach to decision making in employment selection. *Personnel Psychology*, **34**, 55–64.

Haefner, J.E. (1977). Race, age, sex, and competence as factors in employer selection of the disadvantaged. *Journal of Applied Psychology*, **62**, 199–202.

Hakel, M.D. (1982). Employment interviewing. In K.M. Rowland & G.R. Ferris (Eds.), *Personnel Management* (pp. 129–155). Boston: Allyn and Bacon.

Hopper, R. & Williams, F. (1973). Speech characteristics and employability. *Speech Monographs*, **40**, 296–302.

Huffcutt, A.I. & Arthur, W. Jr. (1994). Hunter and Hunter (1984) revisited: Interview validity for entry-level jobs. *Journal of Applied Psychology*, **79**, 184–190.

Huffcutt, A.I. & Roth, P.L. (1997). *Racial group differences in employment interview evaluations*. Paper presented at the twelfth annual conference of the Society for Industrial and Organizational Psychology, St. Louis, MO.

Hunter, J.E. & Hunter, R.F. (1984). Validity and utility of alternative predictors of job performance. *Psychological Bulletin*, **96**, 72–98.

Kalin, R. & Rayko, D.S. (1978). Discrimination in evaluative judgments against foreign-accented job candidates. *Psychological Reports*, **43**, 1203–1209.

Kraiger, K. & Ford, J.K. (1985). A meta-analysis of ratee race effects in performance ratings. *Journal of Applied Psychology*, **70**, 56–65.

Latham, G.P., Saari, L.M., Pursell, E.D. & Campion, M.A. (1980). The situational interview. *Journal of Applied Psychology*, **65**, 422–427.

Ledvinka, J. (1971). Race of interviewer and the language elaboration of Black interviewees. *Journal of Social Issues*, **27**, 185–197.

Lin, T.R., Dobbins, G.H. & Farh, J.L. (1992). A field study of race and age similarity effects on interview ratings in conventional and situational interviews. *Journal of Applied Psychology*, **77**, 363–371.

McDonald, T. & Hakel, M.D. (1985). Effects of applicant race, sex, suitability, and answers on interviewer's questioning strategy and ratings. *Personnel Psychology*, **38**, 321–334.

Motowidlo, S.J., Mero, N.P. & DeGroot, T. (1995). *Predicting and controlling individual variability in interviewers' judgments*. Paper presented at the annual conference of the Society for Industrial and Organizational Psychology, Orlando, FL.

Motowidlo, S.J., Carter, G.W., Dunnette, M.D., Tippins, N., Werner, S., Burnett, J.R. & Vaughan, M.J. (1992). Studies of the structured behavioral interview. *Journal of Applied Psychology*, **77**, 571–587.

Mullins, T.W. (1982). Interviewer decisions as a function of applicant race, applicant quality and interviewer prejudice. *Personnel Psychology*, **35**, 163–174.

Parsons, C.K. & Liden, R.C. (1984). Interviewer perceptions of applicant qualifications: A multivariate field study of demographic characteristics and nonverbal cues. *Journal of Applied Psychology*, **69**, 557–568.

Petty, R.E. & Cacioppo, J.T. (1986). The elaboration likelihood model of persuasion. In L. Berkowitz (Ed.), *Advances in Experimental Social Psychology* (Vol. 19, pp. 123–205). Orlando, FL: Academic Press.

Prewett-Livingston, A.J., Feild, H.S., Veres, J.G. & Lewis, P.M. (1996). Effects of race on interview ratings in a situational panel interview. *Journal of Applied Psychology*, **81**, 178–186.

Pulakos, E.D. & Schmitt, N. (1995). Experience-based and situational interview questions: Studies of validity. *Personnel Psychology*, **48**, 289–308.

Pulakos, E.D., White, L.A., Oppler, S.H. & Borman, W.C. (1989). Examination of race and sex effects on performance ratings. *Journal of Applied Psychology*, **74**, 770–780.

Rand, T.M. & Wexley, K.N. (1975). Demonstration of the effect, "similar to me," in simulated employment interviews. *Psychological Reports*, **36**, 535–544.

Schmitt, N. (1976). Social and situational determinants of interview decisions: Implications for the employment interview. *Personnel Psychology*, **29**, 79–101.

Schneider, B. & Schmitt, N. (1986). *Staffing Organizations*. Glenview, IL: Scott, Foresman.

Scott, W.D. (1915). Scientific selection of salesmen. *Advertising and Selling Magazine*, **25**, 5–6 and 94–96.

Siegfried, W.D. (1982). The effects of specifying job requirements and using explicit warnings to decrease sex discrimination in employment interviews. *Sex Roles*, **8**, 73–82.

Singer, M. & Eder, G.S. (1988). Effects of ethnicity, accent, and job status on selection decisions. *International Journal of Psychology*, **24**, 13–34.

Tepstra, D.E. & Larsen, J.M. (1980). A note on job type and applicant race as determinants of hiring decisions. *Journal of Occupational Psychology*, **53**, 117–119.

Title VII of Civil Rights Act of 1964 (1964). 42 U.S.C.A. § 2000e et seq.

Vance, R.J., Kuhnert, K.W. & Farr, J.L. (1978). Interview judgments: Using external criteria to compare behavioral and graphic scale ratings. *Organizational Behavior and Human Performance*, **22**, 279–294.

Wagner, R. (1949). The employment interview: A critical summary. *Personnel Psychology*, **2**, 17–46.

Walters, L.C., Miller, M.R. & Ree, M.J. (1993). Structured interviews for pilot selection: No incremental validity. *International Journal of Aviation Psychology*, **3**, 25–38.

Webber, A. & Orcutt, J.D. (1984). Employers' reactions to racial and psychiatric stigmata: A field study. *Deviant Behavior*, **5**, 327–336.

Webster, E.C. (1982). *The Employment Interview: A Social Judgment Process*. Schomberg, Ontario: IIP Publications.

Wexley, K.N. & Nemeroff, W.F. (1974). The effects of racial prejudice, race of applicant, and biographical similarity on interviewer evaluations of job applicants. *Journal of Social and Behavioral Sciences*, **20**, 66–78.

Williamson, L., Campion, J., Malos, S., Roehling, M. & Campion, M. (1997). Employment interview on trial: Linking interview structure with litigation outcomes. *Journal of Applied Psychology*, **82**, 900–912.

Wing, H. (1981). Estimation of the adverse impact of a police promotion examination. *Personnel Psychology*, **34**, 503–510.

Part 5

Interviewing for Forensic Purposes

Forensic Interviews of Children

Michael E. Lamb, Kathleen J. Sternberg, Yael Orbach
*National Institute of Child Health and Human Development,
Rockville Pike, Bethesda, Maryland, USA*
Irit Hershkowitz
*University of Haifa, Israel
and*
Phillip W. Esplin
Private Practice, Phoenix, Arizona, USA

FORENSIC INTERVIEWS OF CHILDREN

Sex crimes against children have been alleged with alarming frequency in the last several years (American Association for Protecting Children, 1986; National Society for the Prevention of Cruelty to Children, 1989; Sedlak & Broadhurst, 1996) and this has fostered extensive efforts to improve the quality of forensic investigation so that practitioners can reliably determine whether or not children have been abused. Many experts once believed that medical or physical evidence would prove definitive, but these hopes have not been borne out. In fact, sex crimes against children are extremely difficult to investigate precisely because the only evidence often consists of the victims' and suspects' accounts of the alleged events, and this has increased the importance of obtaining and evaluating information provided by children. Unfortunately, severe criminal penalties increase the temptation to impugn the credibility of young victims, whose statements are not always easy to elicit and can often be misinterpreted or misused. In addition, false allegations of sexual abuse may serve as powerful weapons in the hands of malicious adults, including those engaged in custody disputes (e.g.

Handbook of the Psychology of Interviewing. Edited by A. Memon and R. Bull.
© 1999 John Wiley & Sons Ltd.

Green, 1991; Jones & McGraw, 1987; Jones & Seig, 1988; Thoennes & Pearson, 1987) and this has further increased skepticism about the reports made by young children. All of these factors have fostered intense professional interest in issues related to investigative interviews of children.

Many researchers have begun to study the capacity of young children to provide reliable and valid information about their experiences, with a note-worthy flood of books and articles published in the last decade (Ceci & Bruck, 1995; Ceci, Leichtman & Putnick, 1992; Ceci, Ross & Toglia, 1989; Ceci, Toglia & Ross, 1987c; Dent & Flin, 1992; Doris, 1991; McGough, 1994; Perry & Wrightsman, 1991; Poole & Lamb, 1998; Spencer & Flin, 1993). Unfortunately, researchers have tended to focus on issues that have traditionally been of interest to experimental scientists but may have questionable relevance to sexual abuse (Doris, 1991). Broad variations in the universe of abusive incidents also complicate attempts to design studies whose results elucidate the competencies and limitations of young informants. Despite such limitations, published studies offer increasingly valuable information and insights to forensic interviewers and we review the relevant literature in this chapter.

Our goal in the first section is to summarize our current understanding of the factors that influence children's ability to provide accurate information about events they have experienced. Our focus in this section is thus on the empirical literature concerned with the development of social, communicative and memory capacities, discussed with respect to its relevance to forensic interviewing. We then describe research designed to determine how well investigative interviewers comply with the recommendations drawn from the empirical literature. In the final section, we describe our ongoing efforts to effect improvements by developing and implementing investigative protocols that provide more specific guidance to forensic interviewers.

FACTORS INFLUENCING CHILDREN'S COMPETENCE

Much of the debate over the competency of young witnesses has focused on four topics: fantasy, language, memory and suggestibility. Here, we briefly describe the extent to which variations in children's capacity to distinguish fantasy from reality, express themselves clearly and unambiguously, understand what interviewers say, remember events, and resist suggestion may sometimes affect their competence as informants.

Fantasy

The fantasy lives of children and adults are actually much more similar than was previously believed (Woolley, 1997). Nevertheless, the widely held belief that young children may fantasize about or fabricate allegations of a sexual nature is frequently used to cast doubt on their testimony, even though children over six years of age appear similar to adults in their ability to discriminate between events of internal ("imagined") and external ("experienced") origin (Johnson & Foley, 1984; Lindsay & Johnson, 1987; Roberts & Blades, 1995). In any event, fantastic elements seldom appear in children's accounts of abuse (Dalenberg, 1996), and when they do, they are often elicited by the presence of props (such as toys or dolls) usually associated with fantastic play (Lamb, Sternberg & Esplin, 1994, 1995), or by interviewer prompts that children "imagine" or "pretend". As a result, forensic investigators have been urged to avoid having such props present during investigative interviews and to avoid using such expressions (Lamb, Sternberg & Esplin, 1995, 1998a; Poole & Lamb, 1998). It is also important to distinguish between fantasy, distorted re-collections, deceit or falsehood, and instances in which children are the unwitting or witting tools of manipulative or vengeful adults attempting to fabricate allegations using children as accomplices. Fabrication and false reporting are unrelated to the ability to discriminate between imagined and real events; their occurrence speaks to credibility rather than competence.

Language and Communicative Abilities

Although most children say their first word by early in the second year of life, begin to create two-word sentences by 20 months, and can draw upon an average vocabulary of 8000 to 14 000 words by the time they turn six (Carey, 1978), linguistic and communicative immaturity clearly impede forensic interviewing if only because so few interviewers seem to recognize and understand the gradual pace of communicative development.

Even infants can discriminate between various speech sounds, but children often fail to produce all the sounds of their native language in diverse contexts until the school years. In addition, children do not articulate individual sounds consistently even after they seem to have mastered them (Reich, 1986), and thus it is not uncommon for interviewers to misunderstand children's speech. Mis-understandings also occur because children's rapid vocabulary growth often leads adults to overestimate their linguistic capacities. Despite their apparent maturity, young children – especially preschoolers – frequently use words before they know their conventional adult meaning, they may even use words that they do not understand at all, and they may understand poorly some apparently simple concepts, such as "any", "some", "touch", "yesterday" and "before" (Harner, 1975; Walker, 1994).

In general, the vocabularies of young children are often much more limited and less descriptive than those of adults (Brown, 1973; Dale, 1976; de Villiers & de Villiers, in press). Adjectival and adverbial modifiers are especially likely to be absent in their accounts, which tend to be extremely brief and sparse (Marin et al., 1979), perhaps in partial reflection of children's slow syntactical develop-ment. Unlike adults and older children, furthermore, young children cannot draw upon an array of past experiences to enrich and clarify their descriptive accounts (Johnson & Foley, 1984).

In the process of learning words and the rules for combining words into sentences, children are also learning how to participate in conversations and how to structure story narratives (Warren & McCloskey, 1997). As most parents know, children's conversations often lack the logical structure that adults expect, and loose association and digressions are common. Individual differences are large and developmental changes rapid, however, and interviewers must thus be attentive to the abilities and idiosyncrasies of their conversational partners. The challenge confronting investigators is to obtain accounts that are sufficiently rich in descriptive detail to permit an understanding of the children's testimony. Poole and Lamb (1998) describe a number of concrete strategies that interviewers might adopt to overcome some communicative problems that frequently bedevil interviewers.

As we show in greater detail below, the accuracy of children's accounts is greatly influenced by the linguistic style and the complexity of the language addressed to them by investigators. Interviewers often implicitly and inappropriately ask children to negate adult statements (e.g. "Is it not true that ...?"), expect them to understand passive rather than active sentences, use words that are unfamiliar to children, construct syntactically complex or ambiguous compound sentences, ask children questions they are simply incapable of answering, or ask children to confirm multifaceted "summaries" of their accounts (Dent, 1982; Pea, 1980; Perry & Wrightsman, 1991; Saywitz, 1988; Walker, 1993; Walker & Hunt, 1998; Warren et al., 1996). Roberts & Lamb (in press) showed that when interviewers misrepresent what children say, they are infrequently corrected, and thus the mistakes, rather than the correct information, is recalled later in the interview.

Mismatches between children's abilities and the language addressed to them are not limited to preschoolers, furthermore, as shown when Brennan and Brennan (1988) analyzed the questions asked of 6- to 15-year-old children during cross-examination in court. Overall, fewer than two-thirds of the questions addressed to children were comprehensible to their peers, and lawyers seemed especially likely to overestimate the abilities of 10- to 15-year-olds. As Poole and Lamb (1998, p. 155) warned: "In such cases, we cannot assume that the question the child 'heard' was the one the adult asked. Consequently, if the child later answered a similar question differently, we could not assume that the event had not really happened or that the child was an unreliable witness." Unfortunately, systematic analyses show that, far from being exceptional, inappropriate questioning strategies characterize the vast majority of forensic interviews (e.g. Lamb, et al. 1996a, 1996b; Sternberg et al., 1996; Warren et al., 1996).

Children's accounts of abusive experiences are also influenced by social or pragmatic aspects of communication. Like adults, young witnesses are typically unaware of the amount and type of information being sought by forensic investigators. As a result, interviewers need to communicate their needs and expectations clearly, motivating children to provide as much information as they can. Open-ended questions such as "Tell me everything about that", "Tell me about that from the very beginning", or "Tell me the first thing that happened when you got to [location identified by the child]" encourage children to provide full accounts of their experiences. Interviewers can request additional information by using open-ended prompts such as "Tell me more about [something mentioned by the child]" or "And then what happened". Such open-ended questions and prompts can be used repeatedly until interviewers are satisfied with the scope of information provided.

Years of analyzing forensic interviews have led us, along with forensic linguists such as Walker (1993) and Walker and Hunt (1998), to question widespread assumptions about children's linguistic inabilities and to focus more on the competence, perspective-taking abilities and linguistic styles of investigators. The more impoverished the children's language, the greater the likelihood that their statements will be misinterpreted or that children will misinterpret the interviewers' questions and purposes (King & Yuille, 1987; Perry & Wrightsman, 1991; Walker, 1993). This further underscores the extent to which the interviewers' behavior – particularly their vocabularies, the complexity of their utterances, their suggestiveness, and their success in motivating children to be informative and forthcoming – profoundly influences the course and outcome of their interviews.

Memory

Research on memory development suggests that, as children grow older, the length, informativeness and complexity of their recall memories increase, but the basic structure remains the same (Davies, Tarrant & Flin, 1989; Flin et al., 1992; Nelson & Gruendel, 1981; Saywitz, 1988). In general, young children tend to provide briefer accounts of their experiences than do older children and adults but their accounts are quite accurate (e.g. Goodman & Reed, 1986; Johnson & Foley, 1984; Marin et al., 1979; Oates & Shrimpton, 1991). As time passes, information is forgotten by children just as it is forgotten by adults (Flin et al., 1992). Errors of omission are much more common than errors of commission among both adults and children (Oates & Shrimpton, 1991; Steward, 1993), but are a special problem where children are concerned because their accounts – especially their recall narratives – are often so brief.

Whenever events recur with any regularity, both children and adults tend to blur distinctions among incidents and establish script memories (representations of averaged or typical events rather than particular incidents). Accounts based on script memories are likely to contain fewer distinctive details than are memories of discrete incidents (Nelson & Gruendel, 1981), and the passage of time between experience and recall increases the tendency to rely on scripts (Myles-Worsley, Cromer & Dodd, 1986). Scripts are useful because they help individuals to focus on and remember the important features of repetitive events or sequences while enabling them to ignore less central or repetitious elements (Nelson, 1986; Shank & Abelson, 1977). In addition, scripts may provide the temporal sequence or structure that makes the accounts of specific experiences more comprehensible.

Scripts (like stereotypes) have disadvantages too, however, because they tend to be brief or skeletal and may lead reporters to use general knowledge about a class of events to describe specific events incorrectly. For example, the five- and six-year-olds studied by Martin and Halverson (1983) remembered incorrectly the gender of a character who played a nontraditional gender role, while five- and seven-year-olds studied by McCartney and Nelson (1981) embellished re-statements of stories with items and events that were part of their own scripts. The tendency to do this generally declines with age (Collins, 1970; Collins & Wellman, 1982; Collins et al., 1978), and script-based errors can be reduced by pre-interview counseling or instruction (Saywitz & Snyder, 1993). Children also tend to remember unusual events better than specific events that are congruent with their general or script memories (Davidson, 1991). In investigative contexts, children may nonetheless provide scripted accounts because they are unaware of the level of detail needed by forensic investigators. Interviewers must thus com-municate their needs for narrative accounts of specific incidents and motivate children to be maximally informative witnesses. When children were abused more than once, interviewers can focus the child on specific events by using questions like "Tell me about the last time" or "Tell me about the time in Boston".

In addition to the distinction between script and episodic memory, the dis-tinction between recall and recognition testing is crucial. When adults and chil-dren are asked to describe events from free recall ("Tell me everything you remember. . ."), their accounts may be brief and sketchy, but are more likely to be accurate. When prompted for more details using open-ended prompts like "Tell me more about that" or "And then what happened?", children often recall additional details. When interviewers prompt with leading questions such as "Did he have a beard?", "Did he touch you with his private", or "Did this happen in the day or in the night", however, they shift from recall to recognition testing, and the probability of error rises dramatically (Dent, 1982, 1986; Dent & Stephenson, 1979; Oates & Shrimpton, 1991). Effective interviewers must maxi-mize the reliance on recall memory by offering open-ended prompts so as to minimize the risk of eliciting erroneous information. Recall memories are not always accurate, of course, especially when the events occurred long before the interview or there have been opportunities for either pre- (Leichtman & Ceci, 1995) or post-event contamination (Leichtman & Ceci, 1995; Poole & Lindsay, 1995, 1997; Poole & White, 1993; Warren & Lane, 1995) but accounts based on recall memory are much more likely to be accurate than those elicited from the child using recognition cues or prompts (e.g. Dent, 1986; Oates & Shrimpton, 1991).

It is also important to distinguish between memory performance and memory capacity. Young children's accounts may be brief not only because their memo-ries are poor or because their limited experiences do not provide a rich network of associations from which to draw analogies or metaphors but also because their vocabularies are much more limited and less elaborate than those of adults and because they may not be motivated to reveal what they do remember.

Forensic investigators often dismiss the relevance of experimental research on children's memory by arguing that the stressful nature of sexual abuse makes memories thereof distinctly different. In fact, considerable controversy persists in the experimental literature concerning the effects of increased arousal or stress on the accuracy of children's memory. Deffenbacher (1983) concluded that "forensically relevant" (i.e. high) levels of stress were associated with diminished accuracy, but the relevance of this conclusion to children's testimony is often disputed. Some researchers argue that stress improves children's accuracy (Goodman et al., 1991a, 1991b; Ochsner & Zaragoza, 1988; Steward & Steward, 1996). Steward & Steward (1996), for example, reported that children's ratings of distress were correlated with the completeness and accuracy of their descriptions of medical examinations they had experienced. Other researchers (Oates & Shrimpton, 1991; Ornstein, Gordon & Larus, 1992; Peters, 1987, 1991; Peters & Hagan, 1989; Peterson & Bell, 1996; Vandermaas, 1991) report that arousal either reduces accuracy or has no effect, however. In most of these studies, unfortunately, the children experienced low levels of stress and the ability to recall central elements of experienced events was not assessed. In addition, researchers have not yet studied the effects of stress at the time of recall, although some have studied the effects of social support, which presumably reduce stress (Greenstock & Pipe, 1996; Moston & Engelberg, 1992).

Children are certainly more likely to remember personally meaningful and salient as opposed to meaningless items and events (see Ornstein et al., 1992a, for a review) but this does not mean that incidents of maltreatment will necessarily be recalled better. First of all, not all incidents of sexual abuse are painful or traumatic, and thus the potentially facilitative effects of arousal on the process of *encoding* information cannot be assumed. Second, the context in which the child is asked to *retrieve* information about the experienced event – during interviews with a child protection service worker, a policeman, an attorney, or a judge – *may* be stressful regardless of whether or not the target event was (Goodman et al., 1992). Third, stress may affect different types of memory encoding, processing, and retrieval in different ways.

Even when events are remembered, the process of retrieval is itself complicated and delay may clearly affect it. Flin and her colleagues (Flin et al., 1992) reported that six-year-old children reported less information than nine-year-old children and adults and that, like adults, six- and nine-year-olds reported less information five months after the event. Interestingly, the amount of incorrect information retrieved did not increase over time. Memory is a reconstructive process, however: like adults, children actively work on memory traces in order to retrieve and organize them. Thus when children are repeatedly interviewed, as is often the case when sexual abuse has been alleged, this is likely not only to consolidate the memory (facilitating subsequent recall) but also to shape it (Ornstein, Larus & Clubb, 1992b). In a recent field study of investigative interviews, Lamb et al. (1998b) found that both delay and age affected the amount of information recalled, although in this study it was of course impossible to assess the accuracy of the children's accounts.

In sum, although children clearly *can* remember incidents they have experienced, the relationship between age and memory is complex, with a variety of factors influencing the quality of information provided. For our present purposes, perhaps the most important of these factors pertain to the interviewers' ability to *elicit* information and the child's willingness and ability to *express* it, rather than the child's ability to *remember* it.

Suggestibility

Whatever the vagaries and strengths of children's memories, the competency of child witnesses is often doubted on the grounds that children are too susceptible to influence by misleading questions or other sources of misinformation (Ceci & Bruck, 1993, 1995). Suggestibility is a multifaceted concept that involves social, communicative and memory processes. Children may respond inaccurately because they (a) infer that the interviewer would prefer a particular response (Ceci & Bruck, 1993), (b) do not understand the questions, but are eager to be cooperative (e.g. Hughes & Grieve, 1980), (c) retrieve the most recently acquired information about the event in question, although they might be able to retrieve information about the actual event if prompted to do so (Newcombe & Siegal, 1996, 1997), or (d) suffer from genuine source-monitoring confusion that prevents them from discriminating between the original event and misinformation about it (Poole & Lindsay, 1997).

Given the number of processes that underlie suggestibility it is not surprising that, at first glance, research on children's suggestibility appears to reveal a mixed and confusing picture (Ceci et al., 1987b; Ceci & Bruck, 1993). In a series of studies, Goodman and her colleagues (Goodman & Aman, 1990; Goodman, Aman & Hirschman, 1987; Goodman et al., 1991a, 1990, 1989) showed that children as young as three- to four-years-old were seldom misled by questions such as "Did he keep his clothes on?", "Did he kiss you?", and "He took your clothes off, didn't he?" which suggested actions quite different from those that were witnessed or experienced. Other results might have been obtained if the actions had been more ambiguous and the suggestions more plausible, however (Steller, 1991), or if misleading questions had referred to details observed or experienced in other contexts instead of being totally unfamiliar (Roberts & Blades, 1998). In other laboratory settings, in fact, preschoolers appear especially susceptible to suggestion (e.g. Ceci et al., 1987a, 1987b; King & Yuille, 1987; Toglia, Ceci & Ross, 1989; see McAuliff, Kovera & Viswesvaran, 1998, for a review). These apparently contradictory findings are not difficult to reconcile. In the studies documenting the resistance to suggestion, researchers have not repeated misleading questions over a short time period, exposed children to misleading stereotypes about target individuals, provided incentives to respond falsely, or included conditions that are often associated with recognition errors, such as a combination of specific questions and dolls or instructions to think about nonevents, "pretend," or "guess". All of these experimental conditions increase the susceptibility to suggestion (e.g. Bruck et al., 1995a, 1995b; Cassel, Roebers & Bjorklund, 1996; Ceci et al., 1994; Garven et al., 1998; Leichtman & Ceci, 1995; Thompson, Clarke-Stewart & Lepore, 1997).

Age trends in susceptibility among school-aged children are less clear, with some researchers reporting that suggestibility continues to decline through the early grades (Cohen & Harnick, 1980; Duncan, Whitney & Kunen, 1982; King & Yuille, 1987; Marin et al., 1979) and others suggesting conditions that reverse these age trends (Brainerd & Reyna, in press). Suggestions are less likely to affect children's accounts when they pertain to central or salient details (Dent & Stephenson, 1979; Dodd & Bradshaw, 1980; King & Yuille, 1987) and when interviewers counsel children to report personally experienced events only (Poole & Lindsay, 1997). Unfortunately, little research has been conducted on suggestibility regarding memories of incidents that traumatized or affected individuals profoundly, although Goodman, Hirschman et al. (1991) found that children who were more distressed by inoculations were less suggestible than children who appeared less stressed by the inoculations.

In theory at least, susceptibility to misleading suggestions should vary depending on the child's motivation to be completely accurate and/or comply with the interviewer's implicit or explicit agenda (King & Yuille, 1987). Children may feel obliged to answer adults' questions no matter how bizarre (Hughes & Grieve, 1980) and may assume that the repetition of a question implies that the initial answer was unsatisfactory (Ceci & Bruck, 1993). Subtle differences in the interviewers' style may also affect children's suggestibility. Goodman et al. (1991a) reported that three- to seven-year-olds were equally resistant to suggestions by "nice" and more neutral interviewers, whereas Davis and Bottoms (1998) and Carter, Bottoms and LeVine (1996) found that six- and seven-year-old children interviewed by supportive interviewers made fewer errors in response to misleading questions than did children interviewed by neutral or nonsupportive interviewers. Saywitz, Geiselman and Bornstein (1996) found that "neutral detectives" elicited less inaccurate and more accurate information from eight- to ten-year-old children whereas "supportive detectives" elicited more accurate and inaccurate details. Goodman et al. (1989) reported that seven- and ten-year-old children were surprisingly likely to accept suggestions made "in an atmosphere of accusation" four years after the event being recalled (Goodman & Clarke-Stewart, 1991) and Ceci et al. (1987a, 1987b) reported that preschoolers were more likely to accept suggestions made by an adult than by a seven-year-old confederate. Overall, therefore, the effects of interviewer characteristics are less consistent and impressive than one might expect.

Regardless of the resolution of the various controversies concerning children's suggestibility, most researchers agree that the manner in which children are questioned can have profound implications for what is "remembered", and this increases the importance of careful interviewing (Brainerd & Ornstein, 1991; Lamb et al., 1998a; Poole & Lamb, 1998). Misleading or suggestive questioning can manipulate both young and old witnesses. Such questions are most likely to be influential when the memory is not rich or recent, when the content was

imagined rather than experienced, when the questions themselves are so complicated that the witness is confused, and when the interviewer appears to have
such authority or status that the witness feels compelled to accept his or her
implied construction of the events.

Summary

Fantasy, memory strategies and deficiencies, suggestibility and communication
abilities importantly affect the accounts provided by young children of their
experiences. Many important questions remain unanswered, but some important
conclusions can be offered with a degree of certainty. Specifically, children often
can remember important details of incidents that they have observed or experienced, and although their accounts can be manipulated, sensitive interviewers
who are aware of children's capacities and deficiencies can avoid many of the
problems posed by questions that force children to operate at or beyond the
limits of their capacities.

Evaluation of the information obtained in an investigative interview can only
proceed when there is a complete electronic record – preferably a videotape –
not only of the child's responses but also of the prompts by which they were
elicited and the relative timing within the interview of details derived from recall
memory and those details elicited by more suggestive prompts (Lamb, 1994). (A
suggestive utterance 20 minutes into the interview clearly does not reduce the
value of a narrative description provided earlier in the interview, for example.)
Although there has been considerable professional fear that electronic records
permit defense attorneys to unfairly impugn the value of children's testimony,
the electronic record of a competent interview is clearly of greater value to
prosecutors than to defense attorneys because it permits illustration of the entire
interview process and prevents the selective and unfair focus on single responses
or suggestive questions taken out of context. Furthermore, electronic records of
interviews conducted competently shortly after the alleged events provide a
permanent record of information obtained from a witness whose ability to remember the events is certain to decline over time, and whose account may easily
be affected by post-event contamination in the course of repetitive interviewing
by professionals and family members (Ornstein et al., 1992b). Although electronic records cannot replace in vivo testimony at the time of trial in the United
States, they can prove to be remarkably damning pieces of evidence in the eyes
of juries, judges and even defendants. Moreover, they are admissible as part of
the evidence in chief in some countries, including the United Kingdom. Videotaping may also motivate interviewers to adhere to higher standards and permit
review and evaluation, essential components of quality control.

Because of the nature of the forensic investigation and the way children have
been socialized to communicate with adults, children rarely "volunteer" detailed
and complete accounts of abusive events. Interviewers face the task of eliciting
additional information about the sexual event, the temporal and spatial context

in which it occurred, and the people involved. In this next section, we will attempt to illustrate how much of this information can be obtained using questions and prompts which tap free-recall memory, thus avoiding the risks and errors which often accompany non-spontaneous accounts provided by children.

RESEARCH ON INVESTIGATIVE INTERVIEWS

Linguistic and memorial difficulties do not make children incompetent witnesses, but an understanding of their capacities and limitations should influence the ways in which children are interviewed and the ways in which their accounts are interpreted. Like adults, children can be informative witnesses, and a variety of professional groups and experts have recognized this, offering recommendations regarding the most effective ways of conducting forensic or investigative interviews (e.g. American Professional Society on the Abuse of Children (APSAC), 1990, 1997; Bull, 1992, 1995, 1996; Fisher & Geiselman, 1992; Jones, 1992; Lamb et al., 1994, 1995, 1998a; *Memorandum of Good Practice*, 1992; Poole & Lamb, 1998; Raskin & Esplin, 1991a; Raskin & Yuille, 1989; Sattler, 1998). As Poole and Lamb (1998) pointed out, these books and articles reveal a substantial degree of consensus regarding the ways in which investigative interviews should be conducted, and a remarkable convergence with the conclusions suggested by a close review of the experimental and empirical literature. Clearly, it *is* often possible to obtain valuable information from children, but doing so requires careful investigative procedures as well as a realistic awareness of their capacities and tendencies.

Unfortunately, agreement about the goals and desired characteristics of investigative interviews have not ensured that forensic interviews are typically performed well, as we found when we began undertaking research designed to explore the utility of various investigative utterances in forensic interviews. As noted above, open-ended questions yield the most accurate accounts in the laboratory, although these accounts are often incomplete (Dent, 1982; Dent & Stephenson, 1979; Goodman & Aman, 1990; Goodman et al., 1991b; Ornstein et al., 1992b). The superiority of open-ended questions is attributable to the fact that they are recall probes, whereas many focused or directive questions are recognition probes (Table 1). When recall memory is probed using open-ended prompts, respondents attempt to provide as much relevant information as they "remember", whereas when recognition is probed using focused questions, children may have to confirm or reject information or options provided by the interviewer. Recognition probes refocus the child on domains of interest to the investigator and exert greater pressure to respond, whether or not the respondent is sure of the response. Recognition probes are more likely to elicit erroneous responses in eyewitness contexts because of response biases (e.g. tendencies to say "yes" or "no" without reflection) and false recognition of details that were only mentioned in previous interviews or are inferred from the gist of the experienced events (Brainerd & Reyna, 1996). For these reasons,

Table 1 Comparing open-ended and focused prompts designed to elicit information from children

Summary of allegation: Child told her mother that Uncle Bob "humped her" last week when she visited after school.

Prompts of free recall memory	Prompts of recognition memory
Prompting child for allegation	
Tell me why you came to talk to me.	I heard there may have been some bad touching.
Tell me more about that.	
Tell me everything that happened from the time you got to Uncle B's house.	Does he do things you don't like?
Prompting for more details about the event	
And then what happened?	Did he touch you with his private?
Tell me more about the humping.	Did he put his private inside your private?
Explain what was happening while he was humping you.	Were his clothes on or off?
And then what happened?	Did he say anything when he humped you?
Tell me what happened after he humped you.	
Prompting for context	
Think back to that day when Uncle Bob humped you. Tell me everything that happened from the time you left school until you got to his house.	Was that in the bedroom?
And then what happened.	Was it day or night?
What else can you remember about that day.	Was anybody else there when this happened?

open-ended questions are assumed to yield the most information and the fewest errors in forensic contexts as well, although little systematic research had been done on this topic when we began our research.

Our research has all been conducted using reliable transcriptions of forensic interviews conducted in Israel by "youth investigators", who are statutorily mandated to conduct all investigative interviews of children (Sternberg, Lamb & Hershkowitz, 1996) and in the United States by social workers, sheriffs or police officers. For research purposes, we focus on the portion of each interview concerned with substantive issues, thereby excluding any introductory comments at the beginning of the interview, attempts to establish rapport with the child, and any attempts at the end of the interview to discuss neutral topics. Coders review the transcripts and categorize each interviewer utterance, defined by a "turn" in the discourse.

For the purposes of this summary, we focus on the five types of utterances that consistently comprise around 90% of the interviewer utterances recorded:

1. *Invitations* (using questions, statements or imperatives) for an open-ended response from the child. Such utterances do not delimit the child's focus except in the most general way (for example: "And then what happened?").

2. *Facilitators*. Utterances like "OK", restatements of the child's previous utterance, and nonsuggestive words of encouragement that are designed to prompt continuation of the child's narrative.
3. *Directive utterances*, which focus the child's attention on presumed details or aspects of the event that the child had previously mentioned.
4. *Leading utterances*, which focus the child's attention on details or aspects of the account that the child had not previously mentioned.
5. *Suggestive utterances*, stated in such a way that the interviewer strongly communicates what response is expected, or assumes details that have not been revealed by the child.

The three types of focused utterances (directive, leading, suggestive) thus lie along a continuum of risk, varying with respect to the degree of suggestive influence they exert on children's responses. Note that we use these labels in a distinctive way, such that the utterances we call leading may not be the same as those called leading by other researchers or legal practitioners.

In our research, raters also count the number of words in each utterance and use a technique introduced by Yuille and Cutshall (1986) and elaborated by our research group to tabulate the number of new details conveyed by the child. By definition, details involve the identification and description of individuals, objects, events or actions relevant to the alleged incident.

Our analyses have shown quite consistently that invitations yield responses that are three to four times longer and three times richer in relevant details than responses to focused interviewer utterances (Lamb et al., 1996a, 1996b; Sternberg et al. 1996b). The superiority of invitations is apparent regardless of the age of the children being interviewed. Because most focused questions test recognition rather than recall memory, furthermore, the information elicited is more likely to be inaccurate, and unfortunately focused utterances are much more common in the field than open-ended questions are. In the field sites we studied, for example, more than 80% of the interviewer utterances were focused whereas only 6% were invitations. Research in the United States, the United Kingdom, and Israel shows that the over-reliance on focused questions is evident regardless of the children's age, the nature of the offenses, the professional background of the interviewers, or the utilization of props and tools like anatomical dolls (Craig et al. in press; Lamb et al., 1996a, 1996b; Sternberg et al. 1996b; Stockdale, 1996; Walker & Hunt, 1998; Westcott, Davies & Horan, 1998). Overall, narrative responses are more desirable because they are obtained from free recall, they are more detailed, they are more accurate, and they permit researchers to study supposed indices of credibility like the Criterion-Based Content Analysis criteria (Hershkowitz et al., 1997; Lamb et al., 1997; Raskin & Esplin, 1991a, 1991b).

The findings reported here have important empirical and applied implications, particularly insofar as they confirm the superiority of invitations for eliciting information from children. Most of the experts cited earlier agree that specific or focused questions (directive or leading questions) should only be asked after the child has first been given an opportunity to describe the events in his/her own words, and others suggest that directive and leading utterances should be followed by open-ended prompts that shift the burden to free recall memory (Lamb et al., 1995). Unfortunately, systematic research on the sequence in which questions are asked remains to be conducted, although invitations used early in the interviews we studied appear no more productive than those used in the second half of the interviews (Lamb et al., 1996b).

Because focused questions tend to be so much more common than open-ended prompts, the bulk of the forensically relevant information obtained from young witnesses is usually elicited using these more specific questions, although we do not know how much more information might be obtained if interviewers had employed more open-ended invitations. In addition, we do not know from our field studies whether the overwhelming reliance on focused questions inflates the amount of inaccurate information obtained from young alleged victims. Studies in laboratory contexts have repeatedly shown that errors of commission are much more likely to occur when recognition memory is probed using focused questions, whereas errors of omission are more likely when recall memory is probed using open-ended questions (Dent, 1982, 1986; Dent & Stephenson, 1979; Oates & Shrimpton, 1991).

Because errors of commission are more likely to misdirect further questioning and lead to mistaken conclusions, they can have serious implications. In forensic contexts, the accuracy of individual details can be determined infrequently, but there is no reason to believe that probes of recall and recognition memory would function differently in field and laboratory contexts. It is for this reason that investigators should be urged to probe recall memories using open-ended prompts as extensively as possible, and to avoid strings of focused questions in which the risks of compounded errors are especially serious. Because inaccurate information can be provided in response to open-ended prompts, of course, especially when delays are long or there have been opportunities for post-event contamination (e.g. Leichtman & Ceci, 1995; Poole & Lindsay, 1995, 1997; Warren & Lane, 1995), it is crucially important for investigators to inquire about all relevant interviews and experiences since the alleged event, documenting the evidentiary "chain of custody" as they would when the evidence was a gun or knife (Rosenthal, 1995).

Many researchers have shown that contextual cues can prompt reports of information (e.g. Malpass, 1996; Pipe & Wilson, 1994; Price & Goodman, 1990; Wilkinson, 1988), although forensic investigators have been wary of possible trauma associated with these cues. In a recent study, however, Hershkowitz et al. (1998) reported that no children were anxious about revisiting the scenes at which they had allegedly been abused. In addition, although the children had been exhaustively interviewed at the investigators' offices, they were able to provide many new details (about 25% of the total) when reinterviewed at the scene of the alleged events.

Summary

The results of these field studies show that forensic investigators seldom ask the open-ended questions recommended by experts, relying instead on more focused (and presumably riskier) prompts. Detailed analyses by Bruck and Ceci (1995; Ceci & Bruck, 1995), furthermore, show that other deviations from good investigative practice abound, with preschool children in at least some high-profile cases subjected to suggestive manipulations and coercion. Common sense thus dictates that interviews of preschoolers should be conducted carefully by interviewers with the skills and experiences that help them to avoid such strategies. We can do little about those children who are incompetent, but we can and should improve the quality of interviewing, thereby making it possible to elicit reliable information from those children who are competent.

CHANGING INTERVIEWERS' BEHAVIOR

Changing interviewing practices is quite difficult, however, as our own experiences illustrate quite well. Recognizing that forensic interviewers tended to be too reliant on focused questions, we initially urged interviewers in our workshops to use more open-ended questions in their interviews, particularly when beginning the substantive phase of the interview when narrative accounts of the alleged abuse are very important. In intensive week-long training seminars we described memory processes, reviewed children's linguistic and memory capacities, discussed factors influencing suggestibility, and suggested that interviews be organized so as to include discrete rapport-building and introductory phases, substantive phases, and closure phases in succession. We also reviewed video-tapes of forensic interviews that illustrated the appropriate and inappropriate use of both open-ended and focused questions. Participants were encouraged to ask questions and a great deal of time was devoted to the discussion and review of specific examples and difficult problems. In addition, we described the conceptual bases of Statement Validity Analysis and Criterion-Based Content Analysis as we expected that familiarity with these techniques might improve interview quality, as suggested by Undeutsch (1982, 1989) and Raskin and Yuille (1989).

Despite this training, the interviewers we "trained" continued to rely on focused questions to elicit information from children and we thus designed a study which required forensic interviewers to follow very specific "scripts" in the rapport-building phases of their interviews (Sternberg et al., 1997). The goal of this study was to evaluate the relative effectiveness, in forensic rather than analog contexts, of two techniques for motivating young witnesses to provide detailed accounts of alleged experiences of sexual abuse. In half of the interviews, investigators who were naive with respect to the experimental hypotheses used a script containing many open-ended utterances to establish rapport, whereas in the other interviews the same investigators used a script involving many focused questions. Both introductory scripts took about seven minutes to complete and both ended with the identical open-ended utterance to initiate the substantive phase of the interview. When the resulting interviews were examined, we found that children who had been "trained" in the open-ended condition provided two and one-half times as many details and words in response to the first substantive utterance as did children in the "direct introduction" condition. Children in the "open-ended" condition continued to provide more information in response to subsequent invitations, suggesting that the initial training was successful in conveying the interviewers' desire for detailed description of the alleged events. Evidently, children who had the opportunity to practice providing lengthy narrative responses to open-ended questions in the introductory phase of the interview continued this pattern after the interviewers shifted focus to the alleged incidents of abuse.

We were quite impressed that the richness of children's accounts could be influenced by the interrogatory style modeled in brief introductory segments of the interview, and that a single carefully worded prompt could elicit so much information from the children in both conditions. In Sternberg et al.'s (1997) study, the first substantive question yielded an average of 38 details from children in the direct introduction condition and 91 details from children in the open-ended introduction conditions, whereas in earlier unscripted interviews by the same group of investigators, the average invitation yielded only five details, and the first invitation yielded an average of only six details (Lamb et al., 1996b).

Interestingly, although the open-ended training influenced the response style of the children who participated in this study, it had little effect on the interviewers' style of questioning after the first substantive question was posed. In other words, even when children provided lengthy responses to the first open-ended substantive question, interviewers did not continue to ask open-ended questions but rather shifted to more focused questions. This unexpected finding suggested that it might be valuable to script additional open-ended questions throughout the substantive phase of the interview. We thus developed increasingly detailed scripts for the entire interview (including substantive and non-substantive sections).

Preliminary findings suggest that these extended scripts indeed improve the overall informativeness of forensic interviews. Interviewers retrieve more information using open-ended questions, conduct better organized interviews, and are more likely to follow focused questions with open-ended probes (pairing), as we suggested. Interviewers clearly have difficulty internalizing recommended interview techniques and may need more explicit guidelines than those typically provided in training sessions or manuals, however intensive. In field settings, interviewers who follow scripted protocols seem to elicit more information from recall memory and to avoid more potentially dangerous interviewing practices than do interviewers who improvise, despite the apparent disadvantages of inflexible standardized scripts. In addition, we cannot overemphasize the value of continued peer review, training, role-playing, and the systematic analysis of videotaped and transcribed interviews. We believe that the frequent quality-control meetings between our research staff and the investigators played a crucial role in effecting and maintaining changes in the behavior of interviewers (Horowitz, Hershkowitz, & Hovav, in press).

Summary

The findings reported by Sternberg et al. (1997) are consistent with the results of laboratory/analog studies suggesting that motivational and contextual factors play an important role in shaping children's reports of experienced events (Paris, 1988; Saywitz et al., 1991). Along with the results of our ongoing research, they also suggest that, even in authentic forensic interviews, it is possible to entrain response styles that enhance the richness of information provided by children by providing them with an opportunity to practice providing detailed narrative accounts of experienced events and by reinforcing this style in the pre-substantive portion of the interviews. Richly detailed accounts of abusive events facilitate the more effective investigation of crimes and provide child protection workers with more information upon which to base their evaluations. The results of this study also highlight the value of having interviewers clearly communicate their expectations concerning the child's role. On the other hand, the studies we have conducted thus far have several important limitations. First, although open-ended interview procedures elicit more information from children of all ages studied, we have not been able to evaluate the accuracy of the information provided. It would thus be valuable to compare the direct and open-ended interview scripts in an analog study in which children describe known events. Second, we do not yet know whether our findings can be generalized to children under five years of age. Although there is consensus among researchers and clinicians that children under five are the most difficult to interview, systematic field research on preschoolers in forensic contexts is scarce.

CONCLUSION

Years of systematic research in the laboratory and in authentic forensic settings have helped create a broad and growing understanding of the factors that influence the quality of the information that can be obtained from young children. As we have shown above, children's memorial and communicative capacities are clearly less than those of adults and they (especially preschoolers) are more susceptible than adults to witting or unwitting suggestions by adults. It may often be impossible to differentiate between accurate and inaccurate components of the accounts provided by most three- and many four-year-olds, furthermore, and thus many are likely to be legally incompetent. On the other hand, children can remember and recount their experiences accurately; whether or not their accounts are comprehensible, detailed, and accurate depends on a variety of factors. Perhaps the most important factor is the quality of the investigative

interview conducted to obtain the information. Interviewers who elicit information using open-ended prompts and avoid placing undue cognitive or social
burdens on children are most likely to elicit information, particularly when the
incident occurred more recently, was salient, the child is five or older, and the
child has not been subjected to suggestive interviewing by concerned relatives
and inept investigators.

Unfortunately, research suggests that many forensic interviews are poorly
conducted, and that widespread consensus about the desirable qualities of good
interviews does not guarantee compliance, even by investigators who are confident that their interviews closely follow best-practice guidelines. In our experience, only intensive training which combines use of a scripted interview protocol
with regular reviews of recent interviews has been effective in enhancing the
quality of investigative practice.

ACKNOWLEDGEMENTS

The authors are grateful to Maggie Bruck, Ray Bull, Amina Memon, Kim Roberts and
especially Debra Poole for thoughtful comments on an earlier draft of this chapter.

REFERENCES

American Association for Protecting Children (1986). *Highlights of Official Child Neglect
and Abuse Reporting, 1984.* Denver: Author.
American Professional Society on the Abuse of Children (1990). *Guidelines for Psychosocial Evaluation of Suspected Sexual Abuse in Young Children.* Chicago, IL: Author.
American Professional Society on the Abuse of Children (1997). *Guidelines for Psychosocial
Evaluation of Suspected Sexual Abuse in Young Children* (Revised). Chicago, IL: Author.
Brainerd, C.J. & Ornstein, P.A. (1991). Children's memory for witnessed events: The
developmental backdrop. In J. Doris (Ed.), *The Suggestibility of Children's Recollec-
tions* (pp. 10–20). Washington, DC: American Psychological Association.
Brainerd, C.J. & Reyna, V.F. (1996). Mere testing creates false memories in children.
Developmental Psychology, **32**, 467–476.
Brainerd, C.J. & Reyna, V.F. (in press). Fuzzy-trace theory and children's false memories.
Journal of Experimental Child Psychology.
Brennan, M. & Brennan, R.E. (1988). *Strange Language: Child Victims under Cross
Examination* (3rd edition). Wagga Wagga, NSW, Australia: Riverina Literacy Centre.
Brown, R. (1973). *A First Language.* Cambridge, MA: Harvard University Press.
Bruck, M. & Ceci, S. (1995). Amicus Brief for the case of *State of New Jersey v. Michaels*
presented by committee of concerned social scientists. *Psychology, Public Policy, and
The Law*, **1**, 272–322.
Bruck, M., Ceci, S.J., Francouer, E. & Barr, R. (1995a). "I hardly cried when I got my
shot!" Influencing children's reports about a visit to their pediatrician. *Child Development*, **66**, 193–208.
Bruck, M., Ceci, S.J., Francouer, E. & Renick, A. (1995b). Anatomically detailed dolls do
not facilitate preschoolers' reports of a pediatric examination involving genital touching. *Journal of Experimental Psychology: Applied*, **1**, 95–109.
Bull, R. (1992). Obtaining evidence expertly: The reliability of interviews with child
witnesses. *Expert Evidence*, **1**, 5–12.

Bull, R. (1995). Innovative techniques for the questioning of child witnesses, especially those who are young and those with a learning disability. In M. Zaragoza, J.R. Graham, G.C.N. Hall, R. Hirschman & Y.S. Ben-Porath (Eds.), *Memory and Testimony in the Child Witness* (pp. 179–194). Thousand Oaks, CA: Sage.

Bull, R. (1996). Good practice for video recorded interviews with child witnesses for use in criminal proceedings. In G. Davies, S. Lloyd-Bostock, M. McMarran & C. Wilson (Eds.), *Psychology, Law, and Criminal Justice: International Developments in Research and Practice* (pp. 100–117). Berlin/New York: Walter de Gruyter.

Carey, S. (1978). The child as word learner. In M. Halle, J. Bresnan & G.A. Miller (Eds.), *Linguistic Theory and Psychological Reality* (pp. 264–293). Cambridge, MA: MIT Press.

Carter, C.A., Bottoms, B.L. & Levine, M. (1996). Linguistic and socioemotional influences in the accuracy of children's reports. *Law and Human Behavior*, **20**, 335–358.

Cassel, W.S., Roebers, C.E.M. & Bjorklund, D.F. (1996). Developmental patterns of eyewitness responses to repeated and increasingly suggested questions. *Journal of Experimental Child Psychology*, **61**, 116–133.

Ceci, S.J. & Bruck, M. (1993). Suggestibility of the child witness: A historical review and synthesis. *Psychological Bulletin*, **113**, 403–439.

Ceci, S.J. & Bruck, M. (1995). *Jeopardy in the Courtroom: A Scientific Analysis of Children's Testimony*. Washington, DC: American Psychological Association.

Ceci, S.J., Leichtman, M.D. & Putnick, M.E. (Eds.) (1992). *Cognitive and Social Factors in Early Deception*. Hillsdale, NJ: Erlbaum.

Ceci, S.J., Ross, D.F. & Toglia, M.P. (1987a). Suggestibility of children's memory: Psycholegal issues. *Journal of Experimental Psychology: General*, **116**, 38–49.

Ceci, S.J., Ross, D.F. & Toglia, M.P. (1987b). Age differences in suggestibility: Narrowing the uncertainties. In S.J. Ceci, M.P. Toglia & D.F. Ross (Eds.), *Children's Eyewitness Memory* (pp. 79–91). New York: Springer-Verlag.

Ceci, S.J., Toglia, M.P. & Ross, D.F. (Eds.) (1987c). *Children's Eyewitness Memory*. New York: Springer-Verlag.

Ceci, S.J., Ross, D.F. & Toglia, M.P. (Eds.) (1989). *Perspectives on Children's Testimony*. New York: Springer-Verlag.

Ceci, S.J., Huffman, M.L.C., Smith, E. & Loftus, E.F. (1994). Repeatedly thinking about a non-event: Source misattributions among preschoolers. *Consciousness and Cognition*, **3**, 388–407.

Cohen, R.L. & Harnick, M.A. (1980). The susceptibility of child witnesses to suggestion. *Law and Human Behavior*, **4**, 210.

Collins, W.A. (1970). Learning of media content: A developmental study. *Child Development*, **41**, 1113–1142.

Collins, W.A. & Wellman, H. (1982). Social scripts and developmental patterns in comprehension of televised narratives. *Communication Research*, **9**, 380–398.

Collins, W.A., Wellman, H., Keniston, A. & Westby, S. (1978). Age-related aspects of comprehensive and inference from a televised dramatic narrative. *Child Development*, **49**, 389–399.

Craig, R.A., Sheibe, R., Kircher, J., Raskin, D.C. & Dodd, D. (1996). *Effects of interviewer questions on children's statements of sexual abuse*. Unpublished manuscript, University of Utah.

Dale, P.S. (1976). *Language Development: Structure and Function*. New York: Holt, Rinehart & Winston.

Dalenberg, C.J. (1996). Fantastic elements in child disclosure of abuse. *The APSAC Advisor*, **9** (2), 1, 5–10.

Davidson, D. (1991). Children's *recognition and recall memory for typical and atypical actions in script-based stories*. Paper presented to the meeting of the Society for Research in Child Development, Seattle, WA.

Davies, G., Tarrant, A. & Flin, R. (1989). Close encounters of the witness kind: Children's memory for a simulated health inspection. *British Journal of Psychology*, **80**, 415–429.

Davis, S.L. & Bottoms, B.L. (1998, March). *Effects of social support on children's eyewitness reports.* Paper presented to the American Psychology-Law Society conference, Redondo Beach, CA.

Deffenbacher, K.A. (1983). The influence of arousal on reliability of testimony. In S.M. Lloyd-Bostock & B.R. Clifford (Eds.), *Evaluating Witness Evidence* (pp. 235–251). New York: Wiley.

Dent, H.R. (1982). The effects of interviewing strategies on the results of interviews with child witnesses. In A. Trankell (Ed.), *Reconstructing the Past: The Role of Psychologists in Criminal Trials* (pp. 279–297). Stockholm: Norstedt.

Dent, H.R. (1986). Experimental study of the effectiveness of different techniques of questioning mentally handicapped child witnesses. *British Journal of Clinical Psychology,* **25**, 13–17.

Dent, H. & Flin, R. (Eds.) (1992). *Children as Witnesses.* New York: Wiley.

Dent, H.R. & Stephenson, G.M. (1979). An experimental study of the effectiveness of different techniques of questioning child witnesses. *British Journal of Social and Clinical Psychology,* **18**, 41–51.

de Villiers, J. & de Villiers, P. (in press). Language development. In M.H. Bornstein & M.E. Lamb (Eds.) *Developmental Psychology: An Advanced Textbook* (4th edn). Mahwah, NJ: Erlbaum.

Dodd, D.H. & Bradshaw, J.M. (1980). Leading questions and memory: Pragmatic constraints. *Journal of Verbal Learning and Verbal Behavior,* **19**, 695–704.

Doris, J. (Ed.) (1991). *The Suggestibility of Children's Recollections: Implications for Eyewitness Testimony.* Washington, DC: American Psychological Association.

Duncan, E.M., Whitney, P. & Kunen, F. (1982). Integration of visual and verbal information in children's memories. *Child Development,* **53**, 1215–1223.

Fisher, R.P. & Geiselman, R.E. (1992). *Memory-enhancing Techniques for Investigating Interviewing: The Cognitive Interview.* Springfield, IL: Charles C. Thomas.

Flin, R., Boon, J., Knox, A. & Bull, R. (1992). The effect of a five month delay on children's and adults' eyewitness memory. *British Journal of Psychology,* **83**, 323–336.

Foley, M.A., Johnson, M.K. & Raye, C.L. (1983). Age-related changes in confusions between memories for thoughts and memories for speech. *Child Development,* **56**, 1145–1155.

Garven, S., Wood, J.M., Malpass, R.S. & Shaw, J.S. (1998). More than suggestion: The effect of interviewing techniques from the McMartin Preschool case. *Journal of Applied Psychology,* **83**, 347–359.

Goodman, G.S. & Aman, C. (1990). Children's use of anatomically detailed dolls to recount an event. *Child Development,* **61**, 1859–1871.

Goodman, G.S. & Clarke-Stewart, A.K. (1991). Suggestibility in children's testimony: Implications for sexual abuse investigations. In J. Doris (Ed.), *The Suggestibility of Children's Recollections* (pp. 92–105). Washington, DC: American Psychological Association.

Goodman, G.S. & Reed, D.S. (1986). Age differences in eyewitness testimony. *Law and Human Behavior,* **10**, 317–332.

Goodman, G.S., Aman, C. & Hirschman, J. (1987). Child sexual and physical abuse: Children's testimony. In S.J. Ceci, M.P. Toglia, & D.P. Ross (Eds.), *Children's Eyewitness Memory* (pp. 1–23). New York: Springer-Verlag.

Goodman, G.S., Wilson, M.E., Hazan, C. & Reed, R.S. (April, 1989). *Children's testimony nearly four years after an event.* Paper presented to the Eastern Psychological Association, Boston, MA.

Goodman, G.S., Rudy, L., Bottoms, B. & Aman, C. (1990). Children's concerns and memory: Issues of ecological validity on the study of children's eyewitness testimony. In R. Fivush & J. Hudson (Eds.), *Knowing and Remembering in Young Children* (pp. 249–284). New York: Cambridge University Press.

Goodman, G.S., Bottoms, B.L., Schwartz-Kenney, B.M. & Rudy, L. (1991a). Children's testimony about a stressful event: Improving children's reports. *Journal of Narrative and Life History,* **1**, 69–99.

Goodman, G.S., Hirschman, J., Hepps, D. & Rudy, L. (1991b). Children's memory for stressful events. *Merrill-Palmer Quarterly*, **37**, 109–158.

Goodman, G.S., Taub, E.P., Jones, D.P.H., England, P., Port, L.K., Rudy, L. & Prado, L. (1992). Testifying in criminal court. *Monographs of the Society for Research in Child Development*, **57** (5, Serial no. 229).

Green, A.H. (1991). Factors contributing to false allegations of child sexual abuse in custody disputes. In M. Robin (Ed.), *Assessing Child Maltreatment Reports: The Problems of False Allegations* (pp. 177–190). New York: Haworth Press.

Greenstock, J. & Pipe, M.-E. (1996). Interviewing children about past events: The influence of peer support and misleading questions. *Child Abuse and Neglect*, **20**, 69–80.

Greenstock, J. & Pipe, M.-E. (1997). Are two heads better than one? Peer support and children's eyewitness reports. *Applied Cognitive Psychology*, **11**, 461–483.

Harner, L. (1975). Yesterday and tomorrow: Development of early understanding of the terms. *Developmental Psychology*, **11**, 864–865.

Hershkowitz, I., Lamb, M.E., Sternberg, K.J. & Esplin, P.W. (1997). The relationships among interviewer utterance type, CBCA scores, and the richness of children's responses. *Legal and Criminological Psychology*, **2**, 169–176.

Hershkowitz, I., Orbach, Y., Lamb, M.E., Sternberg, K.J., Horowitz, D. & Hovav, M. (1998). Visiting the scene of the crime: Effects on children's recall of alleged abuse. *Legal & Criminological Psychology*, **3**, 195–207.

Horowitz, D., Hershkowitz, I. & Hovav, M. (in press). The effect of using a scripted interview protocol and training of youth investigators on the quality of interviewing child victims of sexual abuse [Hebrew]. In Y. Vozner, M. Golan & M. Hovav (Eds.), *Evaluation of Intervention in Correctional Services* [Hebrew]. Tel Aviv: Shirikova Press.

Hughes, M. & Grieve, R. (1980). On asking children bizarre questions. In M. Donaldson, R. Grieve & C. Pratt (Eds.), *Early Childhood Development and Education* (pp. 104–114). Oxford, England: Blackwell.

Johnson, M.K. & Foley, M.A. (1984). Differentiating fact from fantasy: The reliability of children's memory. *Journal of Social Issues*, **40**, 33–50.

Jones, D.P.H. (1992). *Interviewing the Sexually Abused Child*. Oxford: Gaskell.

Jones, D.P. & McGraw, E.M. (1987). Reliable and fictitious accounts of sexual abuse to children. *Journal of Interpersonal Violence*, **2**, 27–45.

Jones, D.P. & Seig, A. (1988). Child sexual abuse allegations in custody or visitation disputes. In B. Nicholson (Ed.), *Sexual Abuse Allegations in Custody and Visitation Disputes*. Washington, DC: American Bar Association.

King, M.A. & Yuille, J.C. (1987). Suggestibility and the child witness. In S.J. Ceci, D.F. Ross & M.P. Toglia (Eds.), *Children's Eyewitness Memory* (pp. 24–35). New York: Springer-Verlag.

Lamb, M.E. (1994). The investigation of child sexual abuse: An interdisciplinary consensus statement. *Child Abuse and Neglect*, **18**, 1021–1028.

Lamb, M.E., Sternberg, K.J. & Esplin, P.W. (1994). Factors influencing the reliability and validity of the statements made by young victims of sexual maltreatment. *Journal of Applied Developmental Psychology*, **15**, 255–280.

Lamb, M.E., Sternberg, K.J. & Esplin, P.W. (1995). Making children into competent witnesses: Reactions to the amicus brief *In Re Michaels*. *Psychology, Public Policy, and the Law*, **1**, 438–449.

Lamb, M.E., Hershkowitz, I., Sternberg, K.J., Boat, B. & Everson, M.D. (1996a). Investigative interviews of alleged sexual abuse victims with and without anatomical dolls. *Child Abuse and Neglect*, **20**, 1239–1247.

Lamb, M.E., Hershkowitz, I., Sternberg, K.J., Esplin, P.W., Hovav, M., Manor, T. & Yudilevitch, L. (1996b). Effects of investigative style on Israeli children's responses. *International Journal of Behavioral Development*, **19**, 627–637.

Lamb, M.E., Sternberg, K.J., Esplin, P.W., Hershkowitz, I., Orbach, Y. & Hovav, M. (1997). Criterion-based content analysis: A field validation study. *Child Abuse and Neglect*, **21**, 255–264.

Lamb, M.E., Sternberg, K.J. & Esplin, P.W. (1998a). Conducting investigative interviews of alleged sexual abuse victims. *Child Abuse and Neglect*, **22**, 813–823.

Lamb, M.E., Sternberg, K.J., Esplin, P.W. & Chadwick, D. (1998b). *Effect of age and length of delay on the amount of information provided by alleged abuse victims in investigative interviews*. Unpublished manuscript, National Institute of Child Health and Human Development.

Leichtman, M.D. & Ceci, S.J. (1995). The effects of stereotypes and suggestions on preschoolers' reports. *Developmental Psychology*, **31**, 568–578.

Lindsay, D.S. & Johnson, M.K. (1987). Reality monitoring and suggestibility. In S.J. Ceci, M.P. Toglia & D.F. Ross (Eds.), *Children's Eyewitness Testimony* (pp. 79–91). New York: Springer-Verlag.

Loftus, E.F. (1979). *Eyewitness Testimony*. Cambridge, MA: Harvard University Press.

Malpass, R.S., (1996). Enhancing eyewitness memory. In S.L. Sporer, R.S. Malpass & G. Koehnken (Eds.), *Psychological Issues in Eyewitness Identification* (pp. 177–204). Mahwah, NJ: Erlbaum.

Marin, B.V., Holmes, D.L., Guth, M. & Kovac, P. (1979). The potential of children as eyewitnesses. *Law and Human Behavior*, **3**, 295–305.

Martin, C.L. & Halverson, C.F. (1983). The effects of sex-typing schemas on young children's memory. *Child Development*, **54**, 563–574.

McAuliff, B.D., Kovera, M.B. & Viswesvaran, C. (1998, March). *Methodological issues in child suggestibility research: A meta-analysis*. Paper presented to the American Psychology-Law Society Convention, Redondo Beach, CA.

McCartney, K. & Nelson, K. (1981). Children's use of scripts in story recall. *Discourse Processes*, **4**, 59–70.

McGough, L. (1994). *Child Witnesses*. New Haven, CT: Yale University Press.

Memorandum of Good Practice (1992). London, England: Her Majesty's Stationery Office.

Moston, S. & Engelberg, T. (1992). The effects of social support on children's eyewitness testimony. *Applied Cognitive Psychology*, **6**, 61–75.

Myles-Worsley, M., Cromer, C. & Dodd, D. (1986). Children's preschool script reconstruction: Reliance on general knowledge as memory fades. *Developmental Psychology*, **22**, 2–30.

National Society for the Prevention of Cruelty to Children (1989). *Child Abuse Trends in England and Wales, 1983–1987*. London: NSPCC.

Nelson, K. (1986). *Event Knowledge: A Functional Approach to Cognitive Development*. Hillsdale, NJ: Lawrence Erlbaum Associates.

Nelson, K. & Gruendel, J. (1981). Generalized event representations: Basic building blocks of cognitive development. In M.E. Lamb & A.L. Brown (Eds.), *Advances in Development Psychology* (Vol. 1, pp. 131–158). Hillsdale, NJ: Erlbaum.

Newcombe, P.A. & Siegal, M. (1996). Where to look first for suggestibility in young children. *Cognition*, **59**, 337–356.

Newcombe, P.A. & Siegal, M. (1997). Explicitly questioning the nature of suggestibility in preschoolers' memory and retention. *Journal of Experimental Child Psychology*, **67**, 185–203.

Oates, K. & Shrimpton, S. (1991). Children's memories for stressful and non-stressful events. *Medical Science and Law*, **31**, 4–10.

Ochsner, J.E. & Zaragoza, M.S. (March, 1988). *The accuracy and suggestibility of children's memory for neutral and criminal eyewitness events*. Paper presented to the American Psychology and Law Association, Miami, FL.

Ornstein, P.A., Gordon, B.N. & Larus, D.M. (1992a). Children's memory for a personally experienced event: Implications for testimony. *Applied Cognitive Psychology*, **6**, 49–60.

Ornstein, P.A., Larus, D.M. & Clubb, P.A. (1992b). Understanding children's testimony: Implications of the research on children's memory. In R. Vasta (Ed.), *Annals of Child Development* (Vol. 8, pp. 147–176). London: Jessica Kingsley.

Paris, S.G. (1988). Motivated remembering. In F.E. Weinert & M. Perlmutter (Eds.), *Memory Development: Universal Changes and Individual Differences* (pp. 221–242). Hillsdale, NJ: Erlbaum.

Pea, R.D. (1980). The development of negation in early child language. In D.R. Olson (Ed.), *The Social Foundations of Language and Thought* (pp. 156–186). New York: Norton.

Perry, N.W. & Wrightsman, L.S. (1991). *The Child Witness: Legal Issues and Dilemmas.* Newbury Park, CA: Sage.

Peters, D.P. (1987). The impact of naturally occurring stress on children's memory. In S.J. Ceci, M.P. Toglia & D.F. Ross (Eds.), *Children's Eyewitness Testimony* (pp. 122–141). New York: Springer-Verlag.

Peters, D.P. (1991). The influence of stress and arousal on the child witness. In J. Doris (Ed.), *The Suggestibility of Children's Recollections* (pp. 60–76). Washington, DC: American Psychological Association.

Peters, D.P. & Hagan, S. (April, 1989). *Stress and arousal effects on the child's eyewitness.* Paper presented to the Society for Research in Child Development, Kansas City, MO.

Peterson, C. & Bell, M. (1996). Children's memory for traumatic injury. *Child Development,* **67**, 3045–3070.

Pipe, M.E. & Wilson, C. (1994). Cues and secrets: Influences on children's event reports. *Developmental Psychology,* **30**, 515–525.

Poole, D.A. & Lamb, M.E. (1998). *Investigative Interviews of Children: A Guide for Helping Professionals.* Washington, DC: American Psychological Association.

Poole, D.A. & Lindsay, D.S. (1995). Interviewing preschoolers: Effects of nonsuggestive techniques, parental coaching, and leading questions on reports of nonexperienced events. *Journal of Experimental Child Psychology,* **60**, 129–154.

Poole, D.A. & Lindsay, D.S. (1997, April). *Misinformation from parents and children's source monitoring: Implications for testimony.* Paper presented to the Society for Research in Child Development, Washington, DC.

Poole, D.A. & White, L.T. (1993). Two years later: Effects of question repetition and retention intervals on the eyewitness testimony of children and adults. *Developmental Psychology,* **29**, 844–853.

Price, D.W.W. & Goodman, G.S. (1990). Visiting the wizard: Children's memory of a recurring event. *Child Development,* **61**, 664–680.

Raskin, D.C. & Esplin, P.W. (1991a). Statement validity assessments: Interview procedures and content analyses of children's statements of sexual abuse. *Behavioral Assessment,* **13**, 265–291.

Raskin, D.C. & Esplin, P.W. (1991b). Assessment of children's statements of sexual abuse. In J. Doris (Ed.), *The Suggestibility of Children's Recollections* (pp. 153–164). Washington, DC: American Psychological Association.

Raskin, D. & Yuille, J. (1989). Problems of evaluating interviews of children in sexual abuse cases. In S.J. Ceci, M.P. Toglia & D.F. Ross (Eds.), *Perspectives on Children's Testimony* (pp. 184–207). New York: Springer-Verlag.

Reich, P.A. (1986). *Language Development.* Englewood Cliffs, NJ: Prentice-Hall.

Roberts, K.P. & Blades, M. (1995). Children's discriminations of memories for actual and pretend actions in a hiding task. *British Journal of Developmental Psychology,* **13**, 321–333.

Roberts, K.P. & Blades, M. (1998). The effects of interacting with events on children's eyewitness memory and source monitoring. *Applied Cognitive Psychology,* **12**, 489–503.

Roberts, K.P. & Lamb, M.E. (in press). Children's responses when interviewers distort details during investigative interviews. *Applied Cognitive Psychology.*

Rosenthal, R. (1995). State of New Jersey vs. Margaret Kelly Michaels: An overview. *Psychology, Public Policy, and Law,* **1**, 246–271.

Sattler, J. (1998). *Clinical and Forensic Interviewing of Children and Families.* San Diego, CA: Author.

Saywitz, K.J. (1988). The credibility of the child witness. *Family Advocate,* **10**, 38.

Saywitz, K.J. & Snyder, L. (1993). Improving children's testimony with preparation. In G.S. Goodman & B.L. Bottoms (Eds.), *Child Victims, Child Witnesses: Understanding and Improving Testimony* (pp. 117–146). New York: Guilford.

Saywitz, K.J., Geiselman, E. & Bornstein, G. (1996). Effects of cognitive interviewing, and practice on children's recall performance. *Journal of Applied Psychology*, **77**, 744–756.

Saywitz, K.J., Goodman, G.S., Nicholas, E. & Moan, S.F. (1991). Children's memories of physical examination involving genital touch: Implications for reports of child sexual abuse. *Journal of Consulting and Clinical Psychology*, **59**, 682–691.

Sedlak, A.J. & Broadhurst, D.D. (1996). *Third National Incidence Study of Child Abuse and Neglect: Final Report*. Washington, DC: US Department of Health and Human Resources, Administration for Children and Families.

Shank, R. & Abelson, R. (1977). *Scripts, Plans, Goals, and Understanding*. Hillsdale, NJ: Erlbaum.

Spencer, J. & Flin, R. (1993). *The Evidence of Children* (2nd edn). London: Blackstone Press.

Steller, M. (1991). Commentary: Rehabilitation of the child witness. In J. Doris (Ed.), *The Suggestibility of Children's Recollections* (pp. 106–109). Washington, DC: American Psychological Association.

Sternberg, K.J., Lamb, M.E. & Hershkowitz, I. (1996a). Child sexual abuse investigations in Israel. *Criminal Justice and Behavior*, **23**, 322–337.

Sternberg, K.J., Lamb, M.E., Hershkowitz, I., Esplin, P.W., Redlich, A. & Sunshine, N. (1996b). The relationship between investigative utterance types and the informativeness of child witnesses. *Journal of Applied Developmental Psychology*, **17**, 439–451.

Sternberg, K.J., Lamb, M.E., Hershkowitz, I., Yudilevitch, L., Orbach, Y., Esplin, P.W. & Hovav, M. (1997). Effects of introductory style on children's abilities to describe experiences of sexual abuse. *Child Abuse and Neglect*, **21**, 1133–1146.

Steward, M.S. (1993). Understanding children's memories of medical procedures: "He didn't touch me and it didn't hurt!" In C.A. Nelson (Ed.), *Memory and Affect in Development* (pp. 171–225). Hillsdale, NJ: Erlbaum.

Steward, M.S. & Steward, D.S. (with L. Farquhar, J.E.B. Myers, M. Reinhart, J. Welker, N. Joye, J. Driskill & J. Morgan). (1996). Interviewing young children about body touch and handling. *Monographs of the Society for Research in Child Development*, **61**, (4–5, Serial number 248).

Stockdale, M. (1996). *An evaluation of interview techniques used by police officers and social workers with sexually abused children*. Unpublished Masters Thesis, University of Leicester, Leicester, England.

Toglia, M.P., Ceci, S.J. & Ross, D.F. (April, 1989). *Prestige vs. source monitoring in children's suggestibility*. Paper presented to the Society for Research in Child Development, Kansas City, MO.

Thoennes, N. & Pearson, J. (1987). *Summary of findings from the sexual abuse allegations project*. Unpublished manuscript, Center for Policy Research, Denver.

Thompson, W.C., Clarke-Stewart, K.A. & Lepore, S.J. (1997). What did the janitor do? Suggestive interviewing and the accuracy of children's accounts. *Law and Human Behavior*, **21**, 405–426.

Tulving, E. (1985). How many memory systems are there? *American Psychologist*, **40**, 385–398.

Undeutsch, U. (1989). The development of statement reality analysis. In J.C. Yuille (Ed.), *Credibility Assessment* (pp. 101–120). Dordrecht, The Netherlands: Kluwer.

Undeutsch, U. (1982). Statement reality analysis. In A. Trankell (Ed.), *Reconstructing the Past: The Role of Psychologists in Criminal Trials* (pp. 27–56). Stockholm: Norstedt.

Vandermaas, M. (April, 1991). *Does anxiety affect children's event reports?* Paper presented to the Society for Research in Child Development, Seattle, WA.

Walker, A.G. (1993). Questioning young children in court: A linguistic case study. *Law and Human Behavior*, **17**, 59–81.

Walker, A.G. (1994). *Handbook on Questioning Children: A Linguistic Perspective*. Washington, DC: American Bar Association Center on Children and the Law.

Walker, N. & Hunt, J.S. (1998). Interviewing child victim-witnesses: How you ask is what you get. In C.R. Thompson, D. Herrman, J.D. Read, D. Bruce, D. Payne & M.P. Toglia

(Eds.), *Eyewitness Memory: Theoretical and Applied Perspectives* (pp. 55–87). Mahwah, NJ: Erlbaum.

Warren, A.R. & Lane, P. (1995). Effects of timing and type of questioning on eyewitness accuracy and suggestibility. In M.S. Zaragoza et al. (Eds.). *Memory and Testimony in the Child Witness.* Applied Psychology: Individual, Social and Community Issues. Vol 1 (pp. 44–60). Thousand Oaks, CA: Sage.

Warren, A.R. & McCloskey, L.A. (1997). Language in social contexts. In S.B. Gleason (Ed.), *The Development of Language* (4th edn, pp. 210–258). New York: Allyn & Bacon.

Warren, A.R., Woodall, C.C., Hunt, J.S. & Perry, N.W. (1996). "It sounds good in theory, but . . .": Do investigative interviewers follow guidelines based on memory research? *Child Maltreatment,* **1**, 231–245.

Westcott, H., Davies, G. & Horan, N. (1998, March). *Evaluating investigative interviews for suspected child sexual abuse carried out by English police officers.* Paper presented to the American Psychology-Law Society Conference, Redondo Beach, CA.

Wilkinson, J. (1988). Context effects in children's event memory. In M.M. Gruneberg, P.E. Morris & R.N. Sykes (Eds.), *Practical Aspects of Memory: Current Research Issues* (Vol. 1, pp. 107–111). New York: Wiley.

Woolley, J.D. (1997). Thinking about fantasy: Are children fundamentally different thinkers and believers from adults? *Child Development,* **68**, 991–1011.

Yuille, J.C. & Cutshall, J.L. (1986). A case study of eyewitness memory of a crime. *Journal of Applied Psychology,* **71**, 291–301.

Police Investigative Interviewing

Ray Bull
University of Portsmouth, UK

INTRODUCTION

Just a few years ago a senior British police officer stated that "Unethical be-haviour by interrogators has undermined public confidence and left the police service with a serious skills deficit in its ability to obtain evidence through ques-tioning" and that "Currently, and in particular after any removal of the right to silence, the judges will apply strict criteria before admitting evidence obtained through questioning" (Williamson, 1994, p. 107). Williamson pointed out that "it does not take much skill to beat a confession out of a suspect detained in police custody" nor "much skill to fabricate a confession and allege that it was made during police questioning". However, he noted that "The police in this country would correctly deny that such things happen but unfortunately a considerable proportion of the general public thinks that it happens regularly" (p. 107).

Data concerning the general public's beliefs were gathered in London, Eng-land in the 1980s by the Policy Studies Institute (Smith, 1983) and by Jones, MacLean and Young (1986). Both of these studies found that a notable propor-tion of the public believed police interviewers used physical force and threats when questioning suspects. Williamson (1993) reports an unpublished study by the serving police officer Walkley (1983) who found that almost half of the officers he questioned agreed with the statement "It is sometimes helpful to slap a suspect around the face". However, less than one in ten agreed with the statement "If I think a suspect needs a good hiding to help him think about admitting an offence then I give him one". While just over half agreed with "Police officers should never use any form of violence to get a suspect to speak

Handbook of the Psychology of Interviewing. Edited by A. Memon and R. Bull.

the truth", half also agreed with "Some suspects expect rough treatment in police stations, and, if it suits the circumstances, I don't do anything to allay their fears". Up to the early 1980s almost no substantive guidance was available around the world to police officers on how best to conduct investigative interviews, either with suspects or with witnesses. This dearth of information was one of the reasons for the widespread adoption of the approach to interrogation advocated by the Americans Inbau and Reid (e.g. in the 1986 edition of their book, with the words "interrogation and confession" in its title). Their approach advocated a number of persuasive tactics designed to obtain confessions. (See Kassin (1997), Chapter 5.5 by Gudjonsson in this handbook, Memon, Vrij and Bull (1998) and Gudjonsson (1992) for psychologists' criticisms of these tactics and McKenzie (1994) for a fairly recent comparison of relevant police practices in the USA and England.)

In the 1980s a major development took place in England and Wales regarding police investigative interviewing. The Police and Criminal Evidence Act 1984 (known as PACE, which has accompanying Codes of Practice) requires that police interviews with suspects be recorded on audiotape. Such recording was largely introduced as a way of ensuring that the rights of suspects were safeguarded and initially many police officers were unhappy about this novel development. However, these recordings also allow the exposure of false allegations made by suspects about the way they were interviewed. Nowadays such recording is well accepted by the police service. One extra benefit of this legislation is that it is now possible to listen to these tape-recorded interviews in order to assess them. This sometimes, though not that often, occurs during criminal trials. Somewhat more often the officer(s) who conducted the interview, and sometimes their supervisors, will listen to them. Now and again the police service will allow outside researchers to do so though, understandably, the service is concerned that researchers will arrive at a balanced and informed assessment of what they hear.

Williamson (1994) noted that in England and Wales "The succession of cases which have been overturned by the Court of Appeal is forcing a fundamental reappraisal of the role of the investigator in an adversarial system of justice" (p. 108). In the past police investigators have been tempted to see themselves as part of the prosecution. Indeed, before the introduction of the Crown Prosecution Service (in 1986), which took mounting prosecutions out of the hands of the police, this was almost inevitable. The role of the police investigator is now, Williamson suggested, being redefined as a gatherer of facts and a searcher for the truth. Thus instead of seeing their role as obtaining a confession from a suspect, the police need to realise that they should be seeking quality information from interviewees (whether suspects or witnesses) in order to help determine the truth.

Williamson (1994) pointed out that a "new approach to police interviewing was set out in Home Office Circular 22/1992. The circular laid down certain principles for investigative interviewing which were developed through collaboration between police officers, lawyers and psychologists" (p. 108). The 1993 Royal Commission on Criminal Justice supported this information-gathering rather than confession-obtaining approach. The Commission noted that in the case of the "Cardiff Three" one of the interviews with the suspects contained "a

long and highly repetitive series of questions put . . . in a loud and aggressive way
. . . over a prolonged period leading to damaging admissions by the suspect after
his repeated denials had been ignored" (see Williamson, p. 109). The Lord Chief
Justice said of this: "Short of physical abuse, it is hard to conceive of a more
hostile and intimidating approach by officers to a suspect".

ANALYSES OF INTERVIEWS WITH SUSPECTS

Research in England

Irving (1980) was present at 60 interviews by police detectives of suspects at one
police station in England. He reported that the interviewers used a variety of
persuasive and manipulative tactics and that in the majority of interviews more
than one such tactic was employed. In 1984 PACE outlawed many of these
tactics and in a follow-up study post-PACE, Irving and McKenzie (1989) found
that the frequency of use of such tactics had, indeed, declined as had the frequency of repeatedly interviewing suspects. Most interestingly, they noted that
the proportion of interviews which contained an admission/confession by the
suspect did not change, being 62% pre-PACE and 65% post-PACE.

In 1992 the Home Office published Baldwin's research report, which it had
commissioned, on police interviews with suspects (Baldwin, 1992). Baldwin
(1993) pointed out that little research had been conducted on what goes on
inside the police interview room. He noted that "Before interviews with suspects
were recorded, the police account of what had transpired in the interview room
had to be largely taken on trust" (p. 326). This applied not only to police
accounts of what had been said but also to their opinions about the nature of the
process. Baldwin (1993) contended that police officers believe that most interviews are complex, difficult encounters with awkward, aggressive suspects,
whereas, of the 600 audio or video recorded interviews he analysed, "most were
short and surprisingly amiable discussions in which it often seemed that officers
were rather tentative in putting allegations to a suspect. . . . Indeed in almost
two-thirds of all cases . . . no serious challenge was made by the interviewers to
what the suspect was saying. Even when the suspect denied the allegation, no
challenge was made by the interviewers in almost 40 per cent of cases" (p. 331).
"Over a third of all suspects admitted culpability from the outset" (p. 335). Thus
the majority of interviews seemed relatively straightforward. Baldwin seemed to
be of the opinion that too few challenges were made of the suspects, and he may
well be correct. However, it could be that sometimes the police correctly decided
to accept the suspect's account (e.g. of denial) and release him/her, particularly
since the great majority of suspects answered the police questions. (One wonders
what proportion of suspects typically are wrongly classified as such by the police.)

In only 20 of the 600 interviews that Baldwin examined did suspects "change
their story in the course of an interview. In only nine of these cases was the

change of heart attributable to the persuasive skills of the interviewer, and even here only three involved offences of any seriousness. . . . The great majority of suspects stick to their starting position – whether admission, denial, or some-where in between – regardless of how the interview is conducted" (p. 333). In the light of this finding Baldwin argued for a refocusing of police interview training.

It seemed from Baldwin's seminal analysis of interviews that the police rarely used persuasive interviewing techniques, which could be a result of PACE 1984 successfully outlawing the coercive ones but no techniques having been brought in to replace these. Nevertheless, he argued that it was still a major operational belief among police officers that the aim of an interview with a suspect was to gain a confession. Not only would a confession result in praise from colleagues, it would also be cost effective in that "police officers know that the vast majority of suspects who have confessed will quietly plead guilty" (p. 326) and that "con-siderable amounts of time will not need to be spent interviewing witnesses, preparing lengthy files, and appearing in court" (p. 334). Even though some senior police officers had been attempting to persuade the "rank and file" inves-tigators who conduct most interviews that their role was to obtain evidence, Baldwin pointed out that "If interviewing techniques were to be assessed in terms of the police claim that they are geared to be an objective search for the truth, then they would emerge as thoroughly deficient" (p. 350).

Moston, Stephenson and Williamson (1992) obtained permission to listen to sev-eral hundred tape-recorded London police interviews with suspects. They found that in the majority of these the interviewers spent little time, if any, trying to obtain the interviewee's accounts of events. Instead, the interviewers devoted their time to accusing the interviewee of the offence and asking for his/her response to such accusations. Stephenson and Moston (1994) reported that 80% of the interviewers said that obtaining a confession was the main purpose of the interview, with 73% being sure of guilt prior to interview. Not surprisingly, many interviewees resisted these accusations. Moston et al. found that the accusatory style of interviewing usually took one of three forms. One form merely involved putting the accusation to the interviewee in the hope that he/she would agree that he/she did do it. Another form involved the presentation of evidence suggesting the interviewee's involvement and asking for an explanation. The third was a combination of these two styles. Moston et al. noted that typically, suspects were accused of the crime and informed of the evidence against them. They found, not surprisingly, that when the evidence was strong, confessions were more likely. However, we should note that when the evidence was not strong not only did fewer confessions ensue, the interviewee now knew the strength of evidence against him/her. Given this knowledge, it would be sensible for the interviewee to say little or nothing.

Moston et al. found that the manipulative form of interrogation used pre-viously in England (see Irving, 1980) has been replaced by a confrontational style of questioning where suspects are directly accused of the alleged offence at the beginning of the interview and informed of the evidence against them. One problem with this strategy is that if the suspect denies the allegation interviewers seem (from the research of Moston et al.) not to know what to do next. They noted that interviewers using this tactic often seemed at a loss as to what to do if the suspect did not confess. They also found that the more serious the offences the suspects were being accused of, the less likely they were to reply to accusations and the more likely they were to be silent. Again, from a suspect's point of view this makes sense, especially from a guilty suspect's point of view. (Of course, some "professional" criminals, terrorists and so on may purposely decide to say little or nothing. However, the vast majority of police investigative interviews do not involve such interviewees.) This aside, when interviewing suspects much of the resistance usually met by interviewers is, at least in part, the result of their own behaviour (Cherryman & Bull, 1996).

Even very recently Plimmer (1997) found that experienced English police detectives believed obtaining confessions to be the main aim of interviews with suspects. He reported that many "believed that presumption of innocence tended to lower the quality of interviewing techniques whereas a presumption of guilt tended to strengthen the quality" (p. 17).

Williamson (1993) reported that Moston et al. (1992) found the degree of questioning skill often to be quite low. The interviewers frequently gave up at the slightest obstacle (e.g. the suspect exercising the right to silence and/or saying "no comment"). "Many interviews appeared chaotic and unstructured." In many interviews the "questioning appeared to lack basic preparation and planning. Many of the officers seemed more nervous than the suspect" (p. 98). Preparation and planning was also found to be important in our study of police specialist investigative interviewing skills (Bull & Cherryman, 1996). We were commissioned by the Home Office (i) to provide an agreed definition of what constitutes specialist (or advanced) investigative interviewing, (ii) to provide a list of relevant skills, (iii) to determine the extent to which each of these skills was demonstrated in such interviewing, and (iv) to examine which of these skills differentiated between good and poor interviews with suspects.

In 1993 Baldwin advised that "Anyone seeking to make some evaluation of interviewing practices soon discovers (as do interviewers themselves) that there are very few ground rules. This means that there can be no guarantee that different people would reach the same assessments of the quality of any particular interview" (p. 329). However, in our project we found that expert raters agreed independently in their skill analyses of police interviews and that skilled interviews differed significantly from not-skilled interviews in terms of 11 of the 29 rated skills (e.g. flexibility, communication skills, open-mindedness, use of open questions, use of pauses/silences). Fuller reports of this work can be found in Bull and Cherryman (1996), Cherryman and Bull (in submission, a and b).

Pearse (a serving police officer) and Gudjonsson (1996) listened to 161 police interviews with suspects conducted at two London police stations in 1991 and 1992. They noted that the most common tactic employed by the interviewer was the introduction of evidence, which occurred in three-quarters of the interviews. Attempting to manipulate the self-esteem of the interviewee only occurred very rarely (3%) and much less often than Irving (1980) had found pre-PACE. The interviewers almost always (98%) used open-ended questions (as advocated by relevant police training post-PACE). However, they also often used leading questions (73%). Challenging the suspect (i) about inconsistencies in what he/she had said and/or (ii) that he/she was lying occurred in only 20% of the interviews. Challenging the interviewees in other ways was rare. On average, the interviews lasted only 22 minutes. The suspects were deemed to have been polite in almost all of the interviews (97%), as compliant in most (83%), and as giving full answers in the majority (62%). Very rarely did suspects react in an angry manner. (We should note that 14% of suspects did not give permission for the audio recordings of their interviews to be listened to by the researchers. Whether their interviews would have contained more challenges and less compliance and politeness is unknown.) In just over half of the interviews (58%) an admission or confession occurred. Only very rarely indeed did they find that interviewees changed from denying to admitting an offence either during an interview or from one interview to the next for those suspects interviewed more than once. Pearse and Gudjonsson noted that their admission/confession rate was very similar to those of previous studies, including that of Softley et al. (1980) which was conducted several years pre-PACE. In light of this they contended that "suspects enter a police interview having already decided whether to admit or deny the allegations against them" (p. 73) and that police interview techniques have minimal effects on whether an admission occurs. They speculated that the rare use of tactics beyond putting the allegation to the suspect and revealing the evidence against him/her could be taken to suggest that police officers in England and Wales are still unsure post-PACE (1984) concerning which interviewer behaviours that challenge the suspect will be acceptable or deemed unacceptable by the courts as oppressive or involving coercion. We should note how similar their findings are to those of Baldwin (1993) and of Moston et al. (1992).

Research in the USA

A relatively few years ago Leo (1992) stated that in the USA "Manipulation and deception have replaced force and direct coercion as the strategic underpinnings of information-gathering techniques that police now employ during criminal investigation" (p. 35). His paper offered an account of changes in police interrogation which had occurred since the 1940s. He stated that while courts in the USA "have actively prohibited physical and psychological forms of coercion, they have been reluctant to lay down bright lines about the use of deceptive police methods. Consequently, police are permitted by law to engage widely in trickery and deceit during *both* the investigatory and interrogatory stages of detection" (p. 36). Such police behaviour is not acceptable in some other countries, for example England and Wales where the Police and Criminal Evidence Act 1984 prohibits police use of deceit, coercion and oppression (McKenzie, 1990). Also, it is now recognised by the police in some countries (e.g. Williamson, 1993) that there should not be two separate stages regarding police investigative interviewing (i.e. Leo's "investigatory and interrogatory stages") but only one (i.e. investigatory).

While Leo claimed that "police questioning now consists of subtle and sophist-icated psychological ploys, tricks, stratagems, techniques and methods that rely on manipulation, persuasion, and deception for their efficacy" (p. 37) and that the police "believe that psychological tactics are far more effective at eliciting confessions" (p. 37), he noted that "we know very little about what actually happens during police interrogation" (p. 37). He stated that "interrogation has always been, and continues to be, shrouded in secrecy and mystery . . . most police departments still do not record interrogation sessions" (p. 37). While Leo noted that the state of Alaska requires all custodial interrogations to be elec-tronically recorded, he failed in his lengthy paper to make mention of substantial and very relevant developments in other countries (e.g. in England and Wales where the Police and Criminal Evidence Act 1984 requires the audio recording of police interviews with suspects). Leo pointed out that "only two observational studies of police interrogation exist in the American literature, and both are more than two decades old" (p. 37).

From his interviews with police officers, his reading of interrogation training materials and court cases, and his attendance at interrogation seminars and courses, Leo concluded that "The first rule of modern police interrogation is that the officer must project a sympathetic, friendly, and compassionate per-sonality image. The officer manoeuvres to show the suspect that he respects his dignity and will not condemn his behaviour. By winning the suspect's trust the officer thus creates a conversational rapport with him" (p. 43). We should note that this approach can involve a measure of deception in that the interviewing officer may not genuinely feel sympathetic and compassionate. Even though such an approach is now widely recommended in several countries, the issue of whether it involves coercion seems not yet to have been addressed. Leo also contended that "The goal of the interrogation is to create a psychological atmosphere that will facilitate the act of confessing" (p. 43). The major prob-lem with this, of course, is that an innocent person may falsely confess. Police officers may find this difficult to comprehend. However, a number of famous cases in England and Wales and a full psychological appreciation of what is involved (Gudjonsson, 1992 plus Chapter 5.5 in this handbook) make it clear that false confessions do regularly occur.

Leo (1992) identified eight types of deceptive interrogation including mis-representing the nature or purpose of questioning, misrepresenting the nature or seriousness of the offence, the use of promises, and the use of fabricated evi-dence. He quite rightly pointed out that police use of deception when question-ing suspects poses ethical dilemmas and is influenced by the balance of power between society's needs both for crime control and for due process. He stated that there seemed to be little consensus in the USA about where to draw the line between impermissible and permissible deceptive police investigative interview-ing tactics. While this may still be true in the 1990s in the USA, it seems not to be the case in England and Wales where courts, the Crown Prosecution Service, and now police forces themselves frown upon the purposive use of deception. (See Memon et al., 1988, for more on this.)

In 1994 McKenzie (for many years a police officer and now a highly qualified psychologist) published a comparative study of investigative interviewing in England and the USA. He noted that the Police and Criminal Evidence Act 1984 has, indeed, had a very positive effect on reducing oppressive, coercive and deceptive investigative interviewing practices. He noted that since the mid 1980s English courts have consistently ruled inadmissible confessions obtained via trickery, whereas the situation is not so clearcut in the USA. Thus a "growing distinction between English and American jurisprudence may be clearly seen" (p. 254). He concluded that "the English courts are accepting more readily the work of psychologists and are recognising the malleability of the human psyche as a fact" (p. 251).

ANALYSES OF INTERVIEWS WITH WITNESSES

In 1987 Fisher, Geiselman and Raymond conducted one of the very few studies of police interviewing outside the police station. Some members of the Robbery Division of the Metro-Dade Police Department in Florida agreed to pass to the researchers some audiotape-recorded interviews they conducted with crime witnesses at the crime scene or at the victim's residence. Eleven recorded interviews were available for analysis, a few of which were conducted on police premises. Fisher et al. (1987) reported that these interviews (it is a pity the sample was not larger) differed considerably from each other in structure, though there were some commonalities. Usually the interviewer would briefly introduce himself and then would ask the witness to recall what he/she could remember about the crime. On average, the interviews contained this open-ended question and two other open-ended questions. Unfortunately, the police officers regularly interrupted the witnesses with closed questions while they were still responding appropriately to the open-ended questions. These interruptions occurred around four times per open-ended question.

The interruptions were usually in the form of closed questions which required brief answers (e.g. "Was he wearing jeans?"). Fisher et al. (1987) noted that "answers to open-ended questions were interrupted . . . after only 7.5 seconds of description" (p. 179). They suggested that not only would such constant interruptions disrupt the witness's concentration on retrieving as much as possible in response to the open-ended question, because the interruptions were often unrelated to the preceding open-ended question and to what the witness was presently saying, but they would also force the witness's retrieval processes to jump almost at random from one aspect of the crime to a different, unrelated aspect. Furthermore, the constant interruptions would cause the witness to "learn that he will have only a short period of time in which to give his response before the next interruption" (p. 180). Thus witnesses would learn that short answers to the open-ended questions are required rather than long ones. Fisher et al. argued that this would make it less likely that witnesses would make a concerted effort to retrieve information from memory. The very opposite, presumably, of what the interviewing officer would wish. Similarly, the interviewers rarely allowed there to be pauses/silences in the interviews. The average time between inter-

viewees ceasing their answers to the short-answer closed questions and the interviewer asking the next question was a second. (There was never a pause after
interviewees' responses to open questions because they were always interrupted!) George and Clifford (1992) found a similar thing in England. Fisher et
al. argued that this also would eventuate in the witness reducing his or her efforts
to achieve extensive recall, as would the far greater use of closed questions than
open questions (which was also observed by George & Clifford, 1992). Furthermore, given the style of these interviews, if the interviewer forgot to ask about
something it is unlikely that the witness would mention it.

Fisher et al. also noted that the interviewers asked questions about the suspect
in a rather fixed sequence. First they asked about age then height, weight, body
build, facial characteristics, then clothing. They reported that on one occasion
when the witness began her description with the suspect's height the interviewer
interrupted and asked her to mention the suspect's age first. When Fisher et al.
asked the police detectives why they did this some said they were taught this
sequence at the police academy and that this sequence was compatible with the
form of police report they would be required to fill out! Another officer said " . . .
you just ask them who, what, when, where, why, and how" (p. 178). (Fisher et al.
also made a number of other, lesser criticisms of the interviews they analysed.)
Their paper then made a number of sensible recommendations for improving
police interviewing of witnesses (e.g. promoting focused retrieval, minimising interruptions and distractions, making questions compatible with the witness's recalling of the event) which they incorporated into their enhanced version of the
cognitive interview (Fisher & Geiselman, 1992). (See also Chapter 5.6 by Memon.)
Fisher et al. contended that "The psychology of memory is advanced enough to be
able to contribute positively to effective police interviewing, and there is little
reason for police investigators not to avail themselves of such information" (p.
185). Their paper concluded by recommending to police organisations that "a
major change must be enacted at the institutional level, namely, to introduce
formal training in the science of interviewing cooperative witnesses. This should be
done both at the entry level of the uniformed street police officer, and also as in
house training for the more experienced investigator" (p. 185).

While many police forces in various countries seem to have ignored or be
ignorant of this recommendation, in England and Wales major changes very
much in line with such a recommendation have taken place in the 1990s.

RECENT CHANGES IN POLICE TRAINING

In 1992 the Association of Chief Police Officers and the Home Office jointly
produced two booklets on investigative interviewing to be issued to all 127 000
police officers in England and Wales. One of these booklets described how
investigative interviews should be conducted and one approach recommended
was the cognitive interview procedure (see Chapter 5.6 by Memon), not only for
witnesses and victims but also, where appropriate, for suspects. At the same time

a nationwide initiative of one-week training programmes was set up to train as many officers as possible in the recommended methods (Williamson, 1993, 1994).

1992 also saw in England and Wales new legislation and procedures regarding child witnesses/victims in criminal proceedings, in particular the Government's publication of a guidance booklet detailing how such interviews should be conducted (Home Office and Department of Health, 1992) and specialised training for police officers working in child protection teams. (For more on interviewing children see Bull, 1996, Bull & Davies, 1996, and Chapter 5.1 by Lamb et al.). I will briefly mention here that I am often sent, by defence lawyers, video recordings of police interviews with child witnesses. My expert witness opinion about these interviews is usually that they are quite good.

These three official booklets were very much informed by psychological research and several psychologists (some of whom were also police officers) played a major role in their drafting (Bull, 1992, 1996; Cherryman & Bull, 1996). Such developments demonstrate the substantial contribution that psychology can now make to police investigative interviewing and similar developments should take place in other countries.

DIFFERENCES AMONG POLICE OFFICERS

In his 1993 study (which was part of his 1990 doctoral thesis) the serving senior police officer Williamson (a psychology graduate) analysed the responses of 80 police detectives to his questionnaire on investigative issues (which was administered by a police sergeant). These officers on average had 12 years of police service; 65% were constables, 31% were sergeants and 4% were inspectors. Only 12% said that the main purpose of a police interview was to obtain a confession, with 38% saying the main purpose was to get to the truth and 24% saying it was to seek an explanation.

From his listening to a large sample of audiotaped recordings of police interviews with suspects (i.e. post-PACE 1984) Williamson identified four interrogation styles, these being "collusive" (i.e. a cooperative questioning style to obtain a confession), "dominant" (i.e. a confrontational questioning style to obtain a confession), "business-like" (i.e. a confrontational style to obtain evidence), and "counselling" (i.e. a cooperative style to obtain evidence). A quarter of his respondents identified with the collusive style, a fifth with the counselling style, an eighth with the business-like style and a sixteenth with the dominant style. (The remainder of the respondents seemed not to identify with only one particular style.) When asked to say which style they considered the most unsatisfactory half of the officers chose the dominant style.

Williamson conducted factor analysis on his data in order to reveal the various ways in which these detectives conceptualised the process of questioning suspects. From this, four factors emerged which differentiated somewhat between groups of officers. The older detectives scored highly on "dominance", which indicated a preference for the dominant and business-like styles involving confrontational questioning style with the use of trickery and of quick questioning to put pressure on suspects. The detectives who most frequently interviewed suspects scored highly on "perceived success", which indicated a preference for getting the guilty to confess but by acceptable means. These officers preferred the counselling and collusive styles and had a negative view of trickery and threats. They deemed success to be obtaining confessions, but only truthful ones. (Williamson did not specifically comment on how these interviewers would go about determining whether a confession was true.) The factor "perceived difficulty" indicated variation among the detectives in their degree of pessimism about what interviews with suspects could achieve. The factor "persuasion" demonstrated variation among the respondents in their beliefs that interviewing suspects is a process of bargaining in which untruthful denial by the suspect is common and in which the interviewer by using a familiar manner with the suspect can obtain a confession, frequently when the case is weak. Detectives who scored higher on this factor saw a need for training in persuasive questioning.

Williamson concluded from his findings that "There has been a move away from interviewing primarily for confessions" (p. 97). While this may be so, one wonders to what extent social compliance existed in his study. Did his respondents air their true feelings and beliefs? Even if they did, psychologists (among others) know that what people say they do and believe in may differ from their actual behaviour. Fisher (1995) reported that the detectives Fisher et al. (1987) studied sometimes said one thing but did another. Fortunately, Williamson had very considerable, perhaps almost unique, experience of listening to a very large sample of audiotaped interviews with suspects (e.g. for his own doctoral thesis; see also Moston et al., 1992) and therefore would probably have noticed if the findings reported in his 1993 paper differed from real interviewing behaviour.

Sear and Stephenson (1997) attempted to relate differences among police officers' interviewing behaviours to the officers' personalities. Using regression analysis they found few relationships between officers' overall interviewing skill score (demonstrated in interviews with suspects) and personality measures of dominance, agreeableness, conscientiousness, neuroticism and openness. One reason for this, they suggested, was the similarity in personality among the officers, who exhibited "a cold, calculating and dominating approach to others" (p. 32). When they divided the officers into two groups based on their overall interviewing skill score they again found few effects. Only for openness was there a significant difference, but it was officers with lower openness personality scores who had the higher overall skill scores. Sear and Stephenson then correlated the personality factor of openness with the particular interviewing skills they deemed to be related to openness and found a significant, negative relationship. This led them to note "that *Openness* as a personality trait is not straightforwardly reflected as a behaviour in interviews with suspects" (p. 32). In these interviews with suspects even police officers with higher openness personality scores seemed unable to demonstrate openness in their interviewing behaviours. Sears and Stephenson's recent study suggests that the police culture may be finding it very difficult to replace the confession-obtaining approach with the information-gathering approach.

COOPERATION BETWEEN POLICING AND PSYCHOLOGY

In 1995 Fisher stated that "Despite the importance of eyewitness information in criminal investigation, police receive inadequate training to interview cooperative witnesses. They make avoidable mistakes that minimize the amount of eyewitness information elicited and contribute to inaccurate recollections" (p. 732). He noted that in many crime investigations the main source of information is from witnesses. Such information is not only likely to cause juries and judges to make correct decisions, it is likely to reduce reliance on confessions, while also making perpetrators more likely to confess when the weight of evidence against them is strong (Moston et al., 1992). Fisher commented that from his recent extensive experience of training police officers in the cognitive interviewing procedure he developed with Geiselman (see Fisher & Geiselman, 1992), most police officers seemed not to have received prior training in investigative interviewing, and where they had it had been brief and of poor quality. He noted that textbooks concerned with policing completely ignored this topic or only gave it scant mention. (Prior to the 1990s this unfortunate state of affairs was perhaps understandable given that so little research had been conducted on this topic.) This lack of appropriate training, Fisher argued, had forced officers to follow their own intuition and/or to learn on the job by observing the interviewing behaviour of other officers, not knowing what were good or poor interviewing practices. He noted that (see Fisher et al., 1987) "not until detectives listened to tape recordings of their own interviews were they convinced of their poor technique and motivated to change" (p. 737).

Most of Fisher's 1995 paper is devoted to an explanation and account of the cognitive interview procedure (which is described in Memon's chapter (5.6) in this book) and to a briefer account of police use of hypnosis. Good overviews of the investigatory use of hypnosis are provided by Kebbell and Wagstaff (in press) and Wagstaff (1993), in Chapter 1.2 by Lynn in this handbook, and therefore this topic will not be reviewed here. Fisher concluded his extensive paper by pointing out that "Effective witness interviews depend on a host of psychological factors" but that in the USA "psychological research has been met with only a lukewarm reception by the legal-police community" (p. 758). He noted, however, that in England the police community is "more receptive" (p. 758) to psychological research. I would contend that one reason for this is that some English psychologists have taken the trouble to inform the police community, now over many years, in a positive way of how psychology can help to improve policing (e.g. Bull et al., 1983). Another probable reason is that some of the work on police investigative interviewing in England has either been conducted by police officers with degrees in psychology (e.g. Williamson, McKenzie, Pearse) or funded by official agencies (e.g. the Home Office, which has governmental responsibility for policing).

Fisher (1995) advised that "One method to increase the acceptability of psychological research to the legal-police community is to include members of these groups when initially designing a research project" (p. 759). Doing this may be rare outside England where the contribution of behavioural and social sciences may still be solely to criticise policing rather than to improve it – as used also to be the case in England. Cooperation is becoming ever more the case in England. For example, the project we conducted on police specialist investigative interviewing for the Police Research Group of the Home Office (Bull & Cherryman, 1996) had a helpful advisory board on which sat a very experienced police officer with relevant knowledge, a psychology academic who had prior extensive experience as a police officer, a lawyer, and an internationally renowned social psychologist.

Another example is my being asked by a number of police forces in recent years to advise them on the contribution psychology can make to the courses they are developing on advanced interviewing skills.

To improve investigative interviewing is one of the greatest challenges facing policing. Police officers need the help of psychologists to realise why changes are necessary and what these changes should be. Psychologists need the cooperation of police officers in order to conduct ecologically valid and relevant research.

ACKNOWLEDGEMENTS

The author would like to thank Julie Cherryman and Kim Rigert for their comments on drafts of this chapter.

REFERENCES

Baldwin, J. (1992). *Video taping of police interviews with suspects – an evaluation. Police Research Series Paper number 1*. London: Home Office.

Baldwin, J. (1993). Police interview techniques: Establishing truth or proof? *British Journal of Criminology*, **33**, 325–351.

Bull, R. (1992). Obtaining evidence expertly: The reliability of interviews with child witnesses. *Expert Evidence*, **1**, 5–12.

Bull, R. (1996). Good practice for video recorded interviews with child witnesses for use in criminal proceedings. In G. Davies, S. Lloyd-Bostock, M. McMurran & C. Wilson (Eds.), *Psychology, Law and Criminal Justice*. Berlin: de Gruyter.

Bull, R. & Cherryman, J. (1996). *Helping to Identify Skills Gaps in Specialist Investigative Interviewing: Enhancement of Professional Skills*. London: Home Office Police Department.

Bull, R. & Davies, G. (1996). Child witness research in England. In B. Bottoms & G. Goodman (Eds.), *International Perspectives on Child Abuse and Children's Testimony*. Thousand Oaks, CA: Sage.

Bull, R., Bustin, R., Evans, P. & Gahagan, D. (1983). *Psychology for Police Officers*. Chichester: Wiley.

Cherryman, J. & Bull, R. (1996). Investigative interviewing. In F. Leishman, B. Loveday & S. Savage (Eds.), *Core Issues in Policing*. London: Longman.

Cherryman, J. & Bull, R. (in submission, a). Police officers' perceptions of specialist investigative interviewing skills.

Cherryman, J. & Bull, R. (in submission, b). Identification of skills gaps in specialist investigative interviewing: Analysis of interviews with suspects.

Fisher, R. (1995). Interviewing victims and witnesses of crime. *Psychology, Public Policy and Law*, **1**, 732–764.

Fisher, R. & Geiselman, R.E. (1992). *Memory Enhancing Techniques for Investigative Interviewing: The Cognitive Interview.* Springfield, Illinois: Thomas.

Fisher, R., Geiselman, R.E. & Raymond, D. (1987). Critical analysis of police interview techniques. *Journal of Police Science and Administration*, **15**, 177–185.

George, R. & Clifford, B. (1992). Making the most of witnesses. *Policing*, **8**, 185–198.

Gudjonsson, G. (1992). *The Psychology of Interrogations, Confessions and Testimony.* Chichester: Wiley.

Home Office and Department of Health. (1992). *Memorandum of Good Practice for Video Recorded Interviews with Child Witnesses for Criminal Proceedings.* London: HMSO.

Inbau, F.E., Reid, J.E. & Buckley, J.P. (1986). *Criminal Interrogation and Confessions* (3rd edn). Baltimore: Williams and Wilkins.

Irving, B. (1980). *Police Interrogation, A Case Study of Current Practice. Research Study Number 2, Royal Commission on Criminal Procedure.* London: HMSO.

Irving, B.L. & McKenzie, I. (1989). *Police Interrogation: The Effects of the Police and Criminal Evidence Act.* London: Police Foundation.

Jones, T., MacLean, B. & Young, J. (1986). *The Islington Crime Survey: Crime Victimization and Policing in Inner City London.* London: Gower.

Kassin, S. (1997). The psychology of confession evidence. *American Psychologist*, **52**, 221–233.

Kebbell, M. & Wagstaff, G. (in press). Hypnotic interviewing: The best way to interview eyewitnesses? *Behavioural Science and Law.*

Leo, R. (1992). From coercion to deception: The changing nature of police interrogation in America. *Crime, Law and Social Change*, **18**, 35–59.

McKenzie, I. (1990). Unexpected consequences: Due process v. crime control. *Criminal Justice International*, **6**, 10–12.

McKenzie, I. (1994). Regulating custodial interviews: A comparative study. *International Journal of the Sociology of Law*, **22**, 239–259.

Memon, A., Vrij, A. & Bull, R. (1998). *Psychology and Law: Truthfulness, Accuracy and Credibility.* Maidenhead: McGraw-Hill.

Moston, S., Stephenson, G. & Williamson, T. (1992). The incidence, antecedents and consequences of the use of right of silence during police questioning. *British Journal of Criminology*, **32**, 23–40.

Pearse, J. & Gudjonsson, G. (1996). Police interviewing techniques of two south London police stations. *Psychology, Crime and Law*, **3**, 63–74.

Plimmer, J. (1997). Confession rate. *Police Review*. February 7th, 16–18.

Sear, L. & Stephenson, G. (1997). Interviewing skills and individual characteristics of police interrogators. In G. Stephenson & N. Clark (Eds.), *Procedures in Criminal Justice: Contemporary Psychological Issues.* Leicester: British Psychological Society.

Smith, D.J. (1983). *Police and People in London, (I): A Survey of Londoners.* London: Policy Studies Institute.

Softley, P., Brown, D., Forde, B., Mair, G. & Moxon, D. (1980). *Police Interrogation: An Observational Study in Four Police Stations.* London: HMSO.

Stephenson, G. & Moston, S. (1994). Police interrogation. *Psychology, Crime and Law*, **1**, 151–157.

Wagstaff, G. (1993). What can expert witnesses tell courts about hypnosis? *Expert Evidence*, **2**, 60–70.

Walkley, J. (1983). *Police Interrogation: A study of the psychology, theory and practice of police interrogations and the implications for police training.* Unpublished MSc thesis, Cranfield Institute of Technology.

Williamson, T. (1993). From interrogation to investigative policing: Strategic trends in police questioning. *Journal of Community and Applied Social Psychology*, **3**, 89–99.

Williamson, T.M. (1994). Reflections on current police practice. In D. Morgan & G. Stephenson (Eds.), *Suspicion and Silence. The Right to Silence in Criminal Investigations*, (pp. 107–116). London: Blackstone.

Frames of Mind: Schemata Guiding Cognition and Conduct in the Interviewing of Suspected Offenders

Anna Mortimer *and* **Eric Shepherd**
Investigative Science, East Hendred, Oxfordshire, UK

CRIMINAL INVESTIGATION AND THE INTERVIEWING OF SUSPECTS

The purpose of criminal investigation is to place before the courts an individual against whom there is evidence pointing to that person having committed the offence in question (Weston & Wells, 1980). Investigation involves feedback and feedforward loops of thought and action (Shepherd, 1994) (Figure 1).

Working alone or in groups, investigators at each stage rely on mental maps (Schutz, 1964) or *schemata* (Bartlett, 1932), to guide appropriate cognition and conduct in the search for evidence from people and things to aid the reconstruction of the circumstances of the offence.

Physical evidence is frequently fragmentary and liable to dispute. Testimony is the commonest, most problematic type of evidence. In countries where confession testimony has particular evidential significance, the interviewing of suspects assumes great importance (Ede & Shepherd, 1997).

Criminal investigation exemplifies *naturalistic decision-making* (Zsambok, 1997). It is a real-life situation, involving multiple people, of varying motivation, experience and competence, confronted with an inherently ill-structured problem. Those involved may not have, or share, a coherent *case theory*: a mental

Handbook of the Psychology of Interviewing. Edited by A. Memon and R. Bull.
© 1999 John Wiley & Sons Ltd.

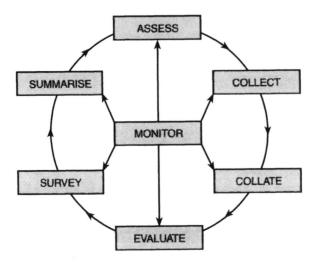

Figure 1   ACCESS-M: a process model of investigation (Shepherd, 1994)

model of "what happened" based on experience, selected detail, and speculation, which influences decisions.

Thought, action and inquiry take place in a dynamic, risky and uncertain environment. Available time, resource, skill and expertise are critical. Reassessment is continuously required. Further stress occurs because the stakes are high and consequences can be serious, since decisions are made in an organisational context (Cooper & Payne, 1988). This defines the "right" way of thinking and acting.

This chapter examines and evaluates the schemata that guide cognition and conduct in the critical investigative task of interviewing the suspect.

SCHEMATA

Individual Schemata

Schemata are cognitive structures. These comprise abridged, generalised, corrigible, organised stereotypical knowledge derived from first- and second-hand experience concerning situations, persons, roles, events, problems, and context-relevant thought and action (Brewer & Nakamura, 1984; Fiske & Taylor, 1984; Louis & Sutton, 1991; Marshall, 1995).

A situation or a set of circumstances triggers a schema that selectively guides attention to incoming information, enabling interpretation, inference, hypothesising and testing. We identify the type of "problem" confronting us by reference to key features. With further selected detail we construct a mental model accounting for the current circumstances (Read, 1987). A *case theory* is such a model, illustrating how we use schemata to fill in gaps and make decisions based on representative and available information (Tversky & Kahneman, 1974).

Our mental model enables projection onto the future through planning, the creation of *scripts* (expectations about behaviour in a situation) (Schank & Abelson, 1977), and setting aims and objectives. Scripts aid planning because they are performance schemata for extended sequences and have a causal character: earlier events produce, or enable, the occurrence of later events (Nisbett & Ross, 1980). Scripts exemplify execution schemata: applying specific knowledge, techniques, skills or routines, affecting the behaviour of others.

Some individuals adopt predominately *top-down* processing (Cacioppo, Petty & Sidera, 1982), particularly when information is inconsistent, ambiguous, complex, emotionally-loaded, or transient. Over-reliance on the schema "solves" idiosyncrasy but through the operation of bias. The individual notices, seeks out or substitutes information that "fits", or confirms, the stereotype and ignores that which does not.

Bottom-up processing implies less reliance on the script, more openness and active attention to actual detail, investigating the missing and the anomalous.

Organisational Schemata

Figure 2 summarises how organisations operate as a system.

Systems create shared schemata (Weick, 1979). These shared cognitive structures – *organisational norms* (Katz & Kahn, 1978) or *organisational "oughts"* (van Maanen, 1976) – communicate *culture* (Louis, 1983; Schein, 1985) and *ethos* tacitly and explicitly. Ethos is the group view, the approved *frame of mind* on the relationship between ends and means. A frame of mind begets "right" schemata to guide individual and collective cognition and conduct.

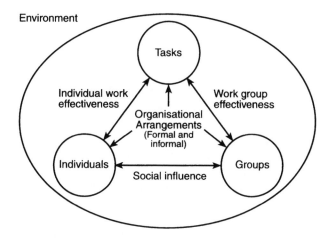

Figure 2 A framework of organisational behaviour (Nadler, Hackman & Lawler, 1979)

In this chapter we examine from a UK perspective two frames of mind in respect of the interviewing of suspects: a long-established, expedient ethos which the police service is seeking to supplant with an ethical alternative. We briefly describe barriers to this process and draw conclusions concerning the future.

INTERVIEWING SUSPECTS: THE EXPEDIENT FRAME OF MIND

In the UK, as in the USA and many other countries, a voluntary confession has prime evidential status. Weston and Wells (1980, p. 201) observed: "A voluntary confession of guilt crowns the evidence structure in any case". However, whilst police suspicions concerning an individual may be based on one or more items of evidence, in many cases guilt may be a matter of belief or opinion. Notions of guilt are also characteristically influenced by knowledge of criminal history (Stephenson & Moston, 1993).

In many cases the available evidence may be insufficient or weak. Resource limitations may constrain the amount of investigation. Irrespective of resource availability there may be little or no prospect of obtaining independent corroboration. Furthermore, there may be public, organisational, group and personal pressures to bring the suspected offender expeditiously before the courts.

Under any or all of these circumstances, given the prime evidential status of voluntary confessions, it is not surprising that a "confession culture" has long prevailed within the police service. Generations of officers have been socialised into an expedient frame of mind. The *end* – a rapid, resource-saving, kudos-enhancing solution to evidential shortcomings, i.e. a confession to the crime and optimally other offences – justifies the *means* – interrogation which overcomes the suspect's resistance by rendering him or her compliant and cooperative (Shepherd, 1991, 1993a, 1996a; Walkley, 1983, 1987).

Two factors ensured that for a very long time this frame of mind went unchallenged. Criminal investigation, and the interrogation of suspects, was the sole preserve of detectives, members of, or aspiring to be admitted to, the Criminal Investigation Department (CID). What happened to suspects in the police station, and during interrogation by CID officers, was not subject to external scrutiny.

Unsystematic Approaches to Interrogation

Historically, officers have learned the practicalities of policing, and questioning suspects in particular, not through formal training but by observing others (Shepherd, 1986b). As a result of this, officers acquired and sought to apply, albeit relatively unsystematically, diverse, disparate and poorly articulated schemata of interrogation.

Traditional wisdom dictated that it was necessary first to create the climate for confession (Deeley, 1971). Typically this would involve the suspect "helping the police with their inquiries" at the police station. In effect, this meant being held incommunicado in a cell, psychologically, socially and physically isolated for a protracted period, until resistance was reduced and desire to talk, to anyone, was elevated. At this point interrogation would begin in earnest.

Detectives learned a conventional, three-stage interrogation script: question on matters *other* than the offence (establishing rapport and creating the habit of answering); focus on the offence; elicit a confession. What occurred within the second and particularly the third stage was a matter of individual judgement.

Observational learning endowed officers with an awareness of available, acceptable *strategies* or *tactics* – the terms themselves being used imprecisely and interchangeably.

Two *strategies* have long been used. To make it "easier" for the suspect to confess officers have traditionally (1) *minimised* the gravity of the offence, the disadvantages of confessing and the worth of resisting, and (2) *maximised* excuses for committing the offence, the worth of confessing, and the advantages of confessing (Inbau & Reid, 1953, 1962, 1967).

In addition, a very wide range of *tactics* have been advocated and applied on an opportunistic, rather than logical, basis. These include: overstating or lying about the amount and strength of incriminatory evidence; emotional blackmail; calls upon morality, conscience, religious beliefs; highlighting lies; lying about implication by fellow suspects; assuming guilt and asking about motives; stressing the relief of "getting it off one's chest"; threatening, or using, physical violence; stressing the endless nature of the interrogation and relief when it ends; anonymity for the suspect if others are denounced; offering inducements, i.e. bail or mitigation (Irving, 1980; Irving & Hilgendorf, 1980; Walkley, 1983).

The common theme throughout was manipulation: the instrumental creation and communication of psychological pressure to induce the suspect to "go along" with the officer, i.e. to cooperate by making the desired confession.

The Emergence of Systematic Interrogation in England and Wales

The expedient interrogation of a mentally handicapped suspect in 1972 led to conviction on the basis of his confession. Following successful appeal the findings of an official inquiry (Fisher, 1977), a Royal Commission on Criminal Procedure (RCCP) (1981) invited Irving to research police interrogation practices.

Irving (1980) identified a number of *interrogation styles* (Table 1), ways of talking rather than scripts, employed by detectives to overcome resistance and to render the suspect compliant and cooperative. Officers indicated to Irving that they selected a style on the basis of "reading" the suspect's "personality" – which amounted to interpreting his or her behaviour. However, it is telling that they were not able to say which suspects were suited to two styles that were observed in 55% of interviews.

Table 1 Interrogation styles (based on data from Irving, 1980)

Style	Characteristic interviewer behaviours	Observed frequency (in 47 interviews)	Type of suspect considered to be suitable for this style
Business-like Professional, brusque, matter of fact	"A job of work like anyone else" Detached Emotionally neutral Neither cold nor friendly	34%	Not stated
Understanding Sympathetic, concerned, warm, personal, overtly befriending	Closer to suspect Looking at the face Softer tone of voice	17%	Overtly frightened Anxious Very guilty
Authoritative Dominating, suspicious, cynical, harsh harrying questioner	Cold Speaking loudly Strong gestures with remarks Table banging Further away from suspect Avoiding casual eye contact Deliberate eye contact (i.e. staring) Rejecting attempts at friendliness or speaking on equal terms	28%	Aggressive "Cocky" "Cheeky" Note: 1. Precludes tactics based on need for reassurance 2. Used with caution ("for right person") by experienced officers
Changing style Mainly authoritative (plus business-like or understanding)		21%	Not stated

A training package developed by Hall in the early 1980s (1983a, 1983b) incorporated:

- Basic social skills (questioning; listening; set induction; reinforcement, or social rewarding)
- The long-established strategies of deceiving the suspect concerning the evidence and making it "easier" for the suspect to confess (*minimising* and *maximising* – as refined and articulated by Inbau and Reid, 1967)
- The existence of behaviours indicative of truth, deception (*lie signs*) and the suspect being at the point of cooperation (*buy signs*) (Inbau & Reid, 1967; Royal & Schutt, 1976)
- A number of interviewing strategies – in effect styles of talking – derived from an Institute of Personnel Management training manual (Hackett, 1978, 1981) which were developments of strategies used in the training and selection of personnel in the wartime Office of Strategic Services (OSS Assessment Staff, 1948) (Table 2)

Many police forces in the UK were attracted by the notion of lie detection and persuasive questioning. They reproduced Hall's early draft materials as local training manuals. The publication of Hall's manuals coincided with Walkley's (1983) report of his research on detective attitudes and behaviours in respect of interrogation. He further endorsed the notion of lie signs and buy signs and the use of strategies.

Table 2   Interrogative strategies (Mortimer, 1994a, after Hackett, 1978, 1981)

Strategy	Main characteristics
Friendly	Self-explanatory
You and me	An extension of *friendly*: • "You can tell me" • "We can work together to show the truth of the matter"
Solution	An extension of *you and me*: • "Let you and me solve this problem" • "We can work out this problem together"
Stress	The opposite of *friendly*: • continuous heavy pressure • undermining confidence • inducing the individual to reveal "true self"
Sweet and sour	*Friendly* alternated with *stress*. *Hard man/soft man* ("Mutt and Jeff")
Tell	Almost complete knowledge by interviewer Undermining the suspect's story by presenting evidence as a stream or bit by bit
Sustained	Doggedly persevering: • being "clinical", objective, unshockable, dispassionate • listening in silence • systematically probing
Strategy mix	Self-explanatory

However, the advice in the manuals was deceptively simple. Many detectives experienced difficulties putting it into effect. For example, there was no guidance as to for which suspects, or when, some of the eight strategies were most appropriate.

In the interim, the work of the RCCP led to the enactment of the Police and Criminal Evidence Act (1984) (PACE), which regulates how police obtain evidence in England and Wales. PACE requires police to be mindful of vulnerability in terms of age, intellect, ability to communicate, and physical and psychological state. They must "act in good faith" when they suspect vulnerability, appointing an "appropriate adult" to protect the individual's interests, who can exercise the right to legal advice on behalf of the suspect (see Chapter 3.2 by Milne).

PACE enables a court to rule inadmissible evidence obtained by methods it considers to be oppressive or unfair. The court is in a better position to make this decision because the law requires the interviewing process to be transparent: it must be recorded, wherever possible electronically, otherwise as contemporaneous notes.

It took several years to install recording equipment, meaning that the interviewing did not become truly transparent until the late 1980s. Before this happened Walkley (1987) had produced the first published interrogation manual, disseminating on a wide scale the notion of lie signs and buy signs and reducing the complexity of strategies to just three: *friendly*, *dominant*, and *hard–soft*.

Meanwhile, one police force went further, adopting and adapting the systematic approach to interrogation devised by Inbau, Reid and Buckley (1986):

- *Behaviour symptoms* – explicit typologies of verbal and non-verbal behaviours (body movements, facial expressions, eye contact, posture, grooming and gestures) deemed to differentiate innocent and deceptive persons.
- *The Behavioural Analysis Interview (BAI)* – a structured set of predetermined behaviour-provoking questions concerning involvement or knowledge of the offence and seeking to elicit verbal and non-verbal symptoms indicative of truth and deception. It is assumed that the innocent suspect will manifest truthfulness, the guilty deception. Using the classification system, each spoken reply, the manner of the reply and accompanying non-verbal behaviour is noted as truthful, deceptive or ambiguous. The individual becomes a probable suspect, and is interrogated, if responses to certain key questions are deceptive.
- *The Nine Steps of systematic interrogation* – to obtain a confession from a suspect deemed to be guilty (1: Positive confrontation; 2: Theme development (i.e. offering reasons or excuses consistent with the strategy of maximising and minimising); 3: Handling denials; 4: Overcoming objections; 5: Procuring and retaining the suspect's attention; 6: Handling the suspect's passive mood; 7: Presenting an alternative question (to obtain the first admission of guilt by asking a question with only two possible, incriminating answers); 8: Detailing the offence (eliciting detailed disclosure); 9: Obtaining a statement.

Problems with the Expedient Frame of Mind

The Fundamental Ethical Problem

Investigation has an ethical dimension. We entrust the police to search lawfully for facts with fidelity, accuracy and sincerity, and to report the results of the search with faithfulness, exactness and probity (Weston & Wells, 1980). We expect and assume integrity: respect for persons and information, and commitment to tell the truth.

However, Inbau, Reid and Buckley (1986, p. xvii) made it clear that the expedient interrogation to obtain a confession from a resistant suspect was, of necessity, unethical:

> Of necessity, therefore, interrogators must deal with criminal suspects on a somewhat lower moral plane than that upon which ethical, law-abiding citizens are expected to conduct their everyday affairs. That plane, in the interest of innocent suspects, need only be subject to the following restriction: Although both "fair" and "unfair" interrogation practices are permissible, nothing shall be done or said to the suspect that will be apt to make an innocent person confess.

In England and Wales judicial rulings since the enactment of PACE have made it clear that the law will not countenance police officers dealing with an individual on a lower moral plane just because he or she is suspected of committing an offence. Any confession obtained by expedient interrogation is liable to be ruled inadmissible. Hence, police officers must not lie about evidence (*R* v. *Mason*, 1988) or use oppressive strategies and tactics no matter how established (*R* v. *Paris and others*, 1993). Protracted interviewing, repetitive questioning, voluble demonstrations of displeasure and continued questioning when a person has clearly broken down are unacceptable (*R.* v. *West*, 1988).

The judge in *R* v. *Heron* (1993) made it clear that the police are not required to accept the first or any answer or answers given. They are entitled to say they do not believe what they are told. Questioning can be persistent, searching and robust but must be fair. Persistence must not develop into bullying. Nor must robustness develop into insulting or gratuitously demeaning questioning, or be taken as a licence to pound with allegations about certainty of the suspect's guilt. Police must bear in mind vulnerability and, yet again, must not lie about evidence.

The "Problem" of Transparency

Inbau, Reid and Buckley (1986) say questioning and interrogation should not be recorded, save the final step of obtaining a confession statement. Arguably their explanation – recording inhibits disclosure – is itself expedient. However, in England and Wales officers have no choice: *all* suspect interviews must be recorded electronically (predominately audio- but increasingly video), and, on those rarer occasions when this cannot be done, must be recorded as contemporaneous notes.

Courts routinely listen to, and watch, the interviewing process, particularly in *voir dire* concerning confession evidence (Wolchover & Heaton-Armstrong, 1996) but often during the main trial. The transparency of recording is a threat to expedient interrogators. It is liable to expose them dealing on a lower moral plane, providing manifest evidence of lack of integrity in handling the individual and information and thus risking exclusion of any confession obtained. Recording reveals interrogators dominating the talking turn and the talking time, treating the suspect's responses as of little or no importance unless they point to, or are, a confession, and disruptive listening – interruption, overtalking, minimal responding and rapid topic changing – to render the suspect silent, submissive and receptive (Shepherd, 1996a).

The Spurious Status of Classification Systems and Assumed Expertise

Ekman (1985, p. 80) spelled out the basic truth:

> *There is no sign of deceit itself* – no gesture, facial expression, or muscle twitch that in and of itself means that a person is lying. There are only clues that the person is poorly prepared and clues of emotions that don't fit the person's line. (Ekman's emphasis in italics).

Overt verbal and non-verbal behaviours have more than one causation. Reducing complexity to a "truth"–"deception" classification system (e.g. Inbau, Reid & Buckley, 1986; Walters, 1996; Zulawski & Wicklander, 1992) is therefore itself deceptive given the findings of empirical research.

Scientific research offers little support: (1) for simplistic "all-or-none" distinctions between deception and truth (Ekman, 1985; Zuckerman & Driver, 1985); (2) that training enhances the detection of deception in real life (Bull, 1989; Chapter 5.4 by Vrij).

Consistently research shows that individuals achieve accuracy around, or worse than, chance, in detecting deception and are only marginally better with truthful responses (e.g. Köhnken, 1990), probably due to their inappropriate beliefs concerning lying behaviour (DePaulo, Stone & Lassiter, 1985; Zuckerman, DePaulo & Rosenthal, 1981). Whilst Ekman (1985) found professionals to be better than lay-people in detecting deception, others have found experienced detectives to be particularly poor in this task (Köhnken, 1987). It would seem that professional investigators differ from lay-people only in being more confident in their performance (DePaulo & Pfeiffer, 1986).

Far from being a simple process, as Friedman and Tucker (1990) pointed out, deception and the detection of deception are abilities that stem from the possession of certain basic communication skills. However, this said, they are a complex interaction of:

- *Deceiver factors* – the deceiver's general communication skills, demographics, personality, past history with the detector, arousal and motivation, emotions, cognitive complexity, and self-control.

- *Behavioural cues* – some of which are usually valid indicators of deception; some of which are often invalid;
- *Detector factors* – motivation to detect, sensitivity to non-verbal cues, cognitive skills, attention (to specific cues), pre-existing stereotypes, and past history with the deceiver.

Interrogation as a Self-fulfilling Prophecy

It is clear from the previous section that classifying behaviours as either "truthful" or "deceptive" is an exercise in self-deception. They are schemata which, in the minds of those who believe them, give rise to biased and spurious assumptions, expectations and hypotheses. This is long-established by schema research and professional interviewing (Millar, Crute & Hargie, 1992). Bias in classifying responses produces *premature closure*. The mind is closed.

In the case of an officer who already believes the suspect to be guilty, even in the absence of evidence, the interrogative task becomes one of confirmation *not* investigation. The aim is to obtain a confession which confirms the suspect's guilt. Confirmatory bias pervades the interrogation creating a self-fulfilling prophecy: behaviour believed to be indicative of guilt is selectively attended to, assumes a distorting salience and is endowed with spurious significance. Those who believe a suspect to be guilty are liable to what Ekman (1985) termed:

- The *Othello error* – interpreting the fear and distress of a truthful person as confirmation of guilt
- The *Brokaw hazard* – misjudging those people who are truthful but who happen to be convoluted and evasive in the way they speak

Furthermore, there are wholly contradictory interpretations of resistance which place the suspect in a "damned if I do – damned if I don't" situation.

Many expedient interrogators consider continued resistance as yet more confirmation of the suspect's guilt. Central is the spurious assumption that continuing resistance proves guilt. This assumption invokes a one-dimensional perspective – *willing/unwilling to talk* – ignoring a second, critical, orthogonal dimension – *ability/inability to tell* (Shepherd, 1993b). It also ignores the contribution of the investigator in fostering, maintaining and increasing resistance: poor conversation management, inappropriate pacing, inappropriate assertion and listening, and inappropriate content of assertions. These reflect the outcome of distorted and distorting pre-interview schemata, endorsing bias and inadequacy in prior investigation and information analysis, and minimising the need for forethought.

Others construe the gradual, or sudden, cessation of resistance and emergence of compliance as confirmation of guilt, and any resultant confession as proving the correctness of their interpretation. It matters not to the expedient interrogator that there is an extensive literature on false confessions (Gudjonsson, 1992; Kassin, 1997; Kassin & McNall, 1991; Kassin & Wrightsman, 1981; see Chapter

5.5 by Gudjonsson). Expediency warrants inattention to, if not opportunistic exploitation of, psychological, intellectual and other forms of vulnerability. The vulnerable are at risk of not understanding the significance of what is put to them or their replies. They may give replies that are invalid and unreliable, particularly in the form of partial or full false confessions.

However, a voluntary false confession is not necessarily the act of a psychiatrically ill, deluded person. Those with a strong desire to be liked and accepted may "go along" with the investigator, responding to unsubtle, suggestive and leading assertions and questioning by making an accommodating-compliant confession. People of all intellectual levels may do this, though the risk is particularly great in those who are intellectually challenged and are excessively compliant (Gudjonsson, 1992). Coerced-compliant false confessions are instrumental confessions: to bring an end to the compressed stresses and cumulative pressures of detention and interviewing, particularly that which is persuasive and oppressive. Some individuals make coerced-internalised false confessions. The stresses and pressures, most particularly police interviewing behaviour, convert the suspect to the police version of "what happened".

In the next section we examine the ethical alternative to the expedient frame of mind: one which does not require police officers to conduct themselves on a lower moral plane just because they are dealing with suspects.

INTERVIEWING SUSPECTS: THE ETHICAL FRAME OF MIND

An ethical frame of mind requires integrity in the handling of information and individuals at *all* stages of an investigation. It implies schemata actively guiding investigators to be open-minded and open in their cognition and conduct, i.e. to reject expediency and *not* to process information instrumentally, *not* to manipulate evidence and suspects (Shepherd, 1991, 1993a).

Investigators need a synthesis of relevant ethical schemata for systematic information analysis and assessment (applied in professional intelligence contexts), ethical schemata for establishing working relationships and coping with resistance (applied in counselling and psychotherapy), and schemata reflecting recognition of research concerning cognitive processes, most particularly distortion and bias (Shepherd, 1988; Shepherd & Kite, 1988).

Prior to an interview schemata framed upon integrity in respect of investigation and information processing enable investigators:

- To conduct fine-grain analyses of information to confront the reality of available evidence
- To use other means of investigation to address identified gaps and anomalies *before* interviewing the suspect
- To guide the setting of goals and objectives based on, and directed at, objectively testable facts

Within the interview investigatory, as opposed to confirmatory and accusatory, schemata enable management of the conversation, the information exchange and processing information.

Conversation Management

Individual police forces and investigators in the public and private sectors as well as the legal profession have adopted an ethical schema, called *conversation management* and summarised by the mnemonic GEMAC (Greeting, Explanation (reasons, route map, routines, expectations), Mutual Activity (monitoring and asserting), Close) (Shepherd, 1986a, 1986b, 1996a, 1996b).

Conversation management reflects the principles of ethical conversation:

- Respect for the suspect – as a fellow human being
- Empathy – sincerely, not exploitatively, adopting the suspect's viewpoint
- Supportiveness – active listening to facilitate and sustain conversation
- Positiveness – continued adherence to the investigative aim and objectives
- Openness – no misrepresentation, dissimulation or disingenuous conduct
- Non-judgmental attitude
- Straightforward talk – mindful of any vulnerability
- Equality – talking across to, not down to, the suspect.

The suspect is left in no doubt that the investigator's sole motivation is the systematic search for the truth. Letting the suspect tell his or her story, allowing sufficient time to reply and monitoring closely and maintaining an accurate record of disclosure, enables:

- Reflection upon potential reasons for the disclosure
- Fine-grain analysis and evaluation of disclosures to detect forensic twaddle and to enable further investigation, including verification

At a national level the police service in the UK has developed a schema summarised by the mnemonic PEACE (Preparation and Planning, Engage and Explain, Account, Closure, and Evaluate), incorporating core features of GEMAC (Central Planning and Training Unit, 1992). A recent revision (National Crime Faculty, 1996) takes account of changes in legislation and a stage where the suspect's account and responses are challenged.

Table 3 summarises the PEACE schema.

Barriers to the Implementation of an Ethical Frame of Mind

Lack of Investigative Knowledge, Skill and Practitioner Systems

PEACE training has highlighted the price paid by the police service, the public and the criminal justice system for the "confession culture", a tradition of

Table 3 PEACE (after National Crime Faculty, 1996)

Stage	Activity	Specific issues
Preparation and planning	*Know the purpose of the interview* To investigate. *Define interview aim* *Either* to obtain evidence to prove or disprove S's involvement in an alleged offence. *Or*, where evidence is available to prove S's involvement, to provide S the opportunity: ● to explain the evidence; ● to test the evidence. *Define interview objectives* May be: ● a list of areas to be covered; ● specific points upon which information is required; ● details which require confirmation. *Assess evidence* Analyse available evidence Assess: ● what evidence is needed; ● where evidence can be obtained – exhaust other possible sources of information rather than rely on the interview. *Check on vulnerability* If vulnerability is suspected, act in good faith, arrange for appointment of appropriate adult. *Think ahead* Consider possible blocks and resistance.	*Investigate with integrity* Empathy and honesty – no lying about evidence. *Essential requirements* Keep an open mind. Separate facts from preconceptions and opinions. Do not dismiss information and evidence: ● which is to S's advantage; ● does not point to S's guilt. Remember witnesses can be wrong.

	Make interview arrangements Location. Timing – taking account of meals, sleep at right time, and, where applicable, attendance of legal adviser and appropriate adult. *Prepare evidence*	Consider using visual representations.

Engage and explain	*Open interview*
	Effect introductions.
	Administer caution.
	State reasons
	● for S's arrest (or the request to attend the police station);
	● for the interview.
	State routines
	● what the police officers might do:
	  – note-taking – how, why and by whom;
	  – introducing and referring to exhibits and other notes;
	  – writing a statement;
	● invite the legal adviser, appropriate adult or second officer to explain their roles.
	Give basic outline of the interview (route map)
	Identify main topics.
		Essential requirements
		Think "first impression".
		Be courteous:
		Treat S in the same way one would like to be treated if in S's position;
		Help S to feel like an individual;
		Use appropriate language.
		Avoid making judgemental statements.

Account	*Fulfil specific legal requirements (PACE)* Introduce significant statements or silence before the interview. Administer special warnings. *Stage 1: Suspect agenda* *When suspect is not motivated to talk* Engage in conversation management: ● Give S the opportunity to give his or her account. ● Obtain the account, without interrupting. ● Review verbally the account, using suspect's own words. ● Question specific points systematically. *When S is very motivated to talk or is vulnerable* Conduct a cognitive interview.	*Timing* On completion consider breaking to prepare for next stage.

Table 3 *Continued*

Stage	Activity	Specific issues
Account (cont. . .)	*Stage 2: Police agenda* Conduct focused questioning of: • facts known to the officer; • points to prove; • possible defences; • additional topics – if appropriate to the offence. *Stage 3: Challenge* Test S's account by: • challenging the detail of what he or she has said; • probing ambiguous answers in the earlier phases; • if evidence exists to prove that S is lying or not telling the full truth, putting this to S; If S gives a new account, commence the conversation management sequence again. If S wishes, take a statement.	*Timing* On completion consider breaking to prepare for next phase. *Essential requirements* A sense of proportion when challenging: • it may be later alleged that too much pressure was placed on S; • challenging should not cause undue pressure such that the admissibility of evidence is placed in doubt. If S continues to deny, do not: • enter into a *Yes, you did, No I didn't* exchange; • continually repeat the strength of the evidence; • engage in repetitive questioning; • labour the point – overly asserting the strength of the evidence.
Closure	*Summarise* State the main points in the interview. Provide S with the opportunity: • to correct; • to alter; • to add to things previously stated.	

Check S's comprehension
Ask S to state what has taken place during the interview.
Encourage S to consider:
- S's present situation and needs;
- S's future situation and needs.

Check S's viewpoint
Give S the opportunity to ask questions or to give feedback:
- responding to S's questions honestly – saying when the answer is not known;
- eliminating any anxiety on the part of S.

Close the interview

Evaluate

Evaluate
Assess:
- the information obtained during the interview;
- the whole investigation in the light of the information obtained during the interview.

Identify areas needing investigation

Assess performance
Reflect on the way the interview was conducted.
Look back at planning and preparation.

Typical considerations
Points to prove the offence.
Identity of the offender.
Legal defences.
Evidence in support of the allegation.
Whether evidence was lawfully obtained.

(S = suspect)

expediency, confirmation bias and cutting corners in investigation and inattention to the quality of *witness* interviewing (Shepherd & Milne, 1999).

The pursuit of confessions has prevented the development of professional systems and effective investigative training. Ede and Shepherd (1997) summarise a wide range of research that shows the following results:

- A generally low level of investigative knowledge and skill, including basic forensic awareness
- Crime reporting and evidence within crime files, testimonials and exhibits that are characterised by gaps, anomalies and questionable accuracy

We would argue that this reflects the extent to which the expedient pursuit of voluntary confessions, preferably expeditiously obtained, has blocked the development of the police service as a professional investigative body. In the next section we describe research which demonstrates the extent to which it has affected the cognitive performance of officers confronted with crime reports and crime files containing forensically significant information.

Barriers to an Open Mind

Mortimer (1994a, 1994b) examined actual investigative interviewing performance by using a field experiment design. Working in collaboration with a large metropolitan police force, standardised crime files were constructed from five real cases. Officers were given a file and, after unrestricted preparation time, conducted a tape-recorded interview of the suspect (an actor). A consistent pattern emerged.

- There was sub-optimal information processing prior to the interview. Officers' performance in extracting forensically relevant information was scored using Shepherd's SE3R (Shepherd, 1996a; Shepherd & Mortimer, 1999). Overall only 41% of information was correctly abstracted (52% event; 32% identity). In the most demanding case information extraction was extraordinarily poor: 31% overall (36% event; 27% identity).
- There were overwhelming perceptions of suspect guilt despite reservations about evidence. Even though evidence was rated as poor, belief that the suspect "did it" was rated as high.
- In the subsequent interviews the stated investigatory aims and objectives were not enacted. Even though officers say they are not seeking a confession, they are fully aware of personal and organisational pressures to succeed by gaining a partial or full admission. This leads many well-intentioned officers, particularly those who have evaluated information poorly and selectively and whose perception of guilt is influenced by knowledge of prior convictions, to adopt a constraining/suggestive, rather than investigatory, schema reflected in their pattern of behaviour in the interview (Mortimer 1994a) (Table 4).

Table 4 shows that a constraining/suggestive schema, in contrast to an investigatory schema, involves behaviours that restrict the response options of the

Table 4 Contrasting interview enactment schemata (Mortimer, 1994a)

Behaviour	Constraining/suggestive pattern	Investigatory pattern
Narrative/probing switch	Early switch from obtaining narrative to direct questioning	Focus on obtaining uninterrupted narrative, postponing direct questioning
Freedom given to the suspect to speak	Suspect hindered by high level of interviewer disruption (i.e. interrupting and overtalking)	Suspect helped by low level of interviewer disruption
Latitude of response afforded to the suspect	Latitude of response content restricted by high level of suggestive questioning (closed yes/no, leading, option, interrogative assertions)	Wide latitude of response given through high level of productive questioning (open, closed identificatory, echo, invitational)

suspect. Furthermore, it limits the likelihood of getting information beyond that already known to the officer prior to the interview. Mortimer found that officers consistently moved from investigatory questioning to confirmatory questioning, i.e. inviting the suspect to confirm the "evidence" the officer had extracted from the crime file. When the suspect blocked this approach officers, in their frustration, would resort to outright accusation, i.e. asserting that the officer "knew" the suspect had committed the offence.

Mortimer (1994a, 1994b) offered a schema-based explanation for these behaviours. Notwithstanding the change to an ethical frame of mind the pressures for "results" remain, i.e. officers are still expected to "solve" crimes by the charging of suspected offenders, optimally with these individuals making admissions to other offences (requesting these to be "taken into consideration" or TIC'd).

Mortimer suggested that inadequacies in reporting and material generated by other officers and lack of resource preventing appropriate investigation *before* interviewing a suspect induce stress in officers already under pressure to perform. Paradoxically, stress is likely to be greater for those who conduct fine-grain analysis and who, as a result of this, know the shortcomings in the police case and evidence before them in the crime report and the crime file.

Mortimer's studies indicated that in such circumstances officers found salvation by behaving in a manner consistent with a powerful organisational schema, the "informal code" which requires officers not to "rock the boat" or to criticise fellow officers (Reuss-Ianni, 1983; Roberg & Kuykendall, 1990). She found the officers' behaviour in her study was indicative of a coping pattern of *defensive avoidance* (Janis & Mann, 1977). To reduce the stress investigators fail to register much of the available information and are biased towards selecting that which "fits".

Shortcomings with the PEACE Model

Whilst PEACE training gives guidance on pre-interview preparation and planning it does not raise officers' awareness of the range of anomaly liable to be found in evidence. Nor does it provide officers with the requisite range of collation systems to enable them to process crime report and crime file information systematically (Shepherd & Mortimer, 1999).

Survival and success in naturalistic decision-making rests on "changing cognitive gears" when the unwanted block on progress occurs (Dowie & Elstein, 1988; Louis & Sutton, 1991; Schön, 1983; Zsambok, 1997). The investigator must have a dynamic mental model to anticipate and cope with resistance, particularly frustrating and discrepant responses, e.g. indignation, anger, tears, arguing, diverting, "blinding with science", non-cooperation, silence, verbal hostility or lying. Flexible, realistic plans rest on conscious modelling before the interview.

PEACE guides officers to anticipate and prepare for blocks but offers no practical schemata, unlike the GEMAC model. If officers construe PEACE as not preparing them for "difficult" suspects its validity (and therefore credibility) is brought into question. When they meet resistance within the interview, frustration is inevitable and the pressures will be great to switch from investigatory to constraining/accusatory questioning.

CONCLUSIONS

The "confession culture" still lives on. Confessions count. Each person charged is another "clear-up", contributing to the numbers which police managers require to demonstrate expeditious and efficient policing (Ede & Shepherd, 1997).

The public at large, the judiciary and juries sustain the expedient frame of mind. That most confessions are true is a pervasive anchoring heuristic (Wagenaar, van Koppen & Crombag, 1993). First instance courts are disposed to admit confessions, rejecting or countenancing manifest evidence of oppression and unfairness. Furthermore, even when people know this, the confession is still persuasive (Kassin & Sukel, 1997). Confessions really do count.

However, confessions count less and integrity matters more as people increasingly value individualism and mutual rights and responsibilities, and demand transparency and accountability in the operation of institutions, and the police service in particular. Legislation, common law and the courts have to articulate these demands unequivocally.

Only this will occasion the evolution of the police service as a professional investigatory body: men and women with systems, resources and, literally above all, schemata guiding ethical cognition and conduct at all stages of an investigation, especially prior to, during, and after investigative interviews with suspected offenders.

REFERENCES

Bartlett, F. (1932). *Remembering*. Cambridge: Cambridge University Press.
Brewer, W. & Nakamura, G. (1984). The nature and functions of schemas. In R. Wyer & T. Srull (Eds.), *Handbook of social cognition* (Vol. 1, pp. 119–160). Hillsdale, NJ: Erlbaum.

Bull, R. (1989). Can training enhance the detection of deception? In J. Yuille (Ed.), *Credibility Assessment*. Amsterdam: Kluwer.

Cacioppo, J., Petty, R. & Sidera, J. (1982). The effects of a salient self-schema on the evaluation of proattitudinal editorials: Top-down versus bottom-up message processing. *Journal of Experimental Social Psychology*, **18**, 324–338.

Central Planning and Training Unit. (1992). *A Guide to Interviewing*. Harrogate, Yorkshire: Home Office.

Cooper, C. & Payne, R. (1988). *Causes, Coping and Consequences of Stress at Work*. Chichester: Wiley.

Deeley, P. (1971). *Beyond Breaking Point*. London: Barker.

DePaulo, B. & Pfeiffer, R. (1986). On-the-job-experience and skill at detecting deception. *Journal of Applied Social Psychology*, **16**, 249–267.

DePaulo, B., Stone, J. & Lassiter, G. (1985). Deceiving and detecting deceit. In B. Schenkler (Ed.), *The Self and Social Life*. (pp. 323–370). New York: McGraw-Hill.

Dowie, J. & Elstein, A. (1988). *Professional Judgment*. Cambridge: Cambridge University Press.

Ede, R. & Shepherd, E. (1997). *Active Defence*. London: Law Society.

Ekman, P. (1985). *Telling Lies*. New York: Norton.

Fisher, H. (1977). *Report of an inquiry by the Hon. Sir Henry Fisher into the circumstances leading to the trial of three persons on charges arising out of the death of Maxwell Confait and the Fire at 27 Doggett Road, London SE6*. London: HMSO.

Fiske, S. & Taylor, S. (1984). *Social Cognition*. Reading, MA: Addison-Wesley.

Friedman, H. & Tucker, J. (1990). Language and deception. In *Handbook of Language and Social Psychology*. Chichester: Wiley.

Gudjonsson, G. (1992). *The Psychology of Interrogations, Confessions and Testimony*. New York: Wiley.

Hackett, P. (1978, 1981). *Interview Skills Training: Practice Packs for Trainers*. London: Institute of Personnel Management.

Hall, E. (1983a). *Investigative Interviewing: a Guide for Instructors*. Ulster: Hall.

Hall, E. (1983b). *Investigative Interviewing: a Guide for CID Officers*. Ulster: Hall.

Inbau, F. & Reid, J. (1953). *Lie Detection and Criminal Interrogation*. Baltimore: Williams and Wilkins.

Inbau, F. & Reid, J. (1962). *Criminal Interrogation and Confessions* (1st edn). Baltimore: Williams and Wilkins.

Inbau, F. & Reid, J. (1967). *Criminal Interrogation and Confessions* (2nd edn). Baltimore: Williams and Wilkins.

Inbau, F., Reid, J. & Buckley, J. (1986). *Criminal Interrogation and Confessions*. (3rd edn). Baltimore: Williams and Wilkins.

Irving, B. (1980). *Police Interrogation: A Case Study of Current Practice. Royal Commission on Criminal Procedure Research Study No. 2*. London: HMSO.

Irving, B. & Hilgendorf, L. (1980). *Police Interrogation: The Psychological Approach. Royal Commission on Criminal Procedure Research Study No. 1*. London: HMSO.

Janis, I. & Mann, L. (1977). *Decision Making: A Psychological Analysis of Conflict, Choice, and Commitment*. New York: Free Press.

Kassin, S. (1997) The psychology of confession evidence. *American Psychologist*, **52**, 221–233.

Kassin, S. & McNall, K. (1991). Police interrogations and confessions. *Law and Human Behaviour*, **15**, 233–251.

Kassin, S. & Sukel, H. (1997). Coerced confessions and the jury: A test of the "harmless error" rule. *Law and Human Behaviour*, **21**, 27–46.

Kassin, S. & Wrightsman, L. (1981). Confession evidence. In S. Kassin & L. Wrightsman (Eds.), *The Psychology of Evidence and Trial Procedure*. London: Sage.

Katz, D. & Kahn, R. (1978). *The Social Psychology of Organisations*. New York: Wiley.

Köhnken, G. (1987).Training police officers to detect deceptive eye-witness statements: Does it work? *Social Behaviour*, **2**, 1–17

Köhnken, G. (1990). *Glaubwürdigkeit: Untersuchungen zu einem psychologischen Konstrukt.* Munich: Psychologie Verlags Union.

Louis, M. (1983). Organisations as culture-bearing milieux. In L. Pondy, P. Frost, G. Morgan & T. Dandridge (Eds.), *Organisational Symbolism* (pp. 39–54). New York: JAI Press.

Louis, M. & Sutton, R. (1991). Switching cognitive gears: From habits of mind to active thinking. *Human Relations*, **44**, 55–76.

Marshall, S. (1995). *Schemas in Problem Solving.* Cambridge: Cambridge University Press.

Millar, R., Crute, V. & Hargie, O. (1992). *Professional Interviewing.* London: Routledge.

Mortimer, A. (1994a). *Cognitive processes underlying police investigative interviewing behaviour.* Unpublished PhD thesis. University of Portsmouth, Department of Psychology.

Mortimer, A. (1994b). Asking the right questions. *Policing*, **10**, 111–124.

Nadler, D., Hackman, J. & Lawler, E. (1979). *Managing Organisational Behaviour.* Boston: Little, Brown.

National Crime Faculty. (1996). *Investigative Interviewing.* Bramshill, Hampshire: National Police Training.

Nisbett, R. & Ross, L. (1980). *Human Inference.* Englewood Cliffs, NJ: Prentice-Hall.

OSS (Office of Strategic Services) Assessment Staff. (1948). *Assessment of Men.* New York: Rinehart.

Police and Criminal Evidence Act. (1984). London: HMSO.

R v. *Heron* (1993) *Judge's Ruling on Voire Dire.* In the Combined Court Centre, Leeds. Unreported.

R v. *Mason (Carl).* (1988).1 WLR 139, CA.

R v. *Paris and others* (1993), 97 CAR, 99.

R v. *West* (1988). *Judge's Ruling on Admissibility of Tape-recorded Police Interviewing.* In the Crown Court at Gloucester. Unreported.

Read, S. (1987). Constructing causal scenarios: a knowledge structure approach to causal reasoning. *Journal of Personality and Social Psychology*, **52**, 288–302.

Reuss-Ianni, E. (1983). *Two Cultures of Policing: Street Cops and Management Cops.* New Brunswick, CONN: Transaction Books.

Roberg, R. & Kuykendall, J. (1990). *Police Organisation and Management: Behaviour, Theory and Processes.* Pacific Grove, CA: Brooks/Cole.

Royal, R. & Schutt, S. (1976). *The Gentle Art of Interviewing and Interrogation: A Professional Manual and Guide.* Englewood Cliffs, NJ: Prentice-Hall.

Royal Commission on Criminal Procedure (1981). *Report.* London: HMSO.

Schank, R. & Abelson, R. (1977). *Scripts, Plans, Goals and Understanding.* Hillsdale, NJ: Erlbaum.

Schein, E. (1985). *Organisational Culture and Leadership.* San Francisco: Jossey-Bass.

Schön, D. (1983). *The Reflective Practitioner.* New York: Basic Books.

Schutz, A. (1964). *Collected Papers II. Studies in Social Theory.* A. Brodersen (Ed). The Hague: Martinus Nijhoff.

Shepherd, E. (1986a). Interviewing development: facing up to reality. *Police Journal*, **59**, 35–44.

Shepherd, E. (1986b). The conversational core of policing. *Policing*, **2**, 294–303.

Shepherd, E. (1988). Developing interviewing skills: a career span perspective. In P. Southgate (Ed.), *New Directions in Police Training* (pp. 170–188). London: HMSO.

Shepherd, E. (1991). Ethical interviewing. *Policing*, **7**, 42–60.

Shepherd, E. (1993a). Ethical interviewing. In E. Shepherd (Ed.), *Aspects of Police Interviewing. Issues in Criminological and Legal Psychology, No. 18* (pp. 46–60). Leicester: British Psychological Society.

Shepherd, E. (1993b). Resistance in police interviews: the contribution of police perceptions and behaviour. In E. Shepherd (Ed.), *Aspects of Police Interviewing. Issues in Criminological and Legal Psychology, No. 18* (pp. 5–12). Leicester: British Psychological Society.

Shepherd, E. (1994). *ACCESS: A process framework for systematic investigation*. East Hendred, Oxfordshire: Investigative Science.

Shepherd, E. (1996a). *Becoming Skilled*. London: Law Society.

Shepherd, E. (1996b). *A Pocket Reference*. London: Law Society.

Shepherd, E. & Kite, F. (1988). Training to interview. *Policing*, **4**, 264–280.

Shepherd, E. & Milne, R. (1999). Full and faithful: ensuring quality practice and integrity of outcome in witness interviews. In A. Heaton-Armstrong, E. Shepherd & D. Wolchover (Eds.), *Analysing Witness Testimony*. London: Blackstone.

Shepherd, E. & Mortimer, A. (1999). Identifying anomaly in evidential text. In A. Heaton-Armstrong, E. Shepherd & D. Wolchover (Eds.), *Analysing Witness Testimony*. London: Blackstone.

Stephenson, G. & Moston, S. (1993). Attitudes and assumptions of police officers when questioning criminal suspects. In E. Shepherd (Ed.), *Aspects of Police Interviewing. Issues in Criminological and Legal Psychology, No. 18* (pp. 30–36). Leicester: British Psychological Society.

Tversky, A. & Kahneman, D. (1974). Judgements under uncertainty: Heuristics and biases. *Science*, **185**, 1124–1131.

van Maanen, J. (1976). Breaking in: socialisation at work. In R. Dubin (Ed.), *Handbook of Work, Organisation and Society*. Chicago: Rand-McNally.

Wagenaar, W., van Koppen, P. & Crombag, H. (1993). *Anchored Narratives: The Psychology of Criminal Evidence*. Hemel Hempstead: Harvester Wheatsheaf.

Walkley, J. (1983). *Police interrogation: A study of the psychology theory and practice of police interrogation and the implications for police training*. Unpublished MSc thesis. Cranfield Institute of Technology, Department of Social Policy.

Walkley, J. (1987). *Police Interrogation: A Handbook for Investigators*. London: Police Review Publishing.

Walters, S. (1996). *Principles of Kinesic Interview and Interrogation*. New York: CRC.

Weick, K. (1979). *The Social Psychology of Organising*. Reading, MA: Addison-Wesley.

Weston, P. & Wells, K. (1980). *Criminal Investigation: Basic Perspectives*. Englewood Cliffs, NJ: Prentice-Hall.

Wolchover, D. & Heaton-Armstrong, A. (1996). *Wolchover and Heaton-Armstrong on Confession Evidence*. London: Sweet & Maxwell.

Zsambok, C. (1997). Naturalistic Decision making: Where are we now? In C. Zsambok & G. Klein (Eds.), *Naturalistic Decision making* (pp. 3–16). Mahwah, NJ: Erlbaum.

Zuckerman, M. & Driver, R. (1985). Telling lies: verbal and non-verbal correlates of deception. In A. Siegman & S. Feldstein (Eds.), *Multichannel Integrations of Nonverbal Behaviour* (pp. 129–148). Hillsdale, NJ: Erlbaum.

Zuckerman, M., DePaulo, B. & Rosenthal, R. (1981). Verbal and non-verbal communication in deception. In L. Berkowitz (Ed.), *Advances in Experimental Social Psychology* (Vol. 14). New York: Academic Press.

Zulawski, D. & Wicklander, D. (1992). *Practical Aspects of Interview and Interrogation*. New York: CRC.

Interviewing to Detect Deception

Aldert Vrij
University of Portsmouth

In this chapter, I will discuss some aspects of how to catch a liar when interviewing. I will start with discussing how good people are at detecting lies. Research has shown that people are generally not very good at detecting lies, and I will give some reasons to explain this. Then I will discuss some guidelines which, I believe, will make people better lie detectors if they take them into account when they try to detect deceit. Finally, I will discuss the accuracy of some scientific lie detecting instruments. More detailed reports concerning these and other deception issues can be found elsewhere (Memon, Vrij & Bull, 1998; Vrij, 1998, 1999).

HOW GOOD ARE PEOPLE AT DETECTING LIES?

There are, in principle, three different ways of catching a liar. The first way is by observing liars' non-verbal behaviour (the movements they make, whether or not they smile or show gaze aversion, their pitch of voice, speech rate, whether or not they stutter, and so on). The second way is by analysing speech content, that is, by analysing what is being said. The third way is by examining physiological responses (blood pressure, heart rate, palmar sweating and so on).

Experimental research has revealed that people are not very good at detecting lies. In a typical deception experiment, observers are exposed to a videotape consisting of a number of people (strangers, friends or partners) who are either telling the truth or not. Observers have to indicate for each person on the videotape whether he or she is lying or not. The accuracy rate (percentage of correct answers) in these studies usually varies between 45 and 60%, whereas a 50% accuracy rate could be expected by chance alone. This means that observers do only just, or do not at all, exceed the level of chance in detecting deceit when they pay attention to someone's verbal and non-verbal behaviour. Research has also shown that lay people, such as college students, and professional lie detectors, such as customs officers and police officers, do not differ in their ability to detect lies. Professional lie detectors, however, are more confident than lay persons in their ability to detect lies (DePaulo & Pfeifer, 1986). In other words, being a professional lie detector makes someone more confident in his or her ability to catch a liar, not more accurate.

WHY ARE PEOPLE POOR AT CATCHING LIARS?

There are three reasons why people are not good at detecting lies, namely (i) lack of motivation to catch a liar, (ii) poor knowledge about how to catch a liar, and (iii) the fact that some people are very good liars, which makes it very difficult to discover their lies.

Lack of Motivation

Some lies remain undetected because observers *do not want* to detect these lies. They would not want this because it is not to their benefit to know the truth or because they do not know what to do if they come to know the truth. Most guests, for instance, don't try to find out whether the host actually likes the present they gave him or her. Because of what to do when the present is not liked? More serious lies also remain undetected for this reason. Many children smoke cigarettes, despite the fact that their parents do not allow them to smoke. Their smoking remains often unnoticed, because their parents do not try to find out whether they are smoking. As soon as they discover that their children smoke, they have to undertake some action. But what can they do? Many parents don't know what to do in such a situation and therefore prefer to be ignorant concerning this issue. Also, a spouse will not always try to find out whether his or her partner is having an adulterous affair. This is because of what can be done if such a thing is discovered? As soon as the spouse tells the partner that he or she has been found out, the partner may feel compelled to choose between the spouse and the other person and may decide to leave the spouse, which may be something the spouse does not want. In short, telling what the spouse has found out may have undesirable consequences, and, realising this, the spouse may therefore decide not to investigate this issue further.

Ekman (1985) suggested that the British prime minister Chamberlain did not want to know the truth when he held talks with Hitler aiming to prevent the Second World War on 15 September 1938. Hitler intended to invade Czechoslovakia but his army was not yet fully prepared. If he could restrain the Czechs from mobilising their army, his own army would be ready for a surprise attack in a couple of weeks. Hitler therefore concealed his real intentions in his meeting with Chamberlain and asssured him that he would not attack Czechoslovakia, if the Czechs did not mobilise their army. Chamberlain did not discover Hitler's lie and tried to persuade the Czechs not to mobilise as long as the negotiations with Hitler continued. After his meeting with Hitler, Chamberlain wrote in a letter to his sister: ". . . in spite of the hardness and ruthlessness I thought I saw in his face, I got the impression that here was a man who could be relied upon when he had given his word . . ." (Ekman, 1985, p. 15/16). In Parliament, Chamberlain said that he was convinced that Hitler did not try to deceive him. It therefore seems as though Chamberlain really trusted Hitler. According to Ekman, Chamberlain did trust Hitler because he had no other choice than to trust Hitler. If he admitted that Hitler was hiding war plans, he also would have to admit that his reconciliation policy had failed and that this policy had brought Europe and the United Kingdom into real danger.

Poor Knowledge

Smiling, Gaze Aversion and Movements

Sometimes the situation is different. The possible purchaser wants to know whether the second-hand car is really as good as the salesman suggests; the employer wants to know whether the candidate is indeed as capable as the candidate says; the customs officer wants to know whether the traveller really has nothing to declare, and the police detective wants to know whether the suspect tells the truth when claiming to be innocent.

But even when people try to detect lies, they often fail to do so. They fail because they often look at the wrong cues to detect a liar. People hold strong beliefs about how liars behave. They think that liars stutter, look away from their conversation partner, smile and make many movements (Vrij & Semin, 1996). The reason for this is that observers expect liars to be nervous and to behave nervously. The behaviours just mentioned are all indicators of nervousness.

Nervous liars, however, quite often do not show nervous behaviours. One reason for this is that they suppress these behaviours. Liars often realise that fidgeting and gaze aversion will make a dishonest impression. They therefore try to avoid showing signs of nervousness and try to react "normally", that is, they try to exhibit the behaviour they usually display when not lying. It is, however, not always easy to control behaviour. People are usually capable of controlling smiling and gaze aversion. The face plays an important role in the exchange of information. People can express via their face whether they feel sad or happy, whether they want to interrupt someone else, whether they understand someone else and so on. As a result of this, people are well trained in controlling their face. Generally, body movements are less important in the exchange of information. As a result, people are less well-trained and less good in controlling their movements. This also emerges from deception research. Liars and truth tellers do not differ from each other regarding gaze aversion and smiling but do differ with respect to subtle, non-functional movements, such as foot and leg movements and hand and finger movements: liars usually make fewer foot, leg, hand and finger movements than truth tellers do (Vrij, 1998).* There are two reasons why liars restrict such movements. Firstly, this is caused by an overcontrol of these movements. Many liars are aware of the fact that observers pay attention to their movements in order to find out whether they are lying or not and they therefore avoid making these movements. This, however, results in an abnormal rigidity, as people usually make some of these non-functional movements in normal circumstances. Secondly, it is sometimes cognitively more difficult to lie than to tell the truth. Liars, for example, have to make sure that they do not contradict themselves. Liars therefore have to think harder when lying compared to when telling the truth. Ekman and Friesen (1972) found that when people are engaged in cognitively complicated tasks, they tend to cease their movements, due to the fact that they neglect their body language. This phenomenon is easy to verify. Ask somebody what they have eaten three days ago. Most people will cease their movements when they are thinking about the answer.

In sum, it is easier to catch a liar by paying attention to movements than by looking at the face. This, however, does not mean that the face does not reveal any information about deception. On the contrary, the face does reveal valuable information about deception, but it is important to ignore smiling and gaze aversion and to pay attention to emotional micro expressions in the face.

Facial Emotional Expressions

Emotions almost automatically activate muscle actions in the face. Joy, for example, activates the zygomatic major muscle, which pulls the lip corners up, bags the skin below the eyes, and produces crow's-feet wrinkles beyond the eye corners; anger results in a narrowing of the lips, and lowering of the eyebrows; eyebrows which are raised and pulled together and a raised upper eyelid and tensed lower eyelid typically mark fear. If a person denies an emotional state which is actually being felt, this person therefore has to suppress these facial expressions. If a scared person claims not to be afraid, the person thus has to suppress the facial micro expressions which typically indicate fear. This is difficult, especially because these emotions arise unexpectedly. People, for instance, don't choose deliberately to become frightened, this happens automatically as the result of a certain event or thought. It is possible that a suspect will become frightened during a police interview at the moment the suspect finds out that the police know more about his or her involvement in the crime than the suspect

---

*This does not mean that all liars make fewer movements than truth tellers. There does not exist typical deceptive behaviour: different liars show different behaviour, and people show different behaviour in different circumstances. All I want to say is that more people show a decrease than an increase in movements during deception.

thought they would know. The moment fright occurs, a fearful facial expression may be shown, which may give the lie away. It is therefore likely that the suspect would try to suppress this emotional expression as soon as this expression appears. People are usually able to suppress these expressions within 1/25th of a second after they begin to appear. This is fast, but it also means that the expression will be present for 1/25th of a second. This means that an alert observer will be able to detect such a facial expression (unless the observer blinks at the moment the liar produces the expression).

The opposite can occur as well. Someone can pretend to experience a particular emotion, whereas in fact this emotion is not felt. A mother can pretend to be angry at her child, whereas in reality she is not angry at all. In order to be convincing, a mother should produce an angry facial expression, that is, she should then try to narrow her lips. This muscle action, however, is very difficult for most people to make. It is also difficult to produce a false smile which looks like a felt smile. False smiles are usually not accompanied by the involvement of the muscles around the eyes; hence, the bagged skin below the eyes and the crow's-feet wrinkles are usually lacking. (See Ekman (1985) for a detailed account of the relationship between facial emotional expressions and deception.)

It is also difficult to simulate an emotion other than the one which is actually felt. An adulterous husband, for instance, can become scared during a conversation with his wife when he realises how much she knows about his affair, but can decide to mask this emotional state by pretending to be angry at his wife; angry because she apparently does not trust him. In order to be convincing, he therefore has to suppress his fearful facial expression and replace it with an angry facial expression. This is difficult, because he has to lower his eyebrows (sign of anger) whereas his eyebrows tend to raise (sign of fear). Paying attention to micro facial expressions may provide a good opportunity to detect lies. I will discuss this issue later.

Good Liars

There are individual differences in deceptive skills: some people are better liars than others. Obviously, the better someone can lie, the more difficult it is to catch that person. What makes someone a good liar? In my view, this is related to cognitive load and emotions which accompany a lie. Good liars do not find it cognitively difficult to lie and do not experience any emotions when they are lying. More precisely, at least four aspects characterise a good liar: (1) being original, (2) thinking quickly, (3) being eloquent, and (4) not experiencing feelings of fear, guilt or "duping delight".

With regard to originality: a liar can be faced with unexpected situations which require an immediate response. For example, a wife confronts her husband with a telephone number and address of a – for her unknown – woman which she found in his pocket; the police detective tells the suspect that the suspect was seen by a witness at the scene of crime directly after the crime occurred; a mother tells her son that, in contrast to what he was saying to her before, the shops were open that day; and an MP who has told investigators that not a businessman but his wife had paid the hotel bill, is facing evidence revealing that his wife could not have visited the hotel on the day she was supposed to have paid the bill. To be a successful liar in these situations – or in similar situations – the liar needs to give a convincing answer, which requires original thinking.

It is essential that the liar does not wait too long before giving an answer, because a delay may make the observer suspicious. Rapid thinking is therefore required.

It will benefit the liar to be an eloquent speaker, as eloquence can help in getting out of awkward situations. People who usually use many words to express themselves, for example, are in an advantageous position. They can commence with giving a long-winded response, which in fact does not answer the question yet. Meanwhile, they can think about the appropriate answer. Or they can use their eloquence to fool the observer, by giving a response which sounds convincing but which, in fact, does not provide an answer to the question. Some politicians are very good at this.

People differ in the emotions they experience when they are lying. One guilty suspect will be very scared when presenting a fake alibi, whereas another guilty suspect will stay calm; one applicant will feel guilty when exaggerating the wages being received from the present employer, whereas another applicant will not feel guilty at all while doing this; one pupil will experience a lot of delight when trying to get the head teacher to believe the excuse, whereas another will not experience such "duping delight" at all. Deceiving others is easier when the liar does not experience feelings of fear, guilt or delight. As long as the liar does not experience any of these emotions, there will not be any emotional behaviour that has to be suppressed while lying and therefore the liar can react naturally. The absence of emotions during deception may be caused by the frequency of lying. The more often someone lies, the less duping delight they will experience and the less guilty they will feel about the fact of lying. Lying frequently will probably make someone a more skilful liar too, which reduces the likelihood of getting caught, and thereby reduces the fear of getting caught.

HOW TO BECOME A BETTER LIE DETECTOR

Detecting lies is difficult, particularly because there do not exist typical non-verbal or verbal cues to deception. Despite the difficulties, I believe that observers can improve their skills in detecting deceit. Hopefully the following remarks will be useful in order to achieve this.

Lies remain undetected because observers have too much good faith: they assume too often that people speak the truth. It is essential for a lie detector to be *suspicious* and to distrust what people are saying. This is difficult, especially when the other is someone they know well, for example, a partner. People usually tend to trust their partners, which is the reason why they are not good at detecting lies told by their partners.

Furthermore, observers should *continue with asking questions* as soon as they suspect somebody of telling a lie. To keep on lying will become increasingly difficult for the liar when the observer keeps on asking questions. There are several reasons for this. The liar must avoid self-contradiction, should not say things which the observer already knows to be untrue, and must remember the things said in case someone asks for a repetition. Moreover, liars have to control their behaviour all the time in order to prevent giving these lies away via non-verbal behavioural cues. These aspects will become more difficult when the observer continues asking questions and therefore forces the liar to keep on lying.

However, to keep on asking questions is not easy. Firstly, asking many questions does not fit with social conversation rules. Someone will become very quickly irritated if the other person questions all the things being said. Secondly, research has shown that, in the first instance, liars make an honest impression as a result of further questioning. That is, when liars – after being challenged by observers – persist in lying, observers have a tendency to believe these liars. The following explanation seems plausible. Observers expect to put liars in an awkward position by further questioning and therefore expect liars to show nervous behaviour (start stuttering, fidgeting and so on). Liars therefore will make an honest impression as long as they succeed in avoiding such nervous behaviour.

It is important for lie detectors not to *reveal too much of their knowledge* to the liar. As I said before, liars have to make sure that they do not say things which the observer knows to be untrue. This task is easier when the liar knows the observer's knowledge about the topic of the lie. The task becomes difficult when the liar does not know the extent of the observer's knowledge. This is so because the liar cannot be sure what to say in order not to get caught.

It makes it easier for the observer to catch a liar when the observer is *well informed* about the topic of the lie. The more details the observer knows, the more likely it is that the liar will say something that the observer knows to be untrue.

There is no typical behaviour that indicates deception, neither do liars say or not say specific things. It is therefore not useful to make judgements about deceit on the basis of stereotypical beliefs (such as "liars show gaze aversion", "liars fidget", "liars stutter", and so on). Observers should judge each case individually. *To look carefully at how someone is behaving and to listen carefully to what someone is saying* is thus essential. A brief emotional expression, an inhibition of subtle movements, a verbal contradiction: all these signs may indicate deception. It is, however, important not to make judgements about someone's untruthfulness too quickly. Suppose that a suspect stops fidgeting as soon as the suspect starts mentioning an alibi. You may well conclude on the basis of this behaviour that something is going on. But it is impossible to say what exactly is going on. It is possible that the suspect stops fidgeting because of lying and is afraid of getting caught. But the suspect may also stop doing this when innocent, because of fear that the police will believe that fidgeting indicates lying. It is therefore impossible to judge whether or not a suspect is lying solely on the basis of the behaviour displayed. The behaviour only reveals that something is probably going on, not what exactly is going on. I believe that police officers are not sufficiently aware of this. In discussions with police detectives, they often come up with statements like: "I am sure that he is lying, because he does not dare to look me straight in the eyes when we discuss the crime". It is too premature to draw this conclusion on the basis of the suspect's behaviour. It may well be the case that something is going on, if a suspect continuously looks away when talking about the crime. It is, however, impossible to say whether or not the suspect is lying. Even innocent suspects may display gaze aversion when they are interviewed about a crime, for instance because they find it hard to accept that they are suspected by the police. In sum, someone has to ask more questions or has to check the information a suspect provides in order to find out whether the suspect is lying. Drawing conclusions about deception solely on the basis of the suspect's behaviour is not reliable.

Looking carefully at someone's behaviour can cause a problem. Looking at movements of hands, fingers, legs and feet can be particularly useful in detecting lies. This means, however, that the observer has to scrutinise the potential liar carefully, and has to observe the potential liar almost literally from head to foot. This is very unusual in conversations and makes an odd impression. We usually restrict ourselves to looking into the eyes of the conversation partner. Eye movements, however, do not give reliable information about deception. It may therefore be a good idea that in police interviews with suspects, a second police officer watches the suspect (e.g. via a video link system in a different room, as this gives the second officer the opportunity to observe the suspect from head to foot, which may not be possible if the second officer is in the interview room).

SCIENTIFIC METHODS OF DETECTING LIES

For a long time people have been trying to develop techniques to detect deception. For example, the Chinese forced suspected liars to chew rice powder and then to spit it out. If the resultant powder was dry then the person was judged to have been lying (Kleinmuntz & Szucko, 1984). Nowadays, there exist several techniques which have been shown to be successful to some extent in detecting lies.

The most detailed and probably most successful non-verbal detection technique (that is, detecting deception via looking at non-verbal cues) has been developed by Ekman and his colleagues. They look at facial micro expressions which are the result of emotions people experience (see above). Ekman and his colleagues have reported accuracy rates of up to 80%; that is, by looking at facial micro expressions they were able to detect 80% of the truths and 80% of the lies (Ekman et al., 1991). Spotting and interpreting facial expressions, however, is not an easy task, as they usually last for only 1/25th of a second. Ekman, however, claims that observers can be trained in this task (Ekman, 1997, personal communication).

The most popular verbal detection technique is called Statement Validity Assessment (SVA). This technique was developed in Germany in the 1980s (Steller & Köhnken, 1989). Trained evaluators examine written statements (transcribed interviews) and judge the presence or absence of each of 19 criteria. Examples of criteria are: "Unstructured production", "Quantity of details", "Unexpected complications during the incident", and "Spontaneous corrections". The presence of each criterion in the statement supports the hypothesis that the account is likely to be based on genuine personal experience. Research has shown that by using this technique 80% of the truths and 65% of the lies can be detected (see Vrij and Akehurst (1998) for a literature review of SVA studies).

Detecting lies by measuring physiological activity can be done with a polygraph. The polygraph (a composition of two Greek words, namely "poly" = many, and "grapho" = to write) is an accurate, scientific measurement device which can display, via ink writing pens onto charts or via a computer's visual display unit, a direct and valid representation of various sorts of bodily activity (Bull, 1988). The most commonly measured activities are palmar sweating, blood pressure and respiration (Ben-Shakhar & Furedy, 1990). Changes in these activities are signs of emotional arousal. The polygraph records these changes accurately, it detects smaller changes than can otherwise be observed, and records activities which are rarely visible (such as heart rate). It does this by amplifying signals picked up from sensors that are attached to different parts of the body. The polygraph is not a lie detector (people sometimes call the polygraph a lie detector but this is misleading). The polygraph measures changes in emotional arousal, and it is assumed that these changes occur during deception. The premise is that telling lies causes some stress or anxiety, and this stress and anxiety is translated into emotional arousal which will be recorded on the polygraph. However, an emotional change typical for lying does not exist (Saxe, 1991). In general, it is not possible to differentiate between emotions through the use of physiological reactions. For instance, conceptually distinctive emotions such as anger, fear, shame or guilt all result in similar physical reactions, and thus, all these emotions will give a similar output on the polygraph charts. In other words while, *the polygraph can tell that some kind of reaction is taking place within the subject, it cannot, however, tell what reaction that is* (Ney, 1988). Polygraph research has shown that, by utilising a special interview technique called the Control Question Technique, 70% of the truths and 90% of the lies can be detected.

CONCLUSION

Detecting lies in interviews is not an easy task. The main problem is that there does not exist typical non-verbal or verbal behaviour which is associated with deception. That is, not all liars show the same behaviour or say the same things. However, this does not mean that detecting lies is impossible. Liars do sometimes give their lies away: micro expressions of emotions, inhibition of subtle non-functional movements, and lack of details in the verbal account are amongst the cues which regularly appear during deception. These cues are more likely to occur when the liar experiences emotions of fear, guilt or delight and when telling the lie requires a lot of mental effort. The interviewer can, to a limited extent, influence these factors by giving the potential liar a hard time during the interview, for example by continuing to ask questions, which forces the liar into further lying. In order to detect deceptive cues, the observer has to watch the potential liar carefully (from head to foot) and has to listen carefully to what has been said. This is easier to do when the lie detector is not the interviewer, as interviewing requires attention, which distracts from observing the potential liar. Therefore, teamwork seems to be appropriate, with one person asking the questions and the other observing the potential liar.

REFERENCES

Ben-Shakhar, G. & Furedy, J.J. (1990). *Theories and Applications in the Detection of Deception.* New York: Springer-Verlag.

Bull, R. (1988). What is the lie-detection test? In A. Gale (Ed.), *The Polygraph Test: Lies, Truth and Science* (pp. 10–19). London: Sage.

DePaulo, B.M. & Pfeifer, R.L. (1986). On-the-job experience and skill at detecting deception. *Journal of Applied Social Psychology,* **16**, 249–267.

Ekman, P. (1985). *Telling Lies.* New York: W.W. Norton.

Ekman, P. & Friesen, W.V. (1972). Hand movements. *Journal of Communication,* **22**, 353–374.

Ekman, P., O'Sullivan, M., Friesen, W.V. & Scherer, K. (1991). Face, voice, and body in detecting deceit. *Journal of Nonverbal Behavior,* **15**, 125–135.

Kleinmuntz, B. & Szucko, J.J. (1984). Lie detection in ancient and modern times: A call for contemporary scientific study. *American Psychologist,* **39**, 766–776.

Memon, A., Vrij, A. & Bull, R. (1998). *Psychology and Law: Truthfulness, Accuracy and Credibility.* Maidenhead: McGraw-Hill.

Ney, T. (1988). Expressing your emotions and controlling feelings. In A. Gale (Ed.), *The Polygraph Test: Lies, Truth and Science* (pp. 65–72). London: Sage.

Saxe, L. (1991). Science and the GKT Polygraph: A theoretical critique. *Integrative Physiological and Behavioral Science,* **26**, 223–231.

Steller, M. & Köhnken, G. (1989). Criteria-based content analysis. In D.C. Raskin (Ed.), *Psychological Methods in Criminal Investigation and Evidence* (pp. 217–245). New York: Springer Verlag.

Vrij, A. (1998). *De psychologie van de leugenaar: Liegen en voorgelogen worden op het werk, in de rechtszaal en thuis.* Lisse: Swets & Zeitlinger.

Vrij, A. (1999, forthcoming). *Telling Lies and Detecting Deceit* (working title). Chichester: John Wiley & Sons.

Vrij, A. & Akehurst, L. (1998). Verbal communication and credibility. In A. Memon, A. Vrij & R. Bull. *Psychology and Law: Truthfulness, Accuracy and Credibility.* Maidenhead: McGraw-Hill.

Vrij, A. & Semin, G.R. (1996). Lie experts' beliefs about nonverbal indicators of deception. *Journal of Nonverbal Behavior,* **20**, 65–80.

Police Interviewing and Disputed Confessions

Gisli Gudjonsson
Institute of Psychiatry, London, UK

INTRODUCTION

A confession made to the police during an interview is sometimes the most powerful evidence against the defendant when the case goes to court. In England defendants can be, and sometimes are, convicted on the basis of their confession alone, even when the confession is disputed at trial. In Scotland and the USA the confession has to be corroborated by some other evidence, although in practice the corroboration criteria allowed by judges are sometimes so weak that they do not constitute an effective safeguard against wrongful conviction. Therefore, a confession made to the police, or to a third party which comes to the attention of the police, can result in a conviction for a serious crime and a lengthy prison sentence. During the present decade there has been growing recognition among the judiciary that wrongful convictions may be occasioned by psychological vulnerability and coercive interviewing. Corre (1995), an English lawyer, attributes the credit for this change in attitudes to the pioneering psychological work that has been conducted in this field in recent years.

As a result of the greater acceptance of expert psychological evidence in court, there are increased demands by defence and Crown for a psychological evaluation of cases involving disputed confessions. The purpose of this chapter is to provide a framework for the psychological evaluation, which will guide psychologists commissioned to provide reports. The first paper to discuss a framework for the psychological and psychiatric evaluation was published by Gudjonsson and MacKeith (1988). The assessment framework was later revised and expanded by Gudjonsson (1992), and recently Gudjonsson and MacKeith (1997)

Handbook of the Psychology of Interviewing. Edited by A. Memon and R. Bull.
© 1999 John Wiley & Sons Ltd.

discuss the role their assessment played in a number of well-publicised cases of miscarriage of justice, including the "Guildford Four", the "Birmingham Six", the "Tottenham Three", and that of Judith Ward.

DISPUTED CONFESSIONS

There are no current figures available which indicate how often confessions are disputed when cases go to court. What is known, however, is that when the confession is the only or main evidence against the defendant the confession is commonly disputed. The reasons why the confession is disputed fall into three broad categories.

1. The confession was allegedly never made

Here the defendant claims that the confession was never uttered and that it was made up by the police or a third party to whom the defendant is alleged to have confessed. So-called "verbals", where police officers claimed that the suspect had made verbal admissions, were common prior to the introduction of the Police and Criminal Evidence Act (PACE) in January 1986. In this group also fall those cases where a confession statement was signed, but the defendant claims that he or she did not know what they were signing, having allegedly never made the confession in the first place.

2. A retracted confession

The defendant accepts that he or she made the confession, but claims that it is a false confession. The reasons given for allegedly making a false confession typically include, being pressured by the police, being promised that they would be allowed to go home after making a confession, and not being able to cope with the demands of the police interview or custodial confinement (Gudjonsson, 1992; Sigurdsson & Gudjonsson, 1996).

3. Disputing a confession that has not been retracted

With the English courts becoming more accepting of psychological evidence, there is a growing trend among defence solicitors, when confession evidence is the only or main evidence against their client, to let the Crown prove the case during a disputed trial, even when the client is making full admissions to the solicitor that he or she was, in fact, involved in the crime. To do this they may employ a psychologist to examine if there are some psychological vulnerabilities, such as a significant intellectual impairment or high suggestibility, in order to get the judge to rule the confession inadmissible, which means that it does not go before the jury. This represents a dilemma for the psychologist, because he or she is colluding with the client being acquitted on the basis of technicality, which raises a number of ethical and professional issues which psychologists should be aware of (Gudjonsson, 1994a; Gudjonsson & Haward, 1998).

The Psychological Evaluation

What often seems to happen in cases of disputed confessions is that the psychologist is instructed to conduct a narrowly focused assessment, where he or she asks the defendant no questions about the confession, and if the defendant happens to repeat the confession to the psychologist then it is not mentioned in the report. Psychologists should not collude with such practice, because it may mislead the court and be instrumental in causing a miscarriage of justice. What psychologists must do at all times is present all relevant evidence in their report, irrespective of whether or not it is favourable to the defendant.

Gudjonsson and MacKeith (1997) point out that while it is important for the courts to accept that psychological vulnerabilities can result in unreliable confessions there is a danger that expert testimony may be misused by the legal profession and becomes a fashionable means for evading justice. There appear to be a growing number of cases where solicitors are commissioning psychologists and psychiatrists in cases where they are trying to get their client acquitted on the basis of psychological vulnerabilities, when these are not relevant to the credibility of the confession. Some psychologists are colluding with this practice, which undermines the integrity and credibility of their profession. Psychological vulnerabilities, even when they are present, are not always relevant to the reasons why suspects confess to the police and each case must be considered on its own merits. As Gudjonsson and MacKeith (1997) state:

> We must be careful not to be carried away on a fashionable "bandwagon" which is likely to increase the Courts' scepticism of expert psychological and psychiatric evidence and eventually undermine the value of such evidence in genuine cases (p. 23).

THE LEGAL PROVISIONS

The law in England and Wales concerning the questioning and treatment of persons by the police is governed by the Police and Criminal Evidence Act 1984 (PACE; Home Office, 1985), which came into effect in January 1986. PACE is supplemented by four Codes of Practice, which provide guidance to the police about procedure and the treatment of suspects (Home Office, 1995). The Codes have legislative power in as far as their breach may result in evidence, including confession evidence, being ruled inadmissible by the judge after hearing legal submissions in the absence of the jury. (This is known as a "*voire dire*" or "trial within a trial".) PACE has not been revised since its implementation in 1986, but the Home Office has published an important revised version of the Codes of Practice which came into force on 10 April 1995 (Home Office, 1995). The most important change since the implementation of PACE is the modification of the right to silence, which means that adverse inferences can be drawn by the court when suspects refuse to answer police questions or exercise their right not to give evidence in court. The current caution has increased the complexity of the decision-making that suspects have to make when questioned by the police (Gudjonsson, 1994b). That is, not only do they have to decide whether or not to answer the questions, they also have to consider the consequences if they refuse to answer a question. In addition, the wording of the caution itself is complicated, with the great majority of persons of below average intellect not fully understanding it (Shepherd, Mortimer & Mobasheri, 1995; Clare, Gudjonsson & Harari, 1998). Of particular concern with regard to the new caution is the fact that many suspects detained at police stations are intellectually disadvantaged (Gudjonsson et al., 1993), which means that many of them are unlikely to understand the new police caution.

Police Interviewing

As far as police interviewing is concerned, the most important aspects of PACE relate to the introduction of tape recording of police interviews and the use of "appropriate adults" during interviews in order to safeguard psychologically vulnerable suspects against giving misleading statements.

The question of fitness to be interviewed is not addressed in PACE or the Codes of Practice, but it is increasingly becoming an issue in cases of mental disorder (Gudjonsson, 1995a; Norfolk, 1997). Gudjonsson (1995a) provides a conceptual framework for the assessment of fitness for interview, which was developed on the basis of a real life criminal case. The case suggested three criteria for evaluating fitness for interview, which relate to the *functional abilities* of the suspect rather than a clinical diagnosis per se. Firstly, is the suspect able to understand the police caution after it has been carefully explained to him or her? Secondly, is the suspect fully oriented in time, place and person? Evidence of disorientation may provide an important insight into the suspect's mental problems and his or her ability to cope with the police interview. Thirdly, is the suspect, because of mental problems, likely to give answers which may be seriously misconstrued by the jury?

The legal issues concerning the admissibility of confession evidence are primarily determined by Sections 76 and 78 of PACE and are concerned with the concepts of "oppression", "unreliability", and "fairness" (Gudjonsson, 1997a). The trial judge will decide on the legal arguments, after hearing all the relevant evidence and legal submissions from the defence and prosecution. If the confession evidence is allowed in evidence then the weight of that evidence will be determined by the jury. This means that the psychologist or psychiatrist commissioned in the case may have to give evidence twice; once in front of the judge, and then again before the jury.

The main difference between Sections 76 and 78 relates to discretionary powers. Section 76 involves "proof of facts", whereas Section 78 involves "the exercise of judgement by the court" (Birch, 1989, p. 96). There is generally the need to establish some kind of police impropriety to operate Section 76 and judges are reluctant to include under this provision unreliability due solely to internal factors (e.g. learning disability, high suggestibility or compliance, drug withdrawal, disturbed mental state). Another difference between Sections 76 and 78 relates to the fact that denials, which can be demonstrated as lies and used against defendants in court, must be excluded under Section 78 (Gudjonsson, 1995a). Section 76 only deals with confession evidence.

Safeguards for Vulnerable Suspects

Section 77 (1) of PACE deals with confessions obtained from persons who suffer from learning disability, referred to in the Act as "mental handicap". The section states that in cases of learning disability where no independent person was present during the police interview, the court must warn the jury that there is special need for caution before convicting the accused solely on the basis of his or her confession. No similar provision is offered in PACE for persons who suffer from other types of mental disorder, such as mental illness. However, there is a general protection for persons suffering from "mental disorder", which is described in detail in the revised Codes of Practice (Home Office, 1995, Code C). The definition used for "mental disorder" is the same as in the Mental Health Act 1983, and means "mental illness, arrested or incomplete development of mind, psychopathic disorder and any other mental disorder or disability of mind" (p. 29). Code C offers important provisions for the detention and interviewing of "special groups", such as foreigners who do not speak much English, juveniles, those who are hard of hearing, and persons who are mentally disordered or handicapped. Where communicating in English is a problem an interpreter must be called to assist. The relevant legal provision for other "special groups" includes: "A juvenile or a person who is mentally disordered or handicapped, whether suspected or not, must not be interviewed or asked to provide or sign a written statement in the absence of the appropriate adult" (Home Office, 1995, p. 55).

An "appropriate adult" is a responsible adult called in by the police in order to offer special assistance to the detainee. The "appropriate adult" can be a relative of the detainee or a professional person such as a social worker. Psychologists and psychiatrists sometimes act in the capacity of an appropriate adult. The detainee's solicitor cannot act as an "appropriate adult".

Where an appropriate adult is present during an interview, he or she shall be informed that they are not there merely as an observer. The purpose of their presence is, first, to advise the person being questioned and secondly to observe whether or not the interview is being conducted properly and fairly, and thirdly, to facilitate communication with the person being interviewed (Home Office, 1995, p. 55).

Juveniles and persons with mental disorder or learning disability are considered "vulnerable" or "at risk", because ". . . they may, without knowing or wishing to do so, be particularly prone in certain circumstances to provide information which is unreliable, misleading or self-incriminating. Special care should therefore always be exercised in questioning such a person, and the appropriate adult should be involved, if there is any doubt about the person's age, mental state or capacity. Because of the risk of unreliable evidence it is important to obtain corroboration of any facts admitted whenever possible" (Home Office, 1995, p. 56).

There are problems with PACE and the Codes of Practice in connection with the generic term "mental disorder". Firstly, there is no operational definition given about what precisely constitutes "mental disorder". Police officers, without any medical training, are expected to be able to identify persons suffering from a condition which is not clearly defined or described in their Codes of Practice. Secondly, the Codes of Practice do not specify how certain characteristics, such as mental illness or learning disability, place suspects "at risk". The implicit assumption appears to be that mental disorder places these persons "at risk" in the sense that they may unwittingly provide the police with unreliable testimony, including a false confession, because they may not fully understand the significance of the questions put to them while being interviewed or the implications of their answers, or that they are unduly influenced by short-term gains (e.g. being allowed to go home) and by interviewers' suggestions and pressure.

ASSESSMENT FRAMEWORK

As far as England, Wales and Northern Ireland are concerned, the psychological assessment in cases of disputed confessions should be relevant to one or more of the legal issues, as specified in PACE, concerned with "oppression", "unreliability" and "fairness". In other jurisdictions, including the Channel Islands, the Isle of Man, Ireland and the USA, the concept of "voluntariness" is used to determine the criteria for admissibility and the weight that the jury can place on confession evidence.

Gudjonsson (1995b) argues that there are a number of problems with the concept of "voluntariness", including the fact that it has primarily to do with the type or intensity of psychological and physical pressure that is legally sanctioned to break down suspects' resistance and their free will during interviewing. What is legally allowed in a given case is adjusted to suit the purpose of a given legal system. This can make the assessment very difficult and it emphasises the importance of taking into consideration the context and country in which the assessment is undertaken. The psychologist has to be familiar with the legal criteria used in the country where he or she is testifying, as well as understanding the court's approach to psychological evidence and disputed confessions. For example, in the USA the law tolerates much greater psychological manipulation and deception by police officers than the English courts, including police officers being commonly allowed to deliberately lie to suspects to induce a confession (Ofshe & Leo, 1997).

Contested Cases

Irrespective of the country where the expert is testifying, confession evidence is typically contested either on the basis of police impropriety, such as police pressure or a technical breach concerning the suspect's legal rights, or because of psychological vulnerabilities, which rendered the suspect "at risk" of giving a misleading statement when interviewed by the police. In most instances the suspect's psychological status will need to be considered and evaluated within the context of the entire case, which includes factors associated with custody and police interviewing. Psychological factors should not be interpreted in isolation from the other aspects of the case. For example, there have been many instances where psychologists have inappropriately challenged the reliability of a confession on the basis of the suspect's demonstrated suggestibility on psychological testing, when it was evident that the police officers had not offered any suggestions to the suspect either prior to or during the police interview. The psychological characteristics identified during the psychological assessment must be relevant and pertinent to the nature of the confession. This is typically the most difficult part of the assessment and requires the psychologist to have good knowledge of the case, including the legal and psychological issues. This requires having studied all the relevant papers in the case, having listened to tape or audio recordings of the police interviews, and having conducted the necessary interview and psychological testing of the defendant.

In most instances the psychological assessment takes place several months, and sometimes years, after the confession was made to the police. The psychologist will need to reconstruct the defendant's mental state and psychological vulnerabilities as they were at the time of the police interview. This can be a difficult process, because over time the defendant's mental state, personality and attitudes may have changed as well as the relevant information not being available at the time of the pre-trial (or post-trial) psychological evaluation (Gudjonsson, 1992).

Each case is different and must be considered on its own merit. Psychological factors often have a bearing on the suspect's capacity to cope with the police interview and confinement.

PSYCHOLOGICAL VULNERABILITIES

Within the context of the police interviewing of suspects, "psychological vulnerabilities" refer to psychological characteristics or mental states which render a suspect prone, in certain circumstances, to providing information which is inaccurate, unreliable (or invalid) or misleading.

Much has been written on the psychological vulnerabilities of suspects detained at police stations (Gudjonsson, 1992; Gudjonsson et al., 1993).

The assessment of psychological vulnerabilities falls into four main groups. These are labelled "mental disorder", "abnormal mental state", "intellectual functioning", and "personality characteristics".

Mental Disorder

The term "mental disorder" implies that the person suffers from a diagnosable psychiatric problem, including mental illness (e.g. schizophrenia, depressive illness), learning disability (also known as "mental handicap") or personality disorder (see Table 1).

In cases of mental illness, perceptions, cognitions, emotions, judgement and self-control may be adversely affected. These may result in misleading information being provided to the police during a police interview. Those suffering from paranoid schizophrenia are sometimes particularly difficult to interview because of their suspiciousness and lack of trust. Breakdown in "reality monitoring" is a salient symptom of mental illness, which means that the patient's ability to differentiate facts from fantasy is adversely affected. In exceptional circumstances this may result in people believing that they have committed crimes of which they are totally innocent. Breakdown in reality monitoring occurs in everyday life in relation to the memory of thoughts, feelings and events (e.g. not being able to differentiate between what one intended to do and what one has done) and it does not require the presence of mental illness. Mental illness makes the breakdown in reality monitoring more extensive and frequent (Bentall, Baker & Havers, 1991).

Depressive illness may cause some people to ruminate and implicate themselves falsely in criminal activity as a way of relieving strong feelings of free-floating guilt. Such attempts only relieve the feelings of guilt temporarily (Gudjonsson, 1992).

Adults suffering from learning disability may experience special problems when interviewed by the police. This problem arises because their condition may impair their ability to give a clear and detailed account of events to the police. They may find it difficult to remember clearly the material event, become confused when questioned, have problems understanding the questions and articulating their answers, not fully appreciating the implications and consequences of their answers, and may feel easily intimidated when questioned by people in authority (Gudjonsson & MacKeith, 1994; Gudjonsson, 1995c).

Interesting papers on identifying witnesses with learning disability and on how to improve their performance during police interviewing have been written by Bull and Cullen (1992, 1993). Clare and Gudjonsson (1995) conclude that persons with learning disability are disadvantaged in many respects. This includes their being less likely to understand their legal rights (including the new police caution), their tendency to be acquiescent and suggestible, and their inability to appreciate fully the consequences of making a misleading statement.

The papers of Tully and Cahill (1984), Dent (1986), Clare and Gudjonsson (1993) and Perlman et al. (1994) show the kind of problems that persons with learning disability have with reporting events by free recall and the extent to which they can be influenced by leading questions. Clare and Gudjonsson (1993) showed that persons with learning disability are particularly susceptible to giving in to leading questions and they are more prone to confabulate with regard to verbal memory recall. (Confabulation is the tendency to fill gaps in one's memory

Table 1 The psychological vulnerabilities of persons with mental illness, learning disability and personality disorder

Mental illness	Learning disability	Personality disorder
Breakdown in reality monitoring	Impaired intellectual capacity and social functioning	Manipulative
Distorted perceptions and beliefs	Poor memory capacity	Lies readily
Impaired judgement	Poor understanding of legal rights	Need for notoriety
Guilt feeling proneness	Greater susceptibility to leading questions	Lack of concern about consequences
Suspiciousness	Heightened acquiescence	Tendency towards confabulation
	Distorted perception of consequences	
	Tendency towards confabulation	

by producing imagined material and it can be measured by the Gudjonsson Suggestibility Scales; Gudjonsson, 1997b.)

"Cognitive interview" techniques developed and refined by Fisher and Geiselman (1992) can enhance the recall of witness, victims and cooperative suspects (see Chapter 5.6 by Memon). Milne and Bull (1996) and Milne, Clare and Bull (in press) provide evidence that the cognitive interview techniques can be effectively used in cases of children and adults with learning disability. This is an area where psychological research has had an important impact on police practice (see Chapter 3.2 by Milne).

The concept of personality disorder was an important psychiatric diagnosis in connection with disputed confessions of Judith Ward, who was wrongfully convicted of terrorist crimes in 1974 and had her conviction quashed by the Court of Appeal in 1992 (Gudjonsson & MacKeith, 1997). She suffered from a personality disorder with histrionic features. A review of medical records concerning her period on remand prior to the trial revealed evidence of severe mental disorder which had not been disclosed by doctors to the Court. Psychological assessment suggested a person of average intellectual abilities who scored highly on a test of suggestibility and exhibited a strong tendency to confabulate in verbal memory recall. Gudjonsson (1992) has discussed the importance of confabulatory tendency in relation to personality disorder. Personality disorder may represent an important psychological vulnerability among some witnesses and suspects in that they appear to have a strong tendency to confabulate in their memory recall (Smith & Gudjonsson, 1995) and more readily make false confessions as a part of their criminal lifestyle (Sigurdsson & Gudjonsson, 1997).

Abnormal Mental State

Suspects may suffer from an abnormal mental state, which may adversely influence the reliability of their testimony, without their having had a history of mental disorder. In a recent study for the Royal Commission on Criminal Justice, Gudjonsson et al. (1993) found that about 20% of the suspects were reporting an abnormally high level of anxiety, but only about 7% reported a history or symptoms of mental illness, mainly that of schizophrenia or depressive illness.

Apart from feelings of extreme anxiety, detainees may experience specific phobic symptoms, such as claustrophobia (i.e. an irrational fear of being locked up in confined space like a police cell) or panic attacks (e.g. drug addicts panicking when they are withdrawing from drugs). In the Royal Commission study (Gudjonsson et al., 1993), extreme fear of being locked up in a police cell was uncommon (i.e. only one case out of 171), although many detainees complained that they were distressed about being locked up at the police station. The most common anxiety was in relation to uncertainties over their current predicament. Detainees expressed concern over what was going to happen to them, they kept asking the researchers for information about their detention, and wanted to know when they were likely to be interviewed by the police.

Occasionally detainees are in a state of bereavement when interviewed by the police due to their having lost a loved one, such as a spouse or a child. This may make them vulnerable to giving unreliable statements because of feelings of guilt and subjective distress that typically accompany the condition. For example, self-blame associated with a state of bereavement can make detainees unwittingly exaggerate their involvement in an offence, especially when they are accused of the loved person's murder (Gudjonsson, 1992).

Alcohol intoxication and withdrawal sometimes occur during interviewing. However, following the introduction of PACE in January 1986 it is uncommon that detainees are nowadays interviewed by the police when under the influence of alcohol (see Gudjonsson et al., 1993). Of course, alcoholics may experience withdrawal symptoms while in detention, but these may in general have no serious effects on the suspect's behaviour during police interviewing (Sigurdsson & Gudjonsson, 1994). More common and problematic, detainees who are high on drugs when arrested may be withdrawing from the drugs while in custody and at the time they are interviewed by the police. Some drug addicts may be vulnerable to giving misleading accounts of events when being asked leading questions and placed under interrogative pressure, in addition to saying things in order to expedite their early release from custody.

In a study among prison inmates in Iceland, Sigurdsson and Gudjonsson (1994) found that being interviewed by the police when suspects are under the influence of drugs or withdrawing from drugs makes them feel confused. This would not normally make them unfit to be interviewed, but it suggests that special care should be taken when interviewing them. Two studies have looked at the effects of drug use and drug withdrawal on interrogative suggestibility. They suggest that opiate users undergoing opiate withdrawal are significantly more suggestible than opiate users who are no longer showing acute withdrawal symptoms (Murakami, Edelmann & Davis, 1996), and there is a subgroup of vulnerable drug addicts who may be more suggestible when under the influence of opiates (Davison & Gossop, 1996).

In a recent follow-up to the Gudjonsson et al. (1993) study for the Royal Commission of Justice, Pearse et al. (in press) found that detainees' reports of taking illicit drugs in the 24-hour period prior to the police interview were the only variable that was significantly associated with making a confession. One possible interpretation of this finding is that withdrawing from drugs encouraged them to make a confession as a way of facilitating their early release from detention.

Medical complaints (e.g. cardiovascular problems, epilepsy, diabetes) can result in a disturbed or abnormal mental state while the person is interviewed by the police. This may adversely influence the accuracy and reliability of their account and their ability to function in a stressful situation.

Intellectual Abilities

Limited intellectual abilities, not amounting to learning disability, can influence the ability of witnesses to understand questions, articulate their answers, and appreciate the implications of their answers.

Many detainees interviewed at police stations are of low intelligence (Gudjonsson et al., 1993). The mean IQ for 160 suspects detained at two police stations was only 82, with the range 61–131, prorating the scores from three subtests of the WAIS-R (Wechster Adult Intelligence Scale; vocabulary, comprehension and picture completion). Nine per cent of the sample had a prorated IQ score below 70, compared with about 2% of the general population, one third (34%) had a prorated IQ score of 75 or below (i.e. bottom 5% of the general population).

It is probable that the IQ scores obtained are an underestimate of the suspects' intellectual abilities due to the circumstances and context of testing (i.e. many of the suspects were anxiously waiting to be interviewed by the police at the time of testing and were preoccupied with their predicament). However, the subtests chosen were those that were least likely to be adversely affected by the stress of being detained for interviewing at the police station. The findings indicate that the police commonly interview suspects of low intellectual abilities.

Gudjonsson (1990a) compared the WAIS-R IQ scores of 100 alleged false confessors and those of 100 other forensic referrals. The mean Full Scale IQ score of the two groups were 80 (SD = 14.6) and 91.4 (SD = 14.8), respectively. These findings suggest that persons referred for a psychological evaluation by solicitors in cases of retracted confessions tend to be substantially below average in their intellectual abilities.

Personality Characteristics

There are a number of personality characteristics that may be relevant and important when evaluating the reliability of confession statements. The three most extensively researched variables are: suggestibility, acquiescence and compliance (Gudjonsson, 1992; Clare & Gudjonsson, 1993).

More recently, confabulation has been investigated in relation to the reliability of verbal accounts given by witnesses (Clare & Gudjonsson, 1993; Sigurdsson et al., 1994). Extreme confabulation has been found in some cases of personality disorder, which was evident in the cases of Joe Giarratano (Gudjonsson, 1992) and Judith Ward (Gudjonsson & MacKeith, 1997). Persons with mental disorder, such as learning disability and severe depression, have impaired memory recall for events, but the accuracy of their accounts is not undermined by a heightened tendency to confabulate (Clare & Gudjonsson, 1993; Sigurdsson et al., 1994).

"Interrogative suggestibility" refers to the tendency of people to yield to leading questions and submit to interrogative pressure. It can be measured by the use of a behavioural test, such as the Gudjonsson Suggestibility Scales. Here subjects are subtly misled in an experimental way and their responses are carefully monitored and compared with those of relative normative groups for the purpose of comparison. If the scores obtained are statistically infrequent, that is, they occur in fewer than 5% of the general population, then the person can be described as being abnormally suggestible on the test (Gudjonsson, 1992, 1997b).

The concept of "compliance" overlaps, to a certain extent, with suggestibility, but it is more strongly associated with eagerness to please and the tendency to avoid conflict and confrontation. It is more difficult to measure compliance than suggestibility by behavioural observation and it is therefore typically measured by a self-report questionnaire (Gudjonsson, 1989). As a result, it is a measure that is easier to falsify than measures of interrogative suggestibility (Gudjonsson, 1997b).

"Acquiescence" refers to the tendency of people, when in doubt, to answer questions in the affirmative irrespective of content. The reason for this tendency appears to be that they answer questions in the affirmative without properly listening to them or fully understanding them. Acquiescence is more strongly correlated with low intelligence than either suggestibility or compliance (Gudjonsson, 1990b).

Suspects are not always open, honest and forthcoming during a police interview or when giving evidence in court. The three main reasons for this are fear of legal sanctions (e.g. being convicted, sentenced), feeling ashamed or embarrassed about the crime, and fear of retaliation by implicating others. Whereas feelings of *shame* inhibit suspects from confessing, feelings of *guilt* facilitate the confession process (Gudjonsson, 1992). Feelings of shame are particularly likely to occur when suspects are interviewed in relation to sexual offending, such as child molestation which carries strong social stigma. Here the police interview will need to focus on ways of overcoming the feelings of shame associated with such offences. These kinds of offender need to be interviewed particularly sensitively if a reliable confession is to be obtained (see Chapter 5.2 by Bull).

A neglected group of people are those who confess falsely to the police in order to protect a significant person in their life from being prosecuted (e.g. a relative, a friend, a peer). These types of false confession are probably quite common and do not come to the notice of the judiciary because they are typically not retracted (Gudjonsson & Sigurdsson, 1994).

CONCLUSIONS

When cases go to court defendants commonly dispute a confession they had previously made to the police. This is most likely to happen when there is little or no evidence against the defendant, apart from the confession. In England defendants can be and sometimes are convicted on the basis of confession evidence alone. Psychologists are increasingly being asked to assess defendants in such cases and the likely reliability of their confession to the police. In this chapter the author has reviewed the relevant literature and provides the reader with a conceptual framework for assessing disputed confession cases as well as providing some practical advice.

REFERENCES

Bentall, R.P., Baker, A.B. and Havers, S. (1991). Reality monitoring and psychotic hallucinations. *British Journal of Clinical Psychology*, **30**, 213–222.

Birch, D. (1989). The pace hots up: confessions and confusions under the 1984 Act. *Criminal Law Review*, 95–116.

Bull, R. & Cullen, C. (1992). *Witnesses who have Mental Handicaps*. Edinburgh: The Crown Office.

Bull, R. & Cullen, C. (1993). Interviewing the mentally handicapped. *Policing*, **9**, 88–100.

Clare, I.C.H. & Gudjonsson, G.H. (1993). Interrogative suggestibility, confabulation, and acquiescence in people with mild learning difficulties (Mental handicap): Implications for reliability during police interrogation. *British Journal of Clinical Psychology*, **32**, 295–301.

Clare, I.C.H. & Gudjonsson, G.H. (1995). The vulnerability of suspects with intellectual disabilities during police interviews: A review and experimental study of decision-making. *Mental Handicap Research*, **8**, 110–128.

Clare, I.C.H., Gudjonsson, G.H. & Harari, P.M. (1998). Understanding of the current caution in England and Wales. *Journal of Community and Applied Social Psychology*, **8**, 323–329.

Corre, N. (1995). *A Guide to the 1995 revisions to the PACE Codes of Practice*. London: Callow Publishing.

Davison, S.E. & Gossop, M. (1996). The problem of interviewing drug addicts in custody: a study of interrogative suggestibility and compliance. *Psychology, Crime and Law*, **2**, 185–195.

Dent, H. (1986) An experimental study of the effectiveness of different techniques of questioning mentally handicapped child witnesses. *British Journal of Clinical Psychology*, **25**, 13–17.

Fisher, R.P. and Geiselman, R.E. (1992). *Memory-enhancing Techniques for Investigative Interviewing: The Cognitive Interview*. Springfield, IL: Thomas.

Gudjonsson, G.H. (1989). Compliance in an interrogation situation: A new scale. *Personality and Individual Differences*, **10**, 535–540.

Gudjonsson, G.H. (1990a). One hundred alleged false confession cases: Some normative data. *British Journal of Clinical Psychology*, **29**, 249–250.

Gudjonsson, G.H. (1990b). The relationship of intellectual skills to suggestibility, compliance and acquiescence. *Personality and Individual Differences*, **11**, 227–231.

Gudjonsson, G.H. (1992). *The Psychology of Interrogations, Confessions and Testimony*. Chichester: John Wiley & Sons.

Gudjonsson, G.H. (1994a). Confessions made to the expert witness: some professional issues. *Journal of Forensic Psychiatry*, **5**, 237–247.

Gudjonsson, G.H. (1994b). Psychological vulnerability: suspects at risk. In D. Morgan and G. Stephenson (Eds.), *Suspicion and Silence. The Right to Silence in Criminal Investigation* (pp.91–106). London: Blackstone Press.

Gudjonsson, G.H. (1995a). "Fitness for interview" during police detention: A conceptual framework for forensic assessment. *Journal of Forensic Psychiatry*, **6**, 185–197.

Gudjonsson, G.H. (1995b). Alleged false confession, voluntariness and "free will": Testifying against the Israeli General Security Service (GSS). *Criminal Behaviour and Mental Health*, **5**, 95–105.

Gudjonsson, G.H. (1995c). "I'll help you boys as much as I can" – how eagerness to please can result in a false confession. *Journal of Forensic Psychiatry*, **6**, 333–342.

Gudjonsson, G.H. (1997a). The Police and Criminal Evidence Act (PACE) and confessions. *British Journal of Hospital Medicine*, **57**, 445–447.

Gudjonsson, G.H. (1997b). *The Gudjonsson Suggestibility Scales Manual*. Hove: Psychology Press.

Gudjonsson, G.H. and Haward, L.R.C. (1998). *Forensic Psychology: A Guide to Practice*. London: Routledge.

Gudjonsson, G.H. and MacKeith, J.A.C. (1988). Retracted confessions: legal, psychological and psychiatric aspects. *Medicine, Science and the Law*, **28**, 187–194.

Gudjonsson, G. & MacKeith, J. (1994). Learning disability and the Police and Criminal Evidence Act 1984. Protection during investigative interviewing: a video-recorded false confession to double murder. *Journal of Forensic Psychiatry*, **5**, 35–49.

Gudjonsson, G.H. and MacKeith, J. (1997). *Disputed confessions and the criminal justice system*. Maudsley Discussion Paper No. 2. London: Institute of Psychiatry.

Gudjonsson, G.H. and Sigurdsson, J.F. (1994). How frequently do false confessions occur? An empirical study among prison inmates. *Psychology, Crime and Law*, **1**, 21–26.

Gudjonsson, G.H., Clare, I., Rutter, S. & Pearse, J. (1993). *Persons at Risk During Interviews in Police Custody: The Identification of Vulnerabilities*. Royal Commission on Criminal Justice. London: HMSO.

Home Office. (1985). *Police and Criminal Evidence Act 1984*. London: HMSO.

Home Office. (1995). *Police and Criminal Evidence Act 1984. Codes of Practice. Revised Edition*. London: HMSO.

Milne, R. & Bull, R. (1996). Interviewing children with mild learning disability with the cognitive interview. In N.K. Clark & G.M. Stephenson (Eds.), *Investigative and Forensic Decision Making*. Issues in Criminological and Legal Psychology, No. 26. Leicester: British Psychological Society, pp. 44–51.

Milne, R., Clare, I. & Bull, R. (in press). Using the cognitive interview with adults with mild learning disability. *Psychology, Crime and Law*.

Murakami, A.T., Edelman, R.J. and Davis, P.E. (1996). Interrogative suggestibility in opiates users. *Addiction*, **91**, 1365–1373.

Norfolk, G.A. (Ed.) (1997). *Fit to be interviewed by the police? Proceedings of the multidisciplinary symposium held at the Stakis Hotel, Blackpool on 10 May 1997*. Harrogate: The Association of Police Surgeons.

Ofshe, R.J. and Leo, R.A. (1997). The social psychology of police interrogation. The theory and classification of true and false confessions. *Studies in Law, Politics and Society*, **16**, 189–251.

Pearse, J., Gudjonsson, G.H., Clare, I.C.H. & Rutter, S. (1998). Police interviewing and psychological vulnerabilities: predicting the likelihood of a confession. *Journal of Community and Applied Social Psychology*, **8**, 1–21.

Perlman, N.B., Ericson, K.I., Esses, V.M. and Isaacs, B.J. (1994). The developmentally handicapped witnesses. Competency as a function of question format. *Law and Human Behavior*, **18**, 171–187.

Shepherd, E.W., Mortimer, A.K. & Mobasheri, R. (1995). The police caution: Comprehension and perceptions in the general population. *Expert Evidence*, **4**, 60–67.

Sigurdsson, J.F. & Gudjonsson, G.H. (1994). Alcohol and drug intoxication during police interrogation and the reasons why suspects confess to the police. *Addiction*, **89**, 985–997.

Sigurdsson, J.F. and Gudjonsson, G.H. (1996). Psychological characteristics of "false confessors". A study among Icelandic prison inmates and juvenile offenders. *Personality and Individual Differences*, **20**, 321–329.

Sigurdsson, J. and Gudjonsson, G. (1997). The criminal history of "false confessors" and other prison inmates. *Journal of Forensic Psychiatry*, **8**, 447–455.

Sigurdsson, E., Gudjonsson, G.H., Kolbeinsson, H. & Petursson, H. (1994). The effects of ECT and depression on confabulation, memory processing, and suggestibility. *Nordic Journal of Psychiatry*, **48**, 443–451.

Smith, P. & Gudjonsson, G.H. (1995). The relationship of mental disorder to suggestibility and confabulation among forensic inpatients. *Journal of Forensic Psychiatry*, **6**, 499–515.

Tully, B. and Cahill, D (1984). *Police Interviewing of the Mentally Handicapped. An Experimental Study*. London: Police Foundation.

Interviewing Witnesses: The Cognitive Interview

Amina Memon
University of Aberdeen, UK

The cognitive interview (or CI) is one of the most exciting developments in psychology in the last ten years. The CI is a forensic tool that comprises a series of memory retrieval techniques designed to increase the amount of information that can be obtained from a witness and may help police officers and other professionals obtain a more complete and accurate report from a witness. The ability to obtain full and accurate information is critical in an investigation; a good interview with a key witness may determine the outcome of a criminal investigation.

The cognitive interview (CI) was initially developed by the psychologists Ed Geiselman (University of California, Los Angeles) and Ron Fisher (Florida International University) in 1984 as a response to the many requests they received from police officers and legal professionals for a method of improving witness interviews. An empirical study of the techniques used by untrained police officers working in a police department in Miami, Florida (Fisher, Geiselman & Raymond, 1987), however, suggested that improving witness memory was only part of the story. There existed some fundamental problems in the conduct of "standard" police interviews that were leading to ineffective communication and limiting interviewer and witness performance. Fisher et al. (1987) document several characteristics of the "standard police interview" among which were constant interruptions (when an eyewitness was giving an account), excessive use of question–answer format and inappropriate sequencing of questions. George (1991) studied the techniques typically used by untrained officers in London and found a remarkably similar pattern among that group. This led to the characterisation of a "standard police interview" as being one of poor quality and stressed the need for an alternative procedure for interviewing

Handbook of the Psychology of Interviewing. Edited by A. Memon and R. Bull.

witnesses. This chapter provides a review of the relevant theory and research that led to the development of the CI. The interview procedure itself will then be fully described with illustrations of the use of the various techniques.

THEORETICAL PERSPECTIVES

The CI represents the alliance of two fields of study: cognitive and social psychology. The CI is based on what psychologists know about the way in which memory works. It also draws upon our knowledge of how best to manage a social interaction and improve communication between an interviewer and interviewee. We will briefly look at the development of the CI procedure, which began with four basic "cognitive" techniques for increasing the amount of information recalled.

The "cognitive" components of the CI draw upon two theoretical principles. Firstly, that a retrieval cue is effective to the extent that there is an overlap between the encoded information and the retrieval cue and that reinstatement of the original encoding context increases the accessibility of stored information (Tulving and Thomson's Encoding Specificity Hypothesis, 1973). Secondly, the Multiple Trace Theory (Bower, 1967) suggests that rather than having memories of discrete and unconnected incidents, our memories are made up of a network of associations and consequently, there are several means by which a memory could be cued. It follows from this that information not accessible with one technique or cue may be accessible with another.

Context Reinstatement

The first cognitive technique in the CI is to reconstruct the physical and personal contexts which existed at the time an event was experienced.

Example

> *Interviewer:* Now what I would like for you to do is close your eyes and take yourself back in time to the event you have described. Take your time . . . Think about the setting where the event took place, recall any sounds you could hear, any smells you associate with the event, try and recall the setting in which the event occurred. For example, who was there [pause], what they were wearing [pause], what they were saying [pause]. Think about your feelings and reactions to the event [pause]. Try and recall as much about the context in which the event occurred as you can by mentally taking yourself back to that context.

Geiselman and his colleagues (Saywitz, Geiselman & Bornstein, 1992) have suggested that it may be helpful for child witnesses to verbalise out aloud when mentally reinstating context. For example, to describe the room as the picture comes to mind, to describe smells, sounds and other features of the context.

There is a substantial body of empirical research on context reinstatement and memory retrieval (see Malpass, 1996, for a recent review).

Report Everything

A second technique of the CI is to ask the witness to report everything. This may well facilitate the recall of additional information, perhaps by shifting criteria for reporting information. For instance, witnesses are encouraged to report in full without screening out anything they consider to be irrelevant or for which they have only partial recall (Fisher & Geiselman, 1992). In addition to facilitating the recall of additional information, this technique may yield information that may be valuable in putting together details from different witnesses to the same crime (see Memon & Bull, 1991).

Example

> *Interviewer*: I would like you to tell me in as much detail as you can, I want you to include every little detail you can remember, try not to edit anything out. Just give me as much information as you can.

Change Perspective

The third CI retrieval aid is to ask for recall from a variety of perspectives. This technique tries to encourage the witnesses to place themselves in the shoes of the victim or of another witness and to report what *they* saw or would have seen. The theoretical assumption is that a change in perspective forces a change in retrieval description, thus allowing additional information to be recalled from the new perspective. Again the aim is to use multiple pathways to retrieval and to increase the amount of detail elicited. There are a number of concerns about the use of the change perspective instruction, in particular the possibility that it could lead to fabricated details and confuse the witness (Memon & Koehnken, 1992; Memon et al., 1996). Police officers have tended not to use the change perspective instruction and some have expressed a concern about the possibility of misleading the witness with this instruction (see Kebbel & Wagstaff, 1996; Clifford & George, 1996).

Example

> *Interviewer*: OK, so you've told me what you saw from where you were. Now I would like you to put yourself in the position of the victim. She was standing on the other side of the room talking to the stranger. Now put yourself in her shoes, and try and describe the scene again from her perspective.

Reverse Order

The fourth component of the CI is the instruction to make retrieval attempts from different starting points. Witnesses usually feel they have to start at the beginning and are usually asked to do so. However, the CI encourages extra focused and extensive retrieval by encouraging witnesses to recall in a variety of orders, from the end, or from the middle or from the most memorable event. This instruction, like the change perspective technique, is assumed to change the retrieval description, resulting in the recall of additional details (Geiselman & Callot, 1990). This technique appears to have the same effect as asking the witness to make a second retrieval attempt (Memon et al., 1997a). In other words, by going through the event for a second time, the witness comes up with some new information not reported earlier. If the witness is probed with questions during their second retrieval attempt, they will report additional information (Milne, 1997).

Example

> *Interviewer*: OK, the last thing you described is that the musician left in a hurry. Now if we start at that point and work backwards, can you describe the event to me in reverse order.
> *Witness*: Where do I start?
> *Interviewer:* Well, the last thing you said was he slammed the door shut. If you start there and work backwards, what happened right before he left?

SOCIAL SKILLS AND THE COGNITIVE INTERVIEW

In order to be able to implement effectively the use of the "cognitive" components of the CI, it is necessary to provide interviewers with the necessary social skills and communication strategies that are required in order to build rapport with a witness. As indicated earlier, research with police officers suggested this was something they lacked. The revised version of the CI (see Fisher & Geiselman, 1992) included the techniques decribed below.

Rapport Building

This is an attempt to get to establish a relationship between the interviewer and interviewee, to put the interviewee at ease and to clarify what the expectations are. An important component of rapport building is for the interviewer to "transfer control" explicitly to the witnesses by (a) making it clear to witnesses that they have to do the work and (b) allowing them time to think and respond. This may facilitate the implementation of the instruction to reinstate context, as described above.

Example

> *Interviewer*: Hello Richard, my name is Linsey. I am a student at Southampton University and I am here to ask you some questions about the event you witnessed last Wednesday.
> *Witness*: Hello Linsey.
> *Interviewer*: Are you comfortable? Good. So you are a student in Biology. Are you enjoying the course? What do you hope to do when you leave college?

Focused Retrieval

The interviewer facilitates eyewitnesses' use of focused memory techniques (i.e. concentrating on mental images of the various parts of the event such as the suspect's face and using these images to guide recall). Fisher and Geiselman (1992) draw a distinction between conceptual image codes (an image stored as a concept or dictionary definition) and pictorial codes (the mental representation of an image). The notion is that images create dual codes or more meaningful elaborations (Paivio, 1971). The "imaging" part of the CI usually occurs in the questioning phase of the interview and assumes that the witness has effectively recreated the context in which an event occurred. The instruction could take the following form: "concentrate on the picture you have in your mind of the suspect, focus on the face and describe it".

In order to effectively engage the witness in focused retrieval, the interviewer needs to speak slowly and clearly, pausing at appropriate points to allow the witness time to create an image and respond.

Example

> *Interviewer*: Now I would like you to concentrate on the man's face, try and form an image of the face, focus in on the various features of the face, and describe to me in detail what you can see.

Witness Compatible Questioning

Finally, the timing of the interviewer's questions is critical (deemed witness compatible questioning). Following principles of encoding specificity and feature overlap, questions should be guided by the witness's pattern of recall rather than the interviewer adhering to a rigid protocol. For example, if a witness is describing a suspect's clothing the interviewer should not switch the line of questioning to the actions of the suspect.

Example

> *Interviewer*: So the person you saw was wearing a light jacket. Tell me about the jacket and any other items of clothing that you recall.

Witness: A casual jacket and blue jeans . . . and shoes . . .
Interviewer: Can you describe his footwear to me?

EMPIRICAL RESEARCH ON THE CI

Between 1984 and 1990 several "simulation" studies of CI were undertaken employing staged and filmed scenarios of forensic relevance, including Los Angeles Police Department training films which depicted "realistic" criminal events. The interviews in some of these studies were conducted by trained and experienced police officers. For example, Geiselman et al. (1985) compared the cognitive interview with the interviews more usually conducted by experienced police officers (the "standard" interview procedure described earlier). The participants (witnesses) were undergraduate students and the interviewers were experienced law enforcement professionals (e.g. police investigators, members of the CIA and private detectives). The training films used in this study were simulations of life-threatening situations which depicted a number of scenarios modelled on real life events. Witnesses were interviewed 48 hours after viewing the film. Interviewers received instructions to follow one of two procedures: (i) their usual procedure or (ii) the cognitive interview, the procedure described earlier.

Geiselman et al. (1985) coded each subject's transcribed report for (1) number of correct items of information recalled, (2) number of incorrect items of information recalled (e.g. describing a person as having blue eyes when they were brown) and (3) number of confabulated items of information recalled (e.g. a description of the suspect's face when the suspect's face was not shown on the film). The CI elicited 35% more correct information than did the standard interview but the two types did not differ on incorrect items or confabulations. Scoring of critical items from the film showed that the CI not only enhanced recall of ancillary facts but also information that could be critical in a criminal investigation.

FIELD STUDIES

To date there have been only two field tests of the cognitive interview. The first was a project that enlisted the assistance of police detectives in Miami, Florida (Fisher, Geiselman & Amador, 1989). The second was a study involving the Hertfordshire police in the UK (George & Clifford, 1996).

The aim of the Fisher et al. (1989) field study was to examine the use of the enhanced CI by trained and "control" police detectives when questioning real life victims and witnesses. The pre-training phase of the study involved the collection of tape recordings of interviews from a sample of detectives using their usual, standard techniques. Half of the group underwent enhanced CI training over four 60 minute sessions. During this time they were given an overview of the procedure and the general psychological principles of cognition, training in specific interviewing techniques, communication techniques and advice on the temporal sequencing of the CI. After the fourth training session each detective tape-recorded a practice interview in the field and received individual feedback from the psychologists on the quality of the interview. The detectives then followed the enhanced CI procedure or "standard interview" procedure (as defined earlier) during the course of their interviews with real witnesses over a period of time. Two measures of the effects of training were taken. Firstly, number of facts elicited before training (i.e. the tapes from the pilot phase) versus after training (thus a within-subjects comparison). Secondly, facts elicited by trained and untrained officers after some had undergone the training programme (between-subjects). The tapes were transcribed by trained research assistants who recorded all the relevant details. Opinionated and irrelevant statements were ignored. The statements included physical descriptions, actions and clothing.

The CI was found to be effective in the before/after comparisons (the within-subjects factor) and in the trained/untrained (between-subjects) comparison. The trained detectives elicited 47% more information after training and significantly more information than detectives not trained in CI. Baseline measures showed there were no differences between the groups prior to training. In order to examine the impact of CI on the amount of incorrect information recalled, it was necessary to examine corroboration rates. (In real crimes, of course, corroborating information from other witnesses, forensic evidence, and so on is not always easily available). When the corroborating source was another witness/ victim, the corroborating interview was always conducted by someone other than the original detective (usually a uniformed officer). Ninety-four per cent of the statements from the interviews in this study were corroborated and there was no difference in the corroboration rates of pre- and post-training interviews, so CI did not appear to increase the amount of incorrect information.

The results of the CI field study are promising. Six of the seven detectives who were trained improved significantly. However, given the relatively small sample size the question as to how representative the trained group were is questionable. The officers were selected for training rather than being randomly assigned to conditions and this is of some concern, especially in light of evidence (see below) that police officers may not be so open to the use of new techniques (Memon et al., 1994; Memon, Bull & Smith, 1995). Finally, there was no trained control group in this field study. This is a limitation of the study because it is hard to tell how much of the CI advantage reflects the use of new techniques and special training and to what extent the effect is a result of the comparison group ("untrained" officers) using poor interviewing techniques.

George and Clifford (1996) reported a field study involving 32 experienced British police officers (see also Clifford & George, 1996). Officers were randomly assigned to one of four conditions: CI, conversation management, CI and conversation management, and a no training control group. Conversation management is a procedure which resembles the structured interview described earlier and includes training in planning the interview, listening skills, conversational styles, question types and summarising. Prior to training, each subject provided a tape recording of an interview they had conducted with a real life witness or victim. Following training each police officer tape-recorded three more interviews with victims or witnesses of street crimes. The tape recordings were transcribed and evaluated for the amount of information provided by the interviewee. The results showed that the CI elicited significantly more information than the standard police interview (25% more than the no training control group). A before and after training comparison showed an increase of 55%. There were no significant differences between conversation management and the untrained control; in fact the conversation management group fared worse, possibly as a result of training overload.

HOW MUCH TRAINING?

The success of the CI depends upon adequate training of interviewers in the techniques described above. It is not clear how much training is needed. Some studies report effects with relatively brief training. Fisher et al. (1989) report benefits after four 60 minute sessions, while George trained officers over two days. Memon et al. (1994) trained officers over a more limited period of time (four hours) and found this was insufficient for officers to use the new techniques effectively, even though non police officers can conduct good CIs after such training. Turtle (1995) has evaluated several one week training courses on the CI for Canadian police officers and found that training has relatively little effect on the use of CI techniques. Clearly, the effects of training are complex and depend not only on length of training, but quality of training, background of interviewer, attitudes towards training and so forth (see Memon et al., 1994).

THE COGNITIVE VS. THE STRUCTURED INTERVIEW

From a practical perspective, it is important to show that the CI is more effective than the techniques currently in use by police officers and others. The selection of untrained police interviewers in the above field studies was a sensible control in the applied setting. However, from a theoretical perspective, an experimental control is needed to demonstrate that the techniques themselves are causing the effects and not some aspect related to training such as motivation, quality of questioning or rapport-building skills.

More recent tests of the CI have compared the CI with a procedure known as the structured interview (SI) procedure where the quality of training in communication and questioning techniques is comparable to the CI training. The training of the structured group follows a procedure that is recommended to professionals who interview children (the Home Office Memorandum of Good

Practice, Home Office and Department of Health, 1992, see Bull, 1992, 1995). The essence of the Memorandum is to treat the interview as a procedure in which a variety of interviewing techniques are deployed in relatively discrete phases proceeding from general to open, to specific, closed-form questions. Rapport-building, through open questions and active listening, are also important components.

So is it possible for an interviewer armed with a range of "good" interviewing techniques and effective communication skills to achieve the same effects as a CI trained interviewer? This question was first addressed by Guenter Koehnken and colleagues in their studies conducted in Germany (Koehnken, Thurer & Zorberbier, 1994; Mantwill, Koehnken & Aschermann, 1995) and in the UK (Memon et al., 1997a, 1997b). In these studies the structured group received training in basic communication skills and use of various types of questioning, as did the CI group. Both SI and CI groups reviewed written and videotaped interview transcripts and engaged in role plays. Only the CI group received special instructions on the cognitive retrieval aids. The training session lasted between four and five hours.

In the German studies (in which the to-be-remembered event was a videotape showing a blood donation) the CI as compared to the SI yielded 25–52% more correct information without any differences in errors and confabulations (Koehnken et al., 1994; Mantwill et al., 1995). In contrast, in one British study (in which the to-be-remembered event was a murder of a child) both the CI and the SI interviewers elicited more total correct information than an untrained group (Memon et al., 1997b). However, this was offset by their producing a significantly higher number of errors and confabulations than the untrained group. It may be inevitable that any technique that increases the amount of information recalled is also going to influence the frequency with which an incorrect item of information is recalled. The most appropriate way of dealing with this is to ensure that the errors are closely monitored and whenever possible the information is checked and corroborated. In the majority of studies, accuracy rates (the proportion of correctly recalled details) are unaffected by the CI (Koehnken et al., in press).

THE COGNITIVE INTERVIEW: AN APPROPRIATE TOOL FOR INTERVIEWING CHILDREN?

The CI and Child Witnesses

Research in this area has been timely given recent developments for child witnesses testifying in criminal trials (e.g. in Britain, the Criminal Justice Acts, 1988, 1991). Among the most significant changes in some countries is the use of video-recorded interviews with children as evidence in criminal trials and the admissibility of the evidence of children under the age of seven years.

There is reasonable evidence to suggest that younger children (ages 6–7) will often recall less information than older children (ages 10–11) (e.g. Davies, Tarrant & Flin, 1989; Memon et al., 1996). Given that the primary aim of CI is to increase the amount of information retrieved it may be an effective procedure to use with children.

Interviewing six- to seven-year-olds

Memon et al. (1993) interviewed 32 six- and seven-year-olds about an eye test. The effectiveness of a CI, comprising the usual four mnemonic techniques, was compared with that of a structured interview. The latter, like the CI, was a good interview procedure and one in which the interviewers used open-ended questions and did not interrupt the witness when he or she was speaking. Children's recall of the event was tested one week after the event and again six weeks later. As mentioned earlier, children had difficulty in understanding interviewer instructions to change perspective and to recall in reverse order such that they became confused about what was expected of them. This may have worked against the CI. Indeed, there were no significant effects of interview type on recall.

Memon et al. (1996) isolated each of the four mnemonic techniques of the CI (context, report in detail, change order and change perspective) and compared them with an instruction to "try harder". Prior to each interview there was a practice session in which each child (aged six to seven years) described a familiar activity using one of the four CI techniques, e.g. context reinstatement. There were no significant differences in correct recall or errors as a function of instruction condition; this suggested that the "try harder" instruction could be as effective as each of the CI techniques. There were a number of interesting differences between the age groups, most notably that the younger children (five-year-olds) performed less well under the CI "context reinstatement" and "change perspective" conditions as compared to the eight-year-olds in the same conditions. A qualitative analysis of the interview transcripts suggested that the children did not fully understand all the techniques and had difficulty using the change perspective instruction. This suggests refinement of the CI is needed for children.

Two main problems in applying the CI with younger children have been identified. First, younger children (six to seven years of age) have difficulty understanding the CI techniques in the form developed for adults. Take the following example:

> *Interviewer*: What I'd like you to try and do is imagine that you are the nurse and that you can see the room from where she was standing, by the wall chart. Just tell me what you can see.
> *Child*: Umm . . . "Did you see the letters, can you see the letters, good." and I said "yes" and that's all she said to me.

The child clearly does not understand what the interviewer is asking of her.

Secondly, the CI interview results may be affected by demand characteristics in that children respond in a way they think may please the interviewer. This is illustrated in the following transcript taken from Memon et al.'s (1993) child witness study:

> *Interviewer*: OK, but what about the day the nurse came? Can you tell me about that? I know you've told me already, but I need to find out more.
> *Child*: Yes, just in case I am saying the right things.
> *Interviewer*: Well no, not exactly, but just in case you remember any more.
> *Child*: Yes, some different things that I forgot to say at all.
> *Interviewer*: Yes. The best thing to do is to start again and tell me everything again.
> *Child*: Well, I can't tell you the same things.

Interviewing eight- to nine-year-olds

Memon et al. (1997a) had eight- to nine-year-olds participate in a live magic show (in small groups). After a delay of two days, some of the children were interviewed about this event using a cognitive or structured interview (the remainder were not interviewed at that time). After a further delay of 12 days all of the children were interviewed (some now for a second time). Four interviewers had been trained in the use of CI techniques (cognitive and social components) and four interviewers had been trained in the use of SI techniques. The children interviewed using CI techniques produced more accurate and inaccurate details. These errors occurred in the questioning phase of the interview and tended to be related to descriptions of persons in the event (the children were asked to describe the magician and the clothing of other children in the event). There are a number of possible explanations for these errors. One is that context reinstatement and imagery instructions encourage children to speculate as they attempt to provide more detailed responses. Another is that children make source monitoring errors in these conditions (i.e. they may confuse what children were wearing on the day of the magic show with what was worn on another day). A more general explanation is that the children in the CI condition feel under pressure to give more information (e.g. to please the interviewer) and they give responses even when they are uncertain (this social effect is well known to psychologists as "demand characteristics"). Interestingly, the children were specifically asked not to guess or make anything up and to say "I don't know" if they were uncertain. The errors, which were quite small in comparison to the amount of correct recall generated with the CI, may have been far higher had this warning not been given.

The CI may be a useful tool in interviewing children over the age of seven (see also Chapter 3.2 by Milne). However, it is important to ensure that interviewers are appropriately trained, are sensitive to demand characteristics and are careful in the questioning phase of the interview. While specific prompts may yield additional details, they may also increase errors. It is important to remind the child that they should not make up answers to questions.

CONCLUSION

It is appropriate that the cognitive interview be included in a handbook on interviewing. The CI is by no means limited to the forensic context. The CI can be used in any situation where a large quantity of information is required from an individual (medical interviews, personnel selection, psychiatric assessments, etc.). The CI can substantially increase the amount of information that is obtained in an investigative context.

Such studies suggest the structured interview may yield as much information as the cognitive. In other words, the CI and the SI have the potential to yield more detailed information without jeopardising the accuracy of that information. The increase in errors may cause concern, although progress has recently been made in identifying where in the interview these occur (Memon et al., 1997a; Milne, 1997). Obviously, the benefits of any innovative technique need to be carefully weighed up against any costs. In a forensic investigation an increase in number of details could be particularly helpful at the information-gathering stage in providing new clues that could lead to a successful conviction. It is up to the investigator to consider when a CI may or may not be helpful and to take particular care when probing the witness for more information.

REFERENCES

Bower, G. (1967). A multicomponent theory of memory trace. In K.W. Spence and J.T. Spence (Eds.), *The Psychology of Learning and Motivation* (Vol. 1). New York: Academic Press.

Brainerd, C. & Ornstein, P.A. (1991). Children's memory for witnessed events. In J. Doris (Ed.), *The Suggestibility of Children's Recollections* (pp. 10–20). Washington, DC: American Psychological Association.

Bull, R. (1992). Obtaining evidence expertly: The reliability of interviews with child witnesses. *Expert Evidence: The International Digest of Human Behaviour, Science and Law*, 1(1), 5–12.

Bull, R. (1995). Innovative techniques for the questioning of child witnesses especially those who are young and those with learning disability. In M. Zaragoza, J.R. Graham, G.C.N. Hall, R. Hirschman & Y.S. Ben-Porath (Eds.), *Memory and Testimony in the Child Witness*. Thousand Oaks, CA: Sage.

Clifford, B.R. & George, R.A. (1996). A field investigation of training in three methods of witness/victim investigative interviewing. *Psychology, Crime and Law*, 2, 231–248.

Davies, G., Tarrant, A. & Flin, R. (1989). Close encounters of the witness kind: children's memory for a simulated health inspection. *British Journal of Psychology*, 80, 415–429.

Fisher, R.P. & Geiselman, R.E. (1992). *Memory Enhancing Techniques for Investigative Interviewing: The Cognitive Interview*. Springfield IL.: Charles C. Thomas.

Fisher, R.P., Geiselman, R.E. & Raymond, D.S. (1987) Critical analysis of police interviewing techniques. *Journal of Police Science and Administration*, 15, 177–185.

Fisher, R.P., Geiselman, R.E. & Amador, M. (1989). Field test of the cognitive interview: Enhancing the recollection of actual victims and witnesses of crime. *Journal of Applied Psychology*, 74(5), 722–727.

Geiselman, R.E. & Callot, R. (1990) Reverse versus forward recall of script based texts. *Applied Cognitive Psychology*, 4, 141–144.

Geiselman, R.E., Fisher, R.P., MacKinnon, D.P. & Holland, H.L. (1985). Eyewitness memory enhancement in the police interview: Cognitive retrieval mnemonics versus hypnosis. *Journal of Applied Psychology*, **70**, 401–412.

George, R. (1991). A field evaluation of the cognitive interview. Unpublished Master's Thesis: Polytechnic of East London.

George, R. & Clifford, B. (1996) The Cognitive Interview: Does it work? In G.M. Davies, S. Lloyd-Bostock, M. McMurran & C. Wilson (Eds.), *Psychology and Law: Advances in Research*. Berlin: De Gruyter.

Kebbel, M. & Wagstaff, G. (1996). Enhancing the practicality of the cognitive interview in forensic situations. *Psycoloquy*, **7**(16).

Koehnken, G., Thurer, C. & Zorberbier, D. (1994). The cognitive interview: Are interviewers' memories enhanced too? *Applied Cognitive Psychology*, **8**, 13–24.

Koehnken, G., Milne, R. Memon, A. & Bull, R. (in press). A meta-analysis on the effects of the Cognitive Interview. Special Issue of *Psychology, Crime & The Law*.

Malpass, R. (1996). Enhancing eyewitness memory. In S.L. Sporer., R.S. Malpass & G. Koehnken (Eds.), *Psychological Issues in Eyewitness Identification*. Mahwah, NJ: Lawrence Erlbaum Associates.

Mantwill, M., Koehnken, G. & Aschermann, E. (1995). Effects of the cognitive interview on the recall of familiar and unfamiliar events. *Journal of Applied Psychology*, **80**, 68–78.

Memon, A. & Bull, R. (1991). The cognitive interview: Its origins, empirical support, evaluation and practical implications. *Journal of Community and Applied Social Psychology*, **1**, 291–307.

Memon, A. & Koehnken, G. (1992). Helping witnesses to remember more: The cognitive interview. *Expert Evidence: The International Digest of Human Behaviour, Science & Law*, **1**(2), 39–48.

Memon, A., Cronin, O., Eaves, R. & Bull, R. (1993). The cognitive interview and the child witness. In G.M. Stephenson and N.K. Clark (Series Eds.) & N.K. Clark and G.M. Stephenson (Vol. Eds.), *Issues in Criminology and Legal Psychology: Vol. 20. Children, Evidence and Procedure*. Leicester: British Psychological Society.

Memon, A., Milne, R., Holley, A., Bull, R. & Koehnken, G. (1994). Towards understanding the effects of interviewer training in evaluating the cognitive interview. *Applied Cognitive Psychology*, **8**, 641–659.

Memon, A., Bull, R. & Smith, M. (1995). Improving the quality of the police interview: Can training in the use of cognitive techniques help? *Policing and Society*, **5**(1), 32–40.

Memon, A., Cronin, O., Eaves, R. & Bull, R. (1996). An empirical test of the mnemonic components of the cognitive interview. In G.M. Davies, S. Lloyd-Bostock, M. McMurran & C. Wilson (Eds.), *Psychology and Law: Advances in Research*. Berlin: De Gruyter.

Memon, A. Wark, L., Bull, R. & Koehnken, G. (1997a). Isolating the effects of the cognitive interview techniques *British Journal of Psychology*, **88**(2), 179–198.

Memon, A., Wark, L., Holley, A., Bull, R. & Koehnken, G. (1997b). Eyewitness performance in cognitive and structured interviews. *Memory*, **5**, 639–655.

Milne, R. (1997). *Application and analysis of the cognitive interview*. Doctoral Dissertation, University of Portsmouth.

Paivio, A. (1971). *Imagery and Verbal Processes*. New York: Holt, Rinehart & Winston.

Saywitz, K.J., Geiselman, R.E. & Bornstein, G.K. (1992). Effects of cognitive interviewing and practice on children's recall performance. *Journal of Applied Psychology*, **77**, 744–756.

Tulving, E. & Thomson, D.M. (1973). Encoding Smith, S. (1988). Environmental context dependent memory. In G. Davies & D. Thomson (Eds.), *Memory in Context: Context in Memory* (pp. 13–34). Chichester: Wiley.

Turtle, J. (1995, July). *Officers: What do they want? What have they got?* Paper presented at the 1st biennial meeting of the Society for Applied Research in Memory and Cognition, University of British Columbia.

Index